# Passing Your Business on to Your Family

## Creating a Lifetime Succession Plan to Meet Your Changing Tax, Estate and Business Needs

Irving L. Blackman

IRWIN
Professional Publishing®
Burr Ridge, Illinois
New York, New York

Originally published as *Transferring the Privately-Held Business* © 1993



ISBN 1-55738-898-9

Printed in the United States of America

BB

1 2 3 4 5 6 7 8 9 0

**To**
**My Children**
Linda
Jeffery
Tammie

**And**
**My Grandchildren**
Ian
Felise
Chad
Brittany
Joshua

Because that's what this book is all about—
transferring the good life to future generations ...

# CONTENTS

# PREFACE

An open letter to my readers.

RESULTS! *Results* is the name of the game. Maybe a better name for this book would be *How to Get the **Results** You Want when Transferring Your Closely-Held Business*.

One day the light went on. It changed my professional life. What? The realization that I don't sell hours. Or advice. Or knowledge. Or even transfer/succession/estate planning. I sell one thing and one thing only—RESULTS!

And how can you learn to get the results—tax, transfer and otherwise—you want? Well, that's what this book is all about. To a large measure, this book represents my life's work: learning how to develop a process that gets the desired results. One purpose of this book is to teach others the process, so they too can get the desired results.

It is my firm belief that the others who learn the process will expand it. Change it. Improve it. And, as a result, improve the *results*. Then I can learn from them.

Except in a few necessary instances, this is not a technical book. It is intended to serve two major groups:

1. Owners of privately-held businesses (sooner or later, transfer/succession is inevitable).
2. The small army of professionals who help and advise business owners (accountants, lawyers, insurance consultants, bankers and others).

# ACKNOWLEDGEMENTS

Most of the concepts written in these pages are not mine. They come from a countless number of lawyers, insurance consultants, accountants, and others who taught me as a young man and continue to teach me today. I am but a catalyst that helps put it all together.

To acknowledge and thank all those who contributed to making this book possible would require pages of names. So let me limit the names to those who were asked to and did make direct contributions of knowledge and effort.

*The insurance industry*. Millard Grauer and Frederick H. Stitt, who encouraged me to write the section of the book dealing with insurance. Rick Knut Nelson, David Greenspahn, and my entire estate-planning study group, most of whom are insurance consultants.

*My lawyers' network*. Donald Russ, who has been a constant inspiration, Howard Denenberg, Richard J. Garvey, Stephen Margolin, Robert O. Middleton, and Jonathan Blattmachr.

*The pension industry*. Gerald Goldstein, Ralph J. Wood, Jr., and Leanne Dear.

*My office, Blackman Kallick Bartelstein*. Paul Lau, Michael Dorman, Janet Zaccari, Jill Balicki, Carol Rendak, and finally, Brian Whitlock, without whom there would be no book.

# PART I

# Getting Started

# INTRODUCTION

## Let's chat.

Speaking, not writing, is my bag. This book really represents the print version of my seminar on "How to Win the Transfer/Succession/Estate Tax Game." Or some similar title.

My quarter century on the lecture circuit is buttressed by years of consulting with owners of closely held businesses and applying the principles and techniques I teach in the seminars. Actually, the seminars are part of a wonderful, much bigger circle: study...add to my base of knowledge...work with other professionals—lawyers, accountants, insurance consultants...learn from them...present my seminars...learn from the audience...consult with business owners from across the United States, learning something from every consultation...and study some more.

So, welcome to the *"Irv Blackman Transfer Seminar."* As much as possible, this book attempts to be an educational experience that you can hear. Put another way, I want to talk to you, one-on-one.

Whenever I give a presentation—a half-hour after-dinner speech or a two-day seminar, whether to a small, local audience or to hundreds of people at a national convention—I'm talking to only one person at a time. Eyeball to eyeball. I actually pick out someone in the audience, look directly at him or her, and talk to that person for a minute, more or less. Then I shift to another person. And so on.

I've done that little one-on-one routine in hundreds of seminars from coast to coast. Why? Because transfer/succession/estate planning is a personal subject. Each person is different. So is each family. Each business.

I tell the audience, "Imagine that this is not a seminar. You are in my office to talk about your personal transfer/succession/estate plan. Maybe you're alone. Chances are your spouse is with you, and very likely one or more of your children. Maybe your lawyer or accountant is there, too. The atmosphere is relaxed. Yet it's clear we have a job to do."

So relax. Imagine you're listening, instead of reading. You are about to have fun while you learn. Remember—it's just the two of us, you and me, eyeball to eyeball. Page to page.

Let's chat.

# 1 Objectives

This chapter is not technical. But, it is timeless.

We're going to start by talking about the most important part, chapter and section in this book. It is the foundation, the keystone, the center of your transfer/succession/estate-planning universe. It discusses a subject that can be clearly described in one word—***objectives.*** But first, a few words about the cost of making a transfer.

## The Transfer Cost—Must It Be High?

The typical closely held family business was founded and is now run by a one-man gang. If he is nothing else, he is an entrepreneur. Bless him. It's guys (or gals) like him, with a strong assist from the IRS, that make tax planning a necessary evil. Let's call him Joe Founder.

Assume that Joe has been in business for a long time, is reaching what he thinks is retirement age and wants to plan how to pass his business on to the next generation.

Planning for the closely held corporation really means planning for the continuation of the business. This type of planning covers two specific timeframes: first, from today to the day Joe will permanently move to the big business in the sky; and second, "the thereafter." Death planning encompasses the instant of death and the thereafter. The first time frame deals with lifetime planning and such things as compensation, business growth, management decisions, diversification and the like. Ultimately, it must deal with the end of business life.

Whether Joe decides to end his business life at an early age (you, the reader, must decide what an "early age" means to you) or procrastinates until it is too late, transfer of ownership is a certainty. It is only a question of when. And the more successful Joe's business becomes, the more the tax cost of the ultimate transfer, since tax rates (both income and estate) move up on a graduated basis.

In transferring the assets of a corporation, you need to be aware of three types of tax-related disasters that can befall you:

- ☐ The transfer does not occur because the founder cannot find a professional who can solve his/her particular transfer problem. The potential tax cost continues to mount.
- ☐ Procrastination.
- ☐ The transfer, although made, was handled poorly from a tax standpoint, and the owner (or the family) has been or will be clobbered taxwise.

You need to solve the procrastination problem. Avoiding the other two tax disaster problems is my job. And in this book, I explain how my office gets the job done.

No, the transfer cost need not be high. But you must know how to make the transfer.

## Procrastination

If you tend to procrastinate (and who doesn't, to some degree), you might identify with the message of an article I wrote for my tax column, which appears in 81 trade journals. Here are some excerpts:

> IS YOUR BUSINESS TRANSFER PLAN BOGGED DOWN?...READ THIS
>
> For years, I have joked that the words "transferring a family business" and "procrastination" are synonymous. Dozens of business owners have told me, "I've been working on my transfer (estate) plan for years." But after spending most of my professional life helping closely held business owners transfer their businesses, it has become painfully clear that one particular reason is usually responsible for the procrastination. What's the reason? Indecision! Yes, this prosperous, decision-making owner who has built a successful business by making the right decisions is frozen with indecision.
>
> Why?...Owners can't get their questions answered. Here are the most common questions I hear year after year: Do I sell to the kids? Should I give them the business? Who keeps control while I'm alive? After I die? How much will the IRS get? How will the IRS value my business? How can my spouse and I be assured a guaranteed income flow?
>
> The answers tend to change every time a different person asks the questions. The answers sometimes change even if given by the same person, because circumstances have changed—your son decides to go into the business or not to, business get substantially better or worse, or a child gets married or divorced.
>
> Why are such simple questions so hard to answer? Simply put, the answers are different for different businesses and different owners who have different family situations and, most of all, different objectives. Here's a fact that almost every business owner with a transfer problem finds exciting: When the owner gets the answers to his/her specific questions, the transfer procrastination disease seems to disappear. Overnight!
>
> Here's the prescription I recommend for every owner afflicted with this debilitation disease: Write down your questions in an organized manner. Divide the questions into three categories based on how the answers will affect (1) you, (2) your business, and (3) each member of your family. Of course, some questions will overlap into more than one category. That's okay. Include all

questions you have about income, gift, and estate taxes. Remember, this is not an exercise in estate planning. You ain't dead yet. So most of your questions should concern lifetime planning. Don't worry about the answers. Your job is to ask the questions.

One of the functions of Parts I and II of this book is to anticipate the questions asked by almost every business owner—the typical owner and the not-so-typical owner. (Sometimes I'm convinced there are more of the latter than the former.) Experience clearly indicates that once a business owner gets his/her basic questions answered, that owner is almost a sure bet to complete his/her transfer/succession/estate plan. Of course, we then proceed to answer the questions posed.

Parts I and II also focus on the characteristics of small-business owners.

## Helter Skelter: A Way of Life

Successful business owners are my favorite people. One way or another, they know how to make a profit.

But three facts continue to amaze me:

1. Most successful business owners try to accumulate wealth without an organized plan. *They do it helter skelter.*
2. Most successful business owners who have a plan to accumulate wealth do not have an organized plan to save income taxes. *They do it helter skelter.*
3. Rarely do successful business owners dovetail their lifetime tax plan (even the few who have one) with their estate plan. *They do it helter skelter.*

The sad, yet predictable result, is that most successful business owners:

- ☐ Do not come close to attaining their wealth potential.
- ☐ Overpay their income tax (year after year).
- ☐ Never put a lifetime tax plan in place.
- ☐ Overpay their estate tax (two-fold, 10-fold or more).

## Let's Begin with the End in Mind

What do we want you to achieve from this book?

- ☐ We want you to maximize your after-tax current income each year. The goal is to have this income exceed your lifestyle needs.
- ☐ Remember that the excess (income over lifestyle expenses) is wealth. We want you to learn how to accumulate wealth.
- ☐ And we want you to learn how to protect and conserve your wealth ***both during your life and AFTER your death.***

The way the American system of taxation works, all three objectives—making money, accumulating wealth and conserving both—are attacked by taxes. I'm talking about federal taxes that can ROB you, your business, and your family of your hard-earned dollars: the income tax, the gift tax, and the estate tax.

We're taking dead aim at all of 'em.

People who attend my transfer/succession/estate planning seminars come to learn how to save tax dollars. And they do. But they quickly learn there's more to winning the transfer game than saving a tax buck.

Which brings us to the most important subject in this book...

## Objectives

Indulge me. You're not reading this book. You're not even attending one of my seminars. You're sitting in my office. We're chatting about tax planning. For you...your business...kids...spouse.

What do you think is my most important objective? *To strive to understand your concerns.*

And here's how I attempt to accomplish my objective.

### Preparation for Meeting

Prior to our meeting, you send me what we call a "four-piece consulting package." It contains:

- ☐ Your company's last tax return and your most recent year-end financial statements.
- ☐ The most recent tax return for you (and your spouse, if applicable), along with a personal financial statement.
- ☐ Your family tree.
- ☐ A copy of your wills (yours and your spouse's) and trusts, if any.

After I review the package, we chat again. Ask some questions. Get some answers. You may send more information. I prepare a detailed and customized "Discussion Agenda" (see examples in Part X) based on the consulting package and our conversations.

We arrange to meet. About 60 percent of the time, this meeting takes the form of a telephone conference. Otherwise, we'll either meet in my office or in the client's office.

Who attends this meeting? Always the business owner. Usually his/her spouse. About half the time, the child or children who will take over for dad. Rarely, the nonbusiness children. Almost 25 percent of the time, the client's CPA, or lawyer, or both. (When a CPA or lawyer refers his/her client to me, that professional almost always attends.)

Where the business is owned by more than one family, a decisionmaker from each family must attend.

### Your Objectives

When we assess your situation, this is how we divide objectives:

I. Length: Short-term (2 to 3 years) or Long-term (4 or more years).

II. Type (with typical objectives shown in parentheses).
   A. *Personal* (maintain or improve current lifestyle, slow down, travel, play more golf, do charity work).
   B. *Business* (diversify, double in size, develop back-up management, sell, transfer to kids).
   C. *Family* (get kids married or educated or both, treat kids fairly, provide for my spouse, keep peace in the family).

But what about *paying less income or estate tax*? Read on.

III. Technical vs. human concerns.
   A. *Technical concerns.* (Shows you how to beat up the IRS, save tax dollars, create wealth. Actually, this is the easy part, and the focus of most of this book.)
   B. *Human concerns.* (This is the hard part. If your professional advisor doesn't explore, understand and deal effectively with human elements, even the most brilliant, money-saving technical plan will fail. Or, most interestingly, the plan will never be signed, completed or fully implemented.)

---

**■ OBSERVATION**

Back to the question about paying less tax. Few people are tax-driven when it comes to considering certain key objectives—such as maintaining one's lifestyle or keeping peace in the family. "The heck with tax dollars—my family comes first," most people tell me.

It's not important to me or other advisors whether you are tax-centered, money-centered, family-centered or whatever. We just want to know. Then we can do the easy part—design a technical plan to accomplish your objectives.

---

## A Pecking Order You Should Know

An overriding factor in almost every business transfer/succession/ estate plan I've handled has been an irresistible force I call "the pecking order."

1. If the business owner/founder has kids in the business, the transfer is to these kids—logical or not.
2. No kids in the business: The owner usually tries to sell to the employees, either by a traditional sale or via an Employee Stock Ownership Plan.
3. No kids in the business/can't sell to employees: Most often, succession means a sale to an outsider. Or, if the business is large and profitable enough, the business goes public or absentee (nonfamily) management takes over from the founder.

## Back to the Agenda

The discussion agenda almost always starts this way:

Objectives (short-term, long-term):

- ☐ Personal
- ☐ Business
- ☐ Family
- ☐ Retirement

It doesn't make much difference what you say, or even if you give good answers. We (my staff and I) just keep on taking notes. If you're hesitant, we know the kind of open-ended questions to ask in a friendly, nonthreatening manner that tend to open up your verbal floodgates.

We ask each family member present to take a shot at the objectives and to pretend that no one else is present. (This tactic usually works, but not always.)

By now you know what we are after—the human concerns of the owner (and those of his/her family members). The road to success in this type of planning is to get the human concerns of the people around the table out in the open. Can you guess what we're looking for? Conflict. If minor, just getting it (or them) out in the open usually solves the rift(s). Normally I can help solve a minor conflict. If solved, fine. We move on. If not, we work until all parties agree to the solution or compromise.

What if the parties don't agree? Logic says your problem is major, not minor. If so, *we end the meeting.* Why? Again, the most brilliant technical plan won't fly if there is a basic underlying conflict that remains unresolved.

---

## ■ COMMENT ON CONFLICT

Fortunately, a major conflict is like lightening. Everyone talks about it, but it rarely strikes. But when it strikes, look out.

Does it happen often? No. Less than two percent of the time. But when it occurs, we consider it serious business and recommend the help of professionals who specialize in conflict resolution.

---

### Using Questions to Discern Objectives

Assume there are no conflicts, or if there were any, they have been clearly resolved. Experience has taught us that the right open-ended questions are the best way to get even the most recalcitrant business owner to open up his mind and his heart.

Years ago, before we knew better, we would give up trying to get close-to-the-vest type owners to talk and would skip to the technical issues—the stuff we were good at. That was a mistake. While our plans may have been good from a technical standpoint, our clients didn't love 'em. We had a plan, but it was rarely the "best" plan for that client.

Today, we take a different tack in such cases. Our unbending rule: Don't touch the technical aspects until you have a complete list of client objectives, confirmed by the client.

We simply tell the client that the failure is ours, not his or hers. It is our job to pinpoint those objectives. We use language like, "We can't fix the clock if we don't know what makes it tick." Then we follow with some general questions, such as: "How did you get into the business?" We keep narrowing our focus. "What are the most important departments (markets, customers, opportunities or similar details about the business) in your company?" And narrower yet: "Why (or how) did Jimmy (the owner's son) wind up running the production department?"

We get most of our questions from two sources:

1. The consulting package the client sends us, together with any verbal comments the client makes during our preliminary chats.
2. From the client's answers (and those from others attending client meetings) to our initial and follow-up questions.

### Questions to Help You Get Started

Here are some sample questions to help clarify your objectives:

1. What is unique about your
   a. Business?
   b. Marketplace?
   c. Family?
   d. Son/daughter (active in business)?
   e. Customer list?
   f. Vendors?
2. Explain your sources of revenue (sales, product lines)
   a. Which make the most money?
   b. Which make the least money?
   c. Which offer the best long-term opportunities?
3. Where do you see your company in five (six, 10, whatever) years?
   a. How will you get there?
   b. Do you have the requisite
      - ☐ Cash flow?
      - ☐ Management?
      - ☐ Capacity?
   c. Does your family agree with your vision?
   d. Does management agree with your vision?
4. What would happen if you took a four-month vacation?
   a. Is this a real possibility?
   b. Who would be in charge? Why him/her?
   c. What would be his/her range of authority?
5. Who will operate the business after you retire? Is there a competent family member or employee within the business to take over? Should an outsider be considered?
6. How will you maintain the income flow you and your family require after you retire? Will it be through dividends or from an established profit-sharing plan? Does such a plan need to be set up now? Can you rent property to the business to receive the needed cash flow?
7. Are you interested in selling the business? If so, is the business salable to an outside party? If so, at what price?
8. Is the business likely to grow in value? In what time frame? By how much? In dollars? Percentage?
9. How about family members not active in the business? Might any of them become active? Do they receive equal or unequal shares? Do they receive part of future growth? How will their interest be converted into cash?
10. How would your plans change if
   a. Your son Joe quit?
   b. You couldn't buy out your nonfamily partner?

While such a list is virtually endless, these questions should get you started.

Sometimes you can vary the question process effectively by asking the same question in a closed-ended way (requires a yes or no answer). By doing so, you are almost certain to get a 'yes' answer. Then, follow up by saying "elaborate." "Explain." "Could you expand on that?"

### Clarifying Objectives

Once such questions are answered, your objectives usually come into sharp focus. If not, keep asking questions. And remember to put the objectives in writing.

A typical set of objectives might look like this:

1. Founder's objectives.
   a. Work until age 60 (founder is now 57).
   b. Then slow down, but remain active in a consulting capacity.
   c. Keep voting control of company until the oldest child (who is now age 30) can assume total responsibility and control.
   d. Have a steady flow of income for retirement without necessity of any compensation from the company after age 65.
2. Corporation's objectives.
   a. Build a strong management team headed by oldest child.
   b. Make sure the company can survive if founder cannot be active for any reason.
   c. Make sure that none of the corporation's assets will be needed to pay taxes at the founder's death.
3. Family's objectives.
   a. Allow founder's spouse to live in manner to which accustomed if founder should die first.
   b. Make certain each of founder's other two children, Tom (age 29) and Mary (27), receives a fair share of founder's estate. (Neither Tom nor Mary is likely to become involved in the business. Both are financially independent.)
   c. Make sure that all the grandchildren—there are nine—have an educational fund set up for them.
   d. Assure that none of the family's real estate or business assets needs to be sold to pay death taxes.

### What to Do Once Objectives Are Set

Review and modify your objectives. If you are advising a client, get final agreement from the primary decisionmaker (usually the owner) and other essential people. (Remember, one of your jobs is to make sure there are no conflicts.)

Explain that the objectives are not set in stone. However, it is common that a client will indicate that certain objectives cannot be changed. So be it.

My strong feeling is that professional consultants should refrain from sharing their views on client objectives except in three cases:

1. To prevent the client from making a tax blunder or doing something that is unwise.
2. It would be dishonest or unethical to do what the client is asking.
3. The professional is directly asked for his/her opinion.

The business owner's objectives are like pegs on which you, the advisor, hang a technical response (use the tools described in the next part of this book). The pegs belong to the client, not the practitioner. The practitioner has no right, unless given permission by the client, to not use a peg, to misuse a peg, or to change or modify a peg.

You and/or your advisor are now ready to start formulating a transfer/ succession/estate plan.

■ **REMEMBER:** Your mission is to put into place a plan that meets your objectives, those of the corporation, and those of your family. Tax considerations only make the right plan better.

### Five-Step Approach

As practiced in my office, transfer of ownership is an organized, five-step process intended to:

1. Restate the business owner's questions, answers, and problems into a series of specific objectives.
2. Identify and discuss the techniques (tools) that meet those objectives.
3. Develop and implement a lifetime plan for the owner.
4. Dovetail the estate plan with the lifetime plan.
5. Maximize the after-tax wealth of the family unit.

You have now completed Step 1 and are ready to attack the remaining four steps—the subject matter of the rest of this book.

Before going on, some observations that pertain to nearly every family-owned business situation—whether you are the owner, a family member, or an advisor to the family:

- ☐ Emotion is always more powerful than logic when applied to a family business problem—real or perceived.
- ☐ Most problems are rational; the solutions are emotional.

## Organizing the Attack

How do you approach a subject as big as "transfer of ownership?"

The subject can be divided into two logical segments:

- ☐ Death planning, and,
- ☐ Lifetime planning

### Death Planning

Bang, bang, Mr. Owner: *YOU ARE DEAD*. This is usually the starting off point for most planners—whether insurance agents, CPAs, lawyers or others. The planner then proceeds to plan the estate using either (1) the dollar value of the estate today or (2) some projected dollar value down the road. This is death planning. Death plans can be easily updated, as needed. For now, set your sights on the future.

### Lifetime Planning

You, Mr. Owner, will live a long, full life...you pick the age—70, 80, 85, whatever—and you will be blessed with good health, a clear mind and a continuing drive to achieve. *This assumption is the heart of this book.*

*"Life,"* not "death," *is our game.* Lifetime planning is our focus. Think for a moment about why lifetime planning is a more logical approach to transfer of ownership than death planning. Jot down your thoughts. Compare them to your newfound approach to transfer of ownership after you finish this book.

## Anticipating Fears

In the context of this book, the terms "objectives" and "fears" are kissing cousins, yet they differ enough to require separate discussion. Objectives can sometimes be stated in purely logical terms; they can even be quantified and reduced to specific numbers. They can also be driven totally by emotion.

Fears, on the other hand, are pure emotion. Here's a list of the most common fears we hear year-in and year-out during our consulting conferences with clients:

**Business Fears**

1. The business will fail without the owner (all kinds of fears here: kids can't run it, taxes, competition, changing conditions).
2. The IRS will sell the business to pay taxes.
3. Fear of losing effective control of the business during owner's lifetime (*this is the most common fear*).

**Family Fears—After Death**

1. Fear that the children will think they were not treated fairly.
2. Fear children will fight.
3. Fear there will not be enough money to:
   a. Meet needs of wife, kids, grandkids, and so on.
   b. Pay taxes.
   c. Pay medical expenses.
4. Fear inflation will erode value of owner's wealth.

How do you deal with a subject as nebulous as fear? In our practice, we tell clients that our approach is designed to solve the easy objectives first, then those that are more difficult.

Usually, all or almost all of a client's objectives are achieved. The right technical solutions, in practice, usually conquer *all* fears.

Here's a job for you. As you read the rest of this book, see which technical tools will overcome the fears listed.

And if you find that one last objective cannot be accomplished, or that a small fear continues to tug at the client's head or heart, don't be alarmed. It simply means that the final transfer/succession/estate plan is imperfect. That's normal.

## A Final Comment

Until human nature changes, the principles discussed in this chapter will continue to stand the test of time. They are, as I see it—*timeless!*

# 2 Basic Concepts/ Problems/Solutions

This chapter is nontechnical. Most of it is timeless.

There are three basic threads—in the form of concepts, problems, and solutions—that are woven into almost every transfer/succession/estate plan. You'll learn what they are in this chapter and throughout this book you'll learn how to sew them into your transfer/succession/estate plan.

Let's start by talking about concerns or problems that ultimately turn into objectives—collectively what I call *the human factors*. For the moment, we'll just list 'em without trying to solve anything.

## Your Concerns and Problems

Typical comments from business owners:

1. "Irv, I don't want my estate to grow. But I don't want to give up *control* just yet."
2. "Irv, I want to *retire* (usually translates to *slow down.*) But I need a flow of income." (The owner owns only one family business and little else.)
3. "Irv, I want to *retire* (usually translates to *slow down*). But I don't want or need any income. It will only increase my estate." (This owner has accumulated wealth outside of the family business.)

   ■ **NOTE:** The owner expresses either #2 or #3, but *never both.*
4. "Irv, I have only one business that cannot be divided. I want to *treat my three kids fairly*. But only Joe Jr. is in the business with me. What can I do about the other kids?" (This scenario probably has about as many versions as there are family businesses.)
5. Other examples of the countless problems and concerns that tug at someone who operates a closely held business and has a family:
   a. "My second wife and my kids..."

b. "My mom is in a nursing home, broke, and none of my brothers or sisters give..."
c. "My son (daughter, grandchild, etc.) needs special care because..."

The list is infinite. In practice, each business owner seems to have some unique twist or turn to his/her concerns and problems.

While I normally don't give my opinion unless I'm asked, let me strongly suggest that you either (1) invite your kids to the final tax-planning meeting or (2) tell them what you have planned. Why? Failure to do so creates after-death problems you can no longer help solve.

In offering counsel, I keep in mind that one or more, but seldom all, of the following considerations are common denominators in every transfer/succession/estate plan.

- ☐ How to maximize your income-tax benefits from this moment forward for as long as you live by dividing income among your family. (This includes such tax techniques as family partnerships, gifts of S corporation stock, and irrevocable trusts.)
- ☐ How to build a retirement fund for you and your spouse that is adequate to fund your lifestyle for as long as you live, assuming both of you enjoy a long life. (This includes your owning and renting business assets to your corporation, creating qualified employee benefit plans and, in general, building wealth outside of your businesses.)
- ☐ How to make sure there are adequate funds to pay death taxes in the event you depart this earth sooner than expected. (In most cases, this means some kind of life-insurance product.)
- ☐ How to freeze the value of your estate as soon as possible during your life to prevent the estate-tax liability from going out of sight. (This is where most of the action is and includes almost all of the "transfer tools" listed in Part II of this book.)
- ☐ How to keep one eye on the contingency plans that must be in place in the event of a divorce in your family—yours, or any of your kids who do or might own stock in the family business, or any other person included in your plan whose divorce would affect your transfer/succession/estate plan. (Actually, your plan should be designed in two ways: one, assuming no divorce, and second, assuming divorce.)

## Tax Rates

Once the human factors (objectives, fears, concerns) are known and present no significant problems, the emphasis shifts from a kinder, gentler approach to an attitude of tax war. Tax rates are both the enemy and our ally. Over time, rates will change—sometimes up, sometimes down—but the principles for dealing with them are timeless.

Let's first list the four rates (for convenience, let's call them "rate tables") you must monitor to maximize your tax savings using the techniques discussed in this book:

1. The income-tax rate tables.
   a. Individual.
   b. Trust and estate.

c. Corporation.

2. Gift-tax rate table.
3. Estate-tax rate table.

■ **NOTE:** You will discover that even though the gift-tax and estate-tax rates come from the same table, in reality the gift tax is a significant money saver when compared with the estate tax.

4. Payroll-tax rate table.

### Current Rates

The exact current rates are not of great importance, but the current rates are the easiest means to use to explain the principles you must learn. What is important—as you will see—is that:

1. The rates (income, gift, estate) are graduated: start low, go high.
2. There are four possible rate tables: avoidance is preferred, but when you must cough up taxes, steer the transaction toward the friendliest table.

But in addition, there are two more "sort of" tables (both very friendly): No-Tax-At-All and Capital Gains.

This book is intended to show you how to beat up the IRS (legally) by playing the rate game as applied to transfer/succession/estate planning. No question about it, this book will make you a tax-rate game winner for the subject matter covered. In addition, by applying the same principles to other tax situations, you will be able to win the rate game in many other tax areas.

## ■ CURRENT RATE TABLES

**INCOME TAX—INDIVIDUALS**

| | Taxable Income* | |
|---|---|---|
| Rate | Joint Return | Single Individual |
| 15% | $37,000 | $22,000 |
| 28% | 90,000 | 54,000 |
| 31% | 90,000 | 54,000 |

*Dollar amounts are rounded to the nearest thousand.

There is a separate table for taxable-income dollar amounts for *estates* and *trusts* which are a bit lower than for *single individuals.*

*Capital gains.* The long-term capital gains rate is currently 28 percent.

**INCOME TAX—CORPORATIONS**

| Taxable Income | Rate |
|---|---|
| 0-$ 50,000 | 15% |
| $ 50,000-$ 75,000 | 25% |
| $ 75,000-$100,000 | 34% |
| $100,000-$335,000 | 39% |
| Over $335,000 | 34% |

**GIFT TAX, ESTATE TAX**

| Taxable Amount | Rate |
|---|---|
| Over $ 600,000 | 37% |
| Over $2,500,000 | 50% |

There are other taxable amounts and rates (see the Appendix) but the above is all we need for the moment.

**PAYROLL TAX**

| | Wage Base | Rates | Cost Per Year |
|---|---|---|---|
| Social Security | $ 57,600 | 6.20% | $3,571 |
| Medicare | 135,000 | 1.45% | 1,958* |
| Total | | | $5,529* |

*This is the amount paid by the employee which must be matched by the employer. The total hit for each employee earning $135,000 or more is $11,058 ($5,529 times 2). Outrageous!

## Using the Rate Tables to Win the Tax Game

Following are the most important rules, concepts, and techniques used in our office to win the rate game.

I. **Bottom fish—income tax.**
   A. Individuals.
      1. *You.* Zero income is never your goal. And paying zero taxes is rarely your goal. Try to engineer your income at a minimum to cover all deductions and exemptions. (Let's call this the "tax-free cup," because the income you have is offset by your deductions and exemptions. Hence, it is tax-free.) It's almost always smart tax planning to pay tax on income that fills the lowest tax bracket cup (now 15 percent) and spills into the next bracket cup (now 28 percent).
      2. *Your low-bracket family members* (such as children and grandchildren). Always try to fill their tax-free cups every year. Filling their 15 percent cups is not such a bad idea, either. Better for the extra 16 percent (say you're in a 31 percent bracket, while your grandson is in a 15 percent bracket) to stay in the family. (Get them income, via trusts, family partnerships, owning S corporation stock, etc.)
      3. *Capital gains.* If you must pay tax, better to pay at the capital-gains rate than the ordinary income-tax rates.
   B. Corporations.
      1. *Rule #1.* Make sure you use all of the lower tax brackets for both yourself and your corporation. For example, if your top bracket is 31 percent and your corporation is in a 15 percent bracket, it makes no sense to trade a 15¢ corporate deduction (say for your increased salary) for a 31¢ tax liability on your individual tax return. You just blew 16¢ per dollar.
      2. *Rule #2.* Do not allow your corporation (say it is a C corporation in a 34-percent tax bracket) to pay at a tax rate greater than your top

individual rate (say you are in a 31-percent tax bracket). Being an S corporation saves you 3 percent; for example, $12,000 on $400,000 of corporate taxable income.

■ **NOTE:** Rule #2 tells you what to do when bottom fishing no longer works. (For example, both you and your C corporation have filled up all of the lower brackets, and you both have taxable income subject to the highest rates).

Rule #2 might be restated to say *"pick the tax rate table that yields the lowest overall income tax."*

II. **Divide.** The concept of *divide* is one of the most important in the how-to-reduce-your-taxes book.

A. Income tax.

*Step #1—Create taxpayers' (taxable entities) trusts (irrevocable) or a corporation (C). Also use every family member with little or no income.* The tax-saving idea is simple: Every live member of your family can pay taxes; get each of them enough income to fill his/her tax-free cup, plus a bit more to bottom-fish the rate table. When you run out of family members, create taxable entities (C corporations, irrevocable trusts) and bottom-fish with each entity.

*Step #2—Divert income from your top tax bracket to family members' zero or low tax brackets.*

B. Don't waste annual tax freebies. It's a shame to waste what the IRS gives you every year:

1. *Income tax.* Every individual (depending on age and other factors) can earn some money tax-free. Sit down with your professional advisor and find out this amount for everyone you support. Then fill the tax-free cups, every year.

   This is using the *divide* concept at its best to win the rate game. Tax dollars are being shifted from your highest tax rate to a zero tax rate.
2. *Gift tax.* Don't waste the $10,000 ($20,000 if you are married) annual exclusion.
3. *Estate tax.* In general, if you don't own it (property), it won't be taxed in your estate. The trick then is to either (a) really not own it (put title in your kids' names or in a trust for their benefit), or (b) give your kids ownership technically, but you control it to the day you die.

III. **Income-tax savers if you need cash.** *Sell high-tax-basis property.* (Say its basis is $1 million, and you can sell it for $1.1 million.) Don't sell during your lifetime. Borrow instead using the property as collateral. The loan proceeds are tax-free. On death, the raised basis (you'll read about this later in the book) avoids any tax when your heirs sell the property for its fair-market value upon your death. *Look for other income savers throughout the book.*

IV. **Income tax vs. estate tax.** This is no contest. Currently, the top estate-tax rate is 55 percent against 31 percent for income tax. If you must pay tax, better to pay income tax than estate tax.

V. **Estate tax vs. gift tax.** Even though the same tax table is used, the gift tax is significantly less (about one-third less) than the estate tax. See Part VII, Chapter Two for exactly how this happens.

VI. **Social security tax vs. no social security tax.** Either the wage base or the rate for social security taxes increases almost every year. Once you are entitled to social security, you lose in two ways by continuing to take a salary from your closely held business. You must pay social security tax, and you lose social security payment benefits you could be entitled to receive. The social security rules are clear: Continuing to work in your business, whether or not you take a salary—so you can draw social security benefits is a no-no. Schemes like having your wife take a large salary (the most common error) or electing S corporation status to take dividends not subject to social security all fail under the law.

If you need cash to live on, arrange to get your after-age-65 cash flow from sources other than compensation. Some options (none is subject to social security taxes or will affect your right to receive benefits):

1. Rent real estate or personal property (i.e., equipment) to your corporation.
2. Establish qualified plans (i.e., profit sharing) as soon as possible.
3. Become an S corporation and
   a. Take dividends from S corporation profits accumulated before you retire, or even after you retire. These dividends are tax-free.
   b. Take S corporation dividends before you retire and loan the money back to your corporation. After you retire, you have two sources of cash flow: the interest (taxable) on these loans and, of course, principal (tax-free) collected on the notes issued when you made the loan. (Note: S corporation dividends are tax-free (you paid the tax personally when the corporation earned the profits). Collection of principal on a note or loan is also income-tax free; it's considered to be a return of capital under the tax law.

The list of methods and techniques used to legally manipulate your tax liability by using the various rate tables as a tax ally is indeed endless. So, too, is the additional list of ways to put you in a pay-no-tax-at-all position, which avoids the tables altogether. (This list of tax savers includes such techniques as shifting income, gifts, the marital deduction and irrevocable life insurance trusts.)

This book is chock-full of ideas, *all legal*, that will save you money on each of the four taxes— income, gift, estate and social security—listed earlier. Use these ideas to lower your taxes.

## The Rule of 72

The Rule of 72 explains the long-term impact of tax savings. To determine how fast tax savings grow over any given time frame, divide the number 72 by the rate of growth or return. The answer indicates how many years it takes for the amount saved to double using that rate of growth. For example, an investment returning (say in your business) 9 percent doubles in 8 years, while one returning 6 percent takes 12 years to double.

This process can also be used to help you determine what rate of growth you need to double your money over a set time period. For example, a 10-year investment will have to return 7.2 percent yearly if you want your money to double in those 10 years, while an investor hoping to double his/her investment in 12 years will require only a 6 percent return.

The Rule of 72 is what drives every qualified employee benefit plan (pension and profit-sharing plans), the insurance industry, the accumulation of wealth by the owner of a privately held business, and the value of that business. The name of the game is actually *the compounding of money over time.*

What's the Rule of 72 lesson? While you're young, invest early and often. You say you're not young? Start today, anyway.

## Control

One of my tax-column articles focused on this topic (for most business owners, the most important subject of all). Some excerpts:

> YES, YOU CAN KEEP CONTROL AFTER TRANSFERRING YOUR BUSINESS
>
> It has been one year longer than 3-1/2 decades since my first consultation with a closely held business owner who had the *its-time-to-transfer-my-business-to-the-kids* itch. And one thing is certain. Nothing has changed.
>
> The two biggest transfer fears of the '50s are still going strong in the '90s. What are they? Here's a hint. The number two fear is taxes—estate taxes that is. And the all-time number one transfer-to-the-kids fear?...CONTROL! Yes, and get this, almost all owners (19 out of 20 to be exact) are frozen with fear when it comes to passing control to their own flesh and blood. So much so, that many go to the big business in the sky and force their surviving families to overpay their estate tax. Why? Well, they held control (over 50 percent) of the business' voting common stock right up to the day they died.
>
> But there are little known, yet easy, ways to beat both fears. We use them year in and year out, and in consultation after consultation. Here's an example.
>
> The owner turns all of his stock (common) into the corporation and takes back two types of common stock in exchange—voting common (say 100 shares) and nonvoting common (say 9,900 shares). This transaction, called a "recapitalization," is tax-free and works for both C corporations (tax-paying) and S corporations. The owner then sells (rarely) or gives (the method used most often) the nonvoting stock to his kids over a period of years. The owner can own as little as 1 percent of all the stock (100 shares of voting stock in this example) and still retain 100 percent of the voting control. Just what he wanted—low value, high control. No fears. Perfect!

Many owners become squeamish and embarrassed when the subject of control comes up. Why? They don't want to admit they are unwilling to step aside and pass control—the right to make the ultimate decisions—down to their son or daughter. This problem is so pervasive that I presume the client/business owner does not want to give up control.

Thus I explain two factors to reassure the client:

1. Wanting to keep control is normal.
2. It is easy to transfer the value of the business for tax purposes, yet keep control via a tax-free, voting/nonvoting stock recapitalization.

Suddenly the client relaxes and turns back into the tiger that made him a success. Then, in the typical case, the rest of the planning agenda is a breeze.

## Divorce

The typical closely held business owner with whom I consult (let's call his business Your Company) is married. This requires two conflicting assumptions on my part:

1. The owner will never divorce.
2. The owner will divorce.

Our ultimate question: If the owner divorces, who gets the stock of Your Company?

Other scenarios obviously must be considered: A single owner might marry and then become a candidate for the abovementioned conflicting assumptions. And, of course, multiple marriages and divorces may occur, forcing more unwelcome opportunities to play the above assumption game and answer the who-gets-the-stock-question. And the same rules apply to the owners kids, married or single, who end up owning stock in Your Company. You get the idea.

*All of these scenarios are covered by one set of rules*, which I addressed in this item from my tax column:

> THINKING OF TRANSFERRING YOUR BUSINESS TO YOUR KIDS?...READ THIS
>
> The transfer-of-ownership meeting at my office was less than five minutes old. The entire family was present: Joe Owner (59), his wife Sue (57), and their two sons, Joe. Jr. (34) and Jake (31). Joe Jr. is married to Peg, and they have one child. Jake is single. The boys run the business on a day-to-day basis.
>
> After the usual exchange of pleasantries, the meeting started. I had prepared a written agenda from data Joe had sent me. The first item on the agenda and my first question was "What are your short-term and long-term objectives for yourself, your business, your family and your retirement?" Joe started to answer, but about two minutes into his response, Sue interrupted him in an emotional outburst. "No, Joe Jr. can never own any stock. I want to make sure Peg never owns stock in our business. Or ever has a say of any kind..." Her emotions spilled over in a torrent of words.
>
> Are such feelings unusual? No. Sometimes it is the father expressing these fears. Sometimes the mother. Sometimes both. The target of these fears is equally spread over sons-in-law and daughters-in-law. Do you share this fear? If so, you're the norm.
>
> When this fear surfaces (and it does most of the time) in a transfer-consulting meeting, it is my job to allay the fear. I simply tell my clients the law:
>
> For these purposes, you must assume your son or daughter will someday be a party to a divorce. If your child never marries, no problem. If your child marries and never divorces, no problem. What happens when one of your children owns stock in the family business and the divorce devil is doing its dance?
>
> Your first job is to determine if the stock is marital property or nonmarital property. If it's nonmarital property, no problem. I've never been involved in or even heard of a case where the judge took nonmarital property away from one spouse and gave it to the other divorcing spouse. Sounds good. And it is.
>
> So when is stock (or any other property) nonmarital property? (1) When your child owned the stock prior to the marriage. (2) When the child received the

stock after the marriage by gift or (3) by inheritance. (4) When your child bought the stock after the marriage with his/her own money (earned before the marriage or received as a gift or by inheritance). But be forewarned, the fourth way may be tough to prove in court. Also, when the marriage is short-term (the definition varies from judge to judge and from state to state), the stock is nonmarital property even if it could have been marital property.

*Now, the most important point of this article:* Start out and keep the stock as nonmarital property. Then you and your children are safe.

Sorry, but everything else is marital property. The stock must be valued (expensive, because each side hires an appraiser) and the court controls if or how it is to be divided. How can stock become marital property? One way is to goof: Put nonmarital property in your spouse's name or in joint tenancy with your spouse. The most common way is when the stock-owning spouse purchases the stock when married with money earned during that marriage.

As soon as any of your children own even one share of stock, a buy-sell agreement is essential. Obviously, there are more problems, rules and exceptions you should know. As far as I know, all of the rules spelled out above are law in all 50 states. *If you know of any differences,* I would welcome your written feedback. This is one area where it pays to get the best professional help available. Always, but always have your lawyer spell out the law in your state.

## ■ NOTE FOR THOSE LIVING IN A COMMUNITY PROPERTY STATE

If you live in a community property state, just substitute the words "separate property" for "nonmarital property" and the words "community property" for the words "marital property."

The following schedule gives a bird's-eye view of the law in this all-important area.

### ■ SUMMARY OF RULES FOR DETERMINING WHETHER PROPERTY IS MARITAL OR NONMARITAL PROPERTY

| | Marital Property if Acquired* | |
|---|---|---|
| How Property Acquired | Before Marriage | After Marriage |
| Gift | No | No |
| Inheritance | No | No |
| Stock Bonus* *+ | No | Yes |
| Purchase | No | Yes/No/? |
| GRIT/GRAT* * *+ | No | No |

* Assumes property acquired and kept in sole name of married individual at all times.
* * While an employee acquires stock of employer.
* * * GRIT (grantor retained interest trust)/GRAT (grantor retained annuity trust).
\+ Concept is explained elsewhere in this book.

My experience is clear with respect to divorce issues: Once the law is explained, the business owner's fear of divorce (relative to stock ownership in the family business) evaporates and the planning meeting proceeds.

## A Short Course in Corporate Stock

To a large extent, this book assumes that your business is incorporated, although most of the discussion so far is equally applicable to an unincorporated business (sole proprietorship or partnership).

*For the balance of this book, it is necessary to assume that you have incorporated your business or will do so in the near future.*

### Shares of Stock and Their Characteristics

Ownership of an interest in a corporation is evidenced by shares of stock. A share of stock has many attributes or characteristics. Let's briefly review the attributes that are important to closely held corporations.

**VOTING POWER.** Stockholders vote to elect the board of directors of a corporation. The directors in turn elect the president and other principal corporate officers. Whether discussing a corporation in which you are the only shareholder (you own 100 percent) or General Motors, this right to vote is a significant attribute of stock ownership. Why? The officers run the day-to-day operations of the corporation.

A corporation may have two or more "classes" of stock, typically common stock and preferred stock. Each class may have voting rights. Often, however, some classes have voting rights, and others do not. If you have only one class of stock, it must be common, and it must be voting.

If you elect S corporation status, you can have only one *class* of stock—common, but you can have two *types* of common stock—voting and nonvoting.

**DIVIDENDS.** The profits of a corporation are distributed among shareholders in the form of *dividends*. Generally, dividends are paid only if the corporation has accumulated earnings. Also, dividends are paid only if the board of directors elects to pay them.

If there is more than one class of stock, dividends may be payable on one class before they can be paid on the other class. In other words, the former class may be preferred as to dividends.

Most family corporations (and other closely held corporations) have only one class of stock—common. Rarely do such corporations pay dividends, which are unattractive taxwise (being taxable to the shareholder but nondeductible by the corporation).

**LIQUIDATION VALUES.** When a corporation is liquidated (i.e., dissolved), each shareholder participates in the net liquidation value (after all debts to creditors have been paid off).

If there is only one class of stock outstanding, each shareholder's distributive share in the liquidation value is proportionate to the number of shares owned.

Where, however, there are two or more classes of stock, the situation is quite different. One or more classes may be preferred as to liquidation value. Thus, each share of "preferred" stock may be entitled to a specific dollar amount of the assets distributed in liquidation (usually "par value," which is explained below). Only if the preferred stock shareholders receive 100 percent of the preferred par value do the common stock shareholders divide up what's left, if anything.

### Additional Characteristics of Stock

Where there are two or more classes of stock, one class is usually assigned a "par value." This is a rather arbitrary number—say $100 per share. Also, each class of preferred stock has a dividend rate, expressed as a percentage (say 8 percent).

Specifying "par value" serves two purposes:

- ☐ First, in the case of preferred stock, it fixes the amount of the liquidation value (say $100 per share).
- ☐ Second, it gives us a numerical base to which we can apply the dividend percentage.

Thus, an eight-percent preferred stock having a $100 par value is preferred as to dividends of up to $8 per share. Hence, each share of preferred stock must be paid an $8 dividend before any dividends can be paid on the common stock.

Preferred stock may be "cumulative" or "noncumulative." Dividends of noncumulative stock must be declared and paid each year. If the board of directors fails to do so, the dividend is lost forever. Cumulative stock carries an annual dividend amount (say $8), which must be paid before dividends can be paid on the common stock. For example, after five years, each preferred share would be entitled to a $40 dividend ($8 x 5) before the common shareholder could receive a dividend.

### Growth

Whether shares of stock will increase in value depends largely on the extent to which the corporation prospers. If, for example, there is only common stock and earnings triple (on a consistent basis), the total value of all outstanding shares is likely to at least triple.

Where, however, there are both common and preferred shares outstanding, improved earnings of the company impact only on the value of the *common* stock. Why? Remember, preferred stock is generally preferred as to dividends and preferred as to liquidation value up to a specified sum. This sum usually serves as a ceiling, as well as a floor, on the extent of participation of the preferred stock. Hence, all growth in value of the corporation, whether due to earnings or otherwise, accrues to the benefit of the common stock, which has neither a floor nor a ceiling limiting its potential future value.

## A Mini-Course in Corporate Finance

Transfer of ownership requires that stock ownership in the family corporation be changed. A quick look at the basic methods of stock transactions will do two things:

- ☐ Give you an overall picture of how stock ownership can be changed.
- ☐ Help you understand how the tools, explained in Part II of this book, are used to meet specific objectives.

In the examples that follow, 100 percent of the stock is always owned by Dad, Mom, Daughter or Son; 200 shares of common stock are owned to start. You can always determine how the example might affect your personal situation by substituting your real names, percentages and number of shares.

**A. SALE OR GIFT**

| Stock Ownership | Shares Owned Before | Shares Owned After |
|---|---|---|
| Dad | 150 | 140 |
| Mom | 50 | 40 |
| Daughter | - | 20 |
| Total Shares | 200 | 200 |

■ **RULE:** The corporation is not involved in the transaction. All shares are transferred among the parties outside of the corporation.

**B. STOCK BONUS**

| Stock Ownership | Shares Owned Before | Shares Owned After |
|---|---|---|
| Dad | 150 | 150 |
| Mom | 50 | 50 |
| Son | - | 2 |
| Total Shares | 200 | 202 |

■ **RULE:** The corporation issues new shares. None of the stockholders (except the stockholder receiving the bonus) is involved in the transaction.

**C. REDEMPTION**

| Stock Ownership | Shares Owned Before | Shares Owned After |
|---|---|---|
| Dad | 100 | 100 |
| Mom | 60 | - |
| Daughter | 40 | 40 |
| Total Shares | 200 | 140 |

■ **RULE:** Only the corporation and the redeeming shareholders (here only Mom) are involved in the transaction. The other shareholders are not involved in the transaction but each has a greater percentage of ownership after the transaction. (Daughter's ownership went from 20 percent "before" to 29 percent "after.")

**D. PREFERRED STOCK DIVIDEND—TAX-FREE**

| | Shares Owned | | |
|---|---|---|---|
| Stock Ownership | Before Common | After Common | After Preferred |
| Dad | 140 | 140 | 280 |
| Mom | 20 | 20 | 40 |
| Son | 40 | 40 | 80 |
| Total Shares | 200 | 200 | 400 |

■ **RULE:** To make the transactions tax-free the corporation and all the stockholders are involved in the transaction. Each stockholder owns exactly the same percentage of all classes of stock before and after the transaction. (For example Dad owned 70 percent of the common "before and owns 70 percent of both common and preferred "after.")

## Dividing Your Assets

### Dividing Assets by Rate of Growth

The assets you own today, the day you start your transfer/succession/estate plan, should be broken down into three logical categories: fast growth, average growth and slow growth (or no growth) assets.

The fast-growth assets are the most important for our purposes. The goal here is to remove them from your estate as quickly as possible to cut off your growing estate-tax liability. At this point, we are examining *what to do*. Later parts and chapters of this book explore *how to do it*.

### Dividing Assets by Tax Basis

Another way of dividing your assets is by tax basis, as follows:

1. Assets with a low tax basis, but a high value. Consider these concepts:
   a. Don't sell 'em. Hold them until death to get a raised tax basis.
   b. Such assets should be owned by the spouse most likely to die first (usually the husband).
   c. These are great assets to gift to charity. (Your profit is not subject to the regular income tax, but you get a charitable deduction equal to the fair market value of the property at the date of the gift.)
2. Assets with a high tax basis but a low value. Consider this concept: Sell 'em. Deduct the loss. Give the proceeds (rather than the property) to charity. You get two deductions from one piece of property.

### Dividing Assets by Business Assets and Nonbusiness Assets

This is the first example in the book showing how a real-life transfer/estate plan can be designed. Be patient. You will see many more.

**STEP #1—DIVIDE YOUR ASSETS BETWEEN BUSINESS ASSETS** *(to be transferred to the business children) and all other assets (to be transferred to the nonbusiness children).* This typical scenario illustrates the problem: Joe has three children—Sam is active in the business; Jack and Jill are inactive. Joe wants to treat the kids "equally," yet would like to give the business assets to Sam and the nonbusiness assets to Jack and Jill. Following is Joe's asset schedule, net of liabilities:

| | VALUE |
|---|---|
| **BUSINESS ASSETS** | |
| Old Company stock (family business) | $1,500,000 |
| New Company stock (recent start-up) | 100,000 |
| Real estate (leased to Old Company)* | 650,000 |
| Total Business Assets | 2,250,000 |
| **OTHER ASSETS** | |
| Cash | 50,000 |
| Marketable securities | 100,000 |
| Main residence | 225,000 |
| Vacation condo | 100,000 |
| Other real estate | 150,000 |
| Life insurance (face value at death) | 250,000 |
| Total Other Assets | 875,000 |
| Total Assets | $3,125,000 |

*Real estate can be converted to a nonbusiness asset. See Step #2 at 2b.

## ■ CAN YOUR PRESENT ASSET MIX MEET YOUR OBJECTIVES?

It is usually very easy to tell—either your present asset mix can or cannot be used to meet your objectives. If it can (for example, you have two children—one, Joe, in the business and one, Sallie, not in the business, and your asset mix is half business assets and half nonbusiness assets). No problem: The business assets go to Joe; the nonbusiness assets to Sallie). If your solution is not so simple, read on.

**STEP #2—CHANGE THE ASSET MIX.** Since you ain't dead yet, start immediately to change your asset mix. You have until the day you die to meet the challenge. Consider combining a number of these approaches. A good rule to remember: Build nonbusiness assets up in value while reducing (or at least freezing) the value of your business assets. Also remember that time is on your side.

1. Purchase more life insurance. (The proceeds are a nonbusiness asset.)
2. Do everything possible to increase your personal wealth (nonbusiness assets) as opposed to the value of the business. Some ideas:
   a. Put away as much as you can in a qualified retirement plan.
   b. Buy real estate and equipment needed in the business in your name. Then, lease it to the business. Note that Joe's real estate ($650,000 value) is listed as a business asset. When dovetailing a transfer plan and an estate plan, such assets can be converted into nonbusiness assets. They can be left to the nonbusiness children, who can lease them to the business.
   c. Elect S corporation status, and take the profits out of the business. If the corporation needs the money, loan it back. Note: The loan (i.e., promissory note) is now a nonbusiness asset and can be left to the nonbusiness children.
   d. Increase your salary (but watch for an unreasonable compensation problem); bank/invest the increase, which is a nonbusiness asset.
3. Plan an annual gift program to the children.
4. Determine your estimated estate tax (federal) and inheritance tax (state) liabilities today and at various estimated dates down the road.
5. Set up a transfer/estate plan as if you might be gone tomorrow.
6. Assume you will live a long time (you pick the age), and set a plan in effect to freeze your estate as much as possible to prevent the estate tax from skyrocketing.
7. Set up a lifetime income tax plan that dovetails with your estate plan to take advantage of the years you have yet to enjoy and fulfill *ALL* of your objectives.

## ■ COMMENT

The abovementioned example shows how a portion of a transfer/estate plan might be structured to solve Joe's problems and meet his objectives. You will learn more about how to treat children fairly in Part III of this book.

You are now ready to begin building your transfer/succession/estate plan. But first you must become familiar with the tools available to get the job done. The balance of this book discusses these tools, how to use them to meet your objectives and deal with your asset mix most effectively.

Don't jump to conclusions. Finish reading the entire book before passing judgment on which tool (or tools) to use. Even then, your best bet is to withhold final judgment until you discuss your situation with an experienced and qualified professional.

# PART II

# The Transfer Tools

II

# INTRODUCTION

## The Right Tools Can Move Your Business World Exactly Where You Want It

There's a famous quote that goes something like this: "Give me a lever long enough and I will move the earth." Well, if you have the right tools, you can move (transfer) your business and wealth to the next generation...the right way.

Of course, you must first learn how to use the tools. Then you can build a transfer/succession plan. The right plan. A plan custom designed for you, your family, and your business. What can the right plan do for you? Accomplish your objectives. Calm your fears. Solve your problems. Eliminate your concerns.

The right plan keeps peace in your family.

What about taxes? The right plan always cuts the overall tax burden—income tax, gift tax, and estate tax. And sometimes the tools can craft a plan to increase your lifetime income and create wealth over and above eliminating the gift tax and the estate tax.

Okay, get your work clothes on. This is your job: Learn what each of the transfer tools is capable of doing. Select only those you need. Learn how to use them. Build your transfer/succession plan. Later you'll learn how to dovetail your transfer/succession plan with your estate plan.

# 1 The Primary Transfer Tools

This chapter is a nontechnical presentation of a technical subject.

This chapter starts the search for answers to meet your objectives. Remember, one size does not fit all.

## Definitions

It's time to define a few terms. The terms "transfer" and "succession" have special meanings. In this book, both terms deal with: (1) moving stock ownership from the current owners of a closely held business to new owners; (2) giving up management control of the business (both day-to-day control and control of all decisions—even decisions that affect the growth, diversification, sale or liquidation of the business); or, (3) both.

"Transfer," for our purposes, means moving ownership, control, or both within the same family, typically from a father to one or more of his children. The consideration for the transfer is usually motivated by love and affection. The person or persons to whom the transfer is made are usually related by blood or marriage to the person making the transfer.

"Succession," for our purposes, means moving ownership, control, or both to nonfamily members. Typically, ownership is moved via a sale to employees or outsiders. In this case the prime motivator for the owner is usually maximizing the after-tax dollars as part of the succession plan. For the most part, the owner has dollar signs in his/her eyes. Emotional issues are clearly subordinate to the how-many-dollars-do-I-wind-up-with-in-my-pocket mentality.

When ownership is retained in the family, but there is no transfer or succession (as defined above), typically day-to-day control is passed to hired management—maybe former employees, maybe entirely new blood. This is another form of succession.

## The Transfer Plan

In most cases, planning the transfer of a closely held corporation simply means accomplishing the business owner's predetermined objectives while minimizing the tax cost. The owner attempts to freeze his estate at its current level and divert future growth (to the extent possible, under law) to the natural objects of his bounty (usually his children and grandchildren). As this book develops, you will see that it is far easier to divert future growth than it is to disgorge wealth that has already been accumulated.

A good transfer plan is part of an overall lifetime plan that attempts to get the asset-freezing process into place as soon as possible. Also, it dovetails with the estate plan. Obviously, if you can cut off (transfer) wealth before it accumulates, you can avoid serious tax problems.

## The Primary Tools

While all tools are important, concentrate on those needed to build your transfer/succession plan. Here is a list of these primary tools:

1. Sale of stock to family members (no-no!).
2. Gifts of stock to the family.
3. Stock bonus to employee (son/daughter).
4. Redemptions (including how to get appreciated property out of your corporation).
5. S corporations.
6. GRATs.
7. Recapitalizations.
8. New activities of the family business.
9. Leasing through passive family partnerships.
10. Combinations.

Scan the list again. Notice that *every item deals with lifetime planning, not* death planning. YOU AIN'T DEAD YET!

---

**■ IMPORTANT**

This chapter is designed to give you a quick nontechnical overview of the transfer tools and how to use them. With a few exceptions, the technical (complex from a tax standpoint) and more sophisticated uses are covered in later parts of this book.

---

## Sale of Stock to Family (No-No!)

Whenever business owners tell me they want to sell their businesses to their children, I shake my head, saying: "No, no, no..." One of my columns explains why.

THINKING OF SELLING YOUR BUSINESS TO YOUR KIDS?...READ THIS

As the years spin by, the message becomes crystal clear: Sooner or later you must transfer your business. And if you're typical, the transfer will be made to one or more of your children. What's the most common form of transfer? Hands down, it's a sale of the business.

Let's follow the triple tax hit to the family when a parent (say dad) sells to his child (say son). Suppose son will pay his dad an amount equal to the fair-market value of the business over a period of years plus current market-rate interest.

The tax tragedy starts with the son. Since he can't deduct the cost of the stock from his current income, he is forced to first earn the money, pay the tax and have only the balance to pay his dad. This is *TAX NUMBER ONE*. By the way, a smart tax move is to elect S corporation status. This accomplishes two purposes: (1) the interest paid to dad becomes deductible by the son, and (2) corporate profits can be withdrawn, free of a dividend tax, to pay dad for the stock.

What happens when dad receives the payments? The interest is fully taxable. The profit on the sale of the stock is taxable as a capital gain. This is *TAX NUMBER TWO*.

Let's review the stock purchase tax damage so far in round numbers. In order to pay dad $1,000, son must earn about $1,500 subject to around a $500 tax bite (including state tax). If dad's tax basis for the stock is $100, he must pay a capital gains tax of about $270 on the $900 profit. What's left?...$730...less than half the $1,500 son had to earn. And remember, son must pay interest on the unpaid balance of the total stock purchase price.

Finally, when dad dies, the after-tax profit from the stock sale ($730 above) will be subject to the estate tax. Probably another 50 percent tax slice (taking $365) and leaving $365 for the heirs. This is *TAX NUMBER THREE*. To summarize: That's $365 left out of $1,500. A lousy tax deal.

## Warning

The sale of stock method is overused because of its simplicity. It should only be used when one of the other methods discussed in this book does not work—a very rare circumstance.

Nevertheless, this method must be explored for two reasons: First, it does sometimes accomplish the family objectives, and second, it is always a good starting point in comparing other methods available.

A sale of stock can be made either for cash or on an installment basis. The easiest way to understand the impact of a sale is by analyzing the cash flow results of a cash sale, as illustrated by Exhibit I.

In this example, Joe Owner's corporation is worth $500,000. Joe wants to sell his son John one percent of the stock, although John does not have any funds with which to make the purchase. All parties—the corporation, Joe and John—are in a 30-percent income-tax bracket. Joe's estate will be in a 50-percent estate-tax bracket.

■ **NOTE:** The exact tax brackets are not as important as the principle illustrated. Use your own brackets in any transaction contemplated.

Look under the column headed "Corporation." In order to get John the money to buy the stock, the corporation pays him a $10,000 bonus. Assume there is no reasonable compensation problem. Notice that the $10,000 is shown opposite "Portion of Salary" as outgoing from the corporation. Since the corporation deducted the $10,000 on its income tax return, the "Net after income and estate taxes" is a net out-of-pocket $7,000 to the corporation.

Next, look at the column under "John." John received a $10,000 salary/bonus, paid $3,000 in taxes and had a "Net after-tax" balance of $7,000. He immediately wrote a check to his father for $7,000 to purchase one percent of the stock. Joe's tax cost for this stock was $1,000, resulting in a $6,000 profit. At a 30-percent tax rate (this is a capital gain; the tax rate will probably go down by congressional action), Joe's tax is $1,800, leaving Joe with $5,200 in cash. Upon Joe's death, that $5,200 will be included in his estate, resulting in a $2,600 estate-tax cost. Joe's "Net after income and estate taxes" is therefore $2,600. When all the smoke clears, the net result of the entire transaction—from the $10,000 bonus to John to the final amount left in Joe's estate—is a $4,400 *cash outflow* ($7,000 out of the corporation, less $2,600 left in Joe's estate)—*A Terrible Tax Result.*

### ■ EXHIBIT I: CASH FLOW—OUTRIGHT SALE

| Details | Corporation | John | Joe |
|---|---|---|---|
| 1. During life | | | |
| a. Portion of salary | $(10,000) | $10,000 | |
| Tax - Saved | 3,000 | - | |
| - Paid | - | ( 3,000) | |
| Net after tax | ( 7,000) | 7,000 | |
| b. Purchase of stock | - | ( 7,000) | $7,000 |
| Tax - assume cost of $1,000, profit of $6,000 x 30% | - | - | (1,800) |
| Net after tax | ( 7,000) | None | 5,200 |
| 2. Estate tax at death of Joe | | | (2,600) |
| Net after income and estate taxes | $( 7,000) | $ None | $2,600 |

Before selling the stock of a closely held corporation to a family member, *work the proposed figures through a tentative cash flow*. In every case, it will be negative.

Then, project the cost of the loss of the use of money. Remember, Joe paid a tax of $1,800 on the $6,000 profit. How much could the family unit have earned with that $1,800 if Joe lived for 10 years after the sale to John?...20 years?...30 years? You get the idea. The lost-opportunity value of money may ultimately be a greater cost than the immediate tax cost. (See the Rule of 72, Part I, Chapter 2).

## Using an Installment Sale

The installment method usually gives better results than a stock sale, but the tax pill is still bitter. And you must make the same cash-flow projections.

Let's look at the pros and cons of an installment sale:

**Advantages**

1. Unquestionably, the future growth of the stock is transferred to John.
2. The interest on the installment sale provides a flow of income to Joe. The principal payment provides an additional flow of funds to Joe.
3. There is no current gift tax or use of the unicredit (in effect, the combined amount of your taxable gifts and taxable estate that can be passed tax free—$600,000). This assumes the stock was sold at its fair-market value.
4. John gets a stepped-up basis for the stock (John could sell the stock for $10,000 without any tax cost).
5. There is tremendous flexibility in the amount of present and future payments. Payments can be adjusted in a number of ways—via the interest rate, by the amount of each principal payment, by adding a prepayment privilege, or by providing for a balloon payment down the road.

**Disadvantages**

1. The portion of the gain realized each year is subject to an immediate tax. Although this gain can be deferred by making the initial principal payments small and putting a balloon at the tail end, sooner or later the tax on the gain must be paid.
2. If Joe dies before receiving full payment of the installment obligations, the obligation is not only included in his estate for estate tax purposes, but the remaining collections are subject to income tax as collected. This is called "income in respect of a decedent," (See Part IX, Chapters 1 and 2 of this book for a complete discussion) causing, in effect, a double tax on the same note receivable.

   ■ **NOTE:** The income taxes paid by Joe on the lifetime installment sale are a waste—they could have been avoided if the stock had been held until Joe's death. John would have received a stepped-up basis equal to the fair-market value of the shares at Joe's death.

3. The interest John pays to Joe could be classified as investment interest, which can only be deducted against investment income. If John has no investment income, the interest is, in effect, nondeductible. Electing S corporation status makes the interest deductible against other ordinary income if John is active in the business.

## Does a Sale to the Kids Ever Make Sense?

Yes, in three circumstances:

1. The stock in the hands of the parent has a high tax basis.
2. The selling parent is in a low-income tax bracket and has a small estate (likely to be free or substantially free of the estate tax).
3. The stock is likely to appreciate rapidly.

For example, let's say Lou's estate is in the 55-percent estate-tax bracket. He owns 100 percent of the stock in a business with tremendous growth potential that he bought for $100,000. He sells the stock to his children for $250,000, its current fair-market value, on the installment basis. The children make a small down payment and do not resell the property within two years. Lou dies six years later, when the fair-market value of the stock is $2 million and the balance on the installment note is $180,000. The only amount includable in Lou's estate is the installment note of $180,000. All the growth passes to the children free of estate tax.

■ **NOTE:** If the children do not hold the stock for at least two years, the IRS can ignore the sale. [See Section 453(e)].

■ **CAUTION:** Trying to use a low-ball price between family members gets you nowhere. The IRS can (and will) ignore your price for tax purposes.

## Gifts of Stock to the Family

The primary advantage of an annual gift program, with either the operating or nonoperating children, is its simplicity. In certain cases (particularly, small estates of about $1,200,000 for a married donor and $600,000 for a single donor), a gift program can be used to accomplish all the family objectives. In most cases, however, because of the high value of the stock involved and the tax consequences, gifts alone cannot do the entire job of transferring ownership and control of a family corporation.

It is helpful to use a checklist of the important items that should be considered when a gift program of stock is contemplated.

**AMOUNT OF GIFT.** The donor (the person making the gift) can make a $10,000 gift to each donee (the person receiving the gift) each year without any gift-tax consequences. If the donor's spouse consents to the gift, the amount can be doubled to $20,000.

**STOCK AS A GIFT.** Property that is likely to appreciate over time, like stock in a closely held corporation, is the perfect gift for members of a younger generation. Future appreciation is removed from the estate of the donor without any tax cost.

**CONTROL OF THE CORPORATION.** Although the founder would like to transfer the ownership of the stock so that it is removed from his/her estate, the founder might not want to transfer control to the children. Three circumstances, in particular, always require attention:

- ☐ The children are minors.
- ☐ Although adult children are active in the business, they are not capable of managing; the management ability of one or more of the adult children is a matter of fierce family disputes; or Dad wants to remain in charge.
- ☐ There are adult children who are not active in the business and who could not, even if given the opportunity, make intelligent voting decisions to direct management.

These problems can usually be solved by putting the stock into a trust, issuing nonvoting stock, or always keeping enough voting stock to stay in control.

■ **NOTE:** See Part VIII, Chapter 3 for a detailed discussion of gifts.

## Stock Bonus to Employees (Son/Daughter)

In most cases, the employee is the son or daughter of the owner or some other close family member active in the corporation. Suppose we give a bonus to Joe Owner's son, John, an employee of the corporation. The bonus is in shares of stock of the corporation. Assume there is no unreasonable compensation problem when the value of the bonus stock is added to John's other compensation.

What are the tax consequences of such a bonus? The answer delights tax practitioners, but owner/clients love it.

1. The employee must pay income tax on the fair-market value of the stock received. See Section 83.
2. The corporation can deduct the fair-market value of the stock that it gives to the employee as compensation. See Revenue Ruling 69-75.

The combination of the Code Section and the Revenue Ruling gives Joe, John, and the corporation tremendous tax advantages.

### Sale of Stock vs. Stock Bonus

Which is best? A sale of stock from Joe Owner to John or use of the stock-bonus method? Obviously, Joe's objectives would have an impact on the answer. Let's compare a sale of stock from Joe to John as opposed to a stock bonus. A comparison shows which method best meets Joe's objectives. Look back at Exhibit I, where Joe sold $7,000 of stock to John, who had received a cash salary of $10,000; paid tax of $3,000, resulting in a $7,000 after-tax amount to John; and finally, transmitted $7,000 to Joe. In Exhibit II, John receives $5,000 in cash and $5,000 in stock as a salary/bonus—a total of $10,000. Look under the column headed "Corporation." Remember, all parties are in 30-percent tax brackets.

**■ EXHIBIT II: CASH FLOW—PARTIAL STOCK BONUS**

| Details | Corporation | John | Joe |
|---|---|---|---|
| During life— | | | |
| a. Cash salary | $(5,000) | $5,000 | $ - |
| b. $5,000 of stock as salary | - | - | - |
| Tax (on $10,000 salary) | | | |
| Saved | 3,000 | - | - |
| Paid | - | (3,000) | - |
| Net After Tax | $(2,000) | $2,000 | $ None |

As Exhibit II indicates, the corporation is out-of-pocket $5,000 because of the cash salary and is in-pocket $3,000 because of the $10,000 it deducted as compensation. Its "Net after-tax" cash flow is a negative $2,000.

Now look under John's column. He received the $5,000 in cash plus $5,000 in stock for a total of $10,000 in compensation and must pay $3,000 income tax for a "Net after-tax" of $2,000.

What about Joe? He had nothing to do with the transaction, other than voting for it as a member of the board of directors.

In this example, the corporation is out-of-pocket $2,000, while John is in-pocket $2,000—a standoff. But, in practice, where the corporation is usually in a higher tax bracket than the family-member employee, the family unit winds up with a net in-pocket gain. Work out your own numbers. You'll like the results.

### Effecting a Stock Transfer Without Making a Real Stock Transfer

In Exhibit II, Joe, the owner, has in fact reduced the value of his interest in the corporation. Assume he owned 100 percent of the corporation before the stock bonus, represented by 100 shares of stock. After the stock bonus of one share to John (since this share is worth $5,000, the total value of the corporation is approximately $500,000), the corporation has 101 shares issued and outstanding. Joe still owns the same 100 shares, but only 99.01 percent of all the stock. In effect, he has transferred almost one percent of the corporation's value—all without a real transfer and, best of all, with zero tax cost.

### Valuation

What if the IRS attacks the stock valuation? For example, if the IRS claims the stock value should have been higher:

1. The corporation would have a larger deduction.
2. John's tax would be larger.
3. The overall cash impact, assuming the same tax bracket for all parties, is still the same—zero. The only danger to guard against is the potential problem of unreasonable compensation (for John).

But let's say the IRS claims a lower value. The result:

1. A smaller deduction for the corporation.
2. A smaller tax for John.
3. Overall, still a zero-cash impact.

■ **NOTE:** A difference in tax brackets, between the corporation and the shareholder, would cause a tax cost or benefit depending on the exact difference in brackets.

## Redemptions

(including how to get appreciated property out of your corporation). This article from my tax column provides a good explanation of redemptions. Two notes:

- ☐ Steps 3, 4 and 5 in the article are collectively considered a "complete redemption" under the income-tax law (explained immediately after the article).
- ☐ The article summarizes several concepts presented in this book and also produces a mini-transfer plan.

HOW KIDS CAN BUY OUT DAD WITHOUT CASH

You've had it. After 10, 15 (well, you fill in the number) or more years of building your business, you want out. More than that, you want some of those nice assets out of the family corporation. Some of those assets—excess cash, investments, land, building—are no longer needed in the business or could be owned outside of the business and rented to the corporation. And one more thing: The kids are ready to run the business, want to buy it and you're willing to sell it, but one little detail is missing. The kids have no real money.

What to do?

The best way to show you how to solve this puzzle is by an example. Here goes: Joe Success, who is married to Jane, owns 100 percent of Go-Go, Inc., which is worth $2,740,000. Go-Go has 2,740 shares of stock, which are worth $1,000 each. Joe's son and daughter—Jon and Jan—have really been running the business for the past five years.

This is the five-step plan the Successes put into effect. Step 1: Joe gives 40 shares (worth $40,000) to Jon and Jan—20 shares each. Step 2: Jane joins in the gift tax return, making the $40,000 gift tax-free. Step 3: Joe sells his remaining 2,700 shares to Go-Go for $2,700,000. Step 4: Go-Go pays for the shares with $200,000 in cash, $500,000 worth of real estate, and a $2-million note payable over 15 years plus interest at a half percent over prime. Step 5: Joe resigns. He's retired.

What's the result? Jon and Jan now own 100 percent of Go-Go, 50 percent each. Joe collects three things from the corporation: rent (for the real estate), interest and principal on the $2-million note. Joe pays only capital gains rates on his stock profits and only as he collects the principal.

The above scenario is very flexible and can be changed in many ways to fit the exact objectives of most family businesses.

## Redemptions Defined

A redemption occurs when a corporation uses its property to acquire its own stock from one or more stockholders. It is immaterial whether the redeemed stock is canceled, retired or held as treasury stock. The term "property" includes money, securities and other property (Section 317).

The vital question: *What will the tax treatment be to the redeeming stockholder—a dividend or capital gain?* Every cent of a dividend, to the extent of retained earnings, is subject to tax. Bad! A capital gain, on the other hand, is tax-free for the full amount of the tax basis (usually cost) of the stock. Good!

The Internal Revenue Code provides a clear answer—Section 302. If the redemption qualifies as a sale or exchange, the excess of the proceeds over the taxpayer's basis is a capital gain. If the redemption does not qualify, the entire amount of the proceeds is a dividend. The Code provides *three redemption methods to attain capital-gain treatment:* complete redemption, substantially disproportionate redemption, and redemptions not essentially equivalent to a dividend.

■ **NOTE:** Only *complete redemptions* have significance in transferring the stock of a closely held business.

## Redemption vs. Sale

A redemption is similar to a sale. What's the difference? In a redemption, the buyer of the shares offered by the seller is the corporation itself, instead of the typical individual taxpayer buyer. This difference dramatically changes the tax consequences.

### Complete Redemption—Stockholders Not Related

These examples typify situations where a corporation redeems part or all of the controlling shareholder's stock and the remaining shareholder is unrelated:

■ **EXAMPLE #1.** Joe Owner owns 70 percent of the stock; the other 30 percent is owned by an unrelated business associate. The corporation, A-Z Inc., is worth $1,000,000. A-Z Inc. redeems 10 percent of Joe's stock for $100,000. Joe is stuck with a $100,000 dividend. (It is not a "complete redemption," and it flunks the complex requirements for a "substantially disproportionate redemption.")

■ **EXAMPLE #2.** A-Z Inc. redeems all of Joe's stock for $700,000. Joe's profit is a capital gain. The redemption price may be paid in a lump sum or in installments. If paid in installments, the redeeming stockholder (Joe in the above example) may elect the installment method.

## How to Get Appreciated Property Out of Your Corporation

*This example illustrates how to get appreciated value out of a firm.* Old Corp. (a C corporation) owns free and clear land and a building that originally cost $300,000. The property's reduced tax basis, due to depreciation, is $100,000; its value, due to appreciation and inflation, is $500,000. Father, the founder of the corporation, owns 40 percent of the stock, while the other 60 percent is owned by members of his immediate family. Father wants to retire. His 40 percent of the stock is worth $500,000. The corporation exchanges the real estate for Father's stock. *Here are the tax consequences:*

1. The corporation realizes a $400,000 profit—$500,000 value less $100,000 basis—just as if the corporation had sold the property.
2. Father has a capital gain equal to the difference between the $500,000 real-estate value and his tax basis for the stock.
3. Father can now turn around and lease the real estate back to the corporation at a fair rental price.
4. Best of all, Father can depreciate the real estate (the building only, not the land) just as if he had purchased it for $500,000.

### Additional Tax-Saving Hints

1. In redemptions, if the property is worth less than the stock being redeemed, the corporation can pay the difference (a) in cash or (b) in notes to be paid over a period of time.
2. An installment election may be available to the stockholder.
3. If the property to be used for the redemption is worth more than the stock, then simply put a mortgage on the property sufficient to reduce its net value to the value of the stock being exchanged.

■ **CAUTION:** If the property is subject to a mortgage (say $250,000) and its tax basis (say $150,000) is less than the liability, the difference ($100,000) is taxable income to the corporation (Section 311(b)(2)).

4. If the only appreciated property available for the exchange is needed in the operation of the business, then exchange the property for that stock anyway. Simultaneously with the exchange, have the corporation lease the property back from the stockholder. Be careful to make the exchange at fair-market value and the lease at a fair rental. I strongly urge you to use an appraiser to fix both the fair-market value and the rent.
5. Any appreciated property—real or personal—can be used. You can even use appreciated securities owned by the corporation. But always project the tax impact on both the corporation and the stockholder.

■ **COMMENT:** This method, besides removing future growth of the family corporation's stock from the founder's estate, also provides a flow of income to him/her in the form of rent (or dividends or interest in the case of securities). And with the property out of the corporation, it is no longer subject to the claims of corporate creditors. This factor alone is reason enough for many founders to use this method.

### Planning Ahead

These favorable tax results are accomplished by the tandem use of two sections of the Code plus a Revenue Ruling.

1. Section 302(b)(3) for a complete redemption gives the stockholder capital gains.
2. Section 311(b) gives the corporation capital gains, except for any depreciation recapture.
3. A shareholder's interest may be deemed terminated under Section 302(b)(3) despite a leaseback of the same property distributed in redemption (Rev. Rul. 70-369).

### Tax-Planning Hint: Incorporation

When you incorporate a business, it is good tax planning to give your spouse and/or children some of the stock because (a) there will be little or no gift tax on the initial low value, (b) dividends paid to the children will be taxed in low brackets, and (c) under the "complete termination" rule (of Section 302), the spouse and/or children can be redeemed out and get a capital gain down the road when the stock value is higher and there are funds in the corporation.

For example, let's say your spouse plays no role in the corporation other than as a 20 percent shareholder. If the corporation buys him or her out, the gain is considered a capital gain. There is no dividend; the original cost basis comes out of the corporation tax-free.

### When and Why to Take Out Appreciated Property

From a tax perspective, distributing appreciated property makes the most sense in certain situations.

I. *At the corporate level.* The corporation has a large carryforward loss, and the gain to the corporation (on the appreciated property distribution) will be offset (all or in part) by the carryforward.

II. *At the stockholder level.*
   A. Capital loss carryforward. As in the corporate situation outlined above, all or part of the gain on the redemption might be wiped out by the carryforward.
   B. Other reasons to take out appreciated property:
      1. You want the property out of the grasp of corporate creditors.
      2. The future depreciation of the property in the hands of the stockholder could provide a real estate tax shelter (passive losses to offset other passive income).
      3. After retirement, the founding stockholder will have a source of income.
      4. An appreciating asset is removed from the corporation for estate purposes. Assume the founder takes appreciating real estate. Then:
         a. These are the tax goodies the family gets:
            - ☐ income sheltered by depreciation during the founder's life;
            - ☐ income-tax-free raised basis (to the property's fair-market value) at the founder's death; and,
            - ☐ the founder's heirs can depreciate the property all over again using the raised basis as a new cost.
         b. The real estate can be left to members of the family who do not work for the family corporation.

In considering whether to take out appreciated property, make projections (for each year, carried out for 10 years or more) showing the tax consequences and cash flows for the corporation and for the redeeming stockholder. These projections will give you the information needed to make the right decision—taking appreciated property out of the corporation via a complete redemption is either a "go" or "no-go."

## S Corporations

S corporations are often the centerpiece of an organized transfer plan. They are also advantageous in many other circumstances.

An S corporation can be compared to a high quality color television set: It's easy to watch and enjoy a clear picture, and you can watch (use) what you want and ignore the rest.

As with a TV set, you don't to know everything about S corporations in order to take advantage of them. Here's what you need to know to enjoy the benefits of an S corporation for our purpose—transfer.

### When to Elect S Corporation Status

You should know *when* to elect S-corporation status. You should also know *why* and, just as important, *when* S corporation status might be a NO-NO. To get you started, here's a list of the pros and cons of S-corporation status:

**ADVANTAGES.** (1) Shareholders retain the limited liability protection of the corporate form. (2) You avoid double taxation, an inherent problem in the corporate form of doing business. However, this can be a tax trap. See discussion below under "The

Double Taxation Myth." (3) Long-term capital gains pass-through to the shareholders. (4) Ordinary losses at the corporate level pass through as ordinary losses at the individual level for shareholders who materially participate in operations. (5) The corporation is not subject to either accumulated earnings tax or personal holding-company tax. (6) Early losses of a new business can be used to offset the stockholders' other income. When operations become profitable, the corporation can terminate the S corporation election. (7) The pass-through of earnings (*pro rata,* based on shares owned) each year makes an S corporation a great way to split income with low-bracket family members. (8) The income of an S corporation, even if the corporation is part of a controlled group, is not added to the income of the other members of the controlled group for the purpose of determining the amount of the group's taxable income. (9) The threat of unreasonable officers' compensation is eliminated. (10) Two types of stock are permitted—voting and nonvoting. (11) If your highest personal bracket is lower than the highest C corporation (a regular tax-paying corporation) tax bracket, your annual tax bill for corporate profits will be less. (12) Beating the "built-in-gains tax" after a "ten-year lookback" (explained later). (13) Allows an inactive shareholder a "stream of income" (really tax-free S corporation dividends) which is not subject to Social Security tax. (14) A shareholder—active or inactive—can allow his/her share of S corporation earnings to (a) accumulate and be used for a rainy day or for retirement, or, (b) be taken as a tax-free dividend and loaned back to the corporation. This allows the shareholder to receive interest income on the note issued by the S corporation and converts a business asset to a nonbusiness asset. Of course, principal payments received on the note are tax-free. (15) The stock of an S corporation can be used to create a grantor retained annuity trust (GRAT, explained later), a magnificent transfer tool.

**DISADVANTAGES.** (1) The net loss of an S corporation is limited by the basis of the shareholder's stock (usually the amount paid for the stock) plus loans to the corporation. (2) When an S corporation stockholder is in the top personal tax bracket, his *pro rata* share of the S corporation income may create a personal tax cost larger than a regular corporation would have paid on the same amount of income. (3) An S corporation is not entitled to the 70 percent dividends-received deduction. (4) Operating losses cannot be carried from an S corporation to a regular corporation. (5) An S corporation is restricted to one class of stock—common. (6) Most fringe benefits are denied to stockholders, but qualified retirement plans are not affected. (7) If a regular corporation uses the LIFO inventory method, the LIFO reserve must be recaptured when electing S-corporation status. Unfortunately, this could be a *major barrier* which may stand in the way of your S election. (8) The right to a fiscal year has been severely restricted. If you still choose a fiscal year, corporate funds must generally be deposited in a noninterest-bearing tax account. (9) Nonactive stockholders are subject to the passive loss rules.

■ **NOTE:** Advantage #11 and Disadvantage #2 are a two-edged sword. To determine if an S corporation or a regular corporation will yield the lowest overall tax, it is essential to make a cash-flow projection.

### Is an S Corporation for You?—Check the Cash Flow

Chances are that the current tax rates, used in the examples that follow, will change before you read these words. However, the concepts illustrated will not change. Use the concepts and the examples—substituting any new tax rates along with numbers for your income and for your corporation's income—to help you determine whether S-corporation status can cut your tax.

For example, let's compare an S corporation that shows a $100,000 profit and is owned 100 percent by Joe Success to a regular corporation. Joe is in a solid 31-percent personal tax bracket and makes over $250,000 a year.

Here are the current corporate rates:

| Income | Rate |
|---|---|
| 0 - $ 50,000 | 15% |
| $ 50,000 - $ 75,000 | 25 |
| $ 75,000 - $100,000 | 34 |
| $100,000 - $335,000 | 39 |
| Over $335,000 | 34 |

**CASH-FLOW EXAMPLE**

| | Regular (C) Corporation | S Corporation |
|---|---|---|
| Corporate Profit | $100,000 | $100,000 |
| Tax Paid by Corporation Joe (31%) | 22,250 | 31,000 |
| Balance after First Tax | 77,750 | 69,000 |
| Second Tax Paid by Joe (28) | 21,770* | None |
| In-Pocket After Second Tax | $ 55,980 | $ 69,000 |

*If Joe liquidates the corporation. (Assume that Joe cannot raise his salary without running into an unreasonable compensation problem.)

Okay, the S corporation looks like the people's choice...*but not always*. Remaining a regular corporation makes sense if you personally are in a high bracket (remember, it can go up to 31 percent under current law and your corporation is in a low bracket, say 15 percent. That's a 16 percent difference between the highest personal rate (31 percent) and the lowest corporate rate (15 percent). Better to save that 16 percent and use the savings inside your corporation to pay debt and build receivables, inventory and other assets needed for growth.

### The Double-Taxation Myth

Before taking a look at the second tax that may have to be paid by a C corporation, keep in mind these two delightful tax-saving facts: *At best, you (or anyone else in your family) will never pay one penny of a second tax. At worst, the second tax can be deferred until you make a taxable sale or transfer of the business*...in effect, an interest-free loan from the tax collector. (See "More Savings," to follow.)

Now let's look at two common scenarios:

1. *In business 'til death do you part.* The second tax will never be paid. Why? Because at death, the stock will be included in your estate at its then fair-market value. The tax basis of the stock is raised instantly to this value. Simply put, death forgives the second tax.
2. *A sale of your business need not be taxable.* Say you want to retire but have no family to whom you want to transfer the business. You are going to sell your business to a third party. The second tax can still be avoided. How? Sell the operating assets of the business, not the stock of your corporation. Then keep the corporation alive (do not liquidate) as a personal holding company until you are called to the big business in the sky. Once again, the raised-basis trick in #1 above saves you from the second tax.

---

■ **TAX-SAVING HINT:** In practice, the second tax is rarely paid *if you get the proper advice*. Although the tax-wise ways of selling your business are beyond the scope of this book, such transactions often can be structured so you pay little or no income tax.

---

Often your greatest tax savings accrue because of a significant economic factor—the time value of money. You should compute the estimated after-tax earnings over time (make a cash-flow projection). These earnings are often more than enough to pay the second tax, substantially enhancing your overall savings. If you are one of the few who in fact pays a second tax, you have had a tax-free loan from the IRS until the tax is paid.

## Technical Considerations: S Corporations

You are not automatically entitled to be an S corporation. These rules should help you assess your situation.

### The One Class of Stock Requirement

True, you can have only one class of stock, but differences in voting rights for that one class are permitted (Section 1361(c)(4)).

■ **PLANNING OPPORTUNITY:** The kids (or anyone else you want to direct income to) can own nonvoting or voting stock.

### Election, Re-Election, and Revocation

*Current-year election.* An election can be effective (for a new corporation or an old C corporation) for the current year only if the election is made on or before the 15th day of the third month of the corporation's taxable year. For example, a new corporation electing S corporation status starts business on July 7 (year-end to be December 31). The election must be made between July 7 and September 15 to be valid for the corporation's first taxable year. ■ **NOTE:** Once an effective election is made, it continues for all succeeding years until the election is terminated.

**NEXT-YEAR ELECTION.** If the condition in the paragraph above (timely election) is not met, the election becomes effective on the first day of the next year (the year following the year in which the untimely election was made). For example, an old C corporation's taxable year is December 31. The 15th day of the third month of the corporation's year is March 15. The election is filed on March 16. The election becomes effective for the next year.

**RE-ELECTION AND REVOCATION.** Once S corporation status is terminated, the corporation cannot make a new election for five years. This means the re-election may not be sought until the fifth taxable year after the year the termination or revocation became effective.

**BUILT-IN GAINS TAX.** A prime benefit to S corporation status is the *one level* of federal income tax—only at the individual shareholder level, none at the corporate level. Congress has always been concerned that a C corporation with substantially appreciated assets (such as a building) could elect S corporation status and avoid double taxation. How does a C corporation get socked for two taxes? Well, under C-corporation status, the first tax is assessed when the corporation sells the building, and the second tax clobbers the individual shareholder when the funds are withdrawn (as a dividend or when the corporation is liquidated).

Can this two-tax horror be beat? Easily. Elect S-corporation status. Not so fast, says the IRS. Under pre-1987 law, Internal Revenue Code Section 1374 was implemented, which provided that capital gains on appreciated property recognized in the *first three years* of an S corporation (which had previously been a C corporation) would be taxed at the top C-corporation rate. Starting in 1987, this rule has been extended to the *first 10 years* of an S corporation that was previously a C corporation.

The first tax is charged at the top corporation rate to the S corporation. The second tax must be paid by the shareholder on the same gain, less the tax paid by the S corporation. This concept of taxing "built-in gains" that have been *realized* economically, but not *recognized* in C-corporation years, closes the old loophole. Let's look at the delightful results when there is no second tax.

Our sample company, Success, Inc., has operated for 15 years. The business has grown, and profits continue to increase. An S-corporation election was made effective for 1985. In 1988, Joe Success (sole shareholder) considered a move to a new and larger factory building. This time, he prefers to own the building personally and lease it to Success, Inc., but he needs the profits on the sale of the current building owned by the corporation as a down payment on the new facility. Under pre-1987 law, Success, Inc. could sell the building and pay one tax on the gain at the shareholder level, as the S-corporation election was effective for three years (1985, 1986, 1987). This is true even though most, if not all, of the appreciation in the building arose in C corporation years. Joe could withdraw the profit in cash and use it as a down payment on the new facility. Under the new law starting in 1987, you must wait 10 years to get the benefit detailed in this example.

An article from my tax column nicely summarizes this section on S corporations. Identify the objectives that might apply to you and the tools needed to meet those objectives.

AN S CORPORATION CAN BE A FRIEND FOR LIFE...AND BEYOND

One of the most interesting realities of consulting with the owners of closely held family businesses is their perception that their succession and tax problems are unique. Sure, most family businesses do have some special problems that require some tailor-made solutions.

But in the hard, practical business world, when I question a business owner (let's call him Joe) about succession, he usually comes up with this typical set of objectives:

1. Joe wants to keep control of the business for as long as he lives.
2. Joe wants his son, Joe, Jr., who has been active in the business for years, to have control after he is gone.
3. Joe, age 59 (substitute your own age), wants to slow down yet keep drawing income from the business for 10 to 15 years (assuming he lives).
4. Joe wants his wife to get income from the business (assuming he dies before her).
5. Joe wants his children (there are two more in addition to Joe, Jr.) to be treated equitably.

Here's a tax-transfer plan that can solve all of the above objectives. First, elect S corporation status. Next, recapitalize your company by exchanging your common voting stock for nonvoting common (say 9,900 shares) and voting common (say 100 shares).

Let's look at your lifetime scenario. You pay tax on the business's earnings. But now you can take all or part of those earnings any time you please without paying a second tax. And once you actually stop working, you can take those earnings just like a salary, without paying any Social Security tax, and draw Social Security benefits, to boot.

And sooner or later, you die. When you die, your wife steps into your shoes—drawing the business earnings. You leave the 100 shares of voting stock to Joe, Jr. He now controls the day-to-day operations of the business.

One more trick can help you save estate taxes. During your life, give some of the nonvoting common stock to all three of the kids. You can give up to $60,000 ($20,000 per child) in stock value per year to the children. Your wills (both husband's and wife's) should leave nonbusiness assets (like cash, stocks of public companies, etc.) to the nonoperating two children and the business assets (the balance of the 9,900 nonvoting shares) to Joe, Jr.

If there are not enough nonbusiness assets to treat the two nonoperating children equitably (a common situation), just give them some of the nonvoting stock. A buy-sell agreement signed by all the children who are stockholders will force Joe, Jr. to buy out his siblings after you and your wife pass on. The agreement can be funded by life insurance, or the payout period can be stretched out for 7 to 10 years or more, in order not to hurt the cash flow of the business. Where does Junior get the money? Again, he draws on the S-corporation earnings. When everything is done, Joe, Jr. has the business and the nonoperating kids have cash.

## Grantor Retained Annuity Trusts (GRATs)

GRATs are explained and discussed in detail in other parts of this book (see the index). For the moment, let's examine the power of a GRAT in transfer planning, as illustrated by excerpts from one of my tax-column articles:

TRANSFERRING YOUR BUSINESS TO THE KIDS?...LIKE A NEW WONDER DRUG, GRATS CURE SEVERE TAX PROBLEMS

There's a wonderful new tax kid on the block...grantor retained annuity trust (his friends call him GRAT).

As you might guess, GRAT is rather complex in theory. Maybe like a car, impossible to build for almost everyone. Ah, but easy to use.

A car can reduce a 50-mile all-day walking trip to an hour or less. A GRAT, when you want to transfer your business to the kids, can reduce a $1-million gift-tax problem (more or less) to $10,000 (more or less). Really! And it's legal. And the IRS can't control the amount of the taxable gift you select. You, with the help of a competent professional, are in complete control.

Maybe a real-life example is the best way to explain the dramatic tax-saving tricks GRAT can do. Here's the story: Jim (age 59), a successful business owner, came to our Chicago office from Pompeno Beach, Florida for a second tax opinion. His original plan was to sell his $4 million business (Success Co., an S corporation) to his three boys, who are all active in the business and who each own 10 percent of Success Co. He wanted to sell his 70 percent of Success Co. stock to the boys for $200,000 per year for life [that is for his life and his wife's—Jan, (age 57)]. We reviewed the tax consequences of his plan. In a word, terrible. Enter GRAT.

First, we decided to recapitalize Success Co.—100 shares of voting stock (70 to Jim; 30 to the boys) and 100,000 shares of nonvoting stock (70,000 to Jim; 30,000 to the boys). Second, Jim gave half (35,000) of his nonvoting shares to Jan. All of these maneuvers are tax-free. Finally, we, using only the nonvoting shares, created two GRATs: one for Jim, the other for Jan.

A GRAT really does only one good tax trick. The trick only works for an S corporation. What's the trick? A GRAT actually divides itself into two separate parts for gift tax purposes.

For example, Jim transferred 25,000 of his nonvoting shares, or 25 percent of the value of Success Co. (worth $1 million) to his GRAT in exchange for a 12 percent annuity (the right to receive $120,000—12 percent times $1 million) for 14 years. Jan's GRAT is identical. This 14-year period is called the "annuity interest." What remains after the 14 years (the GRAT terminates and the kids get the 25,000 shares of nonvoting stock) is called the "remainder interest." The way the law works, the total value of both interests is always the full value (in this case $1 million) of the property put into each GRAT. Logic tells you that the greater the value of the annuity interest, the smaller the value of the remainder interest. Why is this so important? Because the remainder interest is the only part of the GRAT valued for gift tax purposes. You pick the annuity rate (12 percent here) and the length of the annuity (14 years here). The higher the *rate* (it can be eight percent, 10, 15, or you pick it) and/or the *length* (It can be one year or more. Again, you pick it.) of the annuity, the greater the value of the annuity interest...And, of course, the lower the value of the remainder interest. In this case, the value of the two remainder interests (Jim's and Jan's) according to IRS tables is $20,581.

What does this mean? Jim and Jan can pass $2 million of Success Co. stock to their kids and use up only $20,581 of their unified credits (the right of a married couple to give $1.2 million tax free) for gift tax purposes. Fantastic! And did you notice that Jim kept his 70 shares of voting stock, which means he keeps control of Success Co.?

One problem: If you die before the term (14 years here) of the GRAT, the stock plops back into your estate. All the benefits evaporate. To guard against this possibility, we buy life insurance to cover the estimated estate tax liability.

We think GRATs are so terrific that the IRS is likely to ask Congress to change the rules. My advice: Adopt GRAT before a change in the law moves him out of the tax neighborhood.

## Recapitalizations

Three kinds of recapitalizations are used in transfer/succession planning. The types, and frequency of usage:

1. Voting/nonvoting stock: Often
2. Preferred stock dividends: Sometimes
3. Traditional preferred stock: Rarely

### Voting/Nonvoting Stock Recapitalization

The purpose of this type of recapitalization is singular—keep control in the person or persons who want it, usually Dad, the founder. This type of recapitalization is covered in Part I, Chapter Two.

### Preferred Stock Dividends

Preferred stock dividends allow you to take tax-paid dollars out of the corporation and transfer them to low-tax-bracket family members, usually children, grandchildren, or retired parents. Under Section 305, stock dividends are tax-free if declared proportionally to the shareholders. For example, Joe has five grandchildren and would like to use corporate funds to pay for their college educations. He owns 100 percent of Old Co., which declares a $50,000 preferred-stock dividend. Joe gifts all the preferred shares to the five grandchildren—$10,000 each. Assume a 10-percent dividend rate, or $5,000, in total cash dividends. That would be $1,000 per year in cash for each grandchild, which would be tax-free or in a very low bracket.

Summarizing the income-tax consequences:

- ☐ $50,000 in preferred stock is transferred to the grandchildren tax-free.
- ☐ $5,000 of after-tax corporate income is paid out of the corporation in cash each year, with little or no tax to the holders of the preferred stock.
- ☐ There is no gift tax. (You can give up to $10,000 to each grandchild or any other person—each year without gift-tax consequences. The amount is doubled to $20,000 if your wife consents to the gift on a joint gift-tax return).
- ☐ Assume the fair-market value of the common stock is always equal to book value less $50,000 for the preferred stock. The estate-tax consequences: $50,000 is permanently removed from the estate at inception; an additional $5,000 is removed each year because of the cash dividends.

If you cannot meet the requirements for an S corporation, or if becoming an S corporation does not make tax sense (profits are continually under $100,000), then preferred stock dividends are a sure tax winner.

### Traditional Preferred Stock Recapitalization

The traditional recapitalization (often called a "freeze") used by a family-owned corporation is described in Rev. Rul. 67-54:

- ☐ This one corporation issues, as its only class of voting stock, voting preferred stock that is owned and retained by the founder. This stock has a small value. (For this book's purposes, the term preferred stock includes one or more classes of preferred stock or any new class of common stock that might be issued with terms or provisions that are different than the currently issued and outstanding common stock.)
- ☐ The second class of stock to be issued by the corporation is nonvoting preferred stock.

  ■ **NOTE:** Almost the entire value of the corporation at the time of the recapitalization is frozen in the preferred stock.
- ☐ The third class of stock under the recapitalization plan is nonvoting common stock. It constitutes the entire residuary value of the corporation, but has little or no present value. The ownership of this stock goes to those persons in the family who will enjoy the future growth.

This type of recapitalization is now controlled by Chapter 14 (a complex maze) of the Internal Revenue Code. But don't cross these recaps off of your list for complexity alone. They are still capable of doing their old tax magic in certain limited circumstances. When? If your corporation earns more than the current IRS rate of return set by law, then the difference can be transferred free of any gift or estate tax. Simply put, as long as interest rates remain low and your corporation continues to earn in excess of the IRS rate at the time of the freeze, the difference is a tax-free gift. Have your professional advisor check out a traditional recapitalization "freeze." When the weather is right, it is still one of the best tools in the transfer kit.

## New Activities of the Family Business

Let's ask a new question—where do you put something new? Each time the existing family structure is about to undertake any new activity—stop! Determine if the family's best interests will be served by (1) starting the new activity within the present family business structure or (2) allowing family members to whom the family business will ultimately be transferred to start up the new activity in their own names from its inception. The latter approach avoids future transfer problems!

Here are the two basic rules:

1. If the something new can or will result in an operating business (such as a new store, plant or product line), put it into a new entity (like a new corporation). In short, create business income.
2. If the something new is used (as opposed to sold) in the operating business (like real estate or equipment), put it into a family partnership and lease it to your operating entity (old or new). This creates passive income.

## Operating Entity

From this moment forward, you have a new high-level management duty—to look for new opportunities to start new businesses. Profitable businesses. Such activities, done right, are one of the easiest and most tax effective weapons in the entire transfer arsenal.

The idea is simple but effective. Let's say you want to transfer your current business, Success Co., to the kids—now or over a period of time. Let's say a profitable new business opportunity comes along (we'll show you how to identify such opportunities). Don't put the opportunity into Success Co. Instead, start a new business. Call it New Co.

The type of entity (corporation or otherwise) to be used to operate New Co. is not the main concern; ownership of the entity is the issue. If one or more of your kids owns it, you don't own it. So it's not in your estate. In effect, you have made a transfer of a business without ever making a transfer.

Want to keep control while the kids have the value? Easy. Use the voting (you own it)/nonvoting (the kids own it) trick described in Part I, Chapter Two.

If the kids don't have the money to fund the opportunity, lend the kids or New Co. the money. Or guarantee a bank loan.

Now, how do you find that business opportunity? Here's some proven ways:

1. *Expand existing business.* Add a new local store, plant, warehouse or other location. Expand geographically into a new state or country. Or, if your business is purely domestic, enter into the import or export business. ■ **NOTE:** This assumes there is no change in basic products or services.
2. *New products or services.* Expanding product and service lines presents new-business opportunities for changing ownership that are often missed. Some examples: A new line (dresses/auto parts) from a vendor, new or old, domestic or foreign. New services—you now repair, rent and install gizmos as well as sell 'em (consulting services of all types are a natural). Old customers ask you to perform a new function, which requires new equipment; buy the equipment in a new entity to start your new business.
3. *Acquisitions.* Although an acquisition is in your old line of business, operate it in New Co. With entries into new lines of business, ask in what form will the business operate: Corporation?...S or C? Partnership?...General or limited? What about multiple corporations? Trusts? Although this book contains many answers to such questions, professional help is advised for a complete analysis.

By continually putting new activities of an existing family business into another entity, the old business will weaken, or diminish, and the new entity becomes the family's primary profit maker. The result: Success Co. (owned by Dad) lowers in value, New Co. (owned by the kids) increases in value, and Dad's estate taxes are substantially reduced. *This is true long-range planning that is capable of accomplishing most of the transfer/estate planning objectives of the typical family business owner.*

## Leasing Through Passive Family Partnership

In general, we are not talking about a partnership that will operate a business. For our purposes, a passive partnership owns some type of property—either real property or personal property. The partnership rents its property to the family corporation on a "net-net" basis. By "net-net," we mean the corporate lessee (your business) pays only rent to the partnership lessor. The lessee is responsible for paying for such items as insurance, repairs and other expenses of using and operating the property. The activities of the lessor usually are limited to collecting rent, paying any mortgage or loans, and making distributions to the partners.

For simplicity, each partnership is assumed to (1) Own only vacant land; (2) own only improved real estate; or, (3) own only personal property.

It is also assumed that when your children are partners, adult children hold their partnership interests in their own names. Minor children are beneficiaries of an irrevocable trust, and the trust is the partner. Neither the children nor the trust have any other income. Obviously, in actual practice, there can be and often are many variations that differ from these assumptions.

### ■ EXAMPLE #1-VACANT LAND

Vacant land is the simplest example. Assume the family partnership buys a $100,000 piece of vacant land for $20,000 in cash and finances the $80,000 balance. The partners are Father Joe, who owns 100 percent of Joe Industries Inc.; his son, Joe Jr., a 19-year-old college freshman; and Trust #1. Baby Mary, Father Joe's 8-year-old daughter, is the beneficiary of Trust #1. The plan is to have Joe Jr. use his share of the profits to help pay for his college education and to have the trust accumulate its share of the income for Baby Mary's college education down the road. The partners have the following interests in the capital and profits or losses of the partnership:

**Father Joe—10 percent; Joe Jr.—70 percent; and Trust #1—20 percent.**

Father Joe makes a cash gift of $14,000 to Joe Jr. and $4,000 to Trust #1. This cash, together with $2,000 from Father Joe, is deposited in the partnership, which immediately uses the $20,000 as a down payment to buy the vacant land. The land is leased to Joe Industries at a fair rental for 20 years. Assume the partnership makes a $10,000 profit each year. Joe Jr. would receive his share, $7,000, each year. This $7,000 would be taxable income to him and could be used immediately toward his college education.

## ■ EXAMPLE #2-CORPORATION BUILDS ON VACANT

Assume the corporation builds a $300,000 warehouse on the vacant land. The corporation arranges its own financing for the warehouse and takes 100 percent of the depreciation. Follow these delightful results: In 20 years, when the lease expires, the real estate (with a warehouse sitting on it) belongs to the family partnership. The passage of time releases the entire property from the grasp of the corporation (as a tenant) to the partnership (as a landlord) without any tax consequences.

What could go awry with the transactions described in Examples #1 and #2? From our viewpoint, four things could go wrong. The first three deal with a potential IRS problem, while the last item focuses on a potential family concern. The four items: capital, rent, term and control.

1. *Capital.* The IRS could complain if the partners (that is, Father Joe's children or the trusts for their benefit) have no element of risk. In Example #1, 20 percent (or $20,000) of the total price of $100,000 was put up in cash and was at risk. I believe 20 percent or more of the required capital is a safe haven. Less may be okay, but entails risk. For example, if the partnership borrows the entire $100,000 and the corporation subordinates the lease, the partners would have no risk.
2. *Rent.* The rent paid by the family-owned corporation must be a fair rental.
3. *Term.* The term of the lease can be attacked if it is too short. For example, if the partnership winds up owning the $300,000 warehouse after only five years, the IRS could attack the transaction. A reasonable term must be used; any term less than the term of the mortgage on the improvement would be viewed as unreasonable. Remember, at the end of the lease term, the partnership would own the land and warehouse, subject only to any liens on the property.
4. *Control.* Say Father Joe desires to control the property for as long as he likes. The lease term is 20 years. Let's say the 20 years have passed. Father Joe is 60 and still alive. His kids, who control the partnership, want to boot him out. How to deal with such a problem? With options. For example, the lease term might be for 15 years followed by three separate five-year options.

## ■ EXAMPLE #3-PERSONAL PROPERTY

A different partnership (owned 50 percent each by Joe and his wife) buys equipment for $100,000 and leases it to the corporation. Assume $20,000 down and 84 equal monthly payments to pay off the balance at 10 percent interest per annum. The corporation leases the equipment from the partnership for seven years at a $20,000 per year rental.

Your first job is to make two projections for the partnership for the seven-year lease term. One projection will be a cash flow, and the second projection will be taxable loss or income. It is assumed that the partnership will sell the equipment for salvage at the end of the seven-year lease.

Your tax projection will show a loss in the early years, which will turn into a profit in later years. Our objective would be realized best by having Father Joe, alone or with his wife, own 100 percent of the partnership at inception. When the partnership begins to earn a profit, the partnership interests will be gifted to low-bracket family members at the then fair-market value of the equipment. These would be gifts for gift-tax purposes.

■ **WARNING:** If the amount of the loan exceeds the basis of the property, such excess is ordinary income. For example, if on the date the partnership interest is gifted to the children, the tax basis of the equipment is $40,000, and the balance of the loan is $45,000, then the difference ($5,000) is income to Joe and his wife.

■ **EXAMPLE #4-IMPROVED REAL ESTATE**

Another separate family partnership purchases land with a warehouse already on it. The real estate—land and building—is leased to the corporation. This is a hybrid between the vacant-land example and the equipment example. Again, first make your cash-flow and taxable-income projections for the term of the lease. Then, depending on the family objectives, your projection numbers, and other pertinent factors, you will determine who in the family will be a partner and how much of an interest each partner will own.

## Hints for Using Family Partnerships

1. Set up a separate partnership each time a new piece of property is purchased. This gives you flexibility in dealing with changing family circumstances as well as the peculiarities of the property—its purchase, financing, and lease requirements.
2. Make your partnership projections for the entire term of the lease. The projections might look something like this:

CASH FLOW ($ In Thousands)*

| | Year 1 | Year 2 | Year 8 | Year 9 |
|---|---|---|---|---|
| Capital | $31 | | | |
| Rent | 25 | $25 | $25 | - |
| Down payment | (30) | - | - | - |
| Loan payments | (18) | (18) | (18) | - |
| Salvage | - | - | - | $ 5 |
| Cash Flow | $ 8 | $ 7 | $ 7 | $ 5 |

PROFIT OR (LOSS) ($ In Thousands)*

| | Year 1 | Year 2 | Year 5 | Year 8 |
|---|---|---|---|---|
| Rent | $25 | $25 | $ 25 | $25 |
| Depreciation | (21) | (21) | (21) | -** |
| Interest | (18) | (15) | (6) | (3) |
| Profit (loss) | $(14) | $(11) | $ (2) | $22 |

*These schedules are for personal property and assume an eight-year lease. Of courseall years should be shown in your projection.
**The property (equipment) would be fully depreciated in year seven.

3. If a trust is required (because one of the partners is a minor or for any other reason), use an irrevocable trust as the partner.
4. Review the four factors that can go wrong—CAPITAL, RENT, TERM, and CONTROL—for every new piece of property and every partnership.
5. Elderly family members in a low-income-tax bracket make great landlords. When they go to their ultimate rewards, their interest(s) in the partnership will get a raised-tax basis.
6. Remember, the partnership is subject to the passive-loss rules. Plan who in the family should be the original partners and to whom subsequent transfers should be made, based on the projections and where the losses or profits will yield the best tax benefits.
7. In general, direct losses to high-bracket family members and profits to low-bracket family members.

### ■ SUMMARY: FAMILY PARTNERSHIPS

Passive family partnerships are an effective method for:
1. Dividing family income.
2. Reducing estate taxes.
3. Converting business assets into nonbusiness assets that can provide for the nonbusiness children.
4. Providing a flow of income to the founder and his/her spouse after retirement that is not subject to Social Security.

## Combinations

The combinations of methods (tools) for transferring corporate stock are limited only by one's imagination. One example should make the point: An employee stock-bonus plan, continued over a period of years and combined with cash gifts from the business owner, can be very effective in moving substantial portions of stock to one or more members of the family who are employed by the corporation.

For example, let's go back to Exhibit II and change the facts a bit. Assume John is given two shares of stock as a bonus (no cash) with a total +value of $10,000. Now the corporation would be in-pocket $3,000, and John would pay $3,000 in income tax. Joe makes a $3,000 cash gift to John so he can pay his income-tax liability. Joe's $3,000 gift does not have any tax consequences.

If we assume the corporation has a fair-market value of $500,000, then Joe has managed to move approximately two percent of the future growth of the corporation to his son without any current out-of-pocket cost to the family. Why? The corporation is $3,000 in-pocket (because of the $10,000 salary deduction), while Joe and John together are out-of-pocket $3,000 (because the gift to John was used to pay John's current tax liability—30 percent of the $10,000 value of the bonus stock). Net effect: The family, including the corporation, comes out even.

And there is an additional estate-tax saving. Joe's estate will be reduced by about $13,000 ($10,000 for the approximate current value of the stock plus $3,000 in cash). In a 50-percent estate-tax bracket, the family will save another $6,500. Of course, future appreciation of the stock owned by John after the stock bonus also will escape inclusion in Joe's estate.

# 2 The Secondary Transfer Tools and the Support Tools

With few exceptions, this chapter has no technical material.

The only difference between the secondary tools as a group and the primary tools as a group is that the secondary tools are not used in practice as often as the primary tools. All, in their own special ways, are capable of completing all or part of the transfer of stock of a closely held company.

The support tools, on the other hand, are not involved in the transfer of stock, but are used to help implement the total transfer plan.

Here is a list of the secondary transfer as well as support tools discussed in this chapter:

**The Secondary Tools**

1. Employee stock ownership plans (ESOPs)
2. Self-canceling installment debt (SCID)
3. Private annuities (PAs)
4. Multiple corporations

**The Support Tools**

1. Valuation
2. Insurance

**Transfer of Nonbusiness Property (the next four tools)**

3. Trusts, multiple trusts
4. S corporation as a trust that is not a trust
5. Family limited partnerships
6. Grantor retained interest trusts (GRITs)
7. Social Security
8. Buy-sell agreements
9. Employee death benefit agreement
10. Other tools

■ **NOTE:** With the exception of life insurance, *every item on the list deals with lifetime planning*, not death planning. Remember, YOU AIN'T DEAD YET.

## Employee Stock Ownership Plans (ESOPs)

ESOPs are not used often for the pure purpose of transfer/succession planning; but when an ESOP fits, it is capable of accomplishing objectives no other transfer tool can approach.

ESOPs are experiencing phenomenal growth in the United States. Why? In part because Congress has greatly expanded the special tax incentives for employers to adopt ESOPs. The most important of these incentives:

1. An individual may sell sock of a closely held corporation to an ESOP on a tax-deferred basis if (a) the ESOP owns at least 30 percent of the stock of the sponsoring company immediately after the sale; and (b) the sale proceeds are reinvested in stocks and bonds of other U.S. corporations.
2. If a corporation uses an ESOP to obtain a loan, it is entitled to deduct both the interest and the principal payments on the loan, instead of being limited to an interest deduction only, as is the case with a conventional corporate loan. For most companies, this can cut borrowing costs by one-third.
3. A bank may exclude from its taxable income 50 percent of the interest received on a loan to an ESOP that owns more than 50 percent of the stock of the sponsoring employer. As a result, interest rates on loans to such ESOPs usually are lower than the interest rates on other commercial loans.
4. Dividends paid in cash on shares held by an ESOP are deductible by the sponsoring corporation if (a) they are passed through to the participants in the plan, or (b) they are used to pay off a loan taken out to finance the purchase of company stock.

### Tax-Free Rollover: King of the ESOP Tax Hill

The tax incentive that has spurred the most interest in ESOPs for private companies is the opportunity provided under Section 1042 of the Internal Revenue Code: a tax-free "rollover" of the proceeds from a sale of stock to an ESOP if the proceeds are reinvested in securities of other corporations. This special tax treatment is available only with respect to sales of common stock of closely held corporations that you have owned for at least three years. A sale of such stock to an ESOP qualifies for tax-free treatment if the following conditions are met:

1. Immediately after the sale, the ESOP owns at least 30 percent of the total value of the common stock of your company;
2. You reinvest the sales proceeds within 12 months in *qualified replacement property*, a specially defined term; and
3. For certain periods, no portion of the assets of the ESOP attributable to the stock that you sold to the ESOP may accrue for your benefit, for the benefit of any member of your family, or for any other person who owns more than 25 percent of the outstanding stock of the company.

The first requirement for rollover treatment (the plan must own at least 30 percent of the outstanding stock of your corporation) is applied immediately after the sale is closed. Because the 30 percent requirement is applied after the sale, you may establish an ESOP for the purpose of selling all or a significant portion of your stock to the ESOP on a tax-deferred basis.

The second requirement for tax-free rollover treatment (you must reinvest the sale proceeds in certain kinds of property) has two components:

1. The reinvestment must be made within what is referred to in the Internal Revenue Code as the *replacement period*. This period begins three months before the date on which the sale occurs and ends 12 months after the date of the sale. Thus, you enjoy a 15-month tax-planning period.
2. You must purchase *qualified replacement property* with a cost equal to the amount realized on the sale of your stock to the ESOP.

■ **CAUTION:** You are taxed to the extent that the sale proceeds exceed your cost of the replacement property.

Speaking generally, "qualified replacement property" is defined as *stocks and bonds of U.S. operating companies*. Government securities and shares in mutual funds do *not* qualify as replacement property for purposes of this delightful ESOP rollover.

If you satisfy Section 1042, you pay no tax on the sale of your stock to the ESOP. However, your tax basis in the replacement property is reduced by the amount of the untaxed gain on the sale. More simply, the new property has the same tax basis as your old stock. Thus, Section 1042 operates to provide a tax deferral, not a complete avoidance of tax. The deferred gain is taxed when the replacement property is sold.

■ **TAX-SAVING HINT:** THERE IS A WAY TO AVOID EVEN THIS DEFERRED TAX.

Just hold the replacement securities until your death. Your heirs will receive a stepped-up basis (a new tax basis) in the replacement securities equal to their fair-market value at the date of your death. Then they could sell the replacement properties free of any capital-gains tax. For example, Rick Rich owns 100 percent of Success Co. Rick sells $2.2 million of his stock to Success Co.'s ESOP. Rick reinvests the proceeds in a tax-free rollover, which he holds until death. Rick's heirs get a step-up in basis and never pay income tax on the gain.

■ **PLANNING POINTER FOR SENIORS:** Elderly stockholders may prefer a rollover into bonds rather than stock. If so, they should choose bonds with a maturity well beyond their life expectancies. This move effectively locks in gains and gives the taxpayer assets he or she can hold until death to avoid income taxes on the gain entirely.

### Planning Opportunities

Section 1042 allows business owners of closely held businesses to address three common business planning problems on a tax-favored basis.

1. *Sell, but keep control.* An ESOP can be used to buy out the interest of a retiring stockholder and may serve as an attractive alternative to selling a business to outsiders. This is especially true where there is a desire to keep control of the business within a family or key-employee group. If the funds required to

purchase the retiring stockholder's interest must be borrowed, an ESOP can be used to reduce the financing costs.

2. *Diversification.* An owner who has most of his or her wealth tied up in the stock of a closely held corporation may want to diversify his or her investment portfolio before retirement. Section 1042 paves the tax-favored road for doing so.
3. *Buy out of dissident stockholders.* An ESOP is a useful vehicle for buying out dissident stockholders. Because of the tax-free treatment on the sale of the shares, the dissident stockholders may be willing to sell at a reduced price. Also, the tax benefits associated with ESOP loans can reduce the cost of financing the buy-out.

## Voting Rights—The Key Question

The key question is always the same: "Will I lose control of my company if I set up an ESOP?" You'll like the answer. No—for two reasons: First, employee ownership is not an all-or-nothing affair. An ESOP can own all of the stock of your company, but this is not necessary. To the contrary, most ESOPs hold minority interests in their sponsoring employers. In other words, you can set up an ESOP and still retain more than 50 percent of the outstanding stock of your company.

Voting rights with respect to stock of private companies that sponsor ESOPs need to be passed through to the participants only with respect to certain extraordinary transactions—a merger or consolidation, recapitalization, reclassification, liquidation, dissolution, or sale of substantially all of the assets of the business.

The stock contributed by the employer or purchased by the ESOP is voted by the trustee, who may be you, another key officer of the company or, perhaps, a friendly bank. Your employees will not have voting rights with respect to the day-to-day management of the business. *Simply put, you will not be transferring control of your company to your employees when you set up an ESOP.*

## Ownership Succession in Private Companies

The ESOP structure and rules create a private tax haven for controlling stockholders of closely held corporations. These special provisions enable such stockholders to diversify their personal investment portfolios tax free and favorably structure ownership succession transactions. This example puts it all together.

### ■ EXAMPLE 1

Joe Success owns all of the stock of Your Co. He is 70 years old and ready to retire. Joe's son Jim is 40 years old, has been working for the company for 12 years, and is ready to take over management of the business. The fair-market value of Your Co. is $3,000,000. There are several key employees who have worked for the company for many years.

*Joe's objectives are to:*

1. Retire with an adequate and assured income.
2. Transfer control of the business to Jim. And,
3. Protect Your Co.'s long-term employees.

*Jim's objectives are to:*

1. Take over management of the business.
2. Assure retirement security for his dad. And,
3. Provide incentives for the key employees to remain with Your Co.-and to help him expand the business.

This situation suggests several alternatives. First, and most obviously, Joe could arrange to sell Your Co. to a competitor or to another third party. While this would provide him with adequate retirement security, Joe would not be able to pass control of the business to Jim, and there would be no assurance of employment security for the company's long-term employees. Worst of all, Joe would be hit with federal and state taxes equal to one-third or more of the sale proceeds. Assuming that Joe sells his stock for $3 million, and that he has only a nominal basis in his stock, his total tax liability would be about $1 million. Ouch!

As an alternative to selling the business to outsiders, Joe might sell his stock to the corporation (called a "redemption"). In this case, the corporation would probably be required to take out a large bank loan. If the redemption can be financed by the bank, this approach would allow Joe to pass control of the business to Jim and to assure continued employment for the long-term employees.-However, a redemption would be expensive because Joe's stock would have to be repurchased by Your Co. with "after-tax" dollars: Your Co. would have to make about $4.5 million in order to generate $3 million, after taxes, to pay for Joe's shares. And of course, Joe would still get clobbered with the $1 million personal income tax on the sale of his stock back to the corporation.

*Enter the ESOP alternative.* As long as Joe sells at least 30 percent of his Your Co. stock to the ESOP, the sale qualifies for tax-free rollover treatment. For example, if Joe sells one-third of his stock to the ESOP for $1 million, he will save $280,000 in federal capital-gains tax. Put another way, Joe will be able to reinvest the full $1 million in sale proceeds, instead of only $720,000 ($1 million minus $280,000) if he had sold the stock using either of the first two alternatives. Neat!

If Your Co. borrows the funds to repurchase Joe's stock through the use of an ESOP loan, its financing costs will be greatly reduced as compared to the borrowing cost of a conventional corporate stock redemption loan. This is possible because Your Co. can deduct the principal repayments on the loan.

Let's crunch the numbers. Assume that the full $1 million purchase price is borrowed, which entitles Your Co. to $1 million in income tax deductions as the loan is repaid by the ESOP. Result: A tax saving of $340,000 over the term of the loan (assuming that Your Co. is in the 34-percent tax bracket). Now, combine that saving with the $280,000 in taxes that Joe will have deferred, and the total tax savings are $620,000, or 62 percent of the $1 million price. Nothing short of tax magic! And keep adding, because Joe will enjoy additional savings in state income taxes.

So, if an ESOP is used in this typical family-owned business situation:

1. Joe can diversify his wealth.
2. Jim can take over control of the business without jeopardizing Your Co.'s cash flow.
3. The employees will have job security and the incentive of part ownership via the ESOP to increase their productivity.
4. And, most important, the above is accomplished without currently sharing one cent of the family wealth with the IRS.

If Joe does not sell his stock during his lifetime, an ESOP can serve as a means of easing the problems of administering his estate. Assume that the bulk of Joe's estate consists of Your Co. stock. Under normal circumstances, Joe's executor probably would have to raise cash to pay estate taxes by selling a portion of the stock back to the corporation. The sad result: Your Co. would have to use after-tax dollars to redeem Joe's stock.

Once again, apply the magic of an ESOP, which provides a mechanism for Your Co. to redeem Joe's stock on a tax-deductible basis. The ESOP simply purchases the stock from Joe's estate. Then, Your Co. can make tax-deductible contributions to the ESOP to pay for the stock, rather than using after-tax dollars to redeem the shares directly from the estate.

## Self-Canceling Installment Debt (SCID) and Private Annuities (PAs)

SCIDs and PAs are not used often but are accepted ways of freezing the value of your closely held company. In addition, they entirely escape estate tax.

For our purposes, a PA is an arrangement under which an individual (called the *transferor*, we'll call him Joe) transfers stock to a successor (we'll call him John, who is Joe's son) in exchange for John's agreement to make periodic payments in fixed amounts to Joe for the remainder of Joe's life. A SCID is a debt obligation created on the transfer of stock from the transferor-creditor (Joe) to a successor-debtor (John). The debt instrument has a fixed term less than the life expectancy of Joe and contains a provision that automatically voids all future payment obligations on his death.

### SCIDs and PAs Not Covered by Chapter 14

Chapter 14 attacks estate-valuation freeze attempts at the time of the initial transfer through strict gift-tax valuation rules. The use of SCIDs and PAs in stock transfer/ succession planning does not provide for retained right features (Section 2701), is not a transfer of an interest in trust (Section 2702), does not involve an option or buy-sell agreement (Section 2703) and does not contain a lapsing right or restriction used to reduce the value of transferred property (Section 2704).

What's the result of not being covered by Chapter 14? The annuity's value (for a PA) or the note's value (for a SCID) to Joe's estate on the date of his death is zero. Put another way, the annuity or note disappears on the instant of Joe's death for estate-tax purposes. Result: SCIDs and PAs are never subject to an estate tax. ■ **NOTE:** PAs are discussed in detail in Part VIII, Chapter 5; SCIDs are subject to similar rules.

## Multiple Corporations

If a father and mother in the highest tax bracket can transfer $1,000 of their income to each of their three low-tax-bracket children, the family saves tax on this $3,000. How much? The difference between what mom and dad would have paid and the aggregate of what the three children paid. The rule is simple: Shift income from high-tax-bracket family members to low-tax-bracket family members. The identical concept applies to tax-paying C corporations. The idea is to have two (or more) C corporations, each utilizing the lowest tax brackets. Substantial savings are possible every year. The following examples, using 1993 rates (substitute new rates, if there is a change), show the power of this concept.

## ■ EXAMPLE 1

| | One corporation | Two corporations X | | Two corporations Y |
|---|---|---|---|---|
| Earnings | $100,000 | $ 50,000 | | $ 50,000 |
| Taxes: if one | 22,250 | | | |
| if two | | 7,500 | | 7,500 |
| Total taxes | $ 22,250 | | $15,000 | |
| Annual savings | | | $ 7,250 | |

## ■ EXAMPLE 2

| | One corporation | Two corporations X | | Two corporations Y |
|---|---|---|---|---|
| Earnings | $200,000 | $100,000 | | $100,000 |
| Taxes: if one | 61,250 | | | |
| if two | | 22,250 | | 22,250 |
| Total taxes | $ 61,250 | | $44,500 | |
| Annual Savings | | | $16,750 | |

The name of this game is to beat the multiple corporate rules by failing to become a member of a controlled group. The technical rules are beyond the scope of this book, but some examples of "how to beat the rules" should motivate you to start a consultation with your professional advisor.

There are many rules used to determine who is or is not related for the purposes of the multiple corporation rules. Three rules are basic and apply often:

1. *Minors and spouses.* In a tax sense, your minor children and grandchildren (under age 21) and your spouse are related to you. In general, the stock owned by every related party is attributed to (deemed owned by) every other related party. For example, the stock of New Co. is owned as follows:

| Stockholders | Stock Owned |
|---|---|
| Joe Entrepreneur | 40% |
| Joe's wife | 30 |
| Joe's son (age 19) | 20 |
| Joe's grandson (age 3) | 10 |

   For purposes of the multiple corporation rules Joe and his wife each own 100 percent of New Co.

2. *Adult children.* An adult child (21 or older) is not related in a tax sense to his/her parents if the parents own 50 percent or less of the stock. Example:

| Stockholders | Stock Owned |
|---|---|
| Joe Entrepreneur | 20% |
| Joe's wife | 20 |
| Joe's son (age 22) | 60 |

Joe's son is *not related* to his parents.

3. *Siblings.* Brothers and sisters are not related.

In the following examples, all of the corporations escape the multiple corporation rules. All stockholders are unrelated in a tax sense.

### ■ EXAMPLE 1

| | Stock Owned | |
|---|---|---|
| Stockholders | Old Co. | New Co. |
| Joe Entrepreneur | 70% | 20% |
| Total Stranger | 30 | 80 |

Any increase in Joe's share of New Co. or in Total's share of Old Co. would be fatal. The two corporations would be taxed as one.

### ■ EXAMPLE 2

| | Stock Owned | |
|---|---|---|
| Stockholders | Old Co. | New Co. |
| Joe | 77% | 90% |
| Stranger #1 | 23 | None |
| Stranger #2 | None | 10 |

If you substitute *Joe's son (age 22)* for *Stranger #1* the corporations do not escape the multiple corporation rules. Why? Because Joe owns more than 50 percent of Old Co.

### ■ EXAMPLE 3

| | Stock Owned | |
|---|---|---|
| Stockholders | Old Co. | New Co. |
| Joe | 90% | 40% |
| Joe's brother | 10 | 60 |

■ **EXAMPLE 4**

| | Stock Owned | |
|---|---|---|
| Stockholders | Old Co. | New Co. |
| Joe | 100% | 50% |
| Joe's son (age 22) | None | 50 |

An increase of Joe's son's 50 percent share would be okay; any increase in Joe's share would be fatal.

■ **EXAMPLE 5**

| | Corporation | | |
|---|---|---|---|
| Stockholders | A | B | C |
| Father | 100% | 50% | 50% |
| Adult son X | - | 50 | - |
| Adult Daughter Y | - | - | 50 |

This example shows you that a separate new corporation, which escapes the multiple corporation rules, can be formed for each adult child in the family.

■ **EXAMPLE 6**

A father and one adult child can avail themselves of the benefits (three separate surtax brackets) of three noncontrolled corporations.

| | Corporation | | |
|---|---|---|---|
| Stockholders | A | B | C |
| Father | 100% | 50% | - |
| Adult child X | - | 50 | 100% |

■ **NOTE:** The authority for the above examples is at Section 1563(e)(6) and can be used for adult children or grandchildren (who have attained age 21), parents, and grandparents.

These examples are "for starters" only. See a professional tax advisor to explore other ways to beat the multiple corporation rules and slash your corporate taxes.

## Valuation

Any type of transfer that is attempted by the owner of a closely held business requires a valuation of the entire business. Sooner or later, the owner of a closely held corporation and his family must face the valuation problem. It is easier to face the problem while the owner is alive and healthy. It is also easier to face the problem before the corporation has appreciated substantially in value. Delay favors the IRS. And if you manage to escape this life without valuing your business, then death forces the valuation for estate-tax purposes.

Many books address the subject of valuation. The one I recommend,-hands down, is *Valuing the Privately Held Business...The Art & Science of Establishing a Company's Worth*. Written by a fella named Irving L. Blackman. Published by Probus Publishing Company, the publisher of this book.

## Insurance

Read Part V—"The Magic of Insurance."

## Transfer of Nonbusiness Property

All of the primary transfer tools deal with the transfer of a closely held business. Sometimes only the primary tools are needed to complete a transfer plan. But most of the time, business owners have nonbusiness assets they want to transfer. The next four tools tell you how to transfer these types of assets.

## Trusts, Multiple Trusts

This tool, labeled "irrevocable trust," is a delightful tax animal. In general, it is a tax-paying entity. However, to the extent it distributes current income, the trust gets a full deduction.

For example, an irrevocable trust owns nonbusiness property, say a bond, transferred to the trust by Father. The trust has $5,000 in taxable income for the year and distributes $2,000 to the income beneficiary (Sue, Father's daughter) during the year. These are the income tax consequences: Sue has $2,000 of income subject to tax; the trust has only $3,000 subject to tax.

The purpose of this tax tool is to utilize each human taxpayer, usually a child or grandchild, in combination with one irrevocable trust, to give high-bracket taxpayers (in this case Father) two additional small tax brackets (in the above example, $2,000 and $3,000) into which they can stuff their high tax-bracket dollars.

Of course, multiple trusts (say Sue is the beneficiary of more than one irrevocable trust) are possible to create even more low tax brackets. The provisions of the trust can provide flexibility so the income can be distributed (to the beneficiary) or accumulated (in the trust) to attain the lowest overall tax. The tax-saving possibilities of irrevocable trusts should always be explored. See Part VIII, Chapter 2 for a complete discussion of trusts.

## S Corporation as a Trust That Is Not a Trust

An S corporation is a great tactic for transferring nonbusiness assets and slowing estate growth. Here are the six basic steps:

1. Form a corporation (a separate new corporation not connected in any way with your business) and elect S corporation status.
2. Transfer selected (nonbusiness) investment assets to the S corporation. This transfer is tax-free.
3. Capitalize the corporation with both voting and nonvoting common stock: (a) Voting common stock is retained by the parent (or grandparent), who acts as

"Trustee." (b) Nonvoting common stock is gifted to the children (or elderly parents in need of additional support).

4. The S corporation accomplishes two major objectives: (a) It shifts investment income to low-bracket taxpayers. (b) Estate taxes are avoided on value of nonvoting stock gifted plus future growth in the value of the stock.
5. All the above is accomplished without giving up CONTROL:

   Funds accumulated for the children can be used to educate them, pay for weddings, etc.; a proportional share of corporate income is taxed to the child/shareholder, but cash need not be distributed; and, cash continues to be reinvested.
6. The S corporation functions just like a trust without being a trust because the "grantor" still controls the investment (via the voting stock) without being taxed on the income allocated to the holders of the nonvoting stock.

## Family Limited Partnerships

A family limited partnership is capable of freezing the value of any or all of your assets—business as well as nonbusiness assets. In addition, you can stay in complete control of the assets owned by the partnership.

Family limited partnerships are extraordinarily complex. But in the hands of an expert, these partnerships are capable of doing tax tricks not available by any other method. One attorney who is truly an expert is this area is Robert O. Middleton, a partner in the Chicago-based law firm of Nisen & Elliott. These edited excerpts from a memo he wrote to a "John Client" give a good overview of the tax power of a family limited partnership.

> Successful use of a family limited partnership creates benefits under all four federal tax regimes: Income tax, Gift Tax, Estate Tax and Generation-Skipping Tax. Significant non-tax benefits are also available including flexibility and longevity.
>
> I. Tax benefits.
>
> A. *Income tax.* A properly structured limited Partnership among family members is recognized as a Partnership for income tax purposes under Internal Revenue Code Section 704(e). Thus, the Partnership earnings are not subject to federal income tax. Rather, each Partner reports his proportionate share of Partnership income and expenses on his or her tax return. Thus, income from Partnership assets are taxed among the several Partners usually resulting in overall reduced tax liability.
>
> Partnerships are similar to "S" corporations except that Partnerships are more flexible. There are no limitations on who can be a Partner so that trusts, corporations and even other partnerships may own interests in the family Partnership. Partnerships are not limited to one class of Partners so that some Partners may receive preferred income distributions while others receive growth interests or even special allocations of loss items.
>
> Unlike an "S" Corporation, partnership income and assets can be distributed disproportionately to fewer than all partners without tax.

Thus, a distribution can be made to a single Partner to meet specific financial needs. Furthermore, assets can be contributed to or distributed from a partnership without triggering tax. Partnership interests are capital assets and can be redeemed or sold at lower capital gains tax rates.

B. *Gift tax.* Gifts directly to a Partnership are treated as gifts to each Partner. Properly structured, these gifts qualify for the annual gift-tax exclusion.

Partnership interests may also be gifted and/or transferred either outright or in trust. Valuation discounts for voting and transfer limitations as well as discounts for general lack of marketability and minority interests are also recognized.

C. *Estate tax.* Partnership Interests are subject to the estate tax, but unlike "S" corporations the Partnership assets are revalued (receive a stepped-up basis at date of death) so that income taxes can be saved at later disposition. Retention of voting control as a general Partner does not cause previously transferred interests to be included in a decedent's estate.

D. *Generation-skipping transfer tax.* Transfers into Partnerships for the benefit of younger generation Partners can qualify for the generation-skipping transfer-tax exemption. Partnership interests may be transferred into generation-skipping tax-exempt trusts or may be used to make direct skips to younger generation donees.

II. Specific proposal.

A limited partnership will be formed with you and each of your four children as equal Partners. You will be the general Partner. The children will be limited Partners. Minors will own their limited Partnership interests through special minor's trusts until age 21.

Grandfather may transfer up to $100,000 (five donees times $20,000) to the Partnership each year free of gift and generation-skipping transfer taxes. The Partnership will hold and invest the funds much like a trust. Annual distributions may be made to meet the Partners' income tax obligations attributable to the partnership income.

The Partnership may consider entering into a split-dollar life insurance arrangement with any or all of the Partners. The Partnership may also consider executing a freeze (of your business) in the future under the provisions of Chapter 14. The freeze will allow current cash income payments to you (giving you, John Client, a steady source of income) while appreciation of partnership assets accrues to the children.

## Conclusion

A family limited partnership is an ideal vehicle to receive Grandfather's annual gifts to you and your children. First, the gifted assets can remain pooled for more efficient investment. Second, you may control these assets as general Partner so that they are not dissipated by the children. Finally, the assets (in the partnership) will not be taxed in your estate but can be used to aid in the transfer of your family business stock on your death. Of course, the value of your Partnership interest will be subject to estate tax on your death.

To provide you with better insight into the broad capabilities of a limited partnership, here are excerpts from an outline entitled, "The Limited Partnership: the New 'Top Gun' in the Family Estate Planning Arsenal," written by Richard J. Garvey, an estate-planning specialist and a partner in the law firm of McDermott, Will & Emery, Chicago:

I. Property law aspects of partnerships.
  B. Limited partnerships.
    1. ...limited partners have no ability to bind the partnership or other partners, and the death or withdrawal of a limited partner does not affect the partnership entity.
    3. There are differences among state versions of the Uniform Limited Partnership Act (ULPA) and the Revised Act, and there is an ability to choose governing law. Conflicts of laws principles hold that the law of the organization state governs relations among partners in a limited partnership and the liability of partners in a limited partnership. All states, except Louisiana, have adopted some version of ULPA.
    4. There can be substantial restrictions placed on the right to transfer limited partnership interests by the provisions of the agreement. This can guarantee family control of the entity.
    5. These restrictions may make the interests substantially less marketable than the partnership's underlying assets which may be a goal of the older generation for transfer-tax purposes and creditor purposes.

III. Transfer tax advantages of the use of limited partnerships.
  C. In valuing the general partner's interest in an entity, it is usually significant whether or not the general partner can liquidate the entity and reach the value of the underlying assets. This is particularly true when the value of the interest based on cash flow would be much lower than its liquidation value.
  D. Usually a limited partner's right to reach the underlying assets of the partnership (or to withdraw) is restricted. Applying a "willing buyer - willing seller" test to this restricted limited partnership interest can have a substantial depressant effect on value. You may be valuing a minority position with no control and with restrictions on transfer.
  E. If an individual owns both a general partner interest (for control purposes) and a limited partnership interest (for limited liability purposes), the depressant effect on the value of the limited partnership interest can probably be achieved by a second general partner who can prevent liquidation.

IV. Non-tax advantages to the use of limited partnerships.
  A. Management.
    1. The general partner is responsible for operations, but the vote on many issues may require the consent of a majority or super majority of limited partners. Examples—appointment of a new general partner, amendment of agreement, call for capital, etc.
    2. The older generation can set up an S Corp to act as general partner with

a plan for succession as to the vote of the stock at death which enables the older generation to determine who will control the entity.

3. There is a theoretical concern over the application of Section 2036(a) when the donor is in control of distributions of income which should be considered. See Ltr. 9131006.

V. Different types of limited partnerships.

A. Business continuation.

1. The transfer-tax discount should be available from the very beginning of the partnership. For example, assume three individuals create a limited partnership and each of them conveys $1 million to the partnership. In exchange for their $1 million, they receive one-third of the stock in an S Corp, which acts as the general partner, and one-third of the limited partnership interests. Since none of the three is in control of the general partner, none of the three can compel liquidation. Accordingly, their interests should be valued for transfer-tax purposes as a minority position in an S Corp and as a limited partner with substantial restrictions on transfers. Each valuation would be influenced by likely distributions more than underlying asset value.

2. Certain practitioners have suggested that substantially all of a client's assets should be managed through the use of the limited partnership.

3. In a family with varied business interests, separate limited partnerships could be used for each in order to block the reach of creditors from one business to all of the family assets.

4. The discount available for the illiquid position of the limited partner *may* also be available at the death of the older-generation general partner. This would appear to be the case if there was a second general partner who could block liquidation, and this general partner was not a family member.

B. Investment partnerships.

1. The family members of a family business which has been sold may wish to continue their joint investment activities through the use of an investment partnership. The economics of handling various investment advisers and utilizing others to review their performance are enhanced by this vehicle.

2. There may also be a liquidity issue which the older generation may see as advantageous. A grandparent who makes $10,000 annual exclusion gifts to grandchildren may prefer their receiving units in a family partnership controlled by their parents at age 21 rather than marketable assets.

C. Freeze partnerships—Chapter 14.

1. The current low interest rates should permit the older generation to "freeze" their asset values under Chapter 14 using frozen limited partnership interests at rates which they find acceptable.

2. The real trick is to couple a minority discount on the value of the partnership assets before the freeze.

3. The "freeze" is a particularly useful device for assets with substantial appreciation potential (company with good chance of being sold or going public)."

## Grantor Retained Interest Trusts (GRITs)

Often one of the major nonbusiness assets of a business owner is a residence.

A TYPICAL SCENARIO

In a typical scenario, Joan, age 55, owns a closely held business worth $2 million and owns nonbusiness assets worth $1.5 million—a $500,000 securities portfolio and a $1-million home. She paid $250,000 for the home 25 years ago, but it seems to increase in value every year.

Joan has two children, Tim and Tam.

Enter GRIT. Joan transfers the home to a GRIT, retaining the right to live in it for a term of 13 years. For gift-tax purposes, she has made a gift to her children, but the gift (called the "remainder interest," which does not start until after the 13-year term) is much smaller than $1 million. According to IRS tables, the gift is only $346,900 (see schedule, to follow).

When the 13-year term ends, Tim and Tam will own the house. Where will Joan live then? In the house. Joan can rent the house at a fair rental (not a bad idea because the rent stays in the family and is out of Joan's estate).

What can go wrong? If Joan dies during the term of the GRIT, the house will be taxed in her estate at its then fair-market value.-Insurance is the obvious answer to an early death. Tax-wise, Joan's family wins either way. A long life means the home stays out of Joan's estate at tremendous estate-tax savings. A short life for Joan means the family wins the insurance game.

Now let's see how the IRS-GRIT tables work. The following schedule shows the amount of the remainder considered to be a taxable gift (using up a portion of your unified credit) at various ages. The longer the term, the less the value of the gift. When a "100 percent reversion" is used, it further reduces the gift's value. Only a sample of various terms and ages is shown.

**■ VALUE OF GIFT (REMAINDER) FOR A GRIT ($1-MILLION RESIDENCE TRANSFERRED TO GRIT)**

| Term of GRIT (Years) | Without Reversion | With 100% Reversion Age 55 | With 100% Reversion Age 65 |
|---|---|---|---|
| 10 | $517,950 | $452,050 | $381,530 |
| 13 | 425,180 | 346,900 | 269,520 |
| 16 | 349,030 | 261,390 | 182,000 |
| 19 | 286,510 | 192,240 | 115,230 |
| 22 | 235,200 | 137,370 | 67,220 |
| 25 | 193,070 | 94,360 | 35,440 |

**■ NOTE:** *A GRIT without a reversion:* The value of the gift is affected by three factors—(1) rate of treasury-bond interest (not shown above); (2) term of GRIT (the longer the term, the lower the gift value); and (3) the fair-market value of the residence on the date of the gift.

*A GRIT with 100 percent reversion:* In addition to the three factors above, the age of the grantor affects the value of the gift (the older the grantor, the less the value of the gift as shown in the schedule).

What does the term "with 100 percent reversion" mean? A reversion is merely a string attached to the trust (GRIT) that says, if the grantor dies within the term of the trust, then the gift (the residence) is pulled out of the GRIT. Simply, the gift does not come out to the beneficiary (as is the case "without reversion"). Instead, the gift comes back into the grantor's estate. What does this mean? The residence is now subject to the terms of the grantor's will.

But why is the discount greater with a 100 percent reversion? Because the law allows an extra discount for the likelihood that the grantor will die during the term of the trust.

### ■ TAX-SAVING RECOMMENDATION

When you create a GRIT, create it with a 100 percent reversion.-Then draw your will so the residence goes where you want it to go. The clause will only be used if the GRIT fails (you die before the end of the GRIT's term).

## Social Security

Seems odd, but I have seen even multimillionaires chase their Social Security benefits with a vengeance. A worthwhile chase. Avoiding Social Security taxes is another worthwhile pursuit. The goal—winning both chases—is imperative when the business owner has a small or modest amount of wealth and has reached his/her retirement years. Interestingly, the larger the owner's wealth, the easier the goal is to accomplish. Read the text under "Social Security Tax vs. No Social Security Tax" in Part I, Chapter 2.

## Buy-Sell Agreements

This section focuses on how buy-sell agreements are used in the transfer process.

Although such agreements make sense between sisters and brothers, uncle and nephew, unrelated fellow stockholders, and in a host of other situations, these are not our focus. Our discussion centers on a *parent/child buy-sell agreement.*

In this discussion, the trigger event is the death of the owner (Father). Each of these points must be considered to determine the impact on a given situation.

1. *Funds to buy Father's stock.* If the stock has not been transferred to one or more of the children during the father's life, there should be some prearranged assurance that funds equal to the value of the father's stock is available to the surviving shareholders to make the purchase after Father's death. Normally the only way to accomplish this with certainty is via life insurance. However, the age of the owner might make it prohibitively expensive for either the corporation or the child to own and pay for life insurance. Further, the father might not be insurable.

For whatever reason, if there is no insurance funding or the insurance amount is short of the buy-sell price, the most common ways of funding the amount due after the owner's death are:

a. Have the balance due carved out of the inheritance of the child with the buy-sell obligation.
b. Have the balance due payable over a long period of time (usually up to 10 years). Or,
c. Combine options (a) and (b).

2. *Nondeductibility of purchase price.* Whether the corporation purchases stock, via a redemption, or the child purchases the stock personally, neither will get a deduction for the purchase price.
3. *Setting the purchase price.* The objectives of family members often conflict. Since the price of stock (or the formula for determining the price) must be fixed in advance, the father is on the horns of a dilemma. If the price is set too high, it will increase his estate and the financial burden on the family business and the business child. If the price is set too low, it will jeopardize the funds needed to support father's wife and could become unfair to the other nonoperating children in the family. Often, such children must look to the stock value as the sole mechanism for receiving their "fair" share of the estate.

■ **WARNING:** The IRS can and will challenge the business motive and arm's-length terms of any buy-sell arrangement designed to fix an artificially low price. The IRS simply disregards the agreed-upon price for estate- and gift-tax purposes. However, when the business value is fixed by appraisal or other mechanism designed to equal fair-market value, the price should withstand an IRS attack.

No particular formula or fixed price can be guaranteed to establish estate-tax value conclusively. The owner must be careful setting the price in a buy-sell agreement. Otherwise the owner's estate may be obligated to sell at a low price (the price set in the agreement) while required to pay estate tax on a higher value (the value set by the IRS).

*Your best bet: Get a professional appraisal.*

It is rare to find a buy-sell agreement from a business father/mother to a child that triggers a sale to the child *during life*. Such life sales are usually nothing more than an "outright sale," almost always a no-no.

### Using Buy-Sell Agreements to Keep Stock in the Family

A top priority in most family transfer planning is to keep the stock in the family. In a typical transfer scenario, Joe and his wife, Mary, own 80 percent of Big Co. Their four grown children own the balance—five percent each. A brief family tree follows:

| Joe and Mary's Children | Married to | Joe and Mary's Grandchildren |
|---|---|---|
| Alice* | Ralph | 4 |
| Ben | Sue | 0 |
| Carrol | Tom* | 2 |
| Dave* | Divorced | 1 |

*Children or son-in-law active in the business.

Neither Joe nor Mary wants any of the stock to be owned by any person except their family by blood (their children or grandchildren). They are willing to make an exception in the case of a son- or daughter-in-law who actually is employed in the business full-time (Tom). This is how Joe's and Mary's goals are met in the buy-sell agreement. Besides customary buy-sell agreement clauses, additional language would be included to accomplish the following:

1. Instead of four children, there are four groups—the Alice Group, Ben Group, etc.
2. Using the Alice Group as an example, Alice could not transfer (by sale, gift or otherwise) her shares to anyone (not even Ralph), except her four children. The five members of Alice's Group (Alice and her four children) could make transfers among themselves free of the agreement. No dispositions could be made to anyone not in Alice's Group, not even members of the other groups; however, Alice would be able to sell all or part of her shares to Big Co. or to the other groups on a pro rated basis.
3. Various clauses make this group concept totally flexible. For example:
   a. If Alice sells all of the shares she owns, the others in her group are required to sell.
   b. Children who are not active (define as you want) in the business by a certain age (usually about 35) must offer their shares for sale according to the agreement terms.
   c. An in-law who is active in the business (for example, Tom) could own stock transferred to Tom by Carrol as long as Tom remains active in the business.

■ **A BIT OF ADVICE:** Always use this buy-sell group method unless there are overwhelming reasons not to use it. It's amazing how a well-conceived buy-sell agreement using this method seems to keep peace in the family after mom and dad are gone.

Also, see "Restrictive (Buy-Sell) Agreements" in Part III, Chapter 1.

## Employee Death Benefit Agreement

Typically, an employee death benefit agreement (EDBA) is an arrangement where the employer agrees to pay to the employee's heirs, commencing at his death, a certain sum each year for a fixed number of years, if the employee continues in employment until a certain age or until death.

■ **EXAMPLE 1**

If X, an employee, agrees to work for Y, an employer, until X reaches 65 or until his death, Y will pay X's wife, W, an amount equal to two times his annual salary commencing at the time of his death and payable over a period of 10 years.

### Tax Consequences of an EDBA

For income tax purposes, the payments are deductible by the employer as paid and taxable to W as ordinary income as received. For gift- and estate-tax purposes, the employee's benefit is not a taxable gift, nor is it included in the employee's estate.

Bingo! Thus an EDBA is often a better choice than a typical nonqualified deferred compensation agreement, which *is* included in the employee's estate.

■ **WHEN TO USE AN EDBA:** When the owner's estate is small, this is a neat way to get income to the widow without any danger of the value of the EDBA being included in the owner's estate.

When the owner's estate is large, skip the owner's spouse as a beneficiary of the EDBA. Instead, make the children the beneficiaries. This makes the EDBA payments to the children estate-tax free, while the closely held business tends to be worth less for estate-tax purposes because of its EDBA obligation.

## Other Tools

A major problem in writing this book was what to leave out. To cover every aspect of transfer/succession planning would take several large volumes, and even then, not every nuance, exception, rule, and tax problem could be included.

Furthermore, each transfer/succession plan is different. Plans must be tailor-made for *real people* with *real family problems and tax challenges.*

The preceding material covers the most common and important methods for transferring ownership. However, here are some other methods to consider:

### Sale Plus Redemption

1. *To an employee (owner keeps some interest).* For example, say Joe Owner owns 100 percent (1,000 shares) of Success Co. He wants to make Key Employee (not related to Joe) a 50 percent owner. But 50 percent of Success Co. is worth $500,000 and Key simply doesn't have the personal assets to make the deal. So Joe and Key devise this plan:

   Key buys 10 shares of Success Co. stock from Joe for $10,000. He pays $1,000 in cash and gives a 9-year, interest-bearing note for the balance ($9,000). Simultaneously, Success Co. redeems 490 shares from Joe for $490,000, paying $90,000 in cash and a 10-year, interest-bearing note for $400,000.

   The result: Joe sells a 50 percent interest in the corporation for $500,000 ($10,000 + $490,000), walking off with a capital gain. Key acquires a 50 percent interest in the corporation for $1,000 down and nine payments of $1,000 (plus interest).

■ **WARNING:** For this plan to work, Joe must reduce his interest in Success Co. to 50 percent or less. If he keeps more than 50 percent, the funds he takes from the corporation are taxable as a dividend. (See Letter Ruling 8040115).

This is an example of a redemption that is not essentially equivalent to a dividend under Section 302. (See Part II, Chapter 1 under "Redemptions.")

2. *To an outsider (owner sells 100 percent of stock owned).* What happens if the corporation has a large surplus, the buyer is short of cash, and the owner/seller wants an installment sale? In practice, this question often precisely defines the problem. Happily, there is a solution.

■ **EXAMPLE 1**

To illustrate, let's say Corporation X is worth $1 million. The buyer, B, has only $100,000 in cash. X has about $300,000 in cash available. S, the seller and 100-percent owner of X, sells 10 percent of stock to B for $100,000, and S pays tax on the full gain for this portion. S then enters into a contract with X to buy the balance of S's 90 percent of X stock for $900,000, payable at the rate of $100,000 per year plus interest for nine years. S then uses the installment method.

The above method allows the seller to get an installment sale and the buyer (who now owns 100 percent of X) to use the future profits of the business to pay for the purchase. The gain to S is a capital gain, not a dividend. The authority for this tax-saving approach is a very important case—*Zenz v. Quinlivan*.

■ **WARNING:** This arrangement can only be successfully instituted with a nonrelated party, not a family member. The money taken out of the corporation for the redemption, if done with a related family member, causes dividend instead of capital-gain treatment.

### Other Considerations

1. *Lifetime trust.* The business owner creates a revocable trust during his lifetime, establishing as the corpus some part or all of the stock of the business. Under the terms of the trust, further disposition of the business interest may be made to the family after death. This method permits a smooth transition in management of the business after the death of its owner, since the trustee has already been managing prior to death. It also permits the owner to test the trustee's performance during his life.
2. *Outright bequest of the business interest.* If the owner desires to retain ownership, remaining active in the business until death, then bequeathing the business outright at death to an adult beneficiary is the recommended method. However, this method is seldom used alone.

   Normally, another method is used to transfer a portion of the ownership to the next generation (while the owner retains control) during life.
3. *Bequest in trust.* Those persons meant to benefit from the business may not be suited to receive it outright. They may be financially inexperienced or just plain incapable. When the business will be continued under these circumstances, the best vehicle is usually a testamentary trust.

### Premarital Agreements

Although not really a tool (method), premarital agreements are a must to protect the owner of a closely held business who marries for a second (or third, or...) time. The owner is protected in the event of another divorce; the owner's children are protected in the event of the owner's death.

In these agreements, the business should be specifically referenced and should not be treated as a general asset. Any ambiguity can and usually does cause problems in the event of divorce. The disposition of the future appreciation in the value of the business, annual income, profits of the business during marriage, as well as any assets that are integral to the business, but are not part of it (such as real estate and leased machinery), should all be specifically defined.

Even with these agreements there are several pitfalls:

- ☐ The agreement alone does not eliminate a spouse's right to certain retirement interests (more documentation is required);
- ☐ An inaccurate valuation of the business, or incomplete or ambiguous disclosure of other financial interests and obligations, can invalidate the agreement;
- ☐ The agreement must conform to other estate-planning documents;
- ☐ Separate legal counsel should always be used by the two parties.

# PART III

## How to Treat the Children Fairly

# III INTRODUCTION

## Cutting Up the Pie

You've worked your tail off for 25 or more years and have succeeded in building a successful business. You're proud of it. By no means are your ready to cash in your chips. But, from time to time, you've thought about the fact that the kids, or some of them, will eventually take over the business.

Maybe that's the problem: You've only got one business, yet you've got four kids, some in the business, some not. How do you cut up the pie?

Remember, as a child, how your parents always tried hard to treat the kids fairly? There were audible grumblings on the few occasions that they failed. I don't know how it was in your house, but in mine we kids could count. When it came to blueberries, raspberries, or chocolate-covered raisins, it took practically a certified audit to prove to us that we got our fair share.

And when it came to pie, forget it. Sure, we each got one piece, but who got the biggest piece? Our own children, now grown-up adults, are too mature to feel rejected if one gets a smaller piece of the pie than another. Or are they?

The pie in your family oven today is the business/family/other assets pie, more commonly called "a transfer-plan pie." The basic ingredients depend on circumstances and your philosophy. If you have only one child, everything from selecting the ingredients through serving (implementing the plan) is easy.

Do you have more than one child? If so, the transfer-plan pie becomes very difficult, starting from the selection of the ingredients to ultimately dividing the pie among the kids. For example, is each of the kids equally capable of running your business? If the answer is "no," you have a normal problem. Even so, you want to treat them all equally. But is that possible?

Read on. This part of the book will help you define the problems. But, more importantly, it will identify a number of real-life, practical solutions that have helped family businesses survive and prosper into the next generation. Is it easy? No!...Can a perfect succession plan be put in place? Rarely!

Our firm, Blackman Kallick Bartelstein (CPAs), has consulted with and helped family businesses from the four corners of the United States conceive and implement their transfer plans. In over 30 years of this type of work, you might think that we have seen it all. Yet, almost every month we find one more business and family that has a special problem requiring a unique solution.

# 1 Your Business, Its Future, and Your Family

There is not one technical word in this chapter.

If asked what you plan to do with your business, you might reply, "Make a living," "Earn money," "Grow," or "Expand." In all probability, your response to the question will be expressed in terms of prospering financially. You'll probably think in terms of the next few years.

But let's suppose that you've already enjoyed a pretty fair amount of entrepreneurial success and that you are considering the long-term question, "What do you plan to do with your business eventually?"

## Owners with No Children

If you don't have children, you (or your executor) will eventually look for someone to buy you out. While liquidation is sometimes the only choice, selling your business as a going concern usually yields the best results. Indeed, the sales price may often include your continued participation in the business long after the sale.

Like selling a house that no longer fits your needs, selling a business is a matter of finding the right potential buyer who has the necessary purchasing power, then negotiating a mutually satisfactory deal. Often, the most likely buyer is found among your competitors or key employees. Some of your suppliers or customers might even be prospects.

Sorry, but our mission in this book won't permit us to examine the interesting and critical matters involved in finding a buyer and negotiating a satisfactory sale of your business. Our principal concern in this part of the book is with other matters, namely transferring your business to your children, if any.

## Owners with One Child

Let's assume you have only one child. He (or she) is (or is not) of an age, degree of maturity and inclination that makes him (or her) a serious candidate to become your business successor. Obviously, if that only child is an accomplished concert pianist, you shouldn't count too much on having him or her eventually take over your closely held business. If the child is a preschooler, only time will tell. Patience!

If, on the other hand, your kid is now working in the business and doing a good job, he or she is probably your business heir apparent. Even if your kid isn't working for you now, perhaps he/she will eventually reach a degree of maturity, experience and inclination to be a suitable business heir apparent.

Be realistic. If the kid is the man (or woman) for the job, God has blessed you. Give it to him or her, perhaps, piece by piece during your life, so you can have the pleasure of watching your kid and your business grow together, or leave it to him or her in your will.

## Owners with "Equal Children"

Let's explain what we don't mean by "equal children." We don't mean twins, nor do we mean children of the same sex, same size, same intellect or same emotional makeup.

In coining the phrase "equal children," we merely want to identify the possibility that a person may have two or more children with fairly equal interests and propensities to succeed in the business. Obviously, this is dangerous territory. It's almost impossible to identify such "equality," even after your children have been working in the business for five or 10 years—never mind trying to identify it earlier.

But such "equality" is a rarity. An extreme rarity! I have been servicing closely held businesses for my entire professional life and have yet to see it. For the parent who is not so blessed—read on.

## Owners with "Unequal Children"

To parents of more than one child, the expression "unequal children" is redundant. Indeed, no two children are ever alike. They may all be equally lovable, but that's where the equality usually stops. Only time will tell (hopefully) whether your children are "equal" in terms of being suitable business heirs apparent.

So, as a practical matter, we are forced to assume that we are dealing with "unequal children." *This book assumes that you want to transfer your business to one or more of these children* and is directed exclusively at the question of "What do you plan to do with your business eventually?"

At this early stage in the book, the technical aspects (particularly the tax issue) of transferring your business to the kids are rarely troublesome. The human aspects (how to treat the kids fairly) are what creates the problems.

Solve the human aspects, and the technical aspects seem to fall into place.

## Your Business End Game: Four Possible Choices

Okay, you have an established and successful business, two or more children, and you recognize that you are not immortal. What are your choices? You may—

- ☐ Transfer the business,
- ☐ Sell the business,
- ☐ Liquidate the business, or
- ☐ Do nothing.

Let's review these briefly, in reverse order. The reason for reversing the order is so that we can save our discussion of "Transferring the Business" until last. Undoubtedly, this is the preferred alternative for most successful business owners with children.

### Do Nothing

By doing nothing, we mean that you ignore the problem of "what to do with your business eventually." You put it on the "back burner," so to speak. Sooner or later, you must deal with the problem, unless you just ignore it until death. Then the IRS or your executor will do it for you. A lousy choice!

### Liquidate the Business

Nobody is obliged to keep a business going. It's always possible to sell off the assets, pay off the liabilities, and pocket the excess, if any. Often, this is the ultimate "solution" (or rather, dissolution) for a business that no longer has an active and capable leader.

Unfortunately, liquidation prices rarely reflect anything approaching real value. This is usually true with respect to accounts receivable, inventory and equipment—particularly so in the case of a post-death liquidation.

Experience indicates that liquidation should be used only as a solution of last resort. Ordinarily, a going business has far more value than can ever be realized on liquidation.

### Sell the Business

The owner who has no children may eventually sell his business or enter into an agreement for his executor to do so. Also, a sale (or agreement to sell) may be appropriate for the owner who has children if none of them has the interest, inclination or necessary aptitude to run the business.

For many business owners, sale of the business is the only practical answer to the question "What will I do with my business—eventually?" But there is another choice that is generally more consistent with the wishes of the business owner who has children—namely, that of transferring the business.

## Transfer Choices That Treat the Kids Fairly

I often hear my clients say that they want to treat their children "equally" or "fairly" or "equitably," or something like that.

"Fairness" is a tenuous term. It rarely has the same meaning to any two people. It also tends to be short-lived, so that whatever it means today may become inaccurate tomorrow.

"Equality" may be mathematically precise but impractical to implement under most circumstances. Yet that's exactly what most of my business-owner clients want.

To start, let's consider two simple examples, each involving a widower, Joe, with three children and an estate worth $1,500,000. In each example, the objective is to treat the kids equally.

| | Value |
|---|---|
| **EXAMPLE 1** | |
| A portfolio of public company stocks | $1,300,000 |
| 1,000 shares of a publicly listed mutual fund | 75,000 |
| Money fund | 125,000 |
| Total | $1,500,000 |
| **EXAMPLE 2** | |
| Joe's Mercedes | $40,000 |
| Joe's house | 460,000 |
| Joe's business | 1,000,000 |
| Total | $1,500,000 |

Clearly, distribution of Joe's estate in three equal shares is easy in Example 1. But as a practical matter, it is impossible in Example 2. It is most unlikely that co-ownership of a car, a house and a business by three siblings will lead to happiness for any of the kids, much less all of them.

Even though fairness is unattainable and *equality* is impractical, the typical owner wants to treat the children equitably or impartially.

### Partiality as to the Business

Often one or two of the children of the owner show a far greater interest in the business than their siblings. Perhaps they chose their college majors with the business in mind. Perhaps they've already worked for the business constructively.

As to future ownership and management of the business, the owner's partiality for the child who is making a significant contribution to the business seriously conflicts with his natural paternal instinct to treat all of his children equitably.

Let's examine the alternatives available to the owner in resolving the conflict between (1) impartiality of a parent and (2) partiality of an owner to the child who has already "earned his stripes" in the business. But first, let's make sure that we have the problem itself in focus. A case that we recently dealt with may be helpful in this regard.

### Impartiality vs. Partiality to Child in Business: Case in Point

John Owner, age 49, has a wife, Mary (same age), and three children. Son Jerry (age 28) has worked hard for his father for seven years; if necessary, Jerry could run the business. Daughter Jean (age 21) is in college, has never worked in the business, is not interested in it, and is engaged to marry an assistant professor. Son Jimmy (age 14), like his sister, has never worked in the business, and whether he would ever work for the business is uncertain.

John estimates the value of his assets to be as follows:

| | Value |
|---|---|
| Cash and securities | $150,000 |
| Main residence | 250,000 |
| Vacation condo | 150,000 |
| Life insurance | 250,000 |
| Business | 1,200,000 |
| Total | $2,000,000 |

John's wife takes no interest in the business, and that's the way he wants it. Indeed, he wants her to have nothing to do with the business even after his death.

John wants a new will, which would leave the business to his son, Jerry. Everything else goes to his wife, Mary. Then Jean and Jimmy would each get one-half of Mary's share at her death.

■ **NOTE:** The surviving spouse of a married person has a right of election to take a specified share of the deceased spouse's estate rather than to accept the portion left to her (or him) under the will of the deceased spouse. The size of the elective share varies from state to state. One-third of a decedent's estate is quite common. Ask your lawyer what the rule is in your state.

John is fully aware of, and somewhat uncomfortable about the fact, that:

1. Jerry would get three times as big a piece of the pie as Jean and Jimmy each would get, and
2. Jerry would get his share at John's death (even if Mary survived), but Jean and Jimmy would have to wait until both parents died to get their shares.

John was also unhappy that approximately $250,000 in estate taxes would be due at his death because of the $1,200,000 bequest of the business to Jerry. Still, John knew what he was doing (or so he thought), until he was prodded to look a little deeper.

John's advisor asked him to assume that:

1. He had executed a will as described,
2. He died several months or years later, and
3. He looked back at his children from the great beyond years later.

John envisioned a number of scenarios, and his insights made him change his mind. He saw his three children—Jerry (then age 38), Jean (then age 31), and Jimmy (then age 24). Jerry was doing a good job with the business, which appeared to be worth about $2,500,000.

Jimmy had quit college and had been working for his brother for the past three years. Jean was leaving her job at the business to have her third child. She had been working there since the arrival of her second child (three years earlier) in order to help her husband keep their budget balanced.

John saw the problem: Jean's and Jimmy's share is unfairly smaller than Jerry's share; Jean and Jimmy must wait until both John and Mary die. However, John did not see the solution.

Though family situations differ, careful planning can prevent potential disasters.

A number of possible solutions are available in such cases, and each alternative has its own advantages and drawbacks. These possible solutions are the ones most often used in practice.

### Insurance to Equalize

Either corporate or personal dollars can be used to acquire insurance on your life in an amount large enough to provide funds to equalize the ratio of business to nonbusiness assets. This method has the merit of simplicity. Its limitation is that substantial amounts of insurance may be required, or the owner is not insurable, or, even if the owner is insurable, the cost of the insurance is prohibitive (discussed in Part III, Chapter 2).

### Stock Purchase

The children active in the business are provided a life insurance benefit to be used to purchase the business interest from your estate. The proceeds (purchase price) paid to your estate may be left to your spouse and/or the inactive children.

Although not quite as simple to implement as the prior approach, it is nevertheless simple. It can be implemented with somewhat less life insurance (discussed in Part III, Chapter 2).

### Recapitalization—Using Preferred Stock

Amend the corporate charter during life to create two classes of stock—common and preferred. Under your will, the common stock is left to the active children and the preferred stock is left to the inactive children. Or authorize your executor to recapitalize in the same manner after your death.

After your death, the corporation redeems the stock of the inactive children, leaving the active children as the sole owners of the business. This method provides for both the active children (ownership) and the inactive children (cash), but identification of active or inactive can be deferred until after the death of the owner.

### Recapitalization—Using an S Corporation

Amend the corporate charter to create two types of common stock—voting and nonvoting. The voting can be transferred either during life or at death to the active children, and the nonvoting can be similarly transferred to the inactive children. Then, the nonvoting stock can be redeemed as described above under "Recapitalization—Using Preferred Stock."

### Restrictive (Buy-Sell) Agreements

During your lifetime, place restrictions on all shares of stock so that any shareholder's stock may be redeemed at fair-market value except:

- ☐ While he (she) is employed full-time by the business,
- ☐ While he (she) is under age 30 (or some other age), or
- ☐ After he (she) has been employed for 10 (or some other number) successive years.

Then leave your stock to the children in equal shares. The restrictions put the active shareholder child more or less in the driver's seat, which tends to encourage keeping the business in the family.

For an in-depth discussion of buy-sell agreements, see Chapter 2, Part II. Also see Chapter 3, Part III.

■ **WHAT JOHN DID:** John Owner used a combination of life insurance, lifetime gifts and a recapitalization (an S corporation with voting stock, which John kept, and nonvoting stock, gifted to the kids) to put his transfer plan into effect. A restrictive agreement was executed, with the idea that it would be redrafted from time to time to reflect changing circumstances.

# 2 Insurance/Stock Purchase Solution

This chapter is nontechnical.

The problem of equitable treatment of children is nonexistent if the owner has only one child or several children, each with equal standing as the business heir apparent. In the former case, the owner might just transfer the entire business to the only child. Where there are several "equal" (in the mind of the owner) children, the owner might transfer to each of them an equal fractional share of the business. Clearly this would treat them all fairly.

More often than not, there are "unequal" children (in the business sense), but nevertheless the owner has a compelling parental desire to treat them equally! If the value of the business is relatively small compared with the overall size of the owner's wealth, equality of treatment presents no problem.

---

■ **A SIMPLISTIC EXAMPLE**

A widower/owner (Cy) with three children owns a business valued at $400,000. Cy also owns marketable securities valued at $800,000. The $1,200,000 represents the total estate value.

If Cy wants one child to acquire the business, he can leave it to him or her and leave $400,000 of the marketable securities to each of the other two. (It is rare that the amount of nonbusiness assets equals or exceeds the value of the business assets.)

■ **NOTE ON WIVES (AND HUSBANDS):** Many of the examples in this section of the book assume that the business owner is a widower. This assumption is made to avoid complicating the discussion with the matter of bequests to wives versus bequests to children.

---

## An Insurance Solution

In the real world, the business is usually an owner's largest asset, by far. Let's say the business is worth $1,500,000 and the owner has $500,000 of nonbusiness assets.

This situation may not be troublesome. For example, suppose that your daughter is (or is married to) a successful brain surgeon. Notwithstanding the discrepancy in property values, a bequest of the business to your son and the balance ($500,000) of the estate to your daughter is not disturbing.

If, however, the two children are, say, twins (or at least in similar economic circumstances), a bequest of the business to one child (and the balance to the other) may not be attractive if the discrepancy is so large. In such cases, life insurance may be the answer. A $500,000 (or larger) insurance policy on your life, for the benefit of your (nonbusiness) child, can be a most appropriate answer.

In general, then, we can conclude that where disparity in value is small, or the economic circumstances of children differ favorably, value differentials may often be *ignored*. Where the disparity problem is larger, a practical way to *eliminate* the value differential is to insure it. Such life insurance might be provided through parental gifts of premiums to the appropriate children or to trusts for their benefit.

■ **CASH-SAVING IDEA**

In some situations, it may be more economical to provide the insurance protection through a group-term life insurance plan or a so-called split-dollar insurance plan. (See Chapter 3, Part V.)

■ **IMPORTANT:** To the extent that the owner has assets outside of the business, these nonbusiness assets should be used to satisfy amounts needed for the nonbusiness children. To the extent that such assets fall short of what is needed, the planning process should begin immediately. (Read the material under "dividing assets by business assets and nonbusiness assets" at the end of Chapter 2, Part I.)

Then, only the shortfall needed to equalize the values to be distributed to your nonbusiness children requires insurance coverage.

### Pros and Cons of Insurance Solution

The insurance solution has the merit of simplicity. Indeed, it may well be the best solution in cases where the disparity does not exceed a few hundred thousand dollars. Its major shortcoming is that it is too costly (and unnecessarily so) in cases where the disparity is substantial and/or there are too many nonbusiness children.

For example, if the business owner has a $500,000-business, $200,000 of nonbusiness assets, one business heir apparent and four other (nonbusiness) children, eliminating disparities would require $1.8 million ($450,000 x 4) of life insurance in order to produce $2 million in nonbusiness assets ($500,000 for each nonbusiness child).

It should be evident that this life insurance solution is practical only in cases where the value of the business and/or the number of nonbusiness children is fairly small, or the business owner has adequate funds to pay the insurance premiums. Nor is insurance necessarily an all-or-nothing solution. It is often used as a partial solution, in combination with other solutions.

## The Stock-Purchase Solution

A business owner is unlikely to be so careless as to forget mentioning a child in his or her will. Yet, as a practical matter, a child is too often "forgotten."

For example, Joe Owner has a $1 million estate: $450,000 in business assets and $550,000 in other assets. Joe's family includes Sam, who is active in the business; Dana, who is not interested in the business, and his wife, for whom Joe wants to provide after his death.

At Joe's death (absent careful planning), the $1 million estate could be distributed this way:

| Assets | Left To Whom | |
|---|---|---|
| Business | Sam | $ 450,000 |
| Marital deduction | Wife | 500,000 |
| Other assets | Forgotten daughter, Dana | 50,000 |
| Total | | $1,000,000 |

Is there a better way to provide for Dana without compromising the bequest to Sam and Wife? Yes, clearly. By adding $400,000 in life insurance, Joe would make Dana equal to Sam.

### Stock Purchase Using Insurance

Anxious though you may be to pass your business directly to your business heir apparent, what if you don't? Instead, suppose you make Sam buy it! How? One way is to provide Sam with a life-insurance death benefit to be used as part or all of the purchase price. Such an arrangement produces three positive results:

1. It limits (or eliminates) the extent to which you favor the business heir apparent.
2. Cash paid for the purchase price provides nonbusiness assets available to reduce (or eliminate) disparities.
3. The value of the business is "pegged" for purposes of death-tax assessments.

Sam (as owner and beneficiary of the policy) might be provided with a life-insurance benefit of $200,000 (on Joe's life) that he uses to "purchase" the $450,000 business interest at a $200,000 price from Joe's estate. Sam is getting a $250,000 bargain ($450,000 value less $200,000 purchase price). In effect, he receives a $250,000 net bequest.

The estate then has the $200,000 proceeds from the sale of the business interest to add to Dana's $50,000 of other assets. In this way, an equitable distribution is achieved by leaving each child the same $250,000 in value. We made Sam pay for the other $200,000 of business value in the form of paying a life insurance premium. If, of course, the business gives him a hand (in the form of a tax-deductible salary increase equal to the premium amount, net after tax), who is to complain? He undoubtedly earned it.

### Pros and Cons of Stock-Purchase Solution

Although not quite as simple to implement as the prior approach (insurance to equalize), the stock-purchase solution is nonetheless simple. It can usually be implemented with considerably less life insurance. Thus, as a practical matter, it is considerably more attractive than the insurance approach.

## Stock Purchase Without Insurance

For many reasons, insurance may not be available or desirable to implement the stock purchase. Joe Owner's objectives can still be met by leaving his estate as follows:

| Business interest | |
|---|---|
| Sam | $250,000 |
| Dana | 200,000 |
| **Other assets** | |
| Dana | 50,000 |
| Wife | 500,000 |

In his will, Joe can set up the mechanics (different lawyers may do it in different ways in different states) so that Sam must buy Dana's interest for $200,000. The rate of interest and the number of years to pay can be tailored to fit your requirements. Wife's will should be drawn to dovetail with Joe's estate plan. The half that Sam receives from his mother's estate might be used to pay any balance due to Dana.

Such a solution should only be thought of as a beginning.

---

**■ IMPORTANT**

Where necessary, it should be supported by other lifetime and estate tax-planning techniques as detailed throughout this book. For example:

1. A lifetime gift-giving program
2. Utilization of the unified credit
3. Utilization of the marital deduction
4. GRITs, GRATs, and ESOPs
5. Use of an irrevocable life-insurance trust

---

# 3 Restrictive Buy-Sell Agreements

Another nontechnical chapter.

Until all of your kids have matured, you probably cannot decide what rights of stock ownership would be most suitable for each child. You must wait to determine their propensity for business management. Is there a way to treat all the children the same, *temporarily*—yet have a mechanism to change this later on? For example, you might want a child's rights to a share of the business to change depending upon subsequent circumstances—such as the extent of his (or her) activity and interest in the business.

There is, indeed, such a mechanism: Let's call it a "restrictive buy-sell agreement." Such an agreement is highly suitable in cases where some of the children have not yet fully matured. This solution requires only one type of stock.

## A Case Study

The use of a restrictive buy-sell agreement can best be illustrated by a case study. In Chapter 1, this situation was set forth: John Owner has a wife, Mary, and three children. Son Jerry (age 28) could run the business, if necessary. Daughter Jean (age 21) has no interest in the business, and son Jimmy (age 14) is too young to determine his interest in the business and ultimate business ability.

John's estimates of his assets: business, $1,200,000; other assets, $800,000; total, $2,000,000. John's wife takes no interest in the business, and John doesn't want her involved in the business even after his death. His original transfer plan was to leave the business to son Jerry, everything else to his wife, and Jean and Jimmy would each get half of Mary's estate at her death.

After further thought, John recognized that the plan wasn't a suitable solution. Jean and/or Jimmy might eventually work in the business. Yet they could be left out in the cold, as far as any ownership interest is concerned.

John wanted to treat the kids equally, but he also wanted to favor Jerry (the business heir apparent) *as well as* any other child who might get actively involved in the business.

### The Solution

One solution is to leave exactly one-third of the business to each child, but only after a "restrictive buy-sell agreement" has been signed. This agreement [between the present shareholder(s)—John Owner owns 100 percent—and the corporation] contains two important restrictions:

1. It provides that any shares given (during John's life) or bequeathed by John will not be further transferable without first being offered to the corporation at *fair-market value.*
2. All shares of stock will be subject to a call option (i.e., an option to purchase) by the corporation, at *fair-market value,* at any time—EXCEPT under *three* specified circumstances.

The corporation cannot "call" the stock: (1) While a child or his (or her) spouse is a full-time employee of the corporation; (2) while a child is under age 30; or, (3) after a child or his/her spouse has completed *10* consecutive years as a full-time employee of the corporation.

The exact form of the agreement is not important. *The concept is.* Your attorney may prefer a lifetime agreement between stockholder/children (assuming all are adults under local law and each owns at least one share of stock—usually by gift). The agreement could be in the form of an option (given before or after death). Or the stock could be put in trust, and the kids' rights and duties would be spelled out in the trust document.

### Why and How the Solution Works

Our objective is not only to treat the children equally, but also to treat those who are active (now or in the future) in the business "more equally." The call option (or other form used) gives the corporation the power to "kick out" any stockholder by buying his (her) share of the stock for fair-market value.

But maybe you don't *want* to kick a kid out under certain circumstances, say while working for the business, while too young to decide on a career, or after a set number of years of loyal service to the business. Using these three exceptions, the active children (or those who ultimately become active) are indeed protected. Such protection until age 30 is, of course, arbitrary. (It could be to age 25 or 35.) Ten consecutive years of service is also arbitrary. (It could be a shorter or longer period of service.) But unless one of these exceptions applies, each child's future with the company is determined by "the corporation."

■ **NOTE:** The circumstances set forth above are illustrative only—tailor them to your exact needs.

### Who Does the Kicking Out?

The authority to act for a corporation is vested in its board of directors. The directors, in turn, are elected by vote of the stockholders. If the three children are equal stockholders, any two of them could vote to kick out the third (i.e., call his stock at fair-market value).

While this exercise of authority (by majority vote of the children) is legally workable, it may tend to create unnecessary animosity among the children.

Another approach is to leave the stock in trust for the three children or create a voting trust (okay to continue or elect S corporation status). Then, choose trustees who would determine "who does the kicking." For example, in the above case study, three trustees might be named (to act by majority vote): Son Jerry, Mother Mary and the corporation's lawyer.

This will leave Jerry in the driver's seat. He can run the business unimpaired as long as either his mother or the lawyer agrees with him. He can even kick out his brother or sister (with agreement of his mother or the lawyer), except when the EXCEPTIONS to the call option apply.

### Pros and Cons of This Solution

This solution gives the active child practical control. It also gives him the motivation and opportunity to enjoy the fruits of his labors.

The active children have the (corporate) burden of finding cash to redeem the shares of the inactive children. This burden can be lightened by providing appropriate terms (payable over a period of years) in the agreement (or other document).

This approach leaves the inactive children at some potential disadvantage. But the disadvantage is far less than if the entire business is left solely to the active child.

And finally, recognize that you will get better results by not trying to cover every possible contingency in an agreement executed today that, of necessity, must trigger rights and obligations that will not take root until many years down the road.

■ **NOTE:** As circumstances change, the agreement can be modified to provide flexibility. Also, read the material under "Buy-Sell Agreements" in Part II, Chapter 2.

# PART IV

# The Transfer

(This part is a continuing story.)

# IV INTRODUCTION

## My Humbling Profession

The body of knowledge exploded with the dawn of the computer age and shows no sign of stopping. Accounting, taxes, and closely held businesses seem to be at the forefront of this continuing explosion. As a result, even with all my years of experience, I've got to keep on learning. Fast! Just to stay even.

The plain fact is that the more experience I get, and the more I learn, the more help I need from other people to get my job done.

*Yes, my profession is humbling.*

Actually, in my case, the word "experience" means I learned from my mistakes.

Some people consider me the guru of transfer/succession/estate planning. Must admit, it's flattering.

But should the truth be known, the guru is a paper tiger without the help of a small army of other people. He doesn't even know how to prepare his own tax return. It's done by Sandy Soltis, a manager in the tax department of our accounting firm, Blackman Kallick Bartelstein. Bless her.

And talk about our tax department. The nice people (each of the 20 is smart—darn smart—or they couldn't work at Blackman Kallick) in that department do my tax research. Analyze data. Make projections. Write reports. You name it.

The client (sometimes his/her controller or accountant) prepares the data to be used in our consulting meeting.

Appropriate members of my staff help me before, and sometimes during and after the meeting with a variety of details.

The client's accountant is often a source of needed information, as well as insight and wisdom into his/her client's needs. The same for the client's attorney, who also writes the documents—wills, trusts, buy-sell agreements, ESOPs, GRITs, GRATs, and a host of others—to memorialize the transfer/succession/estate plan.

The client's insurance consultant runs the necessary insurance proposals.

What does Irv do? He's the catalyst. Working with all these other people, he blends and shapes the input to satisfy the most important person in the whole world: the CLIENT.

Without the help of all those people, I'm helpless.

*Yes, my profession is humbling.*

But I've loved every minute of it. Past. Present. And hopefully for a long time into the future.

# 1 Meet the Author

Since so much of this book is based upon my interaction with other people, I thought you might like to meet the guy behind the pen. Well, here goes.

I'm a work-hard, play-hard kind of guy with three passions: my family, my work, and my tennis. Actually, a better way to put it is that, after my family, work and tennis are my two passions. But let me point out that my work to me is more often like play. I love my work.

Mark Twain sure got it right when he wrote in *The Adventures of Tom Sawyer*: "Work consists of whatever a body is *obliged* to do...Play consists of whatever a body is *not obliged* to do."

## My First Transfer

It was sometime in the '60s. Don't remember exactly when. A small business owner/client wanted to transfer his business to his kids. This CPA/lawyer didn't have the "foggiest" idea of where to start. So I made calls. Lots of 'em. This was what I learned from my telephone research:

1. Accountants did not do transfer planning.
2. Lawyers did estate planning (death documents) in this area.
3. Insurance consultants searched for the premium dollar.
4. The trust departments of the banks held documents and administered estates.

My plea, that "My client ain't dead yet; this is lifetime planning, not death planning," fell on deaf ears. Well, it's about 30 years later, and not much has changed. Admittedly, my network of knowledgeable professionals has grown through the years, and it is easy to get solid answers to tough questions. But by and large, the four professions identified above still operate today—as far as the subject matter of this book is concerned—the same way they did in the '60s.

This chapter tells a bit about my past and present—as related to the subject of this book, and gives you a peek into my future plans.

## The Past—But Only the Portion That Affects My Professional Future

My college experience started in premed. Mom always wanted me to be a doctor. One day, while a first-semester freshman, my brother Ben (now a retired doctor) introduced me to his friend Earnest. Ben was in medical school at the time. Earnest was his cadaver. The joke was that those doctors-to-be of yesteryear worked in *dead earnest*. That ended my medical career.

The next semester found me in the School of Business majoring in accounting. Four years later (the same year I got my first full-time job in public accounting and entered law school as a night student) the state of Illinois awarded me my CPA certificate.

I worked my "duff" off for the next four years. Worked days. Attended law school at night. Graduated law school after four years. But let it be known that I went straight. I don't practice law. Only accounting.

My early years as a CPA were spent in auditing (of closely held family businesses). But little by little, more of my time was devoted to the practice of taxes, until one day—during the '60s—I became and have remained a full-time tax man.

### The Change in Professional Ethics

The change in the professional ethics (for CPAs) in the '70s changed my professional life. Freedom! At last it was ethical to advertise. To solicit business. To do all the things CPAs could not do before to let the business world know what skills they possessed.

The marketer in me, who had been hidden somewhere in the recesses of my mind, emerged. I began to write (Articles. Columns. Special reports. And eventually books. All in the tax area) and lecture (to anyone who would listen, but mostly to business trade association audiences).

As a result of these educational activities, my tax consulting practice evolved into two distinct disciplines:

1. Business valuation, and
2. Transfer/succession/estate planning.

## The Birth of the Second Tax Opinion

One day the marketing tactic of a second tax opinion occurred to me. We informed every business owner we could. Via my column. Via an ad in my special reports. Via my seminars. Via word of mouth. It worked. This article from my tax column shows one of the many hits from our second-opinion marketing campaign.

> SECOND TAX OPINION SAVES THE DAY
>
> The phone rang. It was a reader (let's call him Joe) of this column. "I need a second opinion," he said. Joe had decided he was at the age (59) when his estate should be put in order. He and his wife, Mary (age 58), had each just signed their own new will and trust agreement. Yet, somehow, Joe still felt uncomfortable.

> I asked Joe a series of pointed questions about such things as his business, his three-child family and his short- and long-term objectives. We decided Joe would send me what we call a "consulting package": copies of his tax returns and financial statements (both business and personal) and copies of the new wills and trusts.
>
> A review of Joe's data revealed several minor problems (easily corrected) and one major problem which is common to business owners like Joe. It's like a disease, but of a very different kind: It doesn't strike until after you are dead. Let me explain.
>
> An analysis of Joe's personal financial statement clearly showed that important parts of Joe's will and trust agreement were worthless. Oh, don't get me wrong. The documents were well written by an experienced lawyer from a large law firm. A good analogy would be a magnificent automobile and no fuel to run it. Here's why. Suppose Joe died first (before Mary). Here's what would have happened to his assets. His IRA, pension plan, and profit-sharing funds would have gone directly to Mary; she is the beneficiary. Same for the substantial life insurance on Joe's life. All of Joe's significant other assets—the business stock, house, condo, investment stocks and some other assets—are held in joint tenancy with Mary. If Joe were to die, Mary would own all of these assets outright—not Joe's executor or trustee.
>
> Simply put, Joe's property would not have flowed through the will and then into the trust. Everything would go directly to Mary. First, a tax disaster—ultimately costing Joe's family about $250,000 in extra estate taxes. Second, Joe's assets would not have been subject to the protection of the trust. Fortunately, we were able to change all that. The trust became the beneficiary instead of Mary. All the joint tenancies were terminated and each asset was put solely into Joe or Mary's name (or their trusts) as dictated by Joe and Mary's objectives.
>
> How do mistakes like the above happen? Joe's case is typical: His accountant planned the business transfer, the insurance consultant suggested the life insurance coverage, and the lawyer did the documents. All experts in their own field. But no quarterback.
>
> How do you cure this problem? Joe showed you the way. Get a second—and independent—opinion.

It's real-people, second-opinion consulting assignments like the above that keep me going professionally.

### The Fax

The fax was (and is) the fuel that boosted my valuation business and second-opinion tax practice into space. In my case, the ground is the greater Chicago area, where my office is located; space is the rest of the United States. (Of the transfer/succession/estate planning business done by me and my accounting firm, Blackman Kallick Bartelstein, 62 percent is done with business owners who live outside of the Chicago area.) Modern communication made it all possible. Another article from my column tells the communication miracle story.

PHONE AND FAX GIVE BIRTH TO NEW TAX TREND

A recent article in the *Wall Street Journal* (March 199_) is titled *'House Calls' By Phone Seen Improving Care*. The article states: "A new study says that patients who received follow-up care by phone reduced their annual medical costs by 28 percent. And they generally fared as well as or better than patients who returned to the doctor's office for face-to-face visits."

A new trend? Could it be that Americans are abandoning that it-must-be-an-eye-ball-to-eye-ball meeting every time they consult with a professional? Yes, is my loud answer. The combination of lowering long distance telephone rates, fax, and the time and cost of travel have revolutionized tax consulting. Shucks, the medical guys are just catching up.

Years ago, only my long-time clients were comfortable with ironing out details over the phone. But even that occurred only after a face-to-face meeting to set the main points of the tax plan.

Not so today. Many tax plans are created by phone, fax and mail (or UPS-like delivery). Often three or more people (the business owners, their families, CPA, lawyer, etc.) simply have a phone conference to achieve the same results that would have been accomplished in a typical old-fashioned office conference.

Why is this subject so important to owners of closely held businesses?...Because now the entire country is opened up to you to help you find the right tax consultant to solve your complex tax problems. You know, problems that can cost huge tax dollars, but don't come up very often...like how to transfer your business, value your business, or eliminate estate taxes. Are you or one of your tax professionals stuck? Need a second opinion? Then, this new phone/fax trend may be the tax-wise way to go.

Jump in. The water's fine.

## My Fantasy

We are in the last decade of the 20th Century. It took an amendment to the constitution in the early 1900s to bring income taxes into being. Income taxes came in like a lamb—low rates and very simplistic. But now income taxes—escorted by gift taxes and estates taxes—have entered the '90s like lions—big, bulky and an unbelievable, complicated maze. Yes, we must still deal with these tax animals, but they are ever-changing. No matter how you slice it, to deal effectively with these special animals means playing the tax-saving game and planning how to win.

Over my professional lifetime, I have developed a process that tames the tax animal kingdom in the transfer/succession/estate planning area. My fantasy is to teach the world—every business owner who could benefit from the process and every professional business advisor who wants to learn—the process.

If modern technology made it possible, I'd love to hold a huge town meeting. Every business owner in the United States would attend. All their professional advisors would be there, too. Only tax cheats would be turned away—they need the kinds of help I don't know how to give.

I'd divide the assemblage into four groups:

**GROUP #1.** Those business owners (and their advisors) who have no transfer/succession/estate plans. (Someday the IRS would eat them or their families alive.)

**GROUP #2.** Those business owners who have been working on a plan for years. This group, though they don't realize it, are essentially part of Group #1. The first order of business would be to give them the courage to fire all of the professionals who have allowed the planning process to go on for all those years.

**GROUP #3.** This group thinks they have a plan, but they don't. This would be a tough group. Each member has a will. Maybe a trust (probably a Living Trust). The toughest members would have one or more Irrevocable Trusts. Sure, they're better off than the first two groups, but my experience is that their death documents (that's all they really have) just scratch the surface of the possible tax-saving opportunities and wealth-creation ideas.

■ **COMMENT:** People in this group think they have it made. They're like sick people getting the right treatment for the wrong disease. And they'll never be cured. The saddest part is that when they die, their families, not them, will pay the tax price.

**GROUP #4.** A small but wonderful group. They're not much different from Group #3, except for one important fact: Its members really do have the right transfer/succession/estate plan that legally beats up the IRS. Meets their financial and tax objectives—for themselves. Their families. And their businesses. Members of this group (and their equally wonderful professionals) could help teach the first three groups how to get the job done right.

Since the technological fantasy described above (the national town meeting) is not possible—at least for the foreseeable future—we'll have to find another way. My hope is that this book will serve the purpose. It is my *town meeting* to attempt to solve the transfer/succession/estate planning problems for every American privately held business owner.

Read and learn at your own pace.

(Another article from my tax column.)

I'VE GOT TO GET SOMETHING OFF MY CHEST BEFORE I EXPLODE

It's almost 100 percent guaranteed. What? There are still huge tax savings to be found when the following words are spoken to me by closely held business owners when they are talking about their transfer of ownership and estate plans:

1. "Irv, some day, I'm going to..."
2. "We've (me and my lawyer or accountant or both) been working for years..."
3. "It's all taken care of. My lawyer did...(that)" and "my accountant did...(this)" and "my insurance agent did...(whatever)."

The business owners in the first and second categories are easy tax-saving targets because they don't have a transfer/estate plan in place. So, of course, we can help 'em. And we do.

But why do I want to explode when I talk to the business owners in the third category (usually readers calling me for a second tax opinion or just chatting with members of the audience from one of my tax seminars)? Because I have found that "done" does not necessarily mean "done right." Rarely, very rarely, does it mean "done best."

Have I ever found that a business owner established a transfer and/or an estate plan and done it "best"? Of course, and in every such case I have found one common denominator: someone has coordinated the efforts of the client, the accountant, the lawyer and the insurance consultant. But for the typical case in which I wind up giving a second opinion, this is what I find: The accountant worked on the current tax liability. The lawyer drafted the death documents. The insurance consultant looked for the premium dollar (usually found it in the corporation). Most of the time all are caring, competent professionals.

But without a leader to take responsibility for coordinating all the professional efforts—dovetailing the lifetime tax plan with the estate plan, and buying or keeping the right type of insurance in the right way to dovetail with the life and death plans—the result is predictable. Yes, the plan is "done," but many techniques—tax-saving and otherwise—were missed.

What can you do to make sure you don't get caught in this same professional tax trap (and keep me from exploding)?...Make sure your professional advisors work together. Critique each other's work. Share ideas. And most important: Select the most knowledgeable and experienced advisor as the leader—responsible for dovetailing everyone's work. Finally, if you are not totally comfortable, *get a second opinion.*

## A Bit of Irv's Philosophy Toward Clients

Maybe I'm out of step with the rest of my profession. But in my opinion, every CPA/lawyer or tax practitioner should be mindful of two important philosophical considerations—"The client's interests vs. the IRS' interests" and "Charging fees when there are no results"—with respect to client relations. Both are discussed below and define the way I practice.

### The Client's Interests vs. Those of the IRS

There's a moth-eaten-looking page in my seminar notes that contains this quote:

> "Tax law has never been a sport for the short-winded.
>
> "If tax law is to remain 'law'...Taxpayers must insist that their tax advisors represent *their* interests, rather than the interests of the Internal Revenue Service, and that they do so with vigor, imagination and professional skill."

I've probably read it hundreds of times to audiences of business owners at tax seminars from coast to coast. It's my philosophy exactly. I don't remember when or where I read it, but for some reason, I kept the quote's cite:

> "See Teschner, 'Expense of Sale: Law-Making by the Commissioner,' 35 Taxes—*The Tax Magazine* 574, August 1957."

Well said, Mr. Teschner. When it come to tax law, and the issue is *who should win,* it's my client over the IRS every time. In my book, it's okay to go for the jugular (vein) of the IRS...but legally and by the rules.

The client owes me something in return: full disclosure. If the potential client wants to cheat, he/she can find another boy.

### Charging Fees When There Are No Results

When doing tax planning—for me that almost always means transfer/succession/estate planning—for the purpose of tax savings, this is my fee philosophy in a nutshell: No tax savings, no fee. Why? Simple. No results. I haven't rendered any service of value. And the same holds true whether the planning is from scratch or a second opinion.

Before you accuse me of being a nice guy, there is something you should know. Only about one matter in 50 results in my telling my consulting client, "Sorry, but I can't help. Your documents are on their way back to you. That's right. There is no charge." Simply put, two-percent failure is well worth flying the *success flag* 98 percent of the time.

## The Present—Irv's Transfer Begins

By the time you read this, the *present* will have become the *past*. Only the future remains. As always.

Through the years, I have helped a long parade of business owners plan their transfer or succession. Now it's my turn. Strange as it seems, it's time for Irv's transfer.

This book—which documents a lifetime of knowledge—is part of my transfer plan.

But my real successor to the transfer/succession/estate planning part of my professional practice is a young man named Brian Whitlock, one of my 19 partners at Blackman Kallick Bartelstein (CPAs and consultants; we do not practice law). Brian is a CPA. A lawyer. A brain. An unbelievable storehouse of technical knowledge. But best of all, he has compassion and empathy. He cares. Clients love him.

Originally, I was Brian's mentor. But now, in terms of technical expertise, the tables are turned. Brian helped me build the transfer part of our practice. We have worked it together for six years, from the day Brian joined the tax department of Blackman Kallick.

Like most of my clients, I am not going to really retire. Just slow down. Brian is already picking up the slack. He sits in on my complex consultations; writes most of the reports (See Part X for many examples); and works his own network (lawyers, insurance consultants and bank trust officers) when he needs expertise that our firm does not have in-house.

Yes, my transfer has begun.

## The Future—Irv's Vision

What happens now? Well, *slow down* to me means to do what I want when I want. Interestingly enough, my passion to work with and help closely held businesses continues to grow. So this is what I intend to do as Brian takes the transfer/succession/estate planning baton and runs with it: Divide my time between slowing-down activities, the present activities, and marketing (my vision).

### Slowing-Down Activities

Play lots of tennis. Spend more time with Sallie, my wife. Travel. Play with my grandchildren. And sometimes just plain *doofilate.* (Don't bother looking it up. It's a word my daughter Linda invented which means *to actively do nothing.*)

### The Present Activities

My intent is to continue doing exactly what I do now for as long as I can draw a breath.

**WRITE.** Continue writing my column, which now goes to eighty trade journals. Update and add to my special-report library; right now there are twenty-five of 'em) fifty to seventy pages each, mostly on how-to-whip-the-IRS tax subjects. Books? Nope. As of now, this book is my last.

**LECTURE.** To me that means give seminars. But not many. I'll pick my spots. Trade associations (catering to closely held businesses) that hold their conventions in warm-climate resort areas that happen to have great tennis facilities would be at the top of the list. Special gatherings where the education environment affords me an opportunity to have a positive impact on the business owners and others attending—whether ten or 1,000 people—will also make my short list.

**CONSULT.** I'll be at the same old desk, in the same old ofice, doing the same old thing. But a new client's problems or situation will have to excite my professional spirit for me to become personally involved. But make the challenge unique, new, big, or complicated, and I will be asking Brian, "Can I work on this one?"

### Marketing

This is where my vision of the future lies—*marketing*. My strong feeling is that businesses that don't market will find it tough to stay alive in the future business environment. Survival. Profits. Success. All will depend on your marketing strategy.

What do I intend to market? Two things. The old. And the new. *First the old:*

1. Brian's transfer/succession/estate-planning department.
2. Blackman Kallick's valuation department.
3. Blackman Kallick's accounting and consulting services.
4. My writing and seminars.

### Now the New

I've met a wonderful man. His name is Jay Abraham. Jay is a marketing genius. My marketing mentor. His marketing principles and methods are not creative, but they are logical. Universal. The methods apply to any business. So far, I have used the principles and methods to market the four services and products listed above. They work.

Let me switch gears for a moment, and then tie this new information back to Jay and marketing. During my countless consulting interviews with business owners, the same type of problem or problems popped up in almost every interview. What kind of problems?...All kinds. The exploding body of knowledge and constantly changing business environment demand skills that the closely held business simply does not have in-house. Why not?...Too expensive to afford the talent needed. What to do?...Hire a consultant. Where do I find the consultant who can do *that*?

The *that* can be anything from transfer/succession/estate planning to marketing; from collecting accounts receivable to a cost-cutting program. The list is endless. So far we have 23 services we intend to market from coast to coast.

What's my vision for the future?...Jay and Irv are joining forces to market such services to business. CPA firms all across the country will play a special part.

See you in the future.

# PART V

# The Magic of Insurance

# V INTRODUCTION

## How to Keep Your Wealth Where It Belongs—In Your Family

If you're typical, the wealth you have accumulated (particularly as a business owner) is nothing more than the result of hard work. Maybe there was a little bit of luck mixed...maybe a lot. Maybe you inherited all or a portion of your wealth.

I have yet to meet a property owner who does not view accumulations as belonging only to him/her and the family, but not necessarily in that order. Sorry...some of that wealth belongs to the government. When you pass to the great beyond, the tax collector will get his pound of flesh...in dollars...your family's dollars. That's the way it is.

Life insurance, and proper planning, can change the sorry result of the last two sentences.

Almost everything that appears in this part of the book is a direct result of what many of my friends in the life-insurance industry have taught me through the years.

This part of the book is about results. It is about how my office uses life insurance to solve transfer / succession / estate-planning problems in practice. Not much theory. Results—not theory—are our goal. You will see that the results are best described by one word—MAGIC!

To get a complete handle on how to use life insurance to get magical results, you must also read the following parts of this book:

| PART | TITLE |
|---|---|
| VI | Low-Load Insurance vs. Traditional Insurance |
| VII | The Irrevocable Life Insurance Trust |
| IX | IRD—The Wealth Killer |

Now the brutal facts. In nine out of 10 consulting cases that come to my office, we find there is either not enough life insurance coverage or there is too much coverage (someone just plain goofed when analyzing the need). Other insurance problems we note:

- The wrong person or entity (usually a corporation) owns the insurance.
- The type of policy is not appropriate.
- The cost of the insurance is too high for the type and amount of coverage.
- The insurance proceeds will be subject to taxes (income or estate; often both), a problem that usually can be easily avoided.

■ **A WORD OF CAUTION:** Just as insurance can work magically for you, it can also work like magic to make your money disappear. Without any benefit to you. You'll read about both kinds of magic in this part of the book.

1

# The Basics of Life Insurance

This chapter is nontechnical, but a little technical stuff sneaks in.

Over the years, life insurance has become one of the major players in estate planning. Almost every estate includes some life insurance. Because of the many types of life-insurance policies and the complex rules that apply to them, planning is essential to maximize after-tax dollars.

Life insurance has many uses for estate planning, including:

1. Providing estate liquidity.
2. Funding repayment of specific debt, whether personal or business, such as a mortgage, a buy-sell agreement, and employee benefit plans—qualified and nonqualified.
3. Providing financial security for beneficiaries by replacing income of the bread-winner.
4. Satisfying spouse's claims in matrimonial settlements.
5. Protecting business against death of a key employee.
6. Providing split-dollar insurance for key employees.
7. Forcing savings through payment of premiums.
8. Providing for special needs, such as payment of college expenses, mortgage balances, or other large capital needs.
9. Use as a credit-building tool; for example, lending institutions and other creditors often use life insurance on a debtor's life as security.
10. Use as an investment; yes, properly used, life insurance is an estate-wealth builder; it is often the best investment you will have made from the start to the end of your life.

## A Basic Life-Insurance Primer

Life insurance is a contract, where, for a stipulated consideration (a premium), one party (the insurer) agrees to pay the other (the insured), or his or her beneficiary, a defined amount on the occurrence of death.

Life insurance forms a part of the financial planning of virtually every business and individual. The rationale for purchasing life insurance extends over a broad area from family planning to business and estate planning.

The variables of life insurance—its need, its use, and both the type and method of purchasing it may change drastically over a period of time, according to the changing financial goals of the purchaser. Key life-insurance factors include the following.

### Cash Surrender Value

The cash surrender value (CSV) is the amount of money the insurance company gives to the owner of the policy if the owner decides to cancel the policy. An ordinary life insurance policy has two components: pure insurance (term insurance) and CSV. For example: Assume a 40-year-old person purchases $100,000 of ordinary life insurance; the relationship between pure insurance and CSV can be seen in this illustration.

**PREMIUMS PAID**

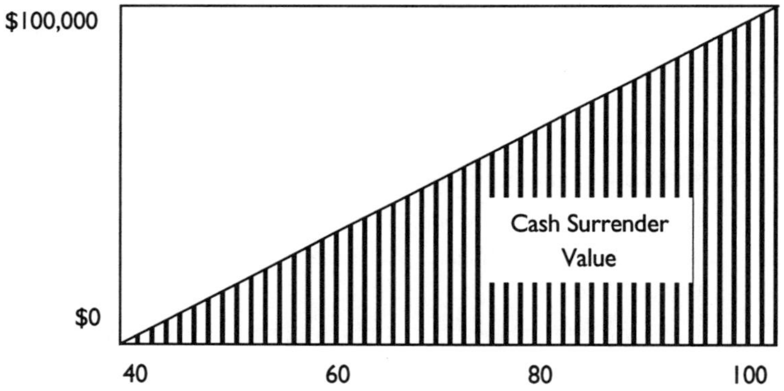


As the pure insurance (term) decreases, the CSV increases. The longer the policy is kept in force, the more the entire arrangement becomes less insurance and more investment. In reality, the CSV is a penalty the insured (you) pay to buy term insurance. Of course, you can recover the CSV by simply canceling the policy (only recommended in rare circumstances), but then you lose the insurance feature. Good sense and economics dictate keeping the policy; ultimately you will die, but then the cash surrender value dies with you. Of course, your beneficiaries receive the insurance proceeds. In the end, the CSV is nothing but rhetoric. It sounds good during the sales pitch; it looks good on policy status reports; but it disappears on your death.

### Loan Value

Loan value means the amount the insurance company will lend the insured. Any portion or all of the CSV at any time may be borrowed on demand by the owner of most permanent life insurance policies. The loan can usually be repaid at any time. Any outstanding balance bears interest. If the insured dies before repaying the loan, the proceeds payable to the beneficiary are reduced by the amount of the loan.

### Ownership of the Policy

The insured may or may not be the owner of the policy. Ownership gives the owner the right to name and change the beneficiary, to cash in the policy, to receive dividends, to borrow against the CSV, and to dispose of some or all of the ownership rights listed. For example, the owner can make an unconditional sale or gift of all ownership rights in the policy (an absolute assignment). When a policy is pledged as collateral for a loan, the assignment is known as a collateral assignment.

### Dividends

Essentially, a dividend is a tax-free refund of part of the premiums paid to the insurance company. The dividend size depends on the relative amount of favorable mortality, interest, and business cost (loading experience) of the company.

The owner can take the dividends in cash or use them to reduce premiums, buy paid-up additional insurance (each dividend buys a small single-premium policy that adds to the coverage of the basic plan), purchase one-year term insurance equal to the cash value of the policy, or pay up the policy to avoid future premium payments. The owner can also elect to leave the dividends with the company to earn interest. This interest is taxable.

### Types of Insurance

The types of life insurance policies available range from annual renewable term insurance, which has the lowest premium, to single-premium policies, which have the highest premiums.

**TERM INSURANCE.** Term insurance buys protection for a stated period—the term of the policy. Renewable term means the policy can be renewed for an additional term without the insured proving insurability (even if the insured just had a heart attack, the insurance company must renew the policy). Annual renewable (one-year) term bears the lowest premium because it typically insures an individual for only one year at a time. The cost for that year would be the cost for insurance for an individual of a certain age in the year. The insurance coverage stays constant, but the premium cost rises each year.

Five-year renewable term carries a premium covering the mortality costs averaged over the five years being insured. Thus, the cost of five-year term is higher than the real mortality cost in the first two years and lower than the mortality costs in later years. The insurance coverage stays constant, but the premium cost rises every five years.

Level-term means the coverage and the premium stay constant throughout the term of the policy.

Convertible-term is a feature that allows the term insurance to be converted to ordinary life insurance in an amount equal to the term insurance coverage without

**PREFERRED RISK (NON-SMOKER) $250,000 TO $499,999**

| ISSUE AGE | | PREMIUM FOR $1,000 OF INSURANCE | | | | | |
|---|---|---|---|---|---|---|---|
| | | YEAR | | | | | |
| M | F | 1 | 2 | 3 | 4 | 5 | 6 |
| | 25 | 0.77 | 0.96 | 1.10 | 1.17 | 1.23 | 1.31 |
| | 26 | 0.77 | 0.96 | 1.10 | 1.18 | 1.24 | 1.33 |
| | 27 | 0.77 | 0.96 | 1.10 | 1.18 | 1.26 | 1.34 |
| | 28 | 0.77 | 0.96 | 1.11 | 1.19 | 1.27 | 1.36 |
| | 29 | 0.77 | 0.96 | 1.11 | 1.20 | 1.29 | 1.37 |
| 25 | 30 | 0.77 | 0.96 | 1.11 | 1.20 | 1.30 | 1.39 |
| 26 | 31 | 0.77 | 0.96 | 1.11 | 1.22 | 1.33 | 1.44 |
| 27 | 32 | 0.77 | 0.96 | 1.12 | 1.25 | 1.37 | 1.49 |
| 28 | 33 | 0.78 | 0.96 | 1.12 | 1.27 | 1.40 | 1.53 |
| 29 | 34 | 0.78 | 0.97 | 1.13 | 1.29 | 1.43 | 1.58 |
| 30 | 35 | 0.78 | 0.97 | 1.14 | 1.31 | 1.47 | 1.63 |
| 31 | 36 | 0.78 | 0.97 | 1.15 | 1.33 | 1.50 | 1.68 |
| 32 | 37 | 0.78 | 0.97 | 1.15 | 1.34 | 1.53 | 1.73 |
| 33 | 38 | 0.78 | 0.97 | 1.16 | 1.35 | 1.56 | 1.78 |
| 34 | 39 | 0.78 | 0.97 | 1.17 | 1.36 | 1.59 | 1.83 |
| 35 | 40 | 0.78 | 0.97 | 1.18 | 1.38 | 1.62 | 1.88 |
| 36 | 41 | 0.82 | 1.03 | 1.27 | 1.51 | 1.79 | 2.08 |
| 37 | 42 | 0.85 | 1.09 | 1.37 | 1.64 | 1.95 | 2.29 |
| 38 | 43 | 0.89 | 1.15 | 1.47 | 1.77 | 2.12 | 2.49 |
| 39 | 44 | 0.92 | 1.22 | 1.57 | 1.90 | 2.29 | 2.69 |
| 40 | 45 | 0.96 | 1.28 | 1.68 | 2.03 | 2.46 | 2.89 |
| 41 | 46 | 1.04 | 1.38 | 1.78 | 2.16 | 2.62 | 3.10 |
| 42 | 47 | 1.10 | 1.48 | 1.88 | 2.28 | 2.78 | 3.30 |
| 43 | 48 | 1.18 | 1.57 | 1.98 | 2.40 | 2.94 | 3.50 |
| 44 | 49 | 1.26 | 1.67 | 2.09 | 2.53 | 3.11 | 3.70 |
| 45 | 50 | 1.34 | 1.77 | 2.19 | 2.66 | 3.27 | 3.90 |
| 46 | 51 | 1.47 | 1.92 | 2.33 | 2.84 | 3.52 | 4.21 |
| 47 | 52 | 1.60 | 2.06 | 2.48 | 3.02 | 3.78 | 4.53 |
| 48 | 53 | 1.73 | 2.22 | 2.63 | 3.21 | 4.03 | 4.84 |
| 49 | 54 | 1.86 | 2.37 | 2.77 | 3.40 | 4.29 | 5.16 |
| 50 | 55 | 1.99 | 2.52 | 2.92 | 3.58 | 4.54 | 5.47 |
| 51 | 56 | 2.11 | 2.69 | 3.19 | 3.92 | 5.00 | 6.06 |
| 52 | 57 | 2.21 | 2.87 | 3.47 | 4.28 | 5.45 | 6.65 |
| 53 | 58 | 2.32 | 3.04 | 3.74 | 4.62 | 5.93 | 7.24 |
| 54 | 59 | 2.43 | 3.22 | 4.02 | 4.97 | 6.39 | 7.83 |
| 55 | 60 | 2.54 | 3.39 | 4.29 | 5.32 | 6.85 | 8.42 |
| 56 | 61 | 2.77 | 3.75 | 4.91 | 6.07 | 7.85 | 9.39 |
| 57 | 62 | 2.99 | 4.10 | 5.53 | 6.84 | 8.88 | 10.36 |
| 58 | 63 | 3.21 | 4.45 | 6.15 | 7.60 | 9.90 | 11.33 |
| 59 | 64 | 3.43 | 4.81 | 6.76 | 8.37 | 10.95 | 12.30 |
| 60 | 65 | 3.65 | 5.16 | 7.38 | 9.16 | 11.99 | 13.27 |
| 61 | 66 | 4.01 | 5.79 | 8.15 | 10.34 | 13.43 | 15.10 |
| 62 | 67 | 4.38 | 6.42 | 8.91 | 11.53 | 14.91 | 16.92 |
| 63 | 68 | 4.74 | 7.05 | 9.68 | 12.74 | 16.38 | 18.75 |
| 64 | 69 | 5.10 | 7.68 | 10.44 | 13.96 | 17.87 | 20.57 |
| 65 | 70 | 5.46 | 8.31 | 11.21 | 15.18 | 19.37 | 22.40 |

The cost for any other type of term insurance is comparable.

proof of insurability on the part of the insured. The premium is identical to what the premium would have been had the insured purchased an ordinary life policy on the conversion date at his exact age on that date.

Reducing-convertible-term (sometimes called decreasing-convertible-term) gives a large amount of coverage initially for a small dollar outlay. In most policies, coverage reduces each year until a specified age (but usually not beyond age 85), when all coverage is gone. However, at any time during the period, this reducing-term policy can be converted to ordinary life insurance. The premium remains constant throughout the entire term.

Group term-life insurance is a group of term policies for which a specific charge for each life is made, based on the age of that life. Very commonly, the premium charged is the average premium for all individuals in a particular group.

No matter how you slice it, *term insurance is a bet*. Die...you win. Live...you lose.

Let's take a look at a one-year pure term policy. You pay your premium for the first year. You live, but you lost the insurance bet. Want to play again? Step up to the window and place your bet. Remember, you are one year older.

You want some credit for last year? Sorry again. Once the year is over, the policy has no value. Those are the rules. If you want to bet again, the cost is higher than last year. Check your program (premium schedule) for rates. And so it goes. Year after year. Unless you win by dying.

Let's look at a top-rated company's premium schedule, "Preferred Risk (Non-Smoker)." You'll quickly get the idea why I call a pure one-year term a pure bet.

### Permanent Life Insurance

There are many varieties of permanent life insurance, often called whole-life insurance. The policies have CSV, and costs vary by the periods of premium payments.

Ordinary life insurance (often called whole life) is the most common type of permanent life insurance. The premium payment period for this type of insurance is the lifetime of the insured, typically to age 100. This policy results in the least outlay of premium for permanent life insurance because the payment period is stretched over a long period. The amount of the coverage and premium remain constant.

A limited-payment life insurance policy, such as a 20-payment life, compresses the premium payment period from the lifetime of an ordinary life policy to a fixed time (in this case, 20 years); thus, premiums are higher, and the CSV is higher in this type of policy.

An endowment, such as a 20-year endowment, also compresses the premium payment period so that at the end of the endowment period (e.g., 20 years), the full face amount of the policy becomes due whether death occurs or not.

### Universal Life Insurance

Universal life insurance is a policy in which the investment (the investment account or CSV), expense, and mortality elements are separately and specifically defined. The insured selects a death-benefit level. The death benefit may be one that increases over time, coinciding with the increased CSV (often called death benefit-option II) or, alternatively, the death benefit can remain level regardless of the CSV changes (often called death-benefit option I). From the premium paid, the company deducts a load amount for contractually defined expenses. The remaining premium is added to the insured's CSV. Mortality charges are deducted. Interest earned on the remaining CSV is then credited at rates based on current investment earnings. (Specific design features vary by company.)

Increased interest rates result in higher CSV, while increased expense loads and increased mortality charges result in lower CSV. Typically, there is a minimum contractual guarantee as to the interest credited, such as 4 or 4.5 percent.

There is no such thing as a predetermined standard universal life plan; each insured selects the level of premium and death benefit desired as well as the length of premium paying period. Significant flexibility in premium payments—when and how much—is possible.

As long as there is enough CSV to pay the expense (loading) charges and mortality costs, the policy will remain in force. If the CSV falls below that level, the policy will terminate. Usually there is a 61-day grace period.

■ **EXAMPLE:** Suppose a universal life policy had a CSV of $10,000 at the beginning of the year and earned $800 during the year. The CSV would be $10,800. If the required premium payment for the current year is $2,000, that premium would be paid out of the CSV, and the CSV to start the next year would be $8,800. If the CSV was only $1,000 and the premium requirement $2,000, the policy would terminate unless the policy owner made a deposit of at least $1,000 to pay the premium.

Universal life has several tax advantages. The insured has great flexibility in arranging premium payments. Once the insurance company's initial requirements are satisfied, the mortality and expense charges, or pure term-insurance charges, may be paid either directly by the insured; from the earnings on the investment account; from the principal in the account; or by any combination of these. Amounts paid or earned in excess of this term-insurance requirement increase the investment account. If the interest earned is enough to pay the entire mortality and expense charges for the year, the arrangement becomes the equivalent of term life insurance paid for with pretax earnings.

There are, however, disadvantages. The insured must accept the risk that short-term interest rates might decline while the expense might rise, with the result that the insurance premium cost to maintain the policy will rise accordingly.

Also, the cash surrender value dies with the insured. The beneficiary collects only the face amount of the policy; the insurance company keeps the cash surrender value.

Universal-life policies are good if the insured wants the flexibility to change the face value of the policy or his premium payment amount from time to time.

You might consider universal life to replace ordinary life policies that have large outstanding loans. You can convert the ordinary life insurance policy, repay the policy loan, and purchase a universal life insurance policy with the net equity in the ordinary life policy. Such an exchange should be nontaxable (Section 1035, based on Rev. Rul. 72-358).

### Variable Life Insurance

A variable life insurance policy resembles a traditional whole life policy with two major distinctions—the death benefit payable on death and the CSV payable during life are not guaranteed. They can increase or decrease, depending on investment performance of the assets underlying the policy.

The death benefit generally cannot decrease below the initial face amount of the policy, as long as all premiums are paid. The insured trades the CSV guarantee of a traditional whole life policy for the potential of value growth by directing the strategy of the policy's investment program.

The insured can direct the investments, depending on the particular company's product, to a money-market style account, a growth-stock account, a bond account, a balanced-fund account, or other types of investment. Typically, the death benefit is adjusted once a year, and the CSV is adjusted daily. Premiums are fixed and remain the same. Since the CSV and death benefit can vary, the product is known as variable life.

If you have the skill to make large investment profits (tax-free as added to the CSV), you can direct where premium dollars are to be invested, as contrasted with typical whole-life or universal-life policies where the insured cannot make such direction.

### Joint and Survivor ("Last To Die" or "Second To Die") Life Policies

A joint and survivor life policy insures the lives of at least two people. The policy may be either whole life, term, universal life, or a combination of two or more types of policies. The death benefit is not realized until the last of the insured individuals (the survivor) dies. Then, the full death benefit becomes payable to the named beneficiary.

This policy is typically confined to husband-wife, parent-child, or two related business people, such as business owners or key employees. The premium cost for a joint policy is usually significantly less than for separate policies on two lives. The full amount of the death benefit is available when needed—after the second death.

---

■ **PLANNING POINTER:** A joint and survivor policy is an effective planning tool to relieve the federal estate tax burden for a couple who has elected to take maximum advantage of the marital deduction. Although there will be no federal estate tax due when the first spouse dies, there will be tax due at the survivor's death.

---

Now, please indulge me. A quick overview of the power of a second-to-die policy can be seen by reading an article that appeared in my tax column in the early '90s.

> A WAY TO BEAT THE TAX COLLECTOR—WELL, ALMOST
>
> Sooner or later, we all will go to that big business in the sky (or that other place). You know how the old saying goes—you can't beat death or taxes. There is a way to eliminate a big chunk of death taxes.
>
> First, let's look at a few basics. The top estate-tax bracket is 55 percent. A common way to pay estate taxes is to buy life insurance equal to the estimated amount of the estate-tax liability. A good idea. But then again life insurance is included in your estate.
>
> Now, let's take a look at a common real life situation. Joe computed that his estate will be short $1,000,000 to pay his estate tax liability. He cleverly

> buys $1,000,000 worth of life insurance to pay the tax. Smart? That $1,000,000 in life insurance will kick up another $550,000 in estate-tax liability. Buy another $550,000 in life insurance? That game can only enrich your happy insurance agent and the IRS. You can defer the tax on your estate by leaving it to your wife, but the IRS will get its pound of flesh when she follows you to heaven.
>
> Here's a method we recommend to our clients to win the insurance/estate game. It's a two-step process. First, Joe should apply for a $1,000,000 second-to-die life insurance policy. It has several different names, but is always easy to recognize: One policy insures two lives (in this case, Joe and his wife), and the $1,000,000 is paid only after the second death. And that's the way it should be in Joe's case because that is when the estate tax is due. This type of policy has one terrific advantage: The premium cost is substantially less than the cost of a single-life traditional policy. Check it out.
>
> Step two is tax heaven. Joe creates an irrevocable life insurance trust. The trustee buys the $1,000,000 second-to-die policy. If properly done, the IRS will not get one cent of that $1,000,000 in insurance proceeds. Not when Joe dies. Not when his wife dies.
>
> If you have any significant potential estate-tax liability, call a competent professional advisor. Don't wait. Time raises the insurance premium cost and favors the IRS.

The premium in such policies is low because the combined survivorship of two people is greater than either one of them individually, so a longer period of time will pass before the policy pays off. The insurance company collects more premiums and earns an investment return on the premiums over a longer period of time.

### Single-Premium Whole-Life

Single-premium whole-life (also called a modified endowment contract) is a policy of investment-advantaged life insurance. Unlike traditional whole-life policies, however, where premiums are due generally until age 90 or 100, a single-premium whole-life policy, as the name implies, requires only one premium.

The insured deposits a single amount in the first policy year. No more premiums are paid. The CSV earns a higher rate than a universal life product, approximately the same as high-grade corporate bonds. The concept is similar to universal life, since the excess over the premium requirement increases the CSV tax-free and escapes the income tax on death (even if the CSV exceeds the original death benefit, which will occur if the insured lives long enough).

Single-premium whole-life insurance is a tax-advantaged product similar to universal life insurance. Both types of policies employ the same term-insurance investment concepts described for universal life. However, while universal life uses tax advantages to carry life insurance, single-premium whole-life uses a life insurance product to carry a tax-advantaged investment.

Single-premium life is treated similarly to annuities for tax purposes. Here are the important rules dealing with withdrawals according to Sections 7702A, 72(e)(10), and 72(v):

1. Withdrawals are treated as first coming from the inside build-up, and therefore are taxable.
2. Any amounts borrowed from the policy are treated as withdrawals, and therefore are taxable.
3. If the policy is pledged as collateral for a loan, the loan proceeds are treated as a deemed withdrawal and are taxable.
4. A 10-percent premature withdrawal penalty is assessed unless (a) the taxpayer has attained age 59 1/2 (b) has become disabled, or (c) the withdrawals are periodic payments for life.
5. The Revenue Reconciliation Act of 1989 made changes in the law where policies are materially changed (Section 7702A(c)(3)(B)), and "last to die" life insurance policies (Section 7702A(c)(6)).

Key benefits of single-premium whole-life policies:

- ☐ With just one up-front premium payment, the policy acquires immediate, substantial cash value. The earnings on the cash value grow and compound free of tax (federal, state and local). As long as the contract stays in force, no income tax is due on the appreciation.

  ■ **PARENTS:** You can buy the policy on the life of a young child (under 14), then gift the policy to the child. Since there is a smaller, pure insurance cost, the balance (cash surrender value) can earn more without being subject to any current tax. The child can surrender the policy after attaining age 14. All the accumulated earnings will be taxed to the child, at his bracket, at that time. Remember, a child under 14 pays tax at his parent's highest rate for unearned income in excess of a base amount.

- ☐ Although interest on policy loans is not tax deductible, most insurers never actually charge interest on single-premium policies. It is simply deducted from the earnings being credited to the policy's inside cash-value buildup. However, policy loans are now taxable.

- ☐ The policy is a tax-sheltered investment. The insurance protection is an added bonus.

- ☐ Single-premium policies are an attractive alternative to municipal bonds. The bulk of the premium goes toward the cash value instead of the cost of the insurance protection. The insurance protection is paid out of the earnings on the cash value. The quoted annual increase in the cash value is a net increase, after deducting the cost of insurance.

  For income tax purposes, when the insured dies, the earnings disappear. The policy proceeds are paid to the beneficiary as an income tax-free life insurance benefit.

- ☐ The policy owner has the ability to name the insured. If the owner is young, he would most likely name himself as the insured to protect his family. If he is older and his family is grown, he may want to insure his wife in order to help pay the estate taxes.

  He can make his children the insured in order to protect his grandchildren. One practical approach is to set up the investment policy with the grandparents as owners and the insurance on the life of their son or son-in-law. By setting up the policy to be owned by the grandparents while they are alive and then to pass, without probate, to the son or daughter, they can create an income tax-free, probate-free investment that passes through three generations.

- Single-premium variable life insurance policies offer a number of investment options, similar to a family of mutual funds. You can invest in one or a combination of funds and can switch from one fund to another. If you switch using regular mutual funds, profits are taxable immediately. Gains on investment switches in single-premium variable policies are not taxable currently.
- Interest build-up on the policy is not included in the calculations that tax up to half of Social Security benefits. Earnings from tax-free municipal bonds, even though not subject to income tax, are included in the Social Security benefits income tax calculations. Also, the interest from certain municipal bonds is subject to the alternative minimum tax (AMT). Switching from municipal bonds to single-premium life and getting retirement income by borrowing allows the owner to avoid tax on part of his Social Security and to also avoid the AMT.
- Investment in a single-premium policy does not increase the risk of an IRS audit. The purchase of the policy is not reported to the Service. But if the owner terminates the policy, the IRS will be notified.

*These policies are not without some disadvantages.* If the owner surrenders the policy, all earnings in excess of cost are taxable immediately. Also, buyers must remember that life insurance costs money. Typically, life insurance has front-end expense charges. All costs of getting in, and getting out, should be examined before buying.

---

■ **SOME PRACTICAL ADVICE:** Don't invest in only one single-premium life contract. Instead build a portfolio of policies. Then you are not at the mercy of one insurance company's investment decisions. Also, if you want to terminate one policy and pay tax on the accumulated earnings, the other policies can continue to work tax-free.

---

### First-To-Die

First-to-die insurance is a new kid on the block. The following letter written to me by an insurance consultant explains "how the First-to-Die policy works." Jeff is really my son and, of course, Sheryl is my daughter-in-law. And I think the consultant is right.

> Dear Irv:
>
> Enclosed please find the First-to-Die proposals for Jeff and Sheryl. I believe the following scenarios will explain how the First-to-Die policy works.
>
> Scenario I: If Jeff predeceases Sheryl, $1,000,000 of death benefit is paid out, and Sheryl has the option of obtaining a $500,000 policy at her attained age, less any CSV that was inside the policy when Jeff passed away. This policy can be obtained regardless of her health.
>
> Scenario II: If Sheryl predeceases Jeff, $500,000 of death benefit is paid out, and Jeff has the option of obtaining an individual insurance policy of $1,000,000

at his attained age, less any CSV that was inside the policy when Sheryl passed away. This policy can be obtained regardless of his health.

Scenario III: If both Jeff and Sheryl die simultaneously, then both death benefits are paid out.

I hope this was helpful in explaining how the First-to-Die policy works. Should you have any questions or need any additional information, please feel free to contact me.

## Tax Consequences of Life Insurance

Life insurance premiums are not deductible; proceeds are not taxable. For gift-tax purposes, only the CSV less any loans on the policy (technically the interpolated terminal reserve, which is slightly higher than CSV) at the time of the gift is a taxable gift.

Face value (proceeds) are included in the insured policy owner's estate: In practice the exceptions, special problems, and variety of techniques developed to provide a better tax rate than that afforded by the general rules has created interesting and exciting opportunities and challenges.

### Income Tax Rules: Deductibility of Premiums

There is no income tax deduction for payment of premiums on personal life insurance because there is nothing in the Code that makes the premiums deductible.

For business life insurance, Section 264(a)(1) succinctly states that no deduction shall be allowed for premiums paid on any life insurance policy covering the life of any officer or employee of the taxpayer or any person financially interested in the taxpayer's business, if the taxpayer is either directly or indirectly a beneficiary under the policy. This rule is strictly applied even if the premiums would have been deductible otherwise as ordinary and necessary business expenses.

For example, the premium is not deductible if the lender requires the business to carry a life insurance policy equal to the amount of the loan on the life of the owner. There are exceptions, however. For example, premiums paid on a policy irrevocably assigned to a charity and the owner reserves no rights to get the CSV are deductible (*Eppa Hunton*, IV, 1 TC 821; 1943).

### Taxing Premiums Paid by an Employer

Generally, if insurance is purchased for the benefit of the employer's business and the insured employee has no interest in the policy, the premiums are not taxable to the employee. For example, when the employer is both the owner and beneficiary of a key-person life insurance policy, the premiums are not income to the employee (*Edward D. Lacey*, 41 TC 329).

However, when the employer pays the premiums on a policy insuring the life of an employee and the employee selects the beneficiary to whom the proceeds will be paid, the premiums are income to the employee (Regulation 1.61-2(d)(2)(ii)).

There are *two important exceptions*:

- ☐ Contributions by an employer to a qualified plan (under Section 401(a)) are not taxable to the employee. Since such contributions are not taxable to the employee, when all or a portion of the contributions are used to purchase insurance for the benefit of the employee, the net effect is tax-free life insurance for the employee. However, an amount representing the so-called PS 58 costs is currently taxable to the employee (see Appendix).

- The first $50,000 of group term life insurance that qualifies for the benefits of Section 79 on each employee is tax-free. The cost of any coverage in excess of $50,000, less any amount paid by the employee, is taxable to the employee. The amount to be included in income is determined from a table (Table 1) set forth in Regulation 1.79-3T.

**TABLE 1. UNIFORM PREMIUMS FOR $1,000 OF GROUP TERM LIFE INSURANCE PROTECTION***

| 5-year age bracket | Cost per $1,000 of protection for 1-month period |
|---|---|
| Under 30 | 8 cents |
| 30 to 34 | 9 cents |
| 35 to 39 | 11 cents |
| 40 to 44 | 17 cents |
| 45 to 49 | 29 cents |
| 50 to 54 | 48 cents |
| 55 to 59 | 75 cents |
| 60 to 64 | $1.17 |
| 65 to 69 | $2.10 |
| 70 and above | $3.76 |

*In using the above table, the age of the employee is his attained age on the last day of his taxable year.

■ **EXAMPLE:** Joe is a 33-year-old employee of Yo-Yo Corporation, which has a group term insurance plan. Joe's policy under the plan is $100,000. The cost for each $1,000 of coverage, per the Regulations, is $1.08 (12 x 9 cents) per year for Joe's age. Joe pays 20¢ per $1,000 and Yo-Yo pays the balance. Joe's income is computed as follows:

| | |
|---|---|
| Cost of insurance coverage over $50,000 ($50,000 x $1.08) | $54 |
| Amount paid by Joe (20¢ x 100) to Yo-Yo | 20 |
| Joe's income | $34 |

The Section 79 rates per $1,000 are significantly less that the PS 58 rates; for example, the PS 58 rate per $1,000 for a 33-year-old is $2.86, as opposed to the 96 cents Section 79 rate.

### Taxing the Increase in Policy Value

A traditional, ordinary life product has the ability to grow in two normal ways: accumulating dividends and increase in cash surrender value. In addition, undrawn dividends may be invested, producing taxable interest.

The recent additions to insurance product lines, including universal life, single-premium whole-life, and combinations, add a whole new dimension. Now the earnings of these products on the excess CSV (the amount in excess of current premium cost) is invested to accumulate tax-free income, which is added to the CSV. In turn, this increased CSV is reinvested again and again to produce more tax-free earnings.

In many cases the annual tax-free increase in the value (from all sources) exceeds the annual cost necessary to keep the policy in force. After a number of years, this value, which becomes the new death benefit, can surpass the original death benefit.

### Collection of Proceeds

Life insurance proceeds are not taxable income to the beneficiary. Section 101(a)(1) expressly provides that amounts received as proceeds from a life insurance contract, whether in one or more payments, are excludable from gross income, if such amounts are received by reason of the death of the insured. The exclusion applies to the full amount of the policy, regardless of who paid the premiums or who owned the policy, and regardless of who the beneficiary might be—an individual, a corporation, a partnership, a trust, or the estate of the insured.

Of course, there are exceptions to the above rule. Income is recognized if the owner of the policy cancels the policy and gets the cash surrender value of the policy. The amount of income recognized by the owner of the policy is the difference between the cash surrender value and the cost (premiums paid) of the policy.

Another situation which generates income is if the beneficiary receives the proceeds of the insurance in payment of a liability owed to him by the decedent. In this case, the proceeds are taxable.

Other important exceptions: when the policy is transferred for value; when the proceeds are received from a qualified deferred compensation plan (discussed later in this chapter); and, when interest earned on the proceeds after the insured's death is paid to the beneficiary and proceeds received by a C corporation may be subject to the alternative minimum tax.

### Transferring a Policy

The transfer-for-value rule created by Section 101(a)(2) provides that if a policy, or any interest in a policy, is transferred for a valuable consideration, the death proceeds are tax exempt only to the extent of the consideration paid by the transferee and the net premiums, if any, paid by the transferee after the transfer. The nonexempt portion of the proceeds is taxable as ordinary income.

There are a number of exceptions that make the rule inoperable (thus reinstating the exemption) in many practical situations. The exemption is reinstated if the transfer is to the insured himself; to a partner of the insured; to a partnership in which the insured is a partner; or to a corporation in which the insured is a shareholder or officer.

### How Are the Benefits to Be Paid?

Most people think of a lump-sum payment upon death, but there are alternatives. Insurance companies will gladly pay the benefits in some manner not involving a lump-sum payment. Here are some options:

1. Life income payments—the benefit is paid over the life of the annuitant. The annuity may be for the life of the recipient alone, for the recipient but with a certain number of payments guaranteed, or for the recipient and survivors.
2. Fixed income—the payment runs for a specified amount of time (attainment of a designated age, a specified calendar date, so many years, etc,). The amount per installment becomes fixed.
3. Fixed period—installments over a designated period of time, with a guaranteed interest rate.
4. Interest payment—leave the benefit with the company and pay only interest earned to the beneficiaries for a specified period of time. Then choose how you want the benefits paid.

Regardless of which payment option is chosen, the present value of the payments is the same, so the beneficiaries can choose the manner in which they want payments made dependent upon their needs.

### Interest Earned on the Proceeds after the Insured's Death

Interest earned on proceeds in the hands of the insurance company is taxable to the beneficiary just as any other interest is. It is taxable to a cash-basis taxpayer on receipt. Such interest is taxable to the beneficiary whether the insured or the beneficiary elected an option to leave the funds with the insurer. The Regulations at 1.101-4(g) provide, in general, that the interest is taxable to the beneficiary in the first year that it can be withdrawn.

### Benefits Received During Life

When the owner receives a lump-sum cash amount in excess of the cost of the policy, the excess is ordinary income and is taxable in the year the policy matures or is surrendered (Section 72(e)). The cost is equal to the total premiums paid, but excludes premiums paid for accidental death benefits or waiver of premium (Section 72(e)(i)(B)). The dividend option selected affects the cost. For example, if dividends are used to purchase paid-up additional insurance, then cost would be the total premiums paid by the owner. The result is the same if dividends are accumulated. But, when dividends are not accumulated or used to purchase paid-up insurance, the total premiums paid must be reduced by dividends received in cash or applied to reduce policy premiums to determine the cost.

Sometimes an owner takes the benefits of a policy while living under a settlement option. Proceeds (other than the interest option) are taxed under the annuity rules of Section 72. These benefits are divided into a nontaxable return of cost, and taxable income. An exclusion ratio, which is the ratio of the total investment (cost) in the policy to the total expected return, is used to determine the two parts, as shown by the following process:

*Step 1:* To determine the expected return, multiply the annual payment by the recipient's life expectancy as shown in Table 2.

**TABLE 2. ORDINARY LIFE ANNUITIES (REGULATION 1.72-9)**

One Life-Expected Return Multiples

| Age | Multiple | Age | Multiple | Age | Multiple |
|---|---|---|---|---|---|
| 5 | 76.6 | 42 | 40.6 | 79 | 10.0 |
| 6 | 75.6 | 43 | 39.6 | 80 | 9.5 |
| 7 | 74.7 | 44 | 38.7 | 81 | 8.9 |
| 8 | 73.7 | 45 | 37.7 | 82 | 7.9 |
| 9 | 72.7 | 46 | 36.8 | 83 | 7.9 |
| 10 | 71.7 | 47 | 35.9 | 84 | 7.4 |
| 11 | 70.7 | 48 | 34.9 | 85 | 6.9 |
| 12 | 69.7 | 49 | 34.0 | 86 | 6.5 |
| 13 | 68.8 | 50 | 33.1 | 87 | 6.1 |
| 14 | 67.8 | 51 | 32.2 | 88 | 5.7 |
| 15 | 66.8 | 52 | 31.3 | 89 | 5.3 |
| 16 | 65.8 | 53 | 30.4 | 90 | 5.0 |
| 17 | 64.8 | 54 | 29.9 | 91 | 4.7 |
| 18 | 63.9 | 55 | 28.6 | 92 | 4.4 |
| 19 | 62.9 | 56 | 27.7 | 93 | 4.1 |
| 20 | 61.9 | 57 | 26.8 | 94 | 3.9 |
| 21 | 60.9 | 58 | 25.9 | 95 | 3.7 |
| 22 | 59.9 | 59 | 25.0 | 96 | 3.4 |
| 23 | 59.0 | 60 | 24.2 | 97 | 3.2 |
| 24 | 58.0 | 61 | 23.3 | 98 | 3.0 |
| 25 | 57.0 | 62 | 22.5 | 99 | 2.8 |
| 26 | 56.0 | 63 | 21.6 | 100 | 2.7 |
| 27 | 55.1 | 64 | 20.8 | 101 | 2.5 |
| 28 | 54.1 | 65 | 20.0 | 102 | 2.3 |
| 29 | 53.1 | 66 | 19.2 | 103 | 2.1 |
| 30 | 52.2 | 67 | 18.4 | 104 | 1.9 |
| 31 | 51.2 | 68 | 17.6 | 105 | 1.8 |
| 32 | 50.2 | 69 | 16.8 | 106 | 1.6 |
| 33 | 49.3 | 70 | 16.0 | 107 | 1.4 |
| 34 | 48.3 | 71 | 15.3 | 108 | 1.3 |
| 35 | 47.3 | 72 | 14.6 | 109 | 1.1 |
| 36 | 46.4 | 73 | 13.9 | 110 | 1.0 |
| 37 | 45.4 | 74 | 13.2 | 111 | .9 |
| 38 | 44.4 | 75 | 12.5 | 112 | .8 |
| 39 | 43.5 | 76 | 11.9 | 113 | .7 |
| 40 | 42.5 | 77 | 11.2 | 114 | .6 |
| 41 | 41.5 | 78 | 10.6 | 115 | .5 |

*Step 2:* Determine the exclusion ratio (or percentage) using the formula

$$\frac{\text{total investment in policy}}{\text{total expected return}}$$

*Step 3:* Multiply the exclusion ratio by each year's total annuity payments to yield the tax-free portion of the total payments received during the year. The balance of the payment is taxable as ordinary income.

TRA-86 amended the law to provide that once the taxpayer's investment is recovered (due to living to their expected life), the balance received under the contract is fully taxable (Section 72(b)(2)). If payments cease before the entire investment is recovered (e.g., the taxpayer's premature death when he had selected a life-only option), the unrecovered investment is deductible in the annuitant's last taxable year (decedent's final return). (Section 72 (b)(3).

If the death proceeds are held by the insurance company and the beneficiary receives only the interest (the interest-only option), the principal amount, when received, is exempt from income taxes. However, the annual interest earned is taxed to the beneficiary as ordinary income (Section 101(c)).

Also, any other options where the beneficiary collects the benefits in installments is subject to the same rules, that is, annual interest is taxable as earned, and the balance (the policy proceeds) is recoverable income tax-free.

### Gift- and Estate-Tax Rules

An insurance policy can be gifted in the same way as any other property and is subject to the same rules.

Section 2042 gathers the insurance proceeds on the life of the insured into the estate if the proceeds are payable to the decedent-insured's estate or executor, or the proceeds are payable to any other beneficiary, and the decedent-insured at the time of his death possesses any of the incidents of ownership, exercisable either alone or in conjunction with any other person.

Where a decedent transfers a policy and does not survive the transfer for three years, the proceeds will be included in his estate (Section 2035(d)(2)).

---

■ **TAX-SAVING IDEA:** Suppose Harold owns a policy with a CSV of $10,000 and face value of $100,000. He can give the policy to his daughter now. The three-year period starts when the policy is given. At no gift-tax cost, after three years Harold will have removed $100,000 from his estate.

---

# 2 Examining Existing Insurance/Buying New Insurance

This chapter is nontechnical.

This chapter, if I had the knowledge, could actually be a book. Someday, perhaps someone with a greater understanding of life insurance—and the industry that sells it—will write a book telling all about how to *examine existing insurance* and *buy new insurance*.

This chapter is a compilation from many sources. It is my method of dealing with the two subjects listed above. It is not intended to be thorough or complete, but will help you get started in this all-important area. But no matter what you read here or anywhere else, there is no substitute for working with an experienced, knowledgeable and honest insurance consultant. The more knowledge you have, of course, the better off you will be, and the better you will be able to determine if, in fact, you are working with the "right" insurance consultant.

Call me a "snob," if you want, but, unless the client insists, I refuse to work with an insurance consultant who does not have at least these three attributes—experience, knowledge, and honesty (which must include integrity). Yet, I'll spend hours teaching young insurance consultants who I sense are honest but need more knowledge and experience (*but I don't want them practicing on my clients*).

## Examining Existing Insurance

An essential piece of information prior to beginning any consultation that includes transfer, succession or estate planning is a schedule of all life insurance owned by the client. If there is more than one client—for example, husband and wife, stockholders, or partners—the schedule should include the policies on each of their lives.

Make a separate schedule for each policy on the insured's life, whether owned by:

1. The insured
2. His/her business

3. A trust—revocable, irrevocable, or by a qualified plan (usually a pension plan or profit-sharing plan)
4. Others; such as wife, children, partners or stockholders.

The schedule should include at least the following information:

---

**BASIC DATA**

Date of policy ______________________________

Name of policy ______________________________

Policy number ______________________________

Type of insurance* ______________________________

Face amount (current death benefit) ______________________________

Annual premium ______________________________

Present cash value ______________________________

Owner ______________________________

Beneficiary ______________________________

Loans on policy ______________________________

Dividend additions ______________________________

Options available ______________________________

Additional features ______________________________

*Whole Life, Universal Life, Term, Group-Term, Split-Dollar

**ADDITIONAL INFORMATION**

A computer run of the policy details until the insured reaches age 95, with year-by-year calculations *using these three assumptions:* (1) current assumptions (the percentage rate of the insurance company's earnings for the most recent year), (2) minimum policy guarantees (usually 4 percent to 4.5 percent), and (3) a rate of earnings between (1) and (2), usually one percent less than the current assumptions—

☐ Premium
☐ Cash surrender value
☐ Death benefit

Also ask (a) when—in what year—the policy will lapse using each of the three assumptions above, and (b) when the premium will vanish (no more premiums required) or the policy will endow (the cash surrender value equals the death benefit).

---

Now the question is, what are you going to do with all this information? First, let's realize that each life insurance policy you own (or control) on your life or the life of some other person is an asset/investment/piece of merchandise. Simply put, you are going to make one of four decisions for each policy (just as you would do if you were examining a stock portfolio or any other investment):

1. Keep the policy.
2. Dump it (pay no more premiums if a term policy; take the cash surrender value if a permanent life policy).
3. Trade it in or replace it.
4. Keep it (maybe), but you won't be happy.

The following analysis may not sound very scientific or precise, but it sure is 100 times better than letting every insurance policy stay, lapse, or be cashed in without any plan or because the whim strikes you.

### Keep the Policy

This is usually obvious because you can compare what you have on hand to what is available at your age and insurability. Simply shop to see if you can get a better deal with a new policy. A policy should never be allowed to lapse or cashed in without a specific reason. So let's see when you should...

### Dump It

This is what you should look for:

1. The policy is permanent insurance and is very old. The cash surrender value (CSV) is about half of the death benefit. You might find this hard to believe, but some times the CSV is 80 percent to 90 percent of the death benefit. And once in a while, the CSV is greater than the death benefit.

   What does this mean? The policy has ceased being pure life insurance and has turned into a part insurance/part investment or a pure investment. A lousy investment to be sure. The decision on such a policy is easy. Dump it.
2. You have term insurance of any kind—an old policy or a new one. Many factors are involved here: Are you insurable?...Is the policy convertible?...Would permanent insurance serve your needs better?...A blend of term and permanent insurance? My experience is that it is an easy decision when you compare the premium cost to age 95 (many term policies don't last that long) to other insurance products available.

### Trade It or Replace It

Often trading (tax-free) one or more of your current insurance policies for a new policy is the perfect answer. Always start by getting a quote for a new policy from the insurance company that issued the current policy.

In most cases if you search the market, you will find that this is your best bet:

1. Cash in (take the CSV) the old policy
2. Use the CSV (all or part of it) as a down payment on a new policy.

Why does trading in or replacing a policy work? Because the insurance industry keeps offering new products that are more cost effective than the old products. However...

■ **CAUTION**

1. Never cash in the old policy until you are covered by a new policy.
2. If the CSV is greater than the amount of premiums you paid, the difference is taxable. In practice, I have never seen this fact change a decision.
3. Replacing a policy (often called "switching") is serious business. Make sure to compare the long-term projections of your current policy to the proposed new one. Don't forget to figure in the costs of getting out of the old policy and into the new one.

### Keep It (Maybe), But You Won't Be Happy

I've never seen it said better than by Jane Bryant Quinn in the July 13, 1992 issue of *Newsweek*:

> "Some cash-value policies were built to last. But...In the cold light of the 1990s, it's clear that cash values didn't grow as fast as was forecast. And here's the bad part: You may not know it!
>
> "When you finally find out, it might cost you many thousands of dollars to bring your policy up to strength. If you don't pay, the coverage will lapse—maybe at the age of 50, maybe at 70; you won't know.
>
> "The first wave of failures is afflicting "vanishing premium" policies. With this type of coverage, you pay extra-high premiums for a few years, after which your insurance is supposed to be paid up for life.
>
> "Thomas...and his wife Dava...bought $240,000 worth of coverage...They intended to pay their $2,287 annual premium for up to five years; after that, said the agent, the policy's cash value would finance the premiums for life...Last February, however, truth broke through. To keep their coverage in force, they'd have to pay an even higher premium for the next 10 years...
>
> "Because contracts like these miss their "vanish" date, their unsoundness is discovered early. But thousands...are unknowingly paying insufficient premiums, on policies they won't think further about for the next 20 years."
>
> ■ **NOTE:** "Vanishing premium" means that after a certain number of years no further premium payments will be required. Why? Because anticipated earnings and dividends are projected to be enough to pay all future premiums.

No question about it: Jane Bryant Quinn is telling it like it is. And that's one of the reasons I always take a close look at all of a client's existing life insurance coverage.

Keeping or dumping a policy should not be made on emotion, but rather your decision should be based on sound principles as explained in this chapter.

## Buying New Insurance—The Insurance Illustration (Proposal)

*NEVER, NEVER FORGET that a typical insurance illustration is a sales tool.* It shows the projected and guaranteed values for the annual premium, number of premiums payable, cash values and death benefit. *Projected values are not guaranteed.* Computer-generated sales illustrations are often confusing because of all the columns and lack of any standard terminology.

Do not rely solely on projected values. *Your decision on which policy to buy must consider what is guaranteed.* Only the guarantees are contained in the policy. The rest is *projected.*

Knowledge, common sense, and an advisor without an axe to grind will always be your best friends when buying new insurance coverage. All insurance is not the same. It is a commodity, like a car. As such, you should try to select the model and make that fits your taste and pocketbook. Then shop, via your trusted professionals, for the "best" coverage at the "best" price. Recognize that best is probably the impossible dream because of the number of companies, types of insurance products, and the endless number of ways in which life insurance can be packaged.

### What Others Say

The best article I have ever seen on the subject of insurance proposals was written by Donald Jay Korn in the March 1991 issue of *Financial Planning*. Its title: "Illustration Wars Still Plague Insurers and Perplex Clients." The subtitle is close to an indictment of the insurance industry: "Competition to come up with the best-looking life insurance policies has produced inflated projections that are haunting the industry as well as policyholders."

These quotes from the article offer sound insight for consumer and advisor alike:

> "Insurance companies know how the game works, too. If Company B can come up with a policy illustration showing the same $2,908 premiums leading to a cash value of $125,000 after 25 years, it likely will get the business. Even better, Company C shows a $150,000 cash value. And so on. This has led to what many in the industry, including Armand de Palo, chief actuary of The Guardian Life Insurance Co., called "Illustration Wars." As he puts it, "Some consumers now are being sold not a better company or a better product, but a better current illustration.
>
> "Another insurance company actuary, Alan Yaeger, senior vice president at Western Reserve Life, adds that 'the majority of insurance companies play games with illustrations, and it's difficult to find the ones that don't.'
>
> 'A lot of policies are sold as 'vanishing premiums' or 'offset' policies," says Hardison-Demuth. "The assumption is that premiums will be paid for a set time period, perhaps seven or eight or ten years. After that, the earnings on the cash value already built up will be enough to keep the policy in force.'...
>
> "But if the insurance company's investment returns can't live up to its assumptions, those early payments may not be enough to cover the ongoing premiums. `The policies may self-destruct or the vanished premiums may 'unvanish,'" says Eugene Grayson, vice president in the Travelers financial services department.
>
> "Don't buy the illustration—buy the best company you can find.'
>
> "No matter what they project, insurers only can pay what they actually earn," said Korn.

And here's another quote from Jane Bryant Quinn that appeared in the August 10, 1992 business section of the *Chicago Tribune* in an article titled, "Insurers' 'illustrations' may paint over the facts."

> "An insurance policy illustration purports to show—apparently to the dollar—what you'll have in cash values and death benefits when you reach old age. But without exception, illustrations are wrong. They're typically based on current interest rates. When interest rates change, so will your policy's ultimate value.
>
> "If rates decline (as they probably will for most policies), you will have to pay higher premiums in the future to keep your insurance in force."

In her column of July 12, 1992 in the *Chicago Sun-Times*, Terry Savage wrote:

> "Many consumers tend to `blank out' when insurance agents go into their sales pitch. The numbers become a blur and there's a tendency to just focus on the dollar amount of the coverage and the cost of the premiums. That could be a huge mistake. As Metzenbaum [A U.S. senator] put it: `It's abundantly clear to me that the life insurance industry designs policy illustrations to be confusing—or worse, unintelligible.' So you're not alone if you're confused!
>
> "The insurance industry is exempt from Truth in Lending laws, and antitrust laws, and the Federal Trade Commission is barred from even studying the industry."

### What I Say

This article was part of my national tax column in August 1991:

> THE INSURANCE-PROPOSAL GAME CAN COST YOU A BUNDLE
>
> "Yesterday, I sold $9 million worth of insurance. Well, I really didn't sell it, but the client actually bought it—about two months later from an insurance agent—as a result of my recommendations.
>
> "Here's the story. A brother and two sisters inherited a family business (one-third of the stock each) from their dad. The brother is active in the business. The sisters are not. The three kids, together with their lawyer and accountant, had been working on a buy-sell agreement for several years. They called me in for a second opinion.
>
> "A series of questions and answers made one objective clear to the siblings: None of them intended to sell their stock until death do they part. Life insurance to fund the buy-sell agreement was an obvious choice. Since the amount of the insurance coverage ($3 million each) was so large, it was decided to get proposals from four different insurance consultants.
>
> "Each of the consultants were told exactly the same thing: The purpose of the insurance, that we wanted permanent insurance (as opposed to term insurance), and the basic assumptions that each proposal must contain. The hope was to make the proposals as comparable as possible. Each consultant was then given an open field to suggest any type of insurance coverage or proposal

that they thought would do a better job than the original marching orders given by me.

"The proposals poured in. I did my comparisons. After much discussion, the client made a decision and the $9 million of coverage is now in force. But I learned something. Something very important to anyone reading this item who will ever buy life insurance or have input when someone else is about to buy any significant coverage. This is my advice: Get at least two proposals. Maybe more. Discard all proposals that are from an insurance carrier that does not have at least a Best's A+ rating and an AA+ from Standard & Poor's or Duff & Phelps or does not clearly explain all assumptions used in the proposals. Remember, you are buying not only the integrity of the consultant, but also the integrity of the insurance company or companies he represents. Some consultants and companies play a proposal game that is designed to sell their products to the unwary, rather than to disclose the true picture of how the particular policy might really perform in the future.

"What's the most important point to learn? Hire a consultant that doesn't sell insurance to analyze the proposals. If you don't chances are you will fall into the trap of the unwary: Buying a better illustration, rather than buying the better company or a better (the right) insurance product. Is it worth all the effort? Yes! Yes! Insurance is the only financial product I am aware of that gives you a combination of tax and economic benefits where you can't lose. Of course, you must buy the right kind of insurance from the right company."

### What to Do with Proposals

Like it or not, the insurance industry is going to keep pumping out proposals. The purpose of this book is not to change the insurance industry, but to learn, as best as we can, how to work with the industry for the benefit of the insurance buyer—you and my clients.

So, I raided my files. Following are a typical "Discussion Agenda" (Schedule #1) and two "Insurance Proposals Summaries" (Schedules #2 and #3). More information is left out than is shown, but what is shown was distilled from a stack of paper about three inches thick. The proposal summaries show the three key elements—premium, death benefit, and cash surrender value—when buying permanent insurance. In a feeble attempt to level the playing field and make the proposal illustrations from the four insurance companies comparable, all the companies were asked to assume eight percent current earnings. At the time, all of the companies were earning well in excess of eight percent. Nothing is changed, except names, the clients and the four insurance companies.

After you look over the agenda and proposals, examine the agenda at point "III, Rationale of Proposals Requested." The target was $2 million in insurance, which we intended to accomplish with the Short-Pay (10 years). (See Schedule #2.) But at the end of the 10-year period, we wanted some flexibility if more insurance was needed. Point III tells you how we might play the game down the road—if Sam is healthy or not.

## A Few Proposal Hints

1. When you ask for proposals, make sure they include:
   a. Current earning assumptions.
   b. Policy guarantee.
   c. A rate between (a) and (b).
2. Get proposals from at least two insurance consultants. Ask the consultants to use at least two different companies. Tell them all to give you the same thing. For example:

**SCHEDULE #1**

**SUCCESS CO.—SAM SUCCESS**
**INSURANCE PROPOSALS**
**DISCUSSION AGENDA**
**APRIL 4, 19__ MEETING**

I. Rating of insurance companies.
   A. Insurance Company A.
   B. Insurance Company B.
   C. Insurance Company C.
   D. Insurance Company D.
   All rated "Best's A+" since 1981.

II. Coverage assumptions.
   A. $2,000,000 initial.
   B. Pay period of premiums.
      1. Short-pay, 10 years.
      2. Long-pay, past age 90.
   C. 8 percent interest (all companies currently earning more).

III. Rationale of proposals requested.
   A. If stay healthy (and need more coverage at or near 10-year point).
      1. Just buy more coverage as needed.
      2. Use cash surrender value to buy better coverage if available.
   B. If not healthy (and need more coverage) continue to pay premiums and death benefit will increase (See Schedule #3).

IV. Proposals.
   A. Review 6-page summary.
   B. Review back-up material if desired.
   C. Make selection of insurance company.

V. Decide on amount of coverage.
   A. Corporation cross-purchase ($2 to $3 million each).
   B. Owned individually outside of corporation ($1 to $2 million each).

**SCHEDULE #2**

## SUCCESS CO.—SAM SUCCESS
## INSURANCE PROPOSALS SUMMARY
## SHORT-PAY (10 YEARS)

| | COMPANY | | | |
|---|---|---|---|---|
| | A | B | C | D |
| **PREMIUM** | | | | |
| Year 1 | $32,670 | $24,000 | $49,735 | $18,870* |
| Year 2 | 32,670 | 24,000 | 17,735 | 18,870 |
| After 10 years | 326,700 | 240,000 | 209,350 | 188,700 |
| After 14 years | 326,700 | 240,000 | 280,290 | 188,700 |
| After 15 years | 326,700 | 240,000 | 280,561 | 188,700 |
| After 20 years | 330,655 | 240,000 | 280,561 | 188,700 |

*Plus $1,000 per million in year 1 only.

| | A | B | C | D |
|---|---|---|---|---|
| **DEATH BENEFIT (8%)** | | | | |
| Year 1 | 2,007,778 | 2,000,000 | 2,119,953 | 2,017,312 |
| Year 10 | 2,269,001 | 2,000,000 | 2,179,387 | 2,235,133 |
| Year 20 | 2,000,000 | 2,000,000 | 1,173,912 | 2,235,133 |
| Age 65 | 2,212,149 | 2,000,000 | 2,018,309 | 2,235,133 |
| Age 70 | ** | 2,149,038 | 2,238,859 | 2,235,133 |

**Not shown.

| | A | B | C | D |
|---|---|---|---|---|
| **CASH SURRENDER VALUE (8%)** | | | | |
| Year 1 | 1,699 | 22,576 | 33,305 | 15,043 |
| Year 10 | 322,248 | 330,764 | 255,783 | 233,628 |
| Year 20 | 628,220 | 685,875 | 557,766 | 472,338 |
| Age 65 | 1,054,647 | 857,804 | 973,342 | 741,015 |
| Age 70 | ** | 1,252,183 | 1,288,898 | 920,256 |

**Not shown.

| **CO. C ONLY—NON GUARANTEED SPECIAL MATURITY DIVIDENDS** | CSV | DB |
|---|---|---|
| Year 1 | $33,305 | $2,119,953 |
| Year 10 | 255,783 | 2,397,325 |
| Year 20 | 612,224 | 2,126,242 |
| Age 65 | 1,156,209 | 2,600,903 |
| Age 70 | 1,596,033 | 2,997,448 |

**SCHEDULE #3**

## SUCCESS CO.—SAM SUCCESS
## INSURANCE PROPOSALS SUMMARY
## LONG-PAY (PAST AGE 90)

| | COMPANY | | | |
|---|---|---|---|---|
| | A | B | C | D |
| **PREMIUM** | | | | |
| Year 1 | $32,670 | $24,000 | $49,735 | $18,870* |
| Year 2 | 32,670 | 24,000 | 17,735 | 18,870 |
| After 10 years | 326,700 | 240,000 | 209,350 | 188,700 |
| After 14 years | 457,380 | 336,000 | 280,290 | 264,180 |
| After 15 years | 490,050 | 360,000 | 280,561 | 283,050 |
| After 20 years | 653,400 | 480,000 | 280,561 | 377,400 |

*Plus $1,000 per million in year 1 only.

| | A | B | C | D |
|---|---|---|---|---|
| **DEATH BENEFIT (8)** | | | | |
| Year 1 | 2,007,778 | 2,000,000 | 2,119,953 | 2,017,312 |
| Year 10 | 2,323,397 | 2,000,000 | 2,179,387 | 2,235,133 |
| Year 20 | 3,048,024 | 2,000,000 | 1,773,912 | 2,762,454 |
| Age 65 | 4,263,770 | 2,807,272 | 2,018,309 | 3,530,744 |
| Age 70 | ** | 4,156,885 | 2,238,859 | 4,129,456 |

**Not shown.

| | A | B | C | D |
|---|---|---|---|---|
| **CASH SURRENDER VALUE (8%)** | | | | |
| Year 1 | 1,699 | 22,576 | 33,305 | 15,043 |
| Year 10 | 349,870 | 330,764 | 255,783 | 233,628 |
| Year 20 | 1,145,147 | 1,069,786 | 557,766 | 762,454 |
| Age 65 | 2,291795 | 2,301,043 | 973,342 | 1,530,744 |
| Age 70 | ** | 3,583,522 | 1,288,898 | 2,129,456 |

**Not shown.

| **CO. C ONLY—NON GUARANTEED SPECIAL MATURITY DIVIDENDS** | CSV | DB |
|---|---|---|
| Year 1 | $33,305 | $2,119,953 |
| Year 10 | 255,783 | 2,397,325 |
| Year 20 | 612,224 | 2,126,242 |
| Age 65 | 1,156,209 | 2,600,903 |
| Age 70 | 1,596,033 | 2,997,448 |

*(List continued from page 144.)*

a. Whole life for
b. $1 million for
c. A female who is
d. 48 years old (give the birthday)
e. Nonsmoker, preferred risk
f. Pay for life
g. Pay for 10 years
h. All three earnings assumptions in 1. above.
i. All only from "top rated companies (You can toss those from companies that do not meet your due-diligence standards and simply refuse to do business with the consultant that submits proposals from sub-standard companies.)
j. Ask the consultant to submit a due-diligence package

3. Until you get a little experience ask for a complete printout of all the assumptions used to get those little numbers in all those columns. Read it. All of it. You can usually tell when something looks fishy.
4. Tell the consultants why you want the illustration and what you intend to do with it. Ask them to recommend an insurance plan, supported by appropriate illustrations, that is better than what you are requesting. (Any recommendation would be in additional to your original request, not a substitute.)

   Not only is this a great way to learn, but sometimes one or more of the consultants has a better idea. How nice.
5. Then ask questions. Most of the insurance consultants I have worked with have been wonderful. The good ones don't mind answering your questions.

Next, let's look at a proposal prepared by an insurance consultant for one of his clients together with the letter (Exhibit #3) that accompanied it. The proposal is presented here word for word (except all names are changed):

☐ Each exhibit (both are identical, except one uses "Current Interest Rates" and the other uses "Interest Rates Lowered 2%") packs a lot of information onto one page, yet is easy to read, and contains most of the significant information needed to make a decision.

☐ Until you develop a better format to show the information you want, I strongly suggest you send copies of these proposals (Exhibits #1 and #2) to the consultants you are working with and ask them to summarize their proposals in the same way these are shown. Doing so will help make the bundle of proposals you receive easier to compare. Of course, you will still ask for all of the information suggested under "A Few Proposal Hints," a few pages back.

■ **NOTE:**
"M" means male.
"F" means females.
"W.L." means whole life.
"Joint and Survivor" means second-to-die.

**EXHIBIT #1**

**INSURED: RON AND MARY PAST (M63, F63)**
**UNDERWRITING CLASS: M-STANDARD, F-PREFERRED**
**AMOUNT: $1,000,000**
**TYPE: JOINT & SURVIVOR**
**CURRENT INTEREST RATES**

| Company | V | W | X | Y | Z |
|---|---|---|---|---|---|
| | **Universal** | **Interest Sensitive WL** | **Modified Premium W.L./Term** | **Universal** | **W.L./Term** |
| A.M. Best Company Rating (1) | A+ | A++ | A++ | A+ | A++ |
| Standard & Poor's Rating (2) | AA | AAA | AAA | AA | AAA |
| **PROJECTED DEATH BENEFIT (3)** | | | | | |
| Years | | | | | |
| 5 | $ 1,000,000 | $ 1,000,000 | $ 1,003,613 | $ 1,000,000 | $ 1,061,703 |
| 10 | $ 1,000,000 | $ 1,000,000 | $ 1,010,729 | $ 1,000,000 | $ 1,184,841 |
| 20 | $ 1,000,000 | $ 1,000,000 | $ 1,029,178 | $ 1,000,000 | $ 1,266,634 |
| **PROJECTED CASH VALUES (3)** | | | | | |
| Years | | | | | |
| 5 | $ 98,594 | $ 85,952 | $ 89,801 | $ 71,371 | $ 98,040 |
| 10 | $ 292,476 | $ 250,586 | $ 237,498 | $ 202,671 | $ 256,070 |
| 20 | $ 491,057 | $ 495,887 | $ 492,316 | $ 391,807 | $ 548,207 |
| Annual Premium | $ 24,489 | $ 22,074 | $ 17,074 | $ 17,743 | $ 19,427 |
| Years to Pay to "Vanish" (4) | 10 | 11 | 10 | 10 | 11 |
| Total Projected Premium Outlay | $ 244,890 | $ 242,814 | $ 170,740 | $ 177,430 | $213,697 |

(1) Source: A.M. Best & Company, Inc. 199__. Independent analysts of the insurance industry since 1899.
(2) Source: Standard & Poor's Insurance Digest, 199__.
(3) Based on insurance company's current assumptions of mortality, expenses, and credited interest rates, which are not guaranteed. Refer to attached insurance company ledgers for guarantees.
(4) "Vanish Point"-Projected values assume election to pay no premium after this year. This is not synonymous with a "paid-up" policy. Based on insurance company's current assumptions of mortality, expenses, and credited interest rates which are not guaranteed. Lower interest rates or increased expenses will require additional premium payments.

This proposal is valid for purchases in Illinois.

**EXHIBIT #2**

**INSURED: RON AND MARY PAST (M63, F63)**
**UNDERWRITING CLASS: M-STANDARD, F-PREFERRED**
**AMOUNT: $1,000,000**
**TYPE: JOINT & SURVIVOR**
**INTEREST RATES LOWERED 2%**

| Company | V | W | X | Y | Z |
|---|---|---|---|---|---|
| | **Universal** | **Interest Sensitive WL** | **Modified Premium W.L./Term** | **Universal** | **W.L./Term** |
| A.M. Best Company Rating (1) | A+ | A++ | A++ | A+ | A++ |
| Standard & Poor's Rating (2) | AA | AAA | AAA | AA | AAA |
| **PROJECTED DEATH BENEFIT (3)** | | | | | |
| Years | | | | | |
| 5 | $ 1,000,000 | $ 1,000,000 | $ 1,001,906 | $ 1,000,000 | $ 1,058,122 |
| 10 | $ 1,000,000 | $ 1,000,000 | $ 1,005,933 | $ 1,000,000 | $ 1,166,865 |
| 20 | $ 1,000,000 | $ 1,000,000 | $ 1,022,748 | $ 1,000,000 | $ 1,337,370 |
| **PROJECTED CASH VALUES (3)** | | | | | |
| Years | | | | | |
| 5 | $ 90,530 | $ 81,102 | $ 84,984 | $ 65,502 | $ 158,185 |
| 10 | $ 256,265 | $ 224,272 | $ 212,644 | $ 176,821 | $ 322,062 |
| 20 | $ 561,920 | $ 562,925 | $ 564,325 | $ 511,591 | $ 590,899 |
| Annual Premium | $ 24,489 | $ 22,074 | $ 17,074 | $ 17,743 | $ 19,427 |
| Years To Pay to "Vanish" (4) | 16 | 18 | 18 | 20 | 18 |
| Total Projected Premium Outlay | $ 391,824 | $ 397,332 | $ 307,332 | $ 354,860 | $ 349,686 |

(1) Source: A.M. Best & Company, Inc. 199__. Independent analysts of the insurance industry since 1899.
(2) Source: Standard & Poor's Insurance Digest, 199__.
(3) Based on insurance company's current assumptions of mortality, expenses, and credited interest rates, which are not guaranteed. Refer to attached insurance company ledgers for guarantees.
(4) "Vanish Point". Projected values assume election to pay no premium after this year. This is not synonymous with a "paid-up" policy. Based on insurance company's current assumptions of mortality, expenses, and credited interest rates (lowered 2%), which are not guaranteed. Lower interest rates or increase expenses will require additional premium payments.

This proposal is valid for purchases in Illinois.

The letter (Exhibit #3) that accompanied the preceding proposals follows. It contains some important information that is not covered elsewhere in this book. It has been slightly edited.

**EXHIBIT #3** (LETTER FROM INSURANCE CONSULTANT TO MR. RON PAST)

Please find enclosed the Joint & Survivor insurance quotes on you and Mrs. Past that we discussed last week. This cover letter will address some of the issues that you will consider when deciding which insurance policy to purchase, such as: insurance company ratings, types of permanent insurance and cost comparison methods.

Insurance Company Ratings - When purchasing insurance you are buying a contract or promise that the insurance company will pay a benefit under the policy's terms. The promise or guarantee is only as strong as the financial strength of the guarantor (the insurance company). Since the financial strength of companies varies widely and the evaluation process is extremely complex, we rely on independent rating services to supply this information. The ratings are only opinions of each company's financial strength and should not be the only criteria for company selection, but it is a good place to start.

The ratings from A.M. Best, Standard & Poor's, Moody's, Duff & Phelps and Weiss Research are included for each company that has been rated by the service. My personal opinion is that the company should have an A+ or A++ (highest) rating from A.M. Best and a AA- (the fourth highest) or better rating from Standard & Poor's. The companies that we have quoted for your insurance have all met these criteria.

Cost of Insurance - All life insurance is based on the same fundamental pricing of RE:2.

| | |
|---|---|
| R=Risk | A portion of the annual cost pays for the risk of death during that policy year. The risk or probability of death increases each year, as you approach normal life expectancy. |
| E=Expenses | Another portion of the annual cost is related to the insurance company's expenses. These expenses include cost of the medical exam, sales commissions, advertising and administration costs. |
| :2 | Represents any dollars that you pay for your life insurance that exceed the annual cost for R and E. |

As an example, if R and E equal $1 for the year's cost of life insurance and you pay more than $1, the insurance company credits you with some of the interest earned.

## TYPES OF PERMANENT OR CASH VALUE INSURANCE

There are basically 4 types of permanent or cash value life insurance contracts. They are whole life, interest-sensitive whole life, universal life, and modified premium whole life.

- **Whole Life** is the most prevalent type of single life contracts in the marketplace. The premium is guaranteed to remain level for the life of the contract and is based on the *guaranteed* risk of mortality rates, expenses, and interest rates found in the contract. Based on these guaranteed rates the premium would remain level and would be paid each year to age 100. The amount of insurance would remain level to age 100, at which time the policy would endow (cash value equals the death benefit). Since insurance companies generally charge the insured lower costs for risk of mortality and expenses along with crediting more interest than the minimum guaranteed level, the whole life policy builds up additional cash value beyond the guaranteed level. The excess interest is retained in the policy by purchasing small amounts of paid-up insurance, until enough extra cash value is accumulated so that this reserve can be used to pay future premiums. This option to cease premium

**EXHIBIT #3** (LETTER FROM INSURANCE CONSULTANT CONTINUED)

payments when sufficient cash values have been accumulated is called "vanish premium." The death benefits on whole life contracts generally increase because the excess interest is retained as small amounts of paid-up insurance. These benefits are called paid-up additions and are added to the base policy.

- ☐ **Interest Sensitive Whole Life** is the same as whole life, except the excess interest is retained in the policy without increasing the basic death benefit. Also, the annual premium can be based on non guaranteed risk of mortality rates, expenses, and the interest rates. The use of non guaranteed pricing assumptions can result in a lower annual premium, but the premium is not guaranteed. These policies generally have a level death benefit from year 1 to age 100, at which time they endow.
- ☐ **Universal Life** is similar to current assumption whole life, except the premium is not fixed. The premium can be adjusted within a range from the minimum to the maximum each year. Most universal life policies are purchased with a premium that duplicates the results of a current assumption whole life contract. However, it does allow for more flexible premium payments, which could include paying a lower premium for a longer number of years. This option is very risky because when minimum premiums are illustrated, they *are not guaranteed*. If the insurance companies do not meet their pricing projections for risk of mortality, expenses, and interest rates, the risk is not just an additional 1 or 2 years of premium payments. The risk is that the premium could be increased several fold.
- ☐ **Modified Premium Whole Life** is the fourth type of contract available for single life insurance. This type of contract is a whole life contract with a lower premium guaranteed for the first 10 or 15 years. Starting in year 11 or 16 the guaranteed premium increases two or three fold and remains at the higher level for the remaining years. This type of contract is usually illustrated with the excess interest used to "vanish" premiums before they increase in year 11 or 16. This is the type of contract where it is very important to look at the guaranteed premium and understand what you are really buying. If premiums don't vanish you will pay a much higher annual premium after year 11 or 15.

The policies we quoted for you include Company V and Company Y which are universal life. Company W is interest sensitive whole life. Company X modified premium whole life, and Company Z is a traditional whole life.

## SPECIFICATIONS FOR INSURANCE QUOTES

Your quotes were prepared using the following specifications:

1. Quote the lowest level annual premium to vanish premiums in 11 years or less.
2. Calculate the premiums based on each company's current projections for risk of mortality, expenses, and interest rates.
3. Based on these projections the policy endows (cash value equals death benefit) for the original amount of insurance at age 100.
4. Term insurance and cash value or paid-up insurance riders are included.
5. Policy loans are not used to "vanish" premiums.

## COMPARISON OF QUOTES

One method of comparison is to look at the total projected premium outlay to vanish premiums. This is a simple method of comparison, but it does not take into account the fact that some whole life contracts have an increasing death benefit while the others have a level death benefit.

**EXHIBIT #3** (LETTER FROM INSURANCE CONSULTANT CONTINUED)

Another method which attempts to correct this deficiency is to calculate the internal rate of return of death benefits. This method calculates the interest rate that would have to be earned on the premiums to equal the amount of the death benefit at a specific year. In theory, a higher internal rate of return would mean you got more interest credited on your premium outlay, or conversely, you paid less in premiums.

The only fault with all these methods is that all of these values are based on the insurance company's projections, which are not guaranteed. That is why the actual net investment yields earned by each company on its invested assets over the last 10 years is included. Although past performance is no guarantee of future performance, this can be useful in selecting an insurance company. The same lesson learned from the S&L industry applies to life insurance...more interest cannot be credited to your policy than is earned by the insurance company.

The quotes have also been recalculated assuming that the current interest rate credited on cash values is reduced by 2%. This illustrates how sensitive the cost is to changes in interest rates.

There is substantial information contained in our proposal for your review and I am sure it will generate some questions...

Sincerely,
Joe Consultant

## Due Diligence

Yes, insurance companies can go broke. And they do. Policyholders can and do lose all or, more likely, part of their benefits. How do you protect yourself? Due diligence!

■ **ADVICE:** Make sure your life insurance company is financially strong. You can't count on regulators to warn you of impending insolvency. Most states lack the resources or even the authority to monitor companies' financial health. And even in states that do monitor the companies, regulators often hush up financial problems so that policyholders won't desert a troubled company and hasten its demise.

Okay, how do you make sure that your life insurance company is financially strong? Due Diligence! Since I am far from an expert in this subject and every insurance consultant I ask has a different opinion (usually one that favors his or her company or supports what he or she likes to sell), I'm not giving you my opinions on due diligence. Instead, this material is taken from due-diligence information submitted to me by insurance consultants along with insurance proposals for my clients.

### Due Diligence Examples

In these examples, nothing is changed or edited, unless noted. My comments or changes, if any, are in parentheses.

**EXAMPLE #1** (IN THE PROMOTION MATERIAL OF A MAJOR INSURANCE COMPANY)

**WHY BUY FROM ANYONE ELSE?**

*Eliminating 93% of the Competition*

Each year the A.M. Best Company rates all life insurance companies doing business in the United States and Canada. The letter ratings assigned are based on the results of a series of financial tests performed by Best's. The highest rating assigned is A+. Of the more than 2,600 legal reserve life insurance companies in North America, A.M. Best rated 1,380 in 1990. 270 companies received Best's A+ rating. Of these 270 companies, only 193 have received Best's A+ rating for the past 10 years.

According to Joseph Belth, a leading insurance consumerist, "to minimize the likelihood of delay, redtape and financial loss, the consumer should only buy life insurance from a company that is financially strong." An A+ rating from Best's is one of the best indicators available that a company is financially strong. Belth recommends that consumers only buy insurance from companies that have received Best's A+ rating for 10 consecutive years. Following is a list of the 193 life insurance companies that have received Best's A+ rating since 1981. With 193 companies to choose from, why buy from anyone else?

(This was followed by a list of the 193 insurance companies, which, of course, included the major insurance company.)

■ **NOTE:** The above clearly tells you that the "A.M. Best Company...highest rating assigned is A+..." Clearly not the whole truth, nothing but the truth...I wonder if it's because this company does not have the really "highest rating"—A++? (see Exhibit #3).

**EXAMPLE #2**

### STANDARD & POOR'S RATINGS

Standard and Poor's (S&P) Insurance Claims Paying Ability Rating is an assessment of an operating company's financial capacity to meet obligations under an insurance policy in accordance with its terms.
The S&P Claims Paying Ability Ratings are as follows:

**Secure Claims-Paying Ability**

**AAA** Superior financial security on both an absolute and relative basis.

**AA** Excellent financial security, capacity to meet policyholder obligations differs only a small degree from insurers rated AAA.

**A** Strong financial security but their capacity to meet policyholder obligations is somewhat more susceptible to adverse changes in economic or underwriting conditions than more highly rated insurers.

### MOODY'S RATINGS

Moody's Insurance Rating is defined as Moody's opinion regarding a company's ability to discharge senior policyholder obligations and claims.
The Moody's Insurance Ratings are as follows:

**Aaa** Best quality - smallest degree of credit risk.

**Aa** High quality - meets all standards.

**A** Upper Medium grade - many favorable investment attributes. Elements may be present which suggest a susceptibility to impairment sometime in the future.

(There are lower ratings for S&P and Moody's, but they are not included above.)

### WEISS RESEARCH, INC. RATINGS

Weiss Research, Inc. is a rating company based in West Palm Beach, Florida. It started rating insurance companies in 1989, and currently rates about 1700 life, health, and annuity companies. Companies receive a rating ranging from A to F, with A and B ratings representing above average, C average, and D and E indicating weakness or potential weakness. The addition of a plus or minus sign indicates a modest possibility that the company could be upgraded or downgraded.

**EXAMPLE #3** (TELLS YOU HOW TO RATE THE RATINGS)

**HIGHEST 8 RATINGS USED BY A.M. BEST, STANDARD & POOR'S, MOODY'S AND DUFF & PHELPS**

| | Ratings | | |
|---|---|---|---|
| Rank | A.M. Best | S&P/D&P* | Moody's |
| 1 | A++ | AAA | Aaa |
| 2 | A+ | AA+ | Aa1 |
| 3 | A | AA | Aa2 |
| 4 | A- | AA- | Aa3 |
| 5 | B++ | A+ | A1 |
| 6 | B+ | A | A2 |
| 7 | B | A- | A3 |
| 8 | B- | BBB+ | Baa1 |

*Standard & Poor's (S&P) and Duff & Phelps (D&P) use the same letter ratings.

*NOTE:* A shorthand for A.M. Best is:

| Rating | Means |
|---|---|
| A++, A+ | Superior |
| A, A- | Excellent |
| B++, B+ | Very Good |
| B, B- | Good |

The above lists only the "highest 8..." The lower ratings are not shown. Why? *You should not even consider buying a policy from a company that falls below the first 6 ratings.*

**EXAMPLE #4** (SECOND-TO-DIE POLICIES; COMPANY NAMES CHANGED)

It is recommended that the companies being considered for their survivorship life (second-to-die) policies pass rigorous scrutiny as to their quality and financial strength. The study is limited to those companies which meet at least three of the four following standards:

1. Licensed in the state of New York
2. Rated Aaa by Moody's
3. Rated AAA by Standard & Poor's
4. Rated A+ by A.M. Best

The following companies meet the above criteria and have been chosen for the study:

A (The company submitting the proposal); B - E (other insurance companies)

**Due Diligence**

The confidence level that you and your clients have in these rate of return projections will depend on the extent to which you have insisted on a thorough analysis of the insurance proposals. The questions that should always be asked about life insurance companies and their products are even more essential for second-to-die policies, both because of the large amounts of insurance often involved and because the success of the estate plan depends on the company and product performing as promised.

1. HISTORY: Past performance does not guarantee future results, but it is probably the best indicator of a life insurer's ability to live up to its projections. There are a number of indicia that are used by state insurance departments, consumer groups, and rating agencies that measure a company's track record—interest-adjusted surrender cost, interest-adjusted payment cost, current and past dividend rates, and treatment of past policyholders as compared to new insureds. The A.M. Best Company's Flitcraft Compend is the primary source for most of this information.

2. RATINGS: There are four main life insurance company rating agencies: A.M. Best & Company (Best's), Moody's, Standard & Poor's, and Duff & Phelps. For years, Best's had the ratings business to itself and today follows about 1400 carriers. However, with the demand for additional detailed financial information on Contracts (GIC's), Moody's and Standard & Poor's entered the field, and Duff & Phelps followed more recently.

Although relatively few companies subscribe to these additional rating agencies, it is important to be able to compare their ratings and analyses with Best's, since Best's gives its top A+ rating to about 200 companies. Fewer than 10 companies have the top rating from Best's, Moody's, and Standard & Poor's; and, today, only two—Company A and Company B—receive the highest marks from all four services.

3. DIVIDENDS: In the case of mutual companies, which, unlike most stock companies, pay dividends, the ratings are based in large measure on the three components of the dividend: investment yield, mortality experience, and company expenses. It is important to look not only at the current dividend and recent trends but also to examine the dividend component to determine a company's relative strengths. An additional benchmark, which contributes to expense performance, is the persistency or the lapse rate of existing business. A low persistency or high lapse rate contributes to high expenses, and may indicate dissatisfaction with a company's performance.

4. FUTURE ASSUMPTIONS: It is important to know whether the projections of policy performance are based on current company experience in the areas of mortality, expenses, and persistency, or whether, as has been true in some cases, companies are assuming improvements in one or more of these categories. For example, some companies with mediocre mortality experience have forecast improvements for second-to-die insureds because of the presumably healthier nature of those policyholders. That ought to be a warning sign.

5. RESERVE PRACTICES AND MORTALITY CHARGES IN BLENDED SECOND-TO-DIE POLICIES: There is a crucial difference between the reserving practices and mortality charges used in the more conservative blended (part term, part whole life) second-to-die policies versus those adopted by the most aggressive companies. The more conservative approach uses joint mortality charges throughout the life of the policy, which combine the lower costs experienced when both insureds are alive with the higher expenses incurred when only one is alive and has reached a more advanced age. This practice results in a higher mortality cost in the earlier policy years and therefore a higher initial premium than is charged by those companies which use lower mortality expenses when both insureds are alive than when only one of them is. This latter practice may offer a lower initial premium, but it also is likely to result in substantial future premium increases.

Similarly, the conservative approach is to charge a high enough premium that the cash value reserves can be increased significantly in the event of an early death, especially of the younger spouse. The higher cash value can generate a dividend sufficient to pay the higher mortality charges and term costs which result from only one living insured without requiring a premium increase. The lower cost policies cannot build up these reserves, and an early death, especially of the younger spouse, could require dramatically higher premiums. Looking at a worst case scenario, ask what would happen to the premium and the rate of return if the younger spouse dies very prematurely and the survivor lives to age 100.

A related inquiry, mentioned earlier, should be whether, in the case of minimum premium policies (where much of the dividend is needed to pay the term costs), a company follows the conservative practice of raising the premium as soon as the dividend goes down. Failure to do so could again lead to much higher premiums down the road.

If you ask all of these questions and receive satisfactory answers to them, you will have performed a necessary, but often overlooked service for your client and will have substantially eliminated the risk of any future malpractice claim.

*(Good stuff, in general. Points (4) and (5) should be mandatory reading when looking at second-to-die proposals. But dig that last paragraph. It suggests two concepts: (a) advisors (other than the insurance consultant) could be liable for a malpractice claim, and (b) doing the due diligence as suggested in his text might protect the advisor from such claims. Nice sales pitch. Could either concept be right? I wonder.)*

## A COMMENT

My files are bulging with due diligence examples submitted by insurance consultants. Most are self serving; some are pure nonsense intended to confuse rather than inform. But the vast majority of the material is well done and informative.

*The real question is, how much due diligence is required before committing real dollars to the trust of a particular insurance carrier?* My answer: Ask the insurance consultants to submit their standard due-diligence packages; ask for more information until you are satisfied you've got the right company; use the right examples in this chapter to help you determine if you have enough and the right information. When in doubt, pass.

Until due diligence standards—probably more of a dream than a reality—are set (so everyone in the industry marches to the same drummer), you are on your own.

**Some advice to insurance buyers:**

1. Stick with the top-rated companies.
2. Work with at least two insurance consultants and have each submit at least two proposals from different insurance companies.
3. Make sure the proposals include at least some of the due-diligence material as outlined in this chapter.
4. Hire an advisor who doesn't sell insurance to look over your selections and help you pick the winning company.

**If you are an advisor:**

1. Develop due-diligence standards with which you are comfortable.

2. Develop a network of other advisors (in or out of your profession), so you can get help when you need it.
3. Join a study group. If you can't find one, organize one.

This entire area—due diligence—is a specialty if I ever saw one. The best answer in my opinion is to develop recognized, licensed, due-diligence experts—like actuaries and CPAs—on whom the rest of us can rely. In the meantime, due diligence is an essential chore for us amateurs in selecting a life insurance product.

# 3 Split-Dollar Insurance

This chapter is mostly technical, but the first two pages explain this wonderful concept in nontechnical language.

Maybe a better title for this chapter would be "The Search for the Premium Dollar." Why? Because insurance consultants are forever searching for the premium dollar. And when it comes to the hero of this book—the owner of a closely held corporation—guess where that premium dollar is, nine out of 10 times? Right! In the corporation.

Split-dollar insurance plans are an efficient, cost-effective way of getting to those premium dollars. Split-dollar is not a kind of life insurance policy, but rather a method of financing the purchase and payments for a life insurance policy.

## Why Split-Dollar Plans Are So Popular

Not only have we found the premium dollar inside the corporation, but every time the corporation pays a premium for the benefit of the employee, he or she is getting, in effect, an interest-free loan.

Split-dollar insurance defined: A split-dollar plan provides for a sharing or "splitting" of policy death benefits and, in most cases, premium payments. Under the classical split-dollar plan, the employer and the employee join in purchasing an ordinary life insurance policy on the life of the employee. The employer agrees to pay the portion of the premium attributable to the annual increase in the cash surrender value (CSV); the employee pays the balance. When the employee-insured dies, the employer receives out of the proceeds an amount equal to the CSV. The employee is given the right to name the beneficiary of the balance of the proceeds. If the employee terminates employment prior to death, either the employer will cancel the policy and receive the CSV from the insurance company or the employee will buy the policy from the employer for the CSV.

A split-dollar plan is used in many ways to help employees purchase life insurance. Our inquiry in this chapter ignores many uses of a split-dollar plan, and zeroes in on how such plans can be used to help the stockholder/employee of a closely held business purchase life insurance for transfer/succession/estate-planning purposes. Further, this chapter assumes you have made all the necessary decisions concerning the insurance: what kind of policy to buy, for how much, from which company and so on. Since you don't want to suffer the full premium load, your decision is easy: Your corporate employer (the company you own) is the best source for the premium dollar. Enter the split-dollar plan.

## The Tax Consequences of Split-Dollar

### Income Taxes: The Employee

1. Because an employee receives life insurance protection under a split-dollar plan, *the value of this life insurance benefit (known as "the value of the economic benefit") is taxable to the employee each year* (Rev. Rul. 64-328).
2. This value is calculated by multiplying the amount of life insurance protection (i.e., the "at risk" portion provided by the employee) times the lower of the P.S. 58 rates (per an IRS table) or the current published premium rates charged by the insurer for individual one-year term insurance available to all standard risks (Rev. Rul. 64-328 and Rev. Rul. 66-110).
3. The amount taxable to the employee each year is reduced by any amount that the employee actually contributes under the plan (Rev. Rul. 64-328).
4. If the employee controls policy dividends or rights to dividend additions, the dividend amount is included in his or her income (Rev. Rul. 66-110).

### Income Taxes: The Employer

1. The employer cannot deduct any portion of the annual premium payment (Section 264(a)(1) and Rev. Rul. 64-328).
2. The employer cannot deduct the value of the economic benefit which is taxable to the employee (Rev. Rul. 64-328).
3. Death benefits received by the employer are income-tax-free (Section 101(a)).

### The Beneficiary (Selected by the Employee)

Death benefits received by an employee's beneficiary are generally income-tax-free (Section 101(a)).

### Gift Taxes

When a split-dollar plan exists between a third party (e.g., an irrevocable trust) and the employer, the insured/employee is deemed to have made a gift to the third party in the amount of the value of the economic benefit reduced by any third-party premium contribution. (Rev. Rul. 78-420).

---

**■ WHAT TO DO**

When the third party (probably an ILIT) receives cash from the insured/employee (you) to make the third party's premium contribution, such transfer from you is a gift, subject to the usual rules.

---

### Estate Taxes

1. If the insured/employee (you) have any incidents of ownership (i.e., right to borrow, or to name a beneficiary) and/or the insurance proceeds are payable to or for the benefit of your estate, the "at risk" portion of the insurance proceeds will be included in your estate (Section 2042).
2. If you own more than 50 percent of the stock of the employer and wish to remove the "at risk" portion from your estate, ask your lawyer to carefully review Rev. Rul. 82-145.

   According to Rev. Rul. 82-145: "...when a decedent's controlled corporation held at the decedent's death the right to borrow against the cash surrender value of a life insurance policy on the decedent's life, the portion of the policy proceeds payable other than to or for the benefit of the corporation is includable in the gross estate under Section 2042(2) of the Code."

   The message is clear: *If you control the corporation and the corporation can borrow against the cash surrender value, you via your control can, in effect, have the right to borrow. That right means you have incidents of ownership. Result: The portion of the split-dollar proceeds paid to your beneficiary are includable in your estate.*
3. If you transfer policy rights under a split-dollar plan to a third party and die within three years from the date of transfer, the "at risk" portion of the proceeds are included in your estate. (Section 2035).

## Common Methods of Policy Ownership

There are four common methods of policy ownership, as follows:

1. **Endorsement Method.** Under this method, the employer owns the policy and, by a policy endorsement, provides that the employee-insured (you) or your transferee has the right to name the beneficiary of the "at risk" portion of the proceeds. Typically, the employer would name itself as the direct beneficiary of an amount of the proceeds equal to the cash value of the policy at the time of your death. In the same endorsement, the employer splits off to you the right to name the beneficiary of the portion of the proceeds in excess of the cash value amount, and you name the beneficiary to receive that portion of the proceeds.
2. **Collateral Assignment Method.** Under this method, you or your transferee own the policy, name the beneficiary or beneficiaries, borrow the premiums from the employer and assign an interest in the policy death benefit and cash value to the employer as collateral for the loan.
3. **Split Ownership Method.** Under this method (also called the "assignment method") you or your transferee own the policy, name the beneficiary or beneficiaries and, by use of an absolute assignment, transfer to the employer specific policy ownership rights over a portion of the policy values equal to the employer's premium payments. You or your transferee retain all other ownership rights.
4. **Sole Ownership Method.** This method is typically used when the insured under the split-dollar plan is a majority shareholder because it can be designed to avoid having any incidents of policy ownership attributed to the shareholder for estate-tax purposes. This method consists of only an "outside" agreement

between the employer and a person/entity other than the insured. The employer has no interest in the policy.

■ **NOTE:** No matter what method is used, the income-tax results of a split-dollar plan are the same if a similar benefit is being provided to the employee (Rev. Rul. 64-328).

*The outside agreement.* The parties must decide how the policy is to be handled while the plan continues in operation and how the policy is to be handled when the plan terminates. These decisions become the basis of an "outside" agreement, which is in addition to the endorsement, collateral assignment, or assignment that is filed with the insurance company's home office or made a part of the policy. When the sole ownership method is used, the outside agreement contains the entire split-dollar arrangement. Normally, the "outside" agreement is not filed at the home office.

A number of very practical problems should be covered in the "outside" agreement. For example, early termination of employment, whether voluntary or involuntary; the termination of the split-dollar arrangement itself; who can terminate the plan, when, and with what form of notice to the other party; whether the insured has a right to purchase the policy in event of termination of employment or on termination of the split-dollar agreement and, if so, at what price; and the amount of the employee's premium contribution, if any.

## Types of Plans

There are many variations to the classical split-dollar plan as described earlier. There are basically two types of plans.

### Noncontributory Plan

The most common type is for the employer to pay the entire premium each year (an "employer pay-all" plan) and charge the employee with income equal to the annual value of the benefit received by the employee or his or her designee.

### Contributory Plan

Alternatively, the employer pays the entire premium except for the value of the annual benefit, which the employee contributes for the payment of the premium.

In certain respects the plans are alike, because in either case, the employer is entitled to receive back, on maturity of the policy, the premiums it paid. The employee, or the designee, is entitled to the balance of the proceeds.

In other respects the plans are not alike because, in the employer pay-all plan, the employee is charged with compensation income in an amount equal to the annual value of the benefit. In the contributory plan, there is no such charge because the employee has paid this amount back to the employer.

## P.S. 58 Rates

Rev. Rul. 64-328 provides that the employee is taxed on the value of the economic benefit received from the employer's participation in the split-dollar plan. The dollar amount of this economic benefit to be included in the gross income of the employee is determined annually by use of the PS 58 rates, or, if lower, determined by reference to the yearly renewable term rates (YRT rates) actually charged by an insurer for comparable term coverage.

■ **NOTE:** The YRT rates as a practical matter are always lower than the P.S. 58 rates. When a second-to-die policy is purchased under a split-dollar plan the "at risk" portion is charged at the so-called P.S. 38 rates. In this chapter the term "P.S. 58" always means the lower of the YRT rates and the insured; P.S. 38 applies when two lives are insured by a second-to-die policy. When one of the parties being insured under a second-to-die policy dies, the P.S. 38 rates are no longer used and the P.S. 58 rates apply to the survivor.

To give you a flavor of just how brutal these rates can become, here is a partial schedule (from a real life case taken from my files) for $1 million under a split-dollar plan prepared for a husband and wife who were age 51 and 52, respectively, in year one of the split-dollar plan.

■ **SCHEDULE OF VARIOUS RATES**

| | | | Single Life | |
|---|---|---|---|---|
| Year of Plan | Ages | P.S. 38 Rates | YRT Rates | P.S. 58 Rates* |
| 1 | 51/52 | $ 110 | $1,780 | $9,970 |
| 5 | 55/56 | 210 | 2,440 | 13,740 |
| 10 | 60/61 | 410 | 3,010 | 19,080 |
| 15 | 65/66 | 1,110 | 4,800 | 31,510 |
| 20 | 70/71 | 2,580 | 6,960 | 48,060 |
| 25 | 75/76 | 5,980 | 12,480 | 73,230 |
| 29 | 79/80 | 11,640 | 18,050 | 102,230 |

*Rate on the husband age 51 in year 1 is $9.97 per $1,000. See P.S. 58 rates table in Appendix for other years.

The P.S. 58 rates are used to compute the current taxable costs of the pure life insurance protection provided to an employee under qualified deferred compensation plans (Section 72(m)(3)(B) and Regulation 1.72-16); split-dollar plans; and tax-sheltered annuities. The amount recognized is the cost of the life insurance protection as determined from the P.S. 58 Table, or the YRT rates, whichever is lower. Only the excess of the face amount of the life insurance contract over its CSV is considered to be life insurance protection. The cost must be computed each year.

■ **A COMMON MISTAKE:** Often too much income is picked up. The rate is only applied to the excess of the face amount payable at death over the CSV of the policy at the end of the year, and not the face amount of the policy. For example, Jim is 55 years old. His $100,000 policy, which is subject to the P.S. 58 rates, has a CSV of $10,000. According to the P.S. 58 rates, the cost per $1,000 is $13.74; per the YRT rates the cost per $1,000 is $2.44. Jim must include $219.60 ($100 – 10 = $90 x $2.44) in his income.

■ **NOTE:** The employee may cause a third-party owner, such as an irrevocable life insurance trust (ILIT), to own the policy in order to remove the policy death benefit from his/her estate. In such a case, the employee must make a gift to the trust each year, to allow the trust to make the required contribution (equal to the annual economic benefit) to the employer. The use of an ILIT in tandem with a split-dollar plan is covered later in this chapter.

Since they are not deductible, the P.S. 58 rates are punishing. The P.S. 38 rates are tolerable (See Exhibit II later in this chapter), but the single-life rates become a bigger burden each year. Remember, if the split-dollar plan is noncontributory, the employee must pay tax on the P.S. 58 costs; if the plan is a contributory plan, the cash drain is worse yet—a nondeductible cash payment equal to the P.S. 58 costs must be made. What to do? Get rid of the P.S. 58 costs. Which brings us to rollout and crawlout.

## Rollout and Crawlout

A split-dollar plan agreement may provide for a termination of the plan prior to death, called a *"rollout"* of the policy, at a certain time. At that time, the employee repays the employer for its premium outlay (usually by withdrawing cash from the policy), and the employee obtains full ownership of the policy. A rollout is usually planned to occur only after the premiums for the policy have "vanished," so that the employee will not pay any more premiums after the rollout. Of course, since the employer is out of the picture, it pays no more premiums either. What's the result? No more P.S. 58 costs.

■ **ROLLOUT MECHANICS:** To "terminate" a split-dollar arrangement when a rollout occurs, two steps are necessary. First, the employee typically pays the employer the total amount of the employer's premium contributions under the plan; and second, any "outside" split-dollar agreement and the insurance policy documents (i.e. collateral assignment) which established the split-dollar arrangement must be terminated.

A variation of the rollout is a *"crawlout."* In this case, the employee continues paying the annual term insurance cost to the employer, even after the premiums have vanished, until the employee's cumulative contributions have repaid the employer for its outlay. Once the employer is repaid, the plan terminates, and the employee has full ownership of the policy.

Now, back to the rollout. Probably the easiest way to understand the first mechanic of a rollout is by a real-life example taken from my client files. The letter (Exhibit I), sent by the insurance consultant together with the two exhibits, refers to Exhibit II (Comparison of Imputed Income Under a Split-Dollar Arrangement), which is self-explanatory, and Exhibit III (Rollout Example), which needs some explanation.

**EXHIBIT I**

Re: Joe and Sue Owner

Dear Irv:

It was a pleasure meeting with you to discuss life insurance alternatives for Joe Owner.

During our meeting we discussed the possibility of using up both Joe's and Sue's (Joe's wife) unified credit, in addition to their annual exclusions, as a source of premium dollars for their irrevocable life insurance trust.

While you expressed concern regarding the economic viability of this alternative, you asked me to send you a comparison of the current rates used for joint lives compared with the rate used for single lives. I have enclosed these rates based on Joe's age of 51 and Sue's age of 52.

The table (Exhibit II) compares the imputed income using Life Table 38 rates while both insureds are living, with the rates currently being used by one of the insurers in our study for a single life. Because their ages are only one year apart the single rate is approximately the same for each of them. I have also indicated the P.S. 58 rate for comparison purposes.

My primary concern with split-dollar and second-to-die life insurance in an irrevocable trust is that at the first death the imputed income is then calculated on the basis of a single life. Therefore, at some point the split-dollar arrangement has to be broken. The only practical way this can happen from an economical standpoint is if additional funds are contributed to the irrevocable trust to reduce the company's investment in the contract. While this may not present a problem with smaller amounts of insurance at younger ages, it could present a difficult cash flow problem with larger amounts of insurance at older ages.

Under this technique, commonly referred to as "rollout", dividend additions would be surrendered at some point in time to pay the corporation.

The enclosed illustration (Exhibit III) was used as an example of the technique at a recent teleconference co-sponsored by the American Society of CLU and the American Bar Association.

I have highlighted the "rollout" point for your review. A more conservative approach would be for the employer to pay a larger portion of the premium so that the arrangement can be "broken" sooner.

If you think this structure has merit, we can work up specific numbers for the Owners.

Best personal regards,

**EXHIBIT II**

## JOE AND SUE OWNER

## $1,000,000

## COMPARISON OF IMPUTED INCOME UNDER A SPLIT-DOLLAR ARRANGEMENT

| | | SINGLE LIFE | |
|---|---|---|---|
| | JOINT LIFE US 38 RATE | INSURANCE COMP. RATE | GOVERNMENT PS 58 RATES |
| 51/52 | 110 | 1780 | 9970 |
| 52/53 | 130 | 1900 | 10790 |
| 53/54 | 150 | 2070 | 11690 |
| 54/55 | 180 | 2260 | 12670 |
| 55/56 | 210 | 2440 | 13740 |
| 56/57 | 250 | 2630 | 14910 |
| 57/58 | 290 | 2820 | 16180 |
| 58/59 | 340 | 2920 | 17560 |
| 59/60 | 410 | 3010 | 19080 |
| 60/61 | 480 | 3130 | 20730 |
| 61/62 | 570 | 3290 | 22530 |
| 62/63 | 670 | 3500 | 24500 |
| 63/64 | 790 | 3870 | 26630 |
| 64/65 | 904 | 4310 | 28980 |
| 65/66 | 1110 | 4800 | 31510 |
| 66/67 | 1310 | 5330 | 34280 |
| 67/68 | 1550 | 5910 | 37310 |
| 68/69 | 1840 | 6240 | 40590 |
| 69/70 | 2180 | 6520 | 44170 |
| 70/71 | 2580 | 6960 | 48060 |
| 71/72 | 3050 | 7760 | 52290 |
| 72/73 | 3610 | 9120 | 56890 |
| 73/74 | 4270 | 10400 | 61890 |
| 74/75 | 5050 | 11390 | 67330 |
| 75/76 | 5980 | 12480 | 73230 |
| 76/77 | 7070 | 13680 | 79630 |
| 77/78 | 8305 | 15010 | 86570 |
| 78/79 | 9860 | 16460 | 94090 |
| 79/80 | 11640 | 18050 | 102230 |

Read the letter and study Exhibit III (the source is identified in the letter and has nothing to do with the Joe and Sue Owner case which we will return to later in the chapter). Pay particular attention to the columns with the arrows near the top of the page. Next, look at the numbers underlined at age 73 (the rollout year) and age 74. It is easy to see that the employee took the $1,974,330 from the insurance company and paid it to the employer. The employer is now out of the plan. The employee is the sole owner. The line opposite age 74 shows the employer getting all of its premium dollar ($1,974,330) outlay back. The "Policy Cash Value and Total Death Benefit" are reduced accordingly.

As you can see, no premium payments are required (the premium vanished) after age 73. This is true even though the $1,974,330 was withdrawn from the policy's CSV. This means that the earnings on the CSV, still left after the withdrawal, will be large enough to pay the annual premium of $78,438 (second column from left). In addition, the earnings are large enough to push the CSV up each year along with the death benefit.

## The Rollout and the Transfer-for-Value Rule

The rollout solves the P.S. 58 problem, but can it create any new problems? Yes...one fact often overlooked concerning a "rollout" is that it actually involves the corporation's transfer of a piece of policy ownership to the employee, and this transfer is for a valuable consideration. Section 101(a)(1) normally excludes life insurance death benefits from income taxation, but Section 101(a)(2) says those proceeds (in excess of premiums and other consideration paid) are taxable income— "...in the case of a transfer for a value consideration...of a life insurance contract or any interest therein..."

The above rule is known as the transfer for value rule. Violate it and you get hit with tax when the insured dies. There are exceptions to the rule: for example, gifts and transfers to the insured are okay. So a rollout to the insured employee does not create any problem.

But what happens when the rollout/transfer is not to the employee? For example, for estate tax or other reasons, the employee has transferred ownership of the policy rights to his/her spouse or other family members, or to a trust for their benefit. Spouses, family members and trusts are not exempt from the transfer-for-value rule. In such situations, two solutions are available to avoid the transfer-for-value rule when a rollout is implemented.

1. *Rollout through the insured.* The corporation transfers its policy interest to the insured/employee, who gifts it to the third party (his/her spouse, family member, or trust). This transaction gets you off of the transfer-for-value rule hook. But now a new problem arises: The three-year rule that causes estate tax under Section 2035. Because an incident of ownership in the policy passes through the insured's hands, he/she must live at least three years past the rollout to keep the policy proceeds from being included in his/her gross estate. *The only way to beat this onerous result is for the insured to live at least three years after the rollout.* Russian Roulette tax planning. Not a good idea.
2. *Use a partnership.* Here's one more exception to the transfer-for-value rule in Section 101(a)(2)(B): "...to a partner of the insured, to a partnership in which the insured is a partner, or to a corporation in which the insured is a shareholder or officer."

**EXHIBIT III**

## ROLLOUT EXAMPLE

| | |
|---|---|
| INSURED: | MR. & MRS. PRESIDENT |
| CORPORATION: | ABC CORPORATION |
| INSURANCE COMPANY: | |
| STARTING AGE: | 45/45 |
| | |
| EMPLOYEE PREMIUM | |
| Starting Employee Premium: | 397 |
| Annual Percentage Increase: | |
| Annual Dollar Increase: | |
| | |
| TOTAL DEATH BENEFIT | |
| First Year of Plan: | 10,000,000 |
| Annual Percentage Increase | 0.0% |

| AGE | NET PREMIUM | PREMIUM PAID BY E'EE | PREMIUM PAID BY E'ER | POLICY CASH VALUE | TOTAL PAID BY E'ER | E'EE CASH VALUE | TOTAL PAID BY E'EE | E'EE DEATH BENEFIT | TOTAL DEATH BENEFIT |
|---|---|---|---|---|---|---|---|---|---|
| 45 | 78,438 | 397 | 78,041 | 0 | 78,041 | 0 | 397 | 9,921,959 | 10,000,000 |
| 46 | 78,438 | 492 | 77,946 | 0 | 155,987 | 0 | 889 | 9,844,013 | 10,000,000 |
| 47 | 78,438 | 586 | 77,852 | 9,600 | 233,839 | 0 | 1,475 | 9,766,161 | 10,000,000 |
| 48 | 78,438 | 682 | 77,756 | 95,211 | 311,595 | 0 | 2,157 | 9,744,671 | 10,056,266 |
| 49 | 78,438 | 778 | 77,660 | 188,783 | 389,255 | 0 | 2,935 | 9,721,441 | 10,110,696 |
| 50 | 78,438 | 873 | 77,565 | 290,880 | 466,820 | 0 | 3,808 | 9,704,532 | 10,171,352 |
| 51 | 78,438 | 1,068 | 77,370 | 401,662 | 544,190 | 0 | 4,876 | 9,705,550 | 10,249,740 |
| 52 | 78,438 | 1,264 | 77,174 | 521,693 | 621,364 | 0 | 6,140 | 9,722,594 | 10,343,958 |
| 53 | 78,438 | 1,463 | 76,975 | 651,176 | 698,339 | 0 | 7,603 | 9,754,863 | 10,453,202 |
| 54 | 78,438 | 1,764 | 76,674 | 790,434 | 775,013 | 15,421 | 9,367 | 9,800,455 | 10,575,468 |

| AGE | NET PREMIUM | PREMIUM PAID BY E'EE | PREMIUM PAID BY E'ER | POLICY CASH VALUE | TOTAL PAID BY E'ER | E'EE CASH VALUE | TOTAL PAID BY E'EE | E'EE DEATH BENEFIT | TOTAL DEATH BENEFIT |
|---|---|---|---|---|---|---|---|---|---|
| 55 | 78,438 | 2,070 | 76,368 | 943,996 | 851,381 | 92,615 | 11,437 | 9,858,035 | 10,709,416 |
| 56 | 78,438 | 2,486 | 75,952 | 1,124,749 | 927,333 | 197,416 | 13,923 | 9,943,196 | 10,870,529 |
| 57 | 78,438 | 2,929 | 75,509 | 1,318,303 | 1,002,842 | 315,461 | 16,852 | 10,098,661 | 11,101,503 |
| 58 | 78,438 | 3,489 | 74,949 | 1,525,505 | 1,077,791 | 447,714 | 20,341 | 10,262,970 | 11,340,761 |
| 59 | 78,438 | 4,279 | 74,159 | 1,747,183 | 1,151,950 | 595,233 | 24,620 | 10,437,335 | 11,589,285 |
| 60 | 78,438 | 4,979 | 73,459 | 1,983,202 | 1,225,409 | 757,793 | 29,599 | 10,372,781 | 11,598,190 |
| 61 | 78,438 | 5,892 | 72,546 | 2,235,617 | 1,297,955 | 937,662 | 35,491 | 10,336,617 | 11,634,572 |
| 62 | 78,438 | 6,916 | 71,522 | 2,505,433 | 1,369,477 | 1,135,956 | 42,407 | 10,321,778 | 11,691,255 |
| 63 | 78,438 | 8,160 | 70,278 | 2,793,682 | 1,439,755 | 1,353,927 | 50,567 | 10,329,539 | 11,769,294 |
| 64 | 78,438 | 9,739 | 68,699 | 3,101,486 | 1,508,454 | 1,593,032 | 60,306 | 10,360,503 | 11,868,957 |
| 65 | 78,438 | 11,562 | 66,876 | 3,429,578 | 1,575,330 | 1,854,248 | 71,868 | 10,415,920 | 11,991,250 |
| 66 | 78,438 | 13,749 | 64,689 | 3,779,118 | 1,640,019 | 2,139,099 | 85,617 | 10,495,247 | 12,135,266 |
| 67 | 78,438 | 16,428 | 62,010 | 4,151,006 | 1,702,029 | 2,448,977 | 102,045 | 10,598,998 | 12,301,027 |
| 68 | 78,438 | 19,738 | 58,700 | 4,546,244 | 1,760,729 | 2,785,515 | 121,783 | 10,727,128 | 12,487,857 |
| 69 | 78,438 | 23,717 | 54,721 | 4,965,695 | 1,815,450 | 3,150,245 | 145,500 | 10,879,430 | 12,694,880 |
| 70 | 78,438 | 28,526 | 49,912 | 5,411,156 | 1,865,362 | 3,545,794 | 174,026 | 11,056,753 | 12,922,115 |
| 71 | 78,438 | 34,350 | 44,088 | 5,883,290 | 1,909,450 | 3,973,840 | 208,376 | 11,262,235 | 13,171,685 |
| 72 | 78,438 | 41,625 | 36,813 | 6,382,719 | 1,946,263 | 4,436,456 | 250,001 | 11,498,637 | 13,444,900 |
| 73 | 78,438 | 50,371 | 28,067 | 6,910,182 | 1,974,330 | 4,935,852 | 300,372 | 11,768,900 | 13,743,230 |
| 74 | (1,974,330) | 0 | (1,974,330) | 5,276,365 | 0 | 5,276,365 | 300,372 | 10,487,101 | 10,487,101 |
| 75 | 0 | 0 | 0 | 5,633,828 | 0 | 5,633,828 | 300,372 | 10,602,200 | 10,602,200 |
| 76 | 0 | 0 | 0 | 6,008,990 | 0 | 6,008,990 | 300,372 | 10,741,932 | 10,741,932 |
| 77 | 0 | 0 | 0 | 6,402,369 | 0 | 6,402,369 | 300,372 | 10,906,618 | 10,906,618 |
| 78 | 0 | 0 | 0 | 6,714,803 | 0 | 6,714,803 | 300,372 | 11,095,471 | 11,095,471 |
| 79 | 0 | 0 | 0 | 7,237,122 | 0 | 7,237,122 | 300,372 | 11,308,035 | 11,308,035 |

This escape hatch takes some preplanning. The employee/insured must enter into a valid partnership with his spouse, family member or trust before the rollout. The partnership must be bona fide. For example, the partnership could invest in small amounts of equipment to lease to the corporate sponsor of the split-dollar plan. The partnership as such need have nothing to do with the life insurance policy. It is probably best to establish the partnership before or at the time the split-dollar plan itself is inaugurated. This particular technique avoids the transfer-for-value problem under the literal language of Section 101.

### ■ THE "EASIEST" WAY OUT

Look back earlier in this chapter under "Sole Ownership Method." Under this method the corporation has no policy ownership rights and the third party has sole ownership from the outset. As a result, there is no transfer at rollout.

## The Majority Stockholder Problem

When the insured/employee is also the sole or controlling stockholder of the corporation, there are special problems when the policy is not owned by the insured. In such cases, the ownership—from the thrust of this book—is in a third party (probably a family member or an irrevocable life insurance trust) for only one reason: to keep the insurance proceeds out of the insured's estate (and, of course, his/her spouse's estate).

Well, here's the problem created by Regulation 20.2042-1(c)(6), which is quoted in part:

> "In the case of economic benefits of a life insurance policy on the decedent's life that are reserved to a corporation of which the decedent is the *sole or controlling stockholder*, the corporation's incidents of ownership will not be attributed to the decedent through his stock ownership to the extent the proceeds are payable to the corporation...*if any part of the proceeds of the policy are not payable to or for the benefit of the corporation...*, any incidents of ownership held by the corporation as to that part of the proceeds will be attributed to the decedent through his stock ownership where the decedent is the sole or controlling stockholder..." (emphasis added)

Actually, the regulation has some logic. If the corporation receives the insurance proceeds, then the proceeds would tend to be reflected in the value of the stock held by the decedent/employee and would be taxed in the estate in that way. But proceeds payable to a beneficiary other than the corporation would escape the tax without the pullback as described in the regulations.

### What to Do—Two Things

1. Follow Rev. Rul. 82-145 to the letter. Eliminate the corporation's right to borrow, but it should retain its right to receive its share of the policy proceeds. This should not trigger incidents of ownership in the shareholder/insured.
2. Use the sole ownership method to eliminate any contention of an incident of ownership being attributed to the controlling shareholder. The third party

(most likely an irrevocable trust for the benefit of the insured's family) owns the entire policy. Under this split-dollar plan, the corporation has a mere unsecured right to receive its premium share back. The third party would be the sole owner of the policy.

## Split-Dollar, S Corporation, and Irrevocable Life Insurance Trust

As a general rule, split-dollar plans and S corporations are not a good mix for employee/shareholders. Why? Because the employee can deal effectively with the policy outside the corporate environment by taking S corporation dividends (nontaxable) to pay the premiums personally. This would avoid the double tax created by P.S. 58 costs and avoid the other problems (even though they can be effectively side-stepped) generated by a split-dollar plan.

But wait. Although a split-dollar plan may not fit for an S corporation shareholder/employee for income-tax purposes, the identical arrangement for gift-tax purposes can yield exciting results. This is how it works:

1. The policy is owned by an irrevocable life insurance trust (ILIT) using the sole ownership method.
2. The employer pays the entire premium to the insurance company in the usual way.
3. The employee gifts the annual P.S. 58 costs (or P.S. 38 costs if a second-to-die policy is involved) to the ILIT.
4. The ILIT, in turn, pays the amount received from the employee to the corporation.

### Tax-Savings

The employee, instead of being forced to gift the entire premium cost to the ILIT each year, is only required to give the P.S. 58 costs, which are almost always a much lesser amount. Assuming the availability of annual exclusions (or possibly the unified credit), this plan generates substantially less gift-tax liability, and maybe no gift tax at all.

Thus a split-dollar, S corporation, and ILIT combination provides maximum leverage for gift-tax purposes.

### Keeping Insurance Proceeds Out of Employee Estates

The insurance proceeds can be kept out of the employees' estate by having (1) a QSST or (2) the employee's children own the policies.

1. The third party could also be a "qualified subchapter S trust" (QSST) with the attributes required by Section 1361(d). The QSST would be irrevocable and would be authorized to buy the corporation's stock from the decedent's estate. Here are the results: (a) The insurance proceeds are free of estate taxes. (b) The S corporation is not terminated. (c) The decedent's estate is liquid. Nice!
2. In this scenario, the children pay the P.S. 58 costs to the QSSTs. They must pay with their own money. A gift to the kids and then to the trust does not do the job. Getting the kids some S corporation stock—probably by gift—will provide the kids with a source of income and funds that only need be large enough to pay the P.S. 58 costs.

Since the kids are beneficiaries of the QSSTs (one child per QSST under the rules), there is no gift tax. Why? You can't make a gift to yourself. This arrangement eliminates gift tax altogether.

### Extending the Concept

Now let's go one step further. Everything is the same, except now the children of the employee/insured create the QSST for the benefit of their children (the grandchildren of the employee). The children are the donors and make a gift to the QSST in an amount equal to the P.S. 58 costs. Of course, annual exclusions can be used to reduce or eliminate any taxable gifts.

This scenario has an added bonus: No generation skipping tax (GST). Why? The employee/insured is not the transferor. His kids are. You don't have a generation-skipping transfer unless the beneficiaries are two generations below the transferor. Since here the beneficiaries are only one generation below the transferor, there is no generation-skipping tax.

### An Even More Sophisticated Variation

If you are interested in transferring wealth by generation-skipping, you can transfer substantial wealth by using split-dollar life insurance. Again, if a combination of an irrevocable insurance trust and an insurance policy owned by the trust established under a split-dollar plan is used, the grantor (you) of the trust can gift each year the value of the economic benefit to the trust. This gift is far less than the actual insurance premium for the policy, and thus allows more insurance death protection to be moved into the trust at lower transfer-tax costs. Since the annual gifts to the trust can be protected from GST by allocating your collective (you and your spouse) $1-million GST exemptions to these gifts, you can see that tremendous tax leverage can be provided using this technique.

*This technique can be used in either an S corporation or C corporation situation.* The grantor would be a grandfather or grandmother passing the benefits of the trust to his/her grandchildren, or even younger generations.

Of course, the future generations that could benefit from such an arrangement would be limited by the rule against perpetuities.

## The Economics of P.S. 58 Costs

The following material has nothing to do with taxes. It is pure economics. Since the P.S. 58 costs grow and grow each year, they ultimately become a financial burden. Look at the P.S. 58 Table in the appendix and keep two goals in mind:

1. Keep the P.S. 58 costs as low as possible, and
2. Get rid of the problem as soon as possible.

The first goal can be easily accomplished by making the policy subject to the split-dollar plan a second-to-die policy. Of course, this presupposes that second-to-die insurance fits into your estate plan. The economic benefit flowing each year to the insureds is not the price of one-life annual term insurance, but the actuarial product of assuming that both deaths occur in the same year. For example, these annual rates per $1,000 of protection would be:

| Younger Age | Older Age | | | | | | |
|---|---|---|---|---|---|---|---|
| | 40 | 45 | 50 | 55 | 60 | 65 | 70 |
| 40 | .02 | .03 | .04 | .06 | .09 | .14 | .22 |
| 45 | | .04 | .06 | .09 | .13 | .20 | .31 |
| 50 | | | .09 | .13 | .20 | .30 | .45 |
| 55 | | | | .19 | .29 | .44 | .68 |

Compare them to the P.S. 58 costs. Pretty low, huh? But there's a fly in the ointment. As soon as one of the insureds dies, the P.S. 58 costs apply to the survivor. Ouch! Which brings us to the second goal—get rid of the P.S. 58 costs as soon as possible.

## ■ IMPORTANT

Whether you start out with a single-life or end up with a single-life when one of the insureds dies in a second-to-die split-dollar plan, the second goal should be part of the plan from the inception.

You might want to take another look at Exhibit III, which appears earlier in the chapter, as a reminder of how the rollout works. There must be enough cash surrender value in the policy so that a portion of the CSV can be used to reimburse the corporation for 100 percent of its contribution to the split-dollar plan and still have enough CSV remaining in the policy so future premiums will stay vanished. Put another way, you want to accelerate the growth of the CSV. This can be done in one of three ways:

1. Have the corporation pay heavier premiums (say $13,000 per year instead of $10,000).
2. Have the insured gift an amount each year in excess of the P.S. 58 costs to the irrevocable life insurance trust that owns the policy. The ILIT in turn pays this excess, together with the P.S. 58 costs to the corporation, that, in turn, pays the excess to the insurance company to fatten up the CSV. In one case, for example, an excess of about $4,000 per year over the P.S. 58 costs hastened the rollout from year 26 to year 16. The projected premium would have been just under $16,000 for 26 years.
3. Use a combination of (1) and (2) above.

### A Special Second-to-Die Problem

What happens when the employee/insured dies before the rollout date? Sure, the P.S. 58 costs (the result would be the same if the spouse of the employee/insured died) start to do their expensive damage, in place of the much lower P.S. 38 costs. But there's a bigger problem: It's somewhat unheard of to continue a fringe benefit (like a split-dollar plan) after the insured employee is dead. On the other hand, if the nonemployee spouse dies, at least the split-dollar plan can continue with the surviving employee/insured even though the P.S. 58 costs would now kick in.

Term insurance on the life of the employee, as a means of providing the funds needed to accomplish the rollout, is the perfect answer. There are two ways of accomplishing this protection for the split-dollar plan.

1. The ILIT purchases and owns a term policy on the life of the employee. The trustee would receive the death proceeds if the employee was the first to die. Such proceeds would give the trustee enough funds to repay the corporation for its interest in the split-dollar plan.

   ■ **A VARIATION:** In a variation, the trustee could purchase a permanent-type, single-life policy on each of the insureds. Then, at the first death, the proceeds—together with the CSV of the single life policy on the surviving insured, could be used to complete the rollout.

2. Include the term insurance as part of the split-dollar plan. This would require the ILIT to pay the corporation not only the P.S. 58 costs, but also the cost of the annual premium for the term insurance on the employee's life. Those are the amounts shown in Exhibit IV (a continuation of the Joe and Sue Owner case shown in Exhibits I and II earlier in the chapter) under "net payment" under "Irrevocable Trust." The "Net Payment" under "Employer" includes both the second-to-die premium and the term premium. Exhibit IV is an exact copy—except the names are changed—of what the insurance consultant submitted to me on a split-dollar plan for one of my clients.

Take another look at Exhibit IV. Notice that the premium vanishes in year 14, but that the rollout (assuming Joe Owner and his wife survive) is not planned to take place until year 20.

**EXHIBIT IV**

## 100% WHOLE LIFE
## (EXCEPT TERM ON JOE OWNER TO COMPLETE PLAN)

ASSUMPTIONS

AGE 51M, NON-SMOKER
AGE 52F, NON-SMOKER

1. BOTH INSUREDS LIVING
2. CURRENT DIVIDEND SCALE
3. LIFE EXPECTANCY - 40 YEARS
4. TERM LIFE ON JOE OWNER TO PAY CORP. AND PREMIUMS TO VANISH

## SUMMARY OF COSTS AND BENEFITS SPLIT-DOLLAR USING SECOND-TO-DIE LIFE INSURANCE ABC INSURANCE CO.

| | EMPLOYER | | | IRREVOCABLE TRUST | | |
|---|---|---|---|---|---|---|
| YEAR | NET* PAYMENT | CASH VALUE | DEATH BENEFIT | NET PAYMENT | CASH VALUE | DEATH BENEFIT |
| 1 | $ 15,674 | $ 3,255 | $ 15,674 | $ 326 | 0 | $1,015,809 |
| 5 | 15,444 | 56,657 | 77,835 | 556 | 0 | 1,075,854 |
| 10 | 14,950 | 153,685 | 153,685 | 1,050 | $ 29,740 | 1,210,845 |
| 13 | 14,362 | 197,438 | 192,438 | 1,538 | 85,795 | 1,318,499 |
| 14 | -1,605 | 195,833 | 195,833 | 1,605 | 110,389 | 1,011,965 |
| 15 | -1,852 | 193,981 | 193,981 | 1,852 | 135,553 | 1,012,942 |
| 20 | -183,244 | 0 | 0 | 0 | 274,099 | 1,011,154 |
| 25 | 0 | 0 | 0 | 0 | 392,819 | 1,017,140 |
| 30 | 0 | 0 | 0 | 0 | 551,974 | 1,025,226 |
| 40 | 0 | 0 | 0 | 0 | 1,115,560 | 1,402,791 |
| TOTAL | 0 | 0 | 0 | $24,655 | | |

*Includes cost of insurance in amount needed to terminate split-dollar plan (buy-out corporation's interest)depending on year of Joe's death plus pay future premium obligations at Joe's death if he dies before the 20th year.

# 4 Junk Money ... How to Multiply Your Wealth

This entire chapter is nontechnical.

The material covered in this chapter is a breakthrough in both lifetime planning and estate planning. The concepts presented can save or make you thousands or millions of dollars after taxes. All without risk.

The concepts apply to

- business owners,
- former business owners who have sold their businesses, and
- other taxpayers who never owned a business.

Sorry, but you must be rich (worth in the $3-million range or more) to even think of playing the junk-money game.

## Junk Money Defined

What's junk money? A very nice thing to have. First a simple definition: Junk money is money you own, but never intend nor will ever have a need to spend, no matter how long you live.

Such "money" is not necessarily cash. It is any kind of property that can be loosely defined as wealth and, if necessary, can be turned into spendable cash. Stocks. Bonds. Real estate. Art. Whatever. Put another way, you are liquid now during your life, and your estate would be liquid if you died. Junk money is always income-tax-paid money/property, free of debt and liens; it is never income in respect of a decedent (See Part IX).

Understand that you have plenty of other money (property/wealth) as a cushion that gives you all the income or capital you need to maintain your lifestyle. Enough to protect you from inflation, ill health and the host of life's other uncertainties—real or imagined. Simply put, junk money is extra money. And obviously, the term "junk money" has different meanings to different people; "extra money" to one person might seem essential to another.

### The Three Kinds of Junk Money

There are three kinds of junk money: precious, semi-precious, and pure.

**PRECIOUS JUNK MONEY.** You have some junk money. Although you can't visualize needing or spending it, you need it to produce income to maintain your lifestyle. This income might even fall short a bit, and you'll have to use a bit of the principal. But you'll still have plenty of surplus money when you and your spouse pass on.

**SEMI-PRECIOUS JUNK MONEY.** No question about it, you have plenty of money to provide enough income to meet the requirements of your current lifestyle, even if you and/or your spouse live to be 120. But you and/or your spouse are worrisome types...Maybe interest-income rates will fall? Tax rates may go up? What about inflation? What about ill health—yours?...the children?...the grandchildren? Or other uninsured losses? Maybe you'll just need some more income someday down the road.

**PURE JUNK MONEY.** There's not even a ghost of a chance in a million that you will ever need one more cent of income, or more property, or more wealth. They could devalue the dollar. Go back to the gold standard. You name it. Besides, your wealth is diversified and hedged, with a large portion stashed in safe-haven foreign countries. It doesn't matter what happens to the rest of the financial world. You're safe.

### What Will Happen to Your Junk Money?

Whether your junk money is precious, semi-precious or pure, if you don't spend it or give it away—to your family, others, or charity—the IRS will take 50 to 55 percent of it. Your family only gets half or less. It could have a better destiny.

You're liquid, so insurance should never be considered. Right?...wrong. Let's look at how junk money can be used to increase your already adequate income, to transfer your estate-tax liability to the insurance carrier, to increase gifts to charity, to create additional wealth for your children and grandchildren, and to function as investment capital. *Insurance is the name of this game.*

When you have junk money, you have investment capital (though most people don't know it). Insurance is the investment. A pure investment.

Your profits are guaranteed. You'll see how. Let's start with a simple example and expand it to cover the three types of junk money.

## Examples—Tax Savings and Wealth Building

#### EXAMPLE #1

Joe, who sold his business two years ago for cash, is 64. His wife Sandi is 59. They have an estate worth $5 million. Roughly $1 million of their estate consists of assets they use ("living assets"), such as residential property, automobiles, jewelry, clothing, furnishings, etc. The balance of their estate is in safe, conservative, liquid investments ("investment assets"). The investment assets earn five percent on average after taxes. With the children out of the house and everything paid for, they live comfortably, spending in the $225,000 to $275,000 range per year. They know that they have enough wealth so that they will never spend it all. *What they don't realize is that they own junk money.*

With the help of their accountant, Sandi and Joe have determined that if they live to their life expectancies, they will consume less than $2 million of their investment assets, leaving a balance of more than $2 million. Okay, allow 50 percent as a margin of error. It is still safe to say that they are not likely to use up anywhere near $3 million of their investment assets during the course of their lives. So, conservatively, the balance—more than $1 million—is their junk money.

Doesn't the term "junk money" fit? They will never spend it, and, in the hands of their heirs, it is worth only 50 cents on the dollar. If they are in the 55-percent estate-tax bracket, the government will take 55 cents out of every dollar. And their state of residence probably will take a piece of the action, too. Put another way, their junk money is worth much less than its face value.

■ **OBSERVATION:** The same basic mechanisms come into play using life insurance with a liquid estate as with an illiquid estate. However, the fact that substantial amounts of cash are available in a liquid estate opens up new planning opportunities not so readily available with an illiquid estate. Done right, it is possible to perform three magical tricks:

1. Increase your spendable cash for as long as you live.
2. Freeze—and even reduce or increase (depending on your objectives)—your estate size.
3. And, make the most of the differences between the estate tax and the gift tax.

And how is this magic performed?

| | THE TRICK | HOW IT'S DONE |
|---|---|---|
| 1. | Increase spendable cash. | Purchase an annuity (explained in this chapter). |
| 2. | Freeze/reduce/increase your estate. | Purchase a life insurance policy (explained in this chapter) that is owned by an irrevocable life insurance trust (ILIT) (see Part VII). |
| 3. | Take advantage of the fact that the gift tax is lower than the estate tax. | Don't use a *Crummey* power (see Part VII). |

Before we look at how these tricks (more properly called an *annuity/insurance plan*) are performed in simulated real-life examples for the three types of junk money, we should take a look at an example that comes up often in practice. For lack of a better name, let's call it the "almost junk money scenario."

For the balance of this chapter, all of the examples that follow use the identical fact pattern presented in Example #1, except the amount of the living assets, the investment assets, and the total estate worth are changed. The annual spending range also changes.

## EXAMPLE #2—AN ALMOST JUNK MONEY SCENARIO

Change only these facts in Example #1:

| | |
|---|---|
| Living assets | $900,000 |
| Investment assets | 2,600,000 |
| Total Estate Worth | $3,500,000 |
| Annual (after-tax) spending range | $200,000 plus |

At current interest rates, which keep income low, and current tax rates, which could realistically go higher, Joe and Sandi do not have any junk money. They must dip into their investment assets to maintain their lifestyle.

Suppose Joe (remember he is 64 years old) buys an annuity contract for $1 million that pays him $108,000 (a real quote from a top-rated insurance company) per year before taxes (assume the income tax cost—both federal and state—is exactly 33_ percent) for as long as he lives.

■ **COMMENT:** All of the insurance quotes in this chapter were prepared by Frederick H. Stitt of A.W. Ormiston & Co., Chicago. Even though insurance is Fred's labor of love, the quotes were a tedious, time-consuming job. Thanks, Fred. In your own real-life situation, warns Fred, current quotes from top-rated companies are a must; both the annuity amounts and premium costs can vary widely depending on interest rates and other factors. I concur.

By the way, Fred gave me a little summary after he reviewed this chapter. Here it is, just the way he wrote it:

**"Suppose—**

- ☐ You have $5MM in net worth.
- ☐ You need the income from your assets to maintain your lifestyle; or, you want all the income from your assets as a hedge against unforeseen future circumstances.
- ☐ You resent the fact that your federal estate tax will be about $2MM and that the marginal rate on increase in your net worth will be 55 percent or, if you are successful enough, 60 percent.

**"How would you like a plan that would—**

- ☐ Secure the income from your assets at current or higher levels.
- ☐ Reduce your federal estate tax by $500,000 or more
- ☐ At no net cost to you?"

Here's the tax picture. *For income tax purposes,* a portion of each annuity payment is considered a return of capital (exclusion ratio) and is tax-free. The balance is subject to tax as ordinary income.

Annuitants (like Joe) with annuity-starting-dates after December 31, 1986 cannot recover (tax-free) more than their investment in the contract. After the entire investment has been recovered, all payments are fully taxable. Thus, the exclusion ratio applies only to a limited number of payments. If an annuitant with an annuity starting date after July 1, 1986 dies before recovering his or her entire investment, a deduction for the unrecovered investment is permitted on the annuitant's final tax return.

---

■ **NOTE:** For those of you just dying to know how the $108,000 annual annuity payment is determined, as well as how the 55.48 percent (in the computation that follows) is determined, here's the answer.

*The $108,000.* Look at the figures under "A. Monthly Annuity Amount for Single Premium of $1 Million" on page 183. Find 64 under "Male, Age" in column D—or $8,994. Multiply $8,994 times 12 (for 12 months), which equals $107,928, the annual annuity payment (rounded to $108,000).

*The 55.48 percent.* The general rule is found in Regulations 1.72-9. Table V in the regulations shows what is called an "expected return multiple" (ERM) of 20.8 for age 64 (the same for male or female). Three simple steps bring you to the 55.48 percent—

**STEP #1**

Multiply the annual payment ($108,000 in our case) times the ERM (20.8). This equals a number called the "expected return," or $2,246,400.

**STEP #2**

Compute the exclusion ratio as follows—

$$\frac{\text{Investment in Contract}}{\text{Expected Return}} = \text{Exclusion Ratio}$$

or

$$\frac{\$1{,}000{,}000}{\$2{,}246{,}400} = \$44.52\%$$

**STEP #3**

Subtract the exclusion ratio (44.52%) from 100%, which equals 55.48% (the portion of each payment subject to tax for the first 20.8 years).

NOTE: See Part V, Chapter One, Table 2 for all ages and a more detailed explanation.

---

We are ready to make the first really important computation: The after-tax increase in *spendable cash*. This is how it is done:

1. Annual annuity payment (based on $1 million paid to the insurance company) to be paid to Joe, age 64, for as long as he lives is $108,000.
2. 55.48 percent of each annuity payment under regulations is taxable.
3. $108,000 times 55.48 percent equals $59,918, the taxable amount of annual annuity payments. (The annuity payments could be monthly, quarterly, semi-annually or annually.)
4. Taxable amount of $59,918 times 33_% tax rate (assume federal and state combined) equals $19,973 of taxes.
5. Amount of annuity (from 1. above) $108,000
   Less—taxes (from 4. above) 19,973
   Net cash after taxes $88,027

| | |
|---|---|
| 6. Less—after-tax income earned by Joe before acquiring the annuity (Assume 6% taxable rate of return—probably high in today's investment market; 4% net after taxes (4% X $1 million)) | 40,000 |
| 7. After-tax increase of spendable cash. | $48,027 |

*What about estate taxes?* There are none. Since the annuity has zero value at the instant of Joe's death, there is nothing to include in his estate.

■ **OBVIOUS OBSERVATION:** The annuity is a good deal if Joe enjoys a long life, but a lousy deal if he dies shortly after the annuity is purchased.

How do you protect yourself against the possibility of such a short-term, lousy deal? Insurance, of course. So, Joe creates an irrevocable life insurance trust (ILIT), which buys a $1-million whole life policy on his life. The annual premium is $30,000, payable until Joe dies.

If Joe dies before Sandi, the ILIT will receive $1 million, which the trustee will invest and distribute the income to Sandi. Sandi will use this income and the income from her other investment assets to maintain her lifestyle. If necessary, the principal from her other investment assets will be used. The ILIT principal could be used, but probably not unless all of the other investment assets were first exhausted. Why? The ILIT funds will pass to Joe's and Sandi's children tax-free.

Another option would be to accumulate the income on the $1 million in the ILIT and have Sandi use her other assets (hers and/or those left to her by Joe—probably in a trust). Again, why? Because, although the ILIT income would be subject to income tax that would be paid by the ILIT, the $1 million, plus the after-tax earnings accumulated in the ILIT until Sandi dies, would go to Joe's heirs free of any estate tax.

Let's summarize the results of Joe's and Sandi's annuity/insurance plan:

**ON JOE'S DEATH (OR AFTER SANDI'S DEATH, IF SHE DIES AFTER JOE)**

| | The Usual Way | Using the Annuity/ Insurance Concept |
|---|---|---|
| Amount of assets or insurance proceeds | $1,000,000 | $1,000,000 |
| Less—Estate tax (assuming 50 percent bracket) | 500,000 | ZERO |
| Amount of Wealth to be Left to Joe's and Sandi's Heirs | $ 500,000 | $1,000,000 |

■ **A NOTE OF CAUTION:** Although we are not sure there would be adverse tax consequences, until there is a firm IRS ruling on the subject, it is strongly suggested that you not buy the annuity and the ILIT's insurance policy from the same insurance company.

So you can get an idea of what the annuity amount might be at various ages, as well as the insurance premium cost, here are schedules on $1-million policies at various ages from various top-rated insurance companies.

**A. MONTHLY ANNUITY AMOUNT FOR SINGLE PREMIUM OF $1 MILLION**

| | Insurance Company | | | |
|---|---|---|---|---|
| Male, Age | A | B | C | D |
| 50 | $ 6,725 | $ 6,130 | $ 6,640 | $ 7,206 |
| 55 | 7,141 | 6,555 | 6,960 | 7,655 |
| 60 | 7,737 | 7,120 | 7,420 | 8,284 |
| 64* | 8,428 | 7,740 | 7,940 | 8,994 |
| 65 | 8,638 | 7,930 | 8,100 | 9,208 |
| 70 | 9,977 | 9,090 | 9,070 | 10,541 |
| 75 | 11,965 | 10,660 | 10,480 | 12,471 |
| 80 | 15,001 | 12,810 | - | 15,368 |

Since the variations in premium costs are endless, and our purpose here is to convey a concept rather than select the "best" insurance, we simply used a whole life policy, assumed that the current rate of return for each company would stay constant, and that the premium would vanish in 10 years. All quotes are from top-rated companies.

**B. ANNUAL INSURANCE PREMIUM FOR A $1-MILLION LIFE INSURANCE POLICY**

| Nonsmoking | Insurance Company | | | |
|---|---|---|---|---|
| Nonrated | | | C—for Years | |
| Male, Age | A | B | 1-5 | 6-10 |
| 50 | $ 22,765 | $18,538 | $18,415 | $ 24,815 |
| 55 | 29,205 | 25,400 | 24,375 | 32,825 |
| 60 | 38,125 | 32,300 | 31,215 | 42,005 |
| 64* | 47,155 | 41,000 | 38,115 | 51,265 |
| 65 | 49,695 | 43,300 | 40,195 | 54,065 |
| 70 | 65,885 | 57,300 | 54,105 | 72,725 |
| 75 | 91,875 | 68,000 | 77,645 | 104,305 |
| 80 | 130,395 | ** | ** | ** |

**Joe
**Maximum age is 75

You might select a 10-year pay as shown above, a 20-year pay, a lifetime pay, or any of the endless other pay options.

■ **A FINAL NOTE:** The above does not attempt to cover every variation, option or other creative ways of using the unique concepts presented.

For simplicity, the time value of the funds used to pay the annual premium on the ultimate estate-tax costs is ignored.

The data shown in the above schedules are used in the following examples.

**EXAMPLE #3—A PRECIOUS JUNK MONEY SCENARIO**

| | |
|---|---|
| Change only these facts in Example #1: | |
| Living assets | $1,200,000 |
| Investment assets | 5,000,000 |
| Total Estate Worth | $6,200,000 |
| Annual (after-tax) spendable range | $ 250,000 to<br>$ 300,000 |

Let's look at a likely annuity/insurance plan:

1. A $2-million single premium annuity (same as Example #2 times 2).
2. A $1-million policy on Joe's life (same as Example #2).
3. A $1-million second-to-die policy on the lives of Joe and Sandi.
4. Two separate ILITs: one to hold each of the $1-million policies described in 2) and 3) above.

Following is a schedule showing the premium cost for a second-to-die policy for $1 million. Since the variations in premium costs are endless, and our purpose here is to convey a concept rather than select the "best" insurance, we simply used a whole life policy, assumed that the current rate of return for each company would stay constant, and that the premium would vanish in 10 years. All quotes are from top-rated companies.

| Nonsmoking, nonrated for ages shown male/female | Insurance Company A | B | C |
|---|---|---|---|
| 50/47 | $11,525 | $10,600 | $11,340 |
| 55/52 | 14,495 | 13,800 | 15,260 |
| 60/57 | 18,295 | 18,186 | 20,700 |
| 64/59* | 20,905 | 21,420 | 24,960 |
| 65/62 | 23,445 | 23,520 | 28,340 |
| 70/67 | 34,025 | 32,540 | 39,270 |
| 75/72 | 50,755 | 45,920** | 55,150 |
| 80/77 | 76,405 | 65,960** | 78,310 |

*Joe and Sandi
**Pay for 9 years

Okay, let's pluck the necessary data that apply to Joe and Sandi out of the various schedules.

| | |
|---|---|
| 1. Annual annuity payment based on $2 million (Example #2 annuity of $108,000 times 2) | $216,000 |
| 2. Net after-tax amount (Example #2 amount of $88,027 times 2) | 176,054 |

| | |
|---|---|
| 3. Annual premium cost of insurance | |
| a. $1-million policy on Joe's life (Company B) | $ 41,000 |
| b. $1-million second-to-die policy (Company A) | 20,905 |
| Total Annual Premium Cost | $ 61,905 |

Let's summarize.

**WHILE JOE IS ALIVE**

| | |
|---|---|
| After-tax spendable cash each year is $176,054, less the insurance premiums of $61,905, or net spendable cash of | $114,149 |
| Less-after-tax income before the annuity | 80,000 |
| Increase in Spendable Cash Every Year | $ 34,149 |

**ON JOE'S DEATH (OR AFTER SANDI'S DEATH, IF SHE DIES AFTER JOE)**

| | The Usual Way | Using the Annuity/ Insurance Concept |
|---|---|---|
| Amount of assets or insurance proceeds | $2,000,000 | $2,000,000 |
| Less—Estate tax cost (assuming 50 percent bracket) | 1,000,000 | ZERO |
| After-Tax Wealth | $1,000,000 | $2,000,000 |

**EXAMPLE #4—A SEMI-PRECIOUS JUNK-MONEY SCENARIO**

| | |
|---|---|
| Change only these facts in Example #1: | |
| Living assets | $2,000,000 |
| Investment assets | 8,000,000 |
| Total Estate Worth | $10,000,000 |
| Annual (after-tax) spending range | $350,000 |

This time Joe:

1. Buys a $4-million single-premium annuity, and
2. A $2-million second-to-die policy.

■ **NOTE:** Go back and look at the definition of semi-precious junk money. In this example, Joe and Sandi are more focused on spendable income than the creation of wealth.

Again, let's summarize.

**WHILE JOE IS ALIVE**

| | |
|---|---|
| Annual annuity payment from $4 million annuity | $ 432,000 |
| Less-income taxes (remember, a portion is tax-free as a return of capital) | 79,892 |
| After-tax spendable cash | 352,108 |
| Less—Insurance premium on $2-million second-to-die policy | 41,810 |
| Net spendable cash | 310,298 |
| Less—after-tax income before the annuity (4% times $4 million) | $160,000 |
| Increase in After-Tax Spendable Cash | $150,298 |

**AFTER THE DEATH OF BOTH JOE AND SANDI**

| | |
|---|---|
| Insurance proceeds | $2,000,000 |
| If the $4 million had stayed in the estate, 55% would have gone for estate taxes and 45% to the family, or | 1,800,000 |
| Increase in After-Tax Wealth | $200,000* |

*For simplicity, the after-tax earnings that might have accumulated during Joe and Sandi's life are ignored; so are any state inheritance taxes.

**EXAMPLE #5—A PURE JUNK MONEY SCENARIO**

Change only these facts in Example #1:

| | |
|---|---|
| Living assets | $4,000,000 |
| Investment assets | 46,000,000 |
| Total Estate Worth | $50,000,000 |
| Annual (after-tax) spending range | $1,000,000* |

*Less than Joe's after-tax income from his investments.

This time Joe:

1. Would not purchase an annuity. He doesn't need the income.
2. He purchases several second-to-die policies totaling $24 million.
   a. $12 million in policies with single premiums totaling $1,379,618, and
   b. $12 million in policies with annual premiums of $143,772, payable until the second death. (The insurance premium quotes for this example were provided by Rick Nelson of R. H. Nelson & Associates, Inc., Northbrook, Illinois.)

■ **COMMENT:** "Several" policies (for example, three $4-million policies) are purchased for diversification as explained in Chapter 2 of this Part.

As explained in detail in Chapter 2, Part VII, the above plan as implemented has two smart new moves not yet discussed: (1) using Joe and Sandi's unified credits during their life instead of waiting for their demise, and (2) making gifts that exceed both the unified credits and the annual gift exclusions ($10,000 per donee per year). A simple explanation for the time being is that the effective gift-tax rates are about 2/3 of the effective estate-tax rates.

What are the results of this plan?

**ON JOE'S DEATH (OR AFTER SANDI'S DEATH, IF SHE DIES AFTER JOE)**

| | The Usual Way | Using the Annuity/ Insurance Concept |
|---|---|---|
| Amount of assets or insurance proceeds | $24,000,000 | $24,000,000 |
| Less—Estate tax cost (assuming 55 percent estate tax bracket) | 13,200,000 | ZERO |
| After-tax wealth | $10,800,000 | $24,000,000* |

*Reduced by use of unified credits and payment of any gift taxes.

### And a Final Summary

The concepts presented in this chapter are, in general, only useful if you are in a 50-percent or higher estate-tax bracket. The following rules will help you implement these unique tax-saving and wealth-building concepts.

| | See Example #s |
|---|---|
| 1. You want more after-tax spendable income, and you | |
| a. Do not want to reduce the amount of wealth to be left to your heirs | 4 |
| b. Want to increase the amount of wealth to be left to your heirs | 2,3 |
| 2. You do not need additional income during your life, but would like to substantially increase the wealth to be left to your heirs | 5 |

## ■ WARNING

The concepts presented in this chapter are capable of doing extraordinary tax-saving and wealth-building tricks. My guess is that some professionals will try to offer the material above as written proof that one or more of the examples in the chapter are exactly what you should do.

Don't listen. The examples are only illustrative of the concepts presented. As a result, the facts on which the examples are based were made purposely simplistic. A true professional can utilize the concepts to give you tremendous spendable income and tax advantages (saving you thousands of dollars or creating after-tax wealth measured by millions of dollars).

But the chances of your particular real-life facts matching the assumptions of one of the five examples is slim to none. Your asset mix, objectives, age, insurability, type of insurance, the insurance companies selected and a host of other factors all must be considered to determine exactly how the concepts should be implemented to give you the greatest benefit.

Get the best expert advice you can find. If you are not sure, get a second opinion.

# 5 Other Things You Should Know about Life Insurance

This chapter is nontechnical, but some technical stuff sneaks in.

This chapter is a potpourri of insurance uses, tax-savings ideas, and various combinations that did not seem to fit elsewhere.

## Insurance and Charity

### Insurance Instead of a Cash Gift

Most large gifts to charity are paid in cash—sometimes in a lump sum, sometimes over a period of years.

---

#### ■ EXAMPLE

For example, Pam pledges $200,000 to her favorite charity, Her College, payable $100,000 now and the balance at $20,000 a year for five years, starting next year. Pam can deduct the payments as a charitable contribution (subject to the contribution limits) as the payments are made.

*But think about this:* Suppose Pam buys a life insurance policy on her life (or maybe a second-to-die policy with her husband Sam) with premium payments to be paid exactly as set forth in the example. Maybe this would buy $1 million of insurance, maybe $2 million, more or less, depending on her age (or Sam's age if a second-to-die policy were purchased). Her College could be made the owner of the policy. Or an irrevocable trust could own the policy with Her College named the beneficiary. Pam would still get the same deductions at the same times as before.

But Her College would ultimately get a huge amount of cash far beyond $200,000. Like I said, think about it.

---

### The Charitable Remainder Trust and Life Insurance

Without getting technical, these are the tax goodies a charitable remainder trust delivers:

1. *Income tax deduction.* Your deduction is equal to a percentage of the fair-market value of the property put in the charitable trust. The percentage is based on your age as set forth in government tables.
2. *Capital gains tax.* When the trust sells the property, you are not subject to capital gains tax.
3. *Estate tax.* There is none. The property is out of your estate.

---

#### ■ EXAMPLE

Harry has various investments—stocks, bonds and vacant real estate—that are worth $500,000 but cost only $150,000. The before-tax earnings average $6,000.

Harry sets up a charitable remainder annuity trust that will pay to him or, upon his death, to his wife, Mary, 6 percent of the $500,000 (or $30,000) per year for the rest of his/her life.

Harry and Mary now have two things they did not have before setting up the trust: a one-time charitable deduction and increased annual income.

---

By now you probably know the next step. Harry buys an insurance policy (probably a second-to-die with Mary in the $500,000-range to replace the value of the property put into the trust) using some of the extra cash generated from the charitable deduction and the increased annual income to pay the premiums. The principal is important, not the exact numbers. Harry's age, Mary's age, their health, how much income they want to retain, and other factors will drive the numbers and the exact amount of insurance to be purchased. Also, there are a number of variations on this theme.

### A Variation: Jack and Jill

Let's look at a variation with some estimated numbers and the steps taken to accomplish Jack and Jill's objectives. Jack is a former business owner who traded his company stock for stock of a public company, Big Co., in a tax-free reorganization. Their objectives are to diversify their portfolio of Big Co. stock, which is worth $6 million, and pay the estate tax of an estimated $3.5 million on their total estate of $8 million.

1. Jack transfers $1.5 million of Big Co. stock to a charitable remainder annuity trust. Jack gets a charitable deduction.
2. The trust sells the stock for $1.5 million. No capital gains tax to Jack.
3. Jack receives $105,000 (7 percent of $1.5 million) per year for life, or $71,000 after taxes.
4. Jack creates an irrevocable life insurance trust (ILIT) for the benefit of his children (or grandchildren if his children do not survive).
5. The ILIT buys a $3.5-million second-to-die policy on the lives of Jack and Jill. The premiums are paid with a portion of the cash generated in #1. and #2.

6. When Jack and Jill pass on, the $3.5 million of insurance proceeds will be received by the ILIT tax-free and will offset the estimated estate-tax liability of $3.5 million.

Again, it is the concept that counts. You must run the numbers to fit your particular situation.

## How to Lower Your Insurance Costs

### Blend Term and Cash-Value Coverage

In the October 15, 1991 issue of the *Wall Street Journal*, an article titled "Blended Life Insurance Policies Can Be Boon or Trap for Buyers" gives the essence of this technique (names of insurance companies changed).

> "The blends can be a boon to budget-conscious insurance shoppers who are worried about insurer safety and want to deal only with the biggest, highest rated companies...
>
> "Blends available from companies such as A Insurance Co. and B Insurance Co. have significantly lower sales commissions than those insurers' regular whole-life policies...
>
> "The workings of any mix-and-match policy depend on the proportions of the parts—whole life, term insurance and the less-known 'paid-up additions'...
>
> "Paid-up additions are the key to creating a souped-up alternative to a company's regular whole-life coverage."

The article goes on to explain that the "policies are designed to look like whole life" because the premiums do not change. If all goes according to the plan, as projected, the whole-life component will pay the term premiums. Ultimately, the term will be replaced by whole life. But be careful, because the premiums are not guaranteed.

■ **COMMENT:** Like universal life, a blend might require higher premiums, a longer payment period, or both to prevent the policy from lapsing. Lower interest rates or rising term charges could be the culprit.

### Get a Rebate

It's legal in two states: California and Florida. Elsewhere, it's illegal. An insurance agent in either state can rebate back to you part of the premium you paid. All you have to do is buy the policy in California, or Florida, even if you just flew in for the day.

The agent's rebate is simply part of his/her commission paid by the insurance company.

■ **NOTE:** The rebate may be taxable income. Until the IRS rules otherwise, it's just not clear. Logically, the rebate should simply be considered a reduction (discount) of the premium cost. Put another way, nontaxable.

## The "Wait-and-See" Trust

The big disadvantage of an irrevocable life insurance trust (ILIT) is that it's irrevocable. If the grantor's circumstances change, it's too bad; the trust still cannot be changed. The wait-and-see trust is an alternative. It is especially appealing to younger clients, and clients involved in a second or third marriage, who want the flexibility to modify their estate plans to meet changing circumstances. An example explains how it works.

■ **EXAMPLE**

Jimmy and Tammy (both 30-something) are married with kids. Let's go through the steps of a wait-and-see trust, explaining as we go along.

Step #1. Jimmy is the owner and the beneficiary of a $1-million policy on Tammy's life; Tammy owns and is the beneficiary of a #1-million policy on Jimmy's life (a simple cross-ownership arrangement).

Step #2. Jimmy's contingent/secondary beneficiary is Tammy's credit shelter trust (under Tammy's will or revocable trust). And, of course, Tammy's contingent/secondary beneficiary is Jimmy's credit shelter trust.

■ **COMMENT:** While Jimmy and Tammy are alive, each owns and controls the other's policy and even could borrow on the cash surrender value. They can wait and see if they want to change their policies or any part of their estate plans.

Step #3. Let's say Jimmy dies first. One of his assets is the $1-million policy on Tammy's life. This policy is now owned by Jimmy's credit shelter trust. But there is no tax (up to $600,000 of CSV). If the CSV of the policy is less than $600,000, other assets in the trust can be used to pay future premiums. When Tammy dies and Jimmy's credit shelter trust collects the $1 million, no part of these proceeds are taxable in Tammy's estate because she had no incidents of ownership in the policy.

■ **NOTE:** Also, remember that when Jimmy died, Tammy received $1 million as the primary beneficiary of Jimmy's policy. Tammy receives this $1 million under the usual rules—no income tax, no estate tax.

When a survivorship rider is available, the owner of the policy is guaranteed the right to purchase more insurance (generally up to four times a much). The rider allows the owner to leverage the amount of insurance purchased because the cost of the rider is much less than insuring immediately for a higher amount.

The couple can purchase insurance on each life with, for example, a $200,000 death benefit. After the first spouse dies, the trustee of the credit shelter trust can increase the insurance on the survivor by four times the original amount to $1 million, without the survivor taking a new physical examination.

In addition, the survivor can leave this additional insurance to his or her family without inclusion in his or her estate. No question about it, an alternative for an ILIT.

What if the trustee does not have enough money in the credit shelter trust to pay the additional premiums? The survivor could lend the money to the trust. Remember, the survivor is sure to have the funds, because he/she receives the proceeds from the policy on the deceased spouse's insurance.

### Compared with Second-to-Die

The wait-and-see approach is similar to second-to-die insurance. Both provide insurance coverage at less cost while increasing the amount of insurance on the death of the surviving spouse. But there are differences too: Second-to-die insurance provides no benefit on the death of the first spouse, only the death of the survivor.

**■ COMMENT**

Unquestionably, second-to-die, combined with ILIT, is more appropriate for an older couple. On the other hand, because they may need greater flexibility, the wait-and-see approach usually makes more sense for a younger couple.

## A Cross-Purchase Agreement and Life Insurance

In a cross-purchase agreement the owners (two or more) of a business entity, either a partnership or a corporation, own the life insurance personally as opposed to the insurance being owned by the entity.

**■ EXAMPLE**

Your Co. has fair market value of $1,000,000. There are two equal stockholders, Larry and Mary. Both stockholders have a basis of $100,000 each for stock acquired in 1977. Larry dies under a fully insurance-funded buy-sell agreement.

| Basis results to survivor, Mary, and additional details | If a stock redemption | If a cross-purchase |
|---|---|---|
| Larry's insurance proceeds paid to | Your Co. | Mary |
| Amount of proceeds | $500,000 | $500,000 |
| Larry's stock acquired for $500,000 by | Your Co. | Mary |
| Mary owns 100% of stock with basis of | $100,000 | $600,000 |

The cross-purchase agreement puts Mary in a position to reduce her potential capital gains on a subsequent disposition of all Your Co. stock by approximately $500,000. Also, the insurance proceeds are free from the grasp of corporate creditors and the potential alternative minimum tax.

### Insurance Funding of New Buy-Sell Agreements

A cross-purchase arrangement in most cases is the choice over a stock redemption arrangement when there are only two shareholders or two major shareholders.

One or more additional shareholders may complicate the issue. Also, the transfer for value rules could cause a problem. For example, assume A, B, and C are equal shareholders with s fully insurance-funded cross-purchase buy-sell agreement. C dies. A and B collect the proceeds and complete the transaction as described in the previous example. C's estate owns policies on the lives of A and B. A and B can acquire these policies from C's estate, but if A acquires the policies on B's life while B acquires the policies on A's life, the transfer for value rules make a portion of proceeds (when A or B dies) taxable as ordinary income. The transfer of insurance policies between stockholders is not protected by the exceptions in Section 101(a) (2) (B).

How can the transfer for value rules be avoided in the ABC situation described above? Frequently a partnership or trust with irrevocable beneficiaries is used at the inception of the buy-sell arrangement. The partnership or trust is a party to the agreement and collects, as well as disburses, the insurance proceeds.

### Existing Redemption Buy-Sell Agreements

There are limited ways to convert an existing traditional corporate stock redemption buy-sell agreement (the corporation owns and is the beneficiary of the existing policies) to a cross-purchase arrangement without running afoul of the transfer for value rules. A transfer by a corporation (C) of the policy insuring X's life to Y is not good; a transfer by C to X of his own policy, together with a like transfer to Y, would be fine, but when X and Y then exchange policies, problems arise again. The Section 101 (a) (2) (B) exceptions are not applicable.

If X and Y are insurable, the answer is to obtain new policies, then keep or cancel the old policies as circumstances dictate. Another alternative would be for X and Y to transfer their life insurance policies to a bona fide partnership which would enter into the buy-sell agreement.

## Taxing Corporate-Owned Life Insurance

### Policy Proceeds Payable to Shareholders

The law is clear: The general rule is amounts received under a life insurance contract paid by reason of the death of the insured are not subject to income tax. This general rule clearly applies when a corporation purchases a key-man life insurance policy on one of its shareholder/officers and the proceeds are paid directly to the corporation. But what happens if the beneficiary of the corporate-owned life insurance policy is the insured's family or estate?

Are the proceeds taxable as a dividend? The IRS would like to think so. Here's some law—cases and rulings—pertaining to the subject:

| Case/Ruling | Who Won |
|---|---|
| 1940—Golden, 113 F2d 590 | The IRS* |
| 1959—Dueros, 272 F2d 49 | Our Side ** |
| 1961—Rev. Rul. 61-134 | The IRS* |
| 1975—Est. of Horne, 64 TC 1020 | See Note*** |
| 1981—Ltr. Ruling 8144001 | Our Side** |

*Proceeds taxable as a dividend
**Proceeds not taxable as a dividend
***Proceeds not taxable as a dividend but taxable—subject to estate tax—in the stockholder's estate

■ **WHAT TO DO:** Because the law is not clear, don't take a chance by having the corporation own the policy and pay the premiums, yet name a beneficiary (usually a family member of the stockholder or a trust created by him/her) other than the corporation.

### Alternative Minimum Tax Consequences

An article from my tax column tells the story.

> NEW TAX LAW CAN REDUCE YOUR LIFE INSURANCE COVERAGE
>
> Changing the rules in the middle of the game isn't allowed. Right? Of Course. But not when it comes to Congress and the tax laws.
>
> Let's set the stage for this tax travesty. Millions of life insurance policies were

sold to corporations where the owners and beneficiaries of the policies were the corporation. Most of the policies were sold as keyman insurance (usually insuring the owner/founder of the corporation) or to fund a buy/sell agreement. The insurance consultant assured the policy purchaser that the proceeds, when received, would be tax free. He was right. Neither he, nor anyone else, ever expected the alternative minimum tax (AMT) imposed on life insurance by the Tax Reform Act of 1986.

In general, this AMT was 10 percent of the amount of life insurance proceeds collected. But, starting in 1990, the rate was boosted to 15 percent. Let's understand just how hard this tax law change hits. The premiums your corporation pays on life insurance policies where it is the beneficiary are not deductible, but the proceeds are subject to the AMT.

Even worse, once the corporation has the after-tax AMT proceeds in hand, your heirs can't get the money out of the corporation unless they pay a second tax on the dividend. All the way around, a lousy deal.

No, you can't beat death, but—in this case, by knowing what to do—you can beat taxes. Here's how. Switch to S corporation status. An S corporation is not subject to the AMT when it is the beneficiary of a life insurance policy. If you cannot elect to be an S corporation for some reason, then each stockholder of the corporation should buy the policies on his life from the corporation for its cash surrender value. Such a purchase will eliminate all income taxes on death. An additional transfer to an irrevocable life insurance trust could even eliminate all estate taxes on the proceeds.

Life insurance and how it is taxed is a very complicated area because of the new rules and the many new insurance products that have become available in recent years. It is imperative that all business owners have their insurance portfolios reviewed. It is not the amount of insurance on your life that counts. It is the after-tax dollars your family winds up with that count.

## Second-to-Die Is Oversold—What's Better and When

Yes, second-to-die insurance is a wonderful product. But it is oversold. Why? Because the marital deduction—the reason for and best friend of second-to-die—is not properly used. And the cost in tax dollars can be big. *Let's examine the two circumstances where second-to-die is the conventional wisdom, but a single-life policy may be the better tax-saving approach.*

### Property That Will Not Appreciate

Let's set the scene. Rick, a retired ex-business owner, and his wife Mary are worth $9 million, all in cash-like investments. For simplicity assume a flat 50-percent tax bracket on the entire $9 million. Also, assume that Rick has other assets to cover his unified credit and estate administration costs. Typically, Rick would leave the entire $9 million to Mary under the protection of the marital deduction. At Mary's death, even though the property is still at $9 million, the estate-tax bite is $4.5 million. The children get the other $4.5 million. So what do you normally do? Buy a $4.5 million second-to-die policy (in an ILIT) to cover the estate-tax damage. Good move? Let's see.

Consider this strategy: Instead, buy a single-life policy on Rick for $3 million (in an ILIT for Mary's benefit). At Rick's death, Mary receives the same $9 million tax-free. Mary immediately gifts $6 million to the kids and pays $3 million in gift taxes. No doubt about it, the children get $1.5 million more, the IRS that much less. The key here is that the gift tax is, in effect, one-third less than the estate tax.

What can go wrong? Rick could double-cross us and outlive Mary. This possibility can be covered by using a first-to-die policy instead of a second-to-die policy. Play with the numbers.

### Appreciating Property

Let's use the same scenario as above with just a few changes: Rick is still in business, and the $9 million is growing at the rate of 12 percent a year; also Mary's life expectancy is 12 years more than Rick's (remember women live about eight years longer than men, according to statistics). In those 12 years, the value of the $9 million compounding at 12 percent would grow to $36 million.

*The rule to burn into your memory is that when dealing with fast growth assets, you want to intercept the estate tax as soon as possible*—at the first death (calls for a single-life policy), not at the second death (calls for a second-to-die policy).

Now, applying the rule to our facts, if Rick were to die today, a $4.5-million single-life policy on Rick covers the estate-tax liability. (For simplicity, let's assume immediate death. The same principles under discussion would apply if we were considering the growth of the $9 million for Rick's life expectancy.) By not using the marital deduction, we cut off the growth of the estate-tax liability at Rick's death. In 12 years, it will take an $18-million second-to-die policy to cover the astronomical estate-tax cost. (With Rick dead, Mary has no marital deduction.)

■ **ONE HINT:** You should figure the present value of the difference between the cost of the two policies—single-life vs. second-to-die. Also, in a real-life situation, the other estate-planning tools discussed in this book would not be ignored.

## Variations of the Basic Insurance-to-Create Leverage-ILIT Game

Some of the ideas that follow are mentioned elsewhere in this book. Some are not. But this little herd of concepts is corralled in one place to make sure you understand each concept in whatever form it may be presented. And what follows is but a sampling of the multitude of possible variations. Each idea assumes an ILIT is the owner and beneficiary of the policy and that the proceeds will be income- and estate-tax-free.

**GIFT OF PROPERTY VS. INSURANCE.** A typical owner of a closely held business often gifts say $1 million in cash, real estate, or stock of the corporation (assume none of the property will appreciate) in order to use up his own and his spouse's unified credits. Instead, purchase a $1-million life insurance policy (single-life or second-to-die depending on the circumstances) to be used for the benefit of the surviving spouse or younger family members. The property retained by the ILIT grantor in excess of the premium payments can be used to maintain the grantor's lifestyle. The $1 million in tax-free insurance proceeds, together with the retained property (amount in excess of the premiums), will always exceed the property gift. Work out the numbers.

**INCREASE $10,000 ANNUAL GIFT-TAX EXCLUSION.** Gift $10,000 ($20,000 if married) to each child and have him/her buy a life insurance policy on his/her mom or dad (or a second-to-die policy).

■ **NOTE:** The identical gift to your grandchildren, who buy the policy on their grandparents, beats the generation-skipping tax.

Or make a gift to your children (second generation) who will buy a policy on their lives which will leave even more money to the grandchildren (third generation) because the children are younger than their parents (first generation), and can buy more life insurance for the same premium dollars. This also avoids the generation-skipping tax.

**SALE OF YOUR BUSINESS.** Say your business is worth $50 million; you started with just about zero 35 years ago (substitute your own numbers). You don't want the risk of staying in business any longer. If you sell and live off of the income, your tax picture looks like this:

| | |
|---|---|
| Selling price | $50,000,000 |
| Less-capital gains tax (rounded) | 15,000,000 |
| Balance | 35,000,000 |
| Less-estate tax (rounded) | 18,000,000 |
| Balance to your heirs | $17,000,000 |

Instead work out the numbers doing something like this:

1. Sell. Now you have $35,000,000 after tax.
2. Buy a $50-million policy (single life or second-to-die), more or less, to replace the sold asset (your business in this case). The proceeds, via the ILIT, will go to your heirs and will be used, if necessary, to pay your estate tax on the balance of your estate.
3. You live off of the balance (what is left after premium payments and any required gift tax). Of course, a portion of the balance could be used to buy annuities to increase your lifetime income.

**TURNING YOUR $600,000 EXEMPTION INTO $2 MILLION, MORE OR LESS (DEPENDING ON YOUR AGE).** Generally, I'm not a great fan of an up-front single-premium payment (as opposed to paying premiums over a period of years) for a life insurance policy. But it may be your best bet in certain circumstances or simply your preference. Since none of the other examples in the book has yet used a single-premium concept, let's use it here.

■ **EXAMPLE**

Richie, who is worth $3.5 million (mostly cash or cash-like investments plus a stock portfolio—since selling his business), is concerned that his wife Rosie might not have enough income if he dies first. He has a typical A/B trust estate plan with $600,000 carved out of his assets to go to his credit shelter trust. To replace it, he puts $600,000 into a trust that buys a $2.8-million policy (you determine the number that applies to you) on his life. At Richie's death the trustee will have $2.8 million to invest for Rosie's benefit, instead of a mere $600,000.

■ **NOTE:** This concept works for an estate of any size.

**LIFETIME INSTALLMENT METHOD OF PAYING ESTATE TAXES.** This is a simple variation of the preceding example.

---

■ **EXAMPLE**

Richie is worth the same $3.5 million. This time he would like to pass the entire $3.5 million on to his children and grandchildren, but his tax advisor told him that his estate tax would be $1.2 million. Richie simply buys a $1.2-million policy (second-to-die, of course, with Rosie).

My recommendation in a case like this is for Richie to plan to short-pay the premiums (say 10 years). After the 10 years, if Richie decides he wants more insurance, he can just keep on paying the annual premium. This will cause the estate-tax-free insurance coverage to rise.

Get an illustration (actually two illustrations: one showing the results for the short-pay period; another that continues the annual premium after the short-pay period until death or the policy endows) for your age. This short-pay idea, plus option to stay short-pay or not, gives delightful results.

---

**THE SPECIAL-FOR-TODAY-ONLY SINGLE-PREMIUM SALES PITCH.** The scenario: I'm an IRS guy selling a one-day Washington special. Your estate is worth $40 million. Your tax, if you die today, will be $22 million. Give me a check for $5 million today and I'll give you a receipt stamped "Paid-in-full for the first $40 million of your estate, no matter when you die." (This scenario assumes a $5-million single premium will buy $22 million of insurance for your ILIT.)

If the concept strikes you, get a run of the numbers for your situation. Include a short-pay (say 10 years) illustration and a long-pay illustration.

## Old Policies and New Policies—The Children as Owners

**ARRANGE FOR POSSIBLE GIFT OF OLD POLICIES TO A TRUST OR THE CHILDREN.** The tax consequences and possible savings change, depending on who owns the insurance (usually on the husband's life)—the husband, the children or a trust. If the after-tax results are better if the children own the policy, then make a gift of the policy.

---

■ **PLANNING POINTER:** Do not make the gift until your advisor has computed the estate-tax impact on both the husband's estate and the wife's estate; determine the impact if the husband dies first.

When the arithmetic proves that the insured should not own the policy, consider giving the policy to another family member.

---

### New Policies

**USE THE CASH SURRENDER VALUE OF OLD POLICIES TO BUY NEW POLICIES.** Often, increased insurance needs can be satisfied without any, or only a small, additional dollar outlay. Determine the cash surrender value available from existing policies. Then get a complete new set of proposals. The new insurance products developed in recent years usually produce greater coverage at a reduced cost.

**THE CHILDREN OR A TRUST AS OWNER.** Have the children or a trust be the designated applicant and the beneficiary. They should be the applicant when the policy is purchased.

---

**■ A TRAP TO AVOID**

If the wife owns the policy on her husband's life, but someone else is the beneficiary (usually the children), a problem arises. Since the wife as owner has the right to designate the beneficiary, she is considered to have made a taxable gift to the actual beneficiary at the instant of her husband's death. At that instant, the gift is completed, because the right to change the beneficiaries has terminated. Also, since the gift is considered made at the time of the husband's death, the gift-splitting provisions are no longer available. Gifts may be split only if both spouses are alive at the time of the gift. Another variation is just as much of a trap: If the wife has the power to revoke the trust, the gift of the policy is not complete until the husband's death, when her power to revoke the trust terminates, and the policy proceeds measure the gift.

---

Each child may be given the policy directly, that is, if he or she is old enough and can safely be entrusted with the responsibility. The proceeds will go directly to the child as owner. If necessary, one policy might be divided into several smaller policies. Thus each child, as a separate beneficiary, can do as he/she likes with his/her share of the proceeds. It might be more economical to give a single policy to multiple donees who become equal owner/beneficiaries.

Use an irrevocable trust (or a separate irrevocable trust for each child) with an independent trustee. If the trust is not irrevocable, the gift-tax objectives are not effective. Only the CSV (less loans) need be considered at the time the irrevocable trust is created.

---

**■ PLANNING POINTERS:** Consider giving the wife the policy during her life by way of a revocable trust (with the wife as trustee), which becomes irrevocable upon either her death (at her death, the policy should fund her credit shelter trust) or her husband's death. Instead of the children becoming the beneficiaries of the trust if the husband dies first, the trust (now under the guidance of an independent trustee) will be residuary (or Q-Tip) type trust, primarily for the benefit of the wife. Also, such a trust can be used to avoid the policy going back into the husband's estate if the wife dies first.

---

And finally, here's a simple summary from my tax column that tells the kids-should-own-the-policy story.

> MORE INSURANCE DOLLARS FOR YOUR FAMILY—LESS FOR THE IRS
>
> There's an old cliché about death and taxes. Death may be certain, but death taxes can sometimes be avoided in whole or in part. More often than not, I see a family's death taxes overpaid by astounding amounts because life insurance was mishandled.
>
> First, some basics. If you own a life insurance policy on your life, the proceeds at death are includable in your estate. That means the IRS can collect up to 55 percent for estate taxes. So for every $100,000 of insurance you own, it's possible that the government can wind up with $55,000 and your family with only $45,000. Suppose a husband makes his wife the beneficiary of a $100,000 policy. The proceeds escape tax at the husband's death because of the marital deduction. Simply put, this deduction allows property to pass from one spouse to the other free of the estate tax. So far so good. But what happens when the surviving spouse (assume the wife) dies? She gets nailed for the estate tax. When there are children, the estate of the last to die (either Mom or Dad) almost always goes to the kids.
>
> Think about this. If the kids had owned the insurance policy in the first place, then it would not have been in either Mom or Dad's estate. The savings on each $100,000 of insurance can be as much as $55,000. One easy way to accomplish this huge tax savings is to gift the insurance policy to the kids, who then become the policy owners as well as the beneficiaries. This is easy to do. Your insurance company will supply the forms. There is an urgency to making the gift. Why? Because the policy owner and insured who makes the gift must survive for a full three years after the gift is completed. Sorry, but if you don't make the three-year period, the insurance proceeds are swept back into your estate.

# PART VI

# Low-Load Insurance vs. Traditional Insurance

# VI INTRODUCTION

## A Developing Story

Some 30 years ago, my back went bad. So I went to the doctor. Well, doctors. Not just any doctors. But orthopedic specialists. After about five years of hospital stays, physical therapy, special exercises, braces and other prescribed treatments, MY BACK STILL HURT. Pain! My athletic career had become sporadic.

What to do? Chiropractors? No. Conventional wisdom said "forget 'em." I went anyway. My back has been fine ever since. Sure, sometimes it goes out. It hurts. But I'm pain-free most of the time. And oh yes, I'm still banging away at tennis balls. Once a week or more.

Why am I telling you this? Because I think we are now engaged in a professional battle that is almost identical. But instead of the organized medical profession battling chiropractors, we have the traditional insurance industry battling the low-load guys.

My purpose in this part of the book is not to take sides, but to open up the subject in order to inform the insurance buyer and my clients that there is a choice.

Of course, just opening up the subject will be enough to have some traditionalists crawling up and down my back. My defense in advance is simple—I have always been a fan of life insurance and I still am. This book supports that fact.

Low-load life insurance is the new kid on the block. It's available. Like chiropractors, it looks like the low-load people are here to stay.

The life insurance products to be bought and who sells them will, as always, be determined by the marketplace. Not me. My job is to let people know what is available.

# 1 The Low-Load Insurance Story

This chapter is easy reading.

## What Others Say

When serving my clients who need insurance products, my client is always at the center of the stage. How others may label certain insurance consultants or companies that are a part of the insurance industry is not my concern. Nor do I think my opinion would or should carry any weight.

So let's turn to what others say. In the June 1992 issue of *Money*, in an article titled "Pssst! Secret Ways to Cut Life Insurance Costs," Walter L. Updegrave said (only the names of the insurance companies are changed):

> "You pay the biggest commissions on whole life, universal life and variable life policies, which link insurance protection with savings accounts known as cash value. The commissions on these policies generally run five times higher than those on term policies...
>
> "With a typical cash-value policy, your agent keeps 55% to 80% of the first year's premium; the company takes another 20% to 45% to cover its other selling expenses. In the second through 10th years, the agent usually siphons off 5% or more of your premiums.
>
> "You don't have to accept such exorbitant fees, though...
>
> BUY LOW-LOAD INSURANCE
>
> "Ten insurance companies, double the number of 1990, employ either salaried telephone representatives or financial consultants who collect only modest commissions or fees for selling policies. Generally, sales fees on these low-load policies amount to roughly 10% to 20% of your first year's premium and 2% or so of subsequent premiums. Most low-load companies are relatively small; the largest, Company A, has $4.4 billion in assets, compared with $38.1 billion

> for a behemoth like Company Z. And some aren't licensed to sell insurance in every state. Nevertheless, most of the 10 discount insurers earn high grades for financial soundness from major ratings companies A.M. Best, Moody's Investors Service and Standard & Poor's. Among the highest rated are (five companies are named). All get A+ grades from A.M. Best, for example."

In the July 13, 1992 issue of *Newsweek,* in an article titled "Buyers Beware," Jane Bryant Quinn said:

> *"Buy low-load (low sales charge) insurance from a company that sells by phone.* It's your best move. Lifetime expenses are a fifth of those on regular policies, which lets you build cash value faster.
>
> *"If you need a customized cash-value policy, buy from a discounter, a low-load agent or an adviser who takes fees in lieu of commissions."*

## What Was Said to Congress

An insurance consultant who sells low-load insurance testified on the subject before the House Committee on the Judiciary on June 13, 1991. Here are excerpts from his prepared testimony:

> "I also learned that most of the leading life insurance companies had developed discount policies which paid a lower commission to the selling agent with the commission savings translating into either a lower premium or greater cash value to the consumer. These discount policies were filed with the state insurance departments for purchase in amounts of $50,000 or $100,000 but as I learned later...agents were discouraged from selling them when not in multi-million dollar amounts.
>
> "I developed a marketing plan to expand my business and serve more consumers. I called myself a `discount life insurance broker' and developed advertisements to inform consumers of the services that could be provided. The ads never included the name of any insurance company...The consumer should decide how much life insurance to buy, what kind and compare the relative cost of similar life insurance policies (copy of guide included). I added to this the idea of lower commissions with discount policies...
>
> "And how did the insurance companies react to me selling th*eir* discount policies to the consumer? My agreements to sell the policies...were canceled...
>
> "In my experience, comparison shopping, and discount policies reduce the cost of life insurance about 20%"

■ **COMMENT:** You can see that the battle lines between low-load insurance consultants and the insurance industry are drawn. The battle is theirs. Not mine. Not yours. I only think it is important to know that the battle exists. Why? Because it has an impact on the insurance products you can buy and from whom. And at what cost.

■ **OBSERVATION:** Unquestionably, the abovementioned testimony on low-load insurance as well as the testimony that follows represent particular points of view. In updates to this book, I will work in other perspectives, as appropriate.

This testimony was given before the U.S. Senate Committee on the Judiciary, June 23, 1992 (names of insurance companies have been changed):

"No one questions the importance of life insurance as a financial tool to protect against the risk of premature death. Consumers recognize the value of life insurance by purchasing more than 13 MILLION new individual life insurance policies last year with first year annual premiums exceeding $10 BILLION. Congress has also acknowledged the importance of this type of insurance by affording the product special tax treatment that is advantageous and enjoyed by no other financial vehicle under the U.S. Tax Code.

"...the life insurance business has developed a dual pricing arrangement based on the most regressive principle of economic discrimination. The very wealthy and executives of FORTUNE 500 companies are courted with the offer of lower cost life insurance while the average consumer pays 20% or more [additional] for the same coverage from the same insurance companies.

"Most of the leading life insurance companies now offer two or more prices for the same amount and type of life insurance. The agent is given a menu of A & B policies from each company. The A's have a full price and the agent receives a full commission or the agent can offer the company's B policy with a cost savings of 20% or more to the consumer and the agent receives a lower commission. The method of obtaining the lower cost quotes varies from company to company. Company V allows the agent to design the price of the policy on his or her computer screen with an input window for the percentage of premium that pays the agent a commission. Company W gives the agent a choice between a full price, full commission policy or designing a lower cost policy by blending or mixing premiums that pay a full commission with premiums that pay little or no commission. The ratio of the mix determines the price to the consumer. Company X recently informed me that they are developing a new life insurance product with 10 different prices for the same type of life insurance varying by the level of commission...

"The act of creating a dual pricing structure for its products was a conscious act by the life insurance companies since they had to file the policies for approval with the various state Insurance Departments and disseminate the rates and product information to the agents."

## What a Low-Load Insurance Consultant Says

HOW TO SAVE MONEY WITH A DISCOUNT LIFE INSURANCE BROKER

"Most life insurance is sold to the consumer in today's marketplace. The agent plays a multitude of roles in this process and a substantial amount of effort is directed towards planning. Retirement planning, estate planning, and financial planning are just some of the services that most agents use as their vehicle to sell life insurance. The planning is provided for free and the life insurance is recommended as one of the financial products that needs to be purchased to complete the planning process. The agent is then compensated for the planning services from the commissions generated by the life insurance sale.

"But what happens if you have accountants and attorneys already handling your planning and during the course of their work the purchase of life insurance is recommended? In that situation, you move from someone being sold to a buyer. Now that you are a buyer of life insurance, two facts will become evident. The first deals with the cost for planning services and dictates that since you are already paying your accountant for the planning services, you don't want to pay the insurance agent for the same function. Simply, you want to avoid being charged twice for the planning. The second fact is that as you move towards being a buyer, the price of the life insurance becomes a more important issue. Under the first scenario where the agent is supplying the planning service and is compensated in the sale of the life insurance, the price of the planning service is bundled with the price of the insurance policy. Now that you are a buyer you are more interested in segregating the cost for planning services from the cost of acquiring or buying the policy. This will lead you to focus more on price and introduces a new set of challenges for the buyer.

"These challenges can be best illustrated by a recent case which involved our firm. One of the nation's largest investment banking firms was interested in buying two $16-million life insurance policies on a husband and wife. The couple were in their early 60's and the investment banking firm was entering into a very complex financial deal with the two. Their financial arrangements would cause a substantial liability to the firm when each of the spouses died and life insurance was determined to be the best financial product to fund the liability. I, along with another agent, were invited to submit quotes on the life insurance. Particulars about the insured's age and health status were provided to each of us along with financial criteria for selection of the insurance companies.

"The general counsel from the investment banking firm called me after receiving all of the quotes. He gave me the bad news that my quotes were not the lowest and added insult to injury by saying that my premiums were over $250,000 higher than [those of] my competitors for the same coverage. For most consumers and agents, the matter would have ended with the sale going to my competitor and the client assuming they saved more than $250,000 in annual premiums. However, I had quoted all of the leading insurance companies and knew that my quotes could not possibly be that far off the mark. I also knew that the general counsel was a very astute attorney, but did not know how to buy life insurance. I asked the attorney how many years of coverage were illustrated on the winning quotes. He responded that premiums, cash values, and death benefits were shown for 20 years (20 years of values is all that is required to be illustrated under most state laws). I suspected why my quotes appeared high and to spring the trap I asked the general counsel to request that the other agent submit the same insurance company's quotes, but illustrate values for more than 20 years.

"A week later the general counsel called back after reviewing the revised quotes and confirmed my suspicions. The coverage ended after 20 years. The competing agent had quoted a universal life policy which provided $32 million of life insurance coverage for 20 years and none thereafter.

"The general counsel was not amused by the revelation and questioned why there weren't more safeguards or disclosure requirements when buying life insurance. After all, he dealt with the SEC and NASD on a daily basis concerning these same issues on investment products. He explained that when selling an investment, great lengths are taken to try and level the playing field when comparing types of products. There is also much more emphasis on the contractual guarantees and risks associated with the product.

"The same rules do not apply to life insurance, and that causes life insurance buyers to be confronted with two challenges. First, there are very few rules restricting how the life insurance policy can be illustrated so a buyer-beware atmosphere is created. Secondly, most consumers are not given enough information to make an informed purchase and the burden is placed on the consumer to ask the right questions.

"You can remedy this situation and become an informed buyer by following a few simple rules.

1. Get the financial ratings for each insurance company from all the leading rating agencies, which include A.M. Best, Standard & Poor's, Moody's, Duff & Phelps, and Weiss Research. Remember that ratings are just opinions of financial strength and strong ratings are not a guarantee that the company's products are low cost. They are also just opinions, which might change over time, but it is the best place to start your search.
2. Comparison shop among the leading insurance companies for the type and amount of coverage you plan to buy. Costs for the same type and amount of life insurance vary by 100% among the leading companies, so comparison shopping is a must.
3. Get all the quotes in writing and make sure the illustrated values are shown to age 95 or 100.
4. Have all quotes recalculated assuming credited interest rates are reduced 1% or 2%.
5. Consider using a discount broker to further increase your savings.

"Life insurance is a financial product that will be sold to most consumers and bought by a few. If you invest a little time to become familiar with the product, organize the quotes for an apples-to-apples comparison, and exercise the same good judgement used to purchase other goods and services, the savings can be substantial."

■ **OBSERVATION:** The low-load portion of the insurance industry is tiny at this writing. Only a handful of insurance companies sell low-load products. And the number of insurance consultants who specialize in selling low-load insurance is still slim.

■ **A CAUTION:** Low-load policies can be a scam product offered by weak insurance companies. Do your due diligence (see Part V, Chapter Two).

The choice of products, knowledge, size and strength of the companies selling traditional insurance products is overwhelming today. So, no doubt, the traditional companies and the consultants who represent them are and will continue to be on my long list.

But I intend to keep an open mind as far as low-load insurance is concerned. There are more choices if you want to lower your insurance costs. Make sure you read the material in Part V, Chapter 5, under "How to Lower Your Insurance Cost."

### A Final Comment

Remember—I'd like to hear from any interested parties with points of view on the material presented in this chapter.

# PART VII

# The Irrevocable Life Insurance Trust

# VII INTRODUCTION

## The Super Trust...Saves Taxes, Creates Wealth

*True or False: Two Things You Can Always Be Sure of—Death and Taxes*

False! Death, yes. Taxes, no. So let's make an assumption. When death comes, you will owe lots of taxes. Estate taxes, that is. Unless you plan well, the tax collectors will receive more of your estate than your heirs.

This is actually a happy part of this book. After your death and after all the smoke clears, using what you will learn in this part, here are the results:

1. The insurance company sells you insurance.
2. You transfer your estate tax liability to the insurance company.
3. The IRS gets its taxes.
4. And you arrange it all so your heirs get your wealth without paying, in effect, one dime of estate taxes.

If you are insurable, it's a slam dunk. If you are not, we probably can use someone else, whose life is insurable, to get the job done.

At best, you will learn how to eliminate all estate taxes. At worst, you will learn how to mushroom your after-tax wealth. How is it all done? With a super trust with the not-so-fancy name of "Irrevocable Life Insurance Trust."

Most of the material in the part that follows is, of necessity, technical. It's intended for your professional. If you want to skip the *how to* parts and get right to the *results*, just read Part VII, Chapter 1, and the last pages of Part VII, Chapter 2, starting at "Funding the ILIT."

You'll love it. I guarantee it.

1

# How to Lower Your Estate Tax Cost to 7.28 Percent ... or Less

This very short chapter tells the *irrevocable life insurance trust* story in an easy-to-read fashion. It is a quick fix, intended for the nonprofessional. Actually, it is an exact copy of an article that originally appeared in my tax column.

HOW TO LOWER YOUR ESTATE TAX COST TO 7.28 PERCENT...OR LESS

Do you think $1 million is a lot of money? How much must you earn to leave your family $1 million?...Roughly $3 million. Try this: You make $3 million. Income taxes take one-third (or $1 million) and the remaining $2 million gets halved for estate tax purposes. Some deal: The IRS gets $2 for every $1 your family keeps. Is there any way to beat this tax confiscatory game? Yes! This article shows you how.

This tax magic act requires two tricks working in tandem: First, generate income free of the income tax and, second, pass this income to your heirs free of the estate tax. And that's exactly what I set up when called in to give a second opinion on a family business transfer plan near Buffalo, New York.

The business owner, Joe, is 62 years old. His wife, Mary, is 56. Joe and Mary's estates, after both are gone, will be left to their two sons, John and Jack. The estate tax liability is estimated at $2 million. Now, the first trick. Buy a *$2-million second-to-die* life insurance policy. These policies do not pay off until the second insured dies. The premiums for this type of policy are remarkably low, and will vanish in 10 years (not even one cent more in premium payments) based on an 8 percent dividend scale. For Joe and Mary (premium cost is obviously determined by your ages and health) the premium cost—to the insurance company—will be $32,366 per year. Joe elected the 10-year payment schedule because it suited his budget. He could have elected to have the premiums vanish sooner (causing higher premiums) or later (more than 10 years or even for life, reducing the annual premium cost). Okay, after 10 years Joe and Mary will have paid in $323,660 (10 X $32,366). Then what happens? The earnings on the cash surrender value will pay all future premiums for year number 11 and each year thereafter.

Now, watch this: The proceeds of a life insurance policy ($2 million in this case) are *tax-free income* under the Internal Revenue Code. End of trick number one.

There are two basic ways to do trick number two. But first, let me assure you that if you own the life insurance on your life, the IRS will collect *estate tax* on the proceeds, unless the proceeds are left to your spouse. When the second of Joe and Mary goes to the big business in the sky, there will be no spouse alive to receive the insurance estate tax free. And second, let me tell you, if the proceeds are paid to the kids—John and Jack—the IRS will get their pound of estate tax flesh. What to do? Now the trick. Give the policy away. One way is to have the policy owned by an irrevocable life insurance trust. I like to call them *super trusts*. Joe elected to do a simple version of the trick—have John and Jack each own $1 million of the policies from inception. Since neither Joe nor Mary will own the policies at their deaths, the boys will get the entire $2 million estate tax free.

To sum up, $323,660, plus the cost of money on this account, paid at the rate of only $32,366 per year for 10 years will do the work of earning $6,666,666 for Joe. Some trick! Oh yes, in Joe's case, that lowers his estate tax cost from 55 percent to 7.28 percent. (You see, $4,444,444 is left after $2,222,222 in income tax on the $6,666,666. Now, watch again—55 percent times the $4,444,444 for estate taxes robs Joe's family of another $2,444,444, leaving $2 million. The exact amount of the insurance! Yes sir, 7.28 percent of $4,444,444 equals $323,660. The exact amount of the insurance cost!)

By the way, if either Joe or Mary make it to age 95, the policy will pay John and Jack a total of $3,142,234 tax free. That's right. Not one cent of income tax or estate tax. Now here's your challenge...figure your reduced estate tax percentage. Check with a competent professional to see how nicely the numbers work in your case.

2

# The Irrevocable Life Insurance Trust: The Cornerstone of Life Insurance as an Estate Tax Killer or Wealth Multiplier

This chapter is interspersed with technical and nontechnical material.

## A Plan to Eliminate the Estate Tax, Create Wealth, or Both

Wouldn't it be nice if a taxpayer could—in effect—completely bypass the tax collector? For example, if a taxpayer had enough life insurance to pay his estate tax, and the life insurance was not taxable to him, his estate, or his spouse's estate, wouldn't he, in effect, be getting a pass on the estate tax? Of course! This chapter explains how to accomplish this tax-planning maneuver legally, by properly using an irrevocable life insurance trust (ILIT), sometimes called a *super trust*.

What else can an ILIT do? Create wealth. Keep reading.

## A Super Trust

A super trust is an irrevocable trust that owns life insurance and is the beneficiary of the policy it owns. Sometimes, the trust does not own the policy, but is only the beneficiary. For example, the trust might be the beneficiary of a group term insurance policy provided by the employer.

The basic operation and results of a super trust are very simple. During the life of the insured (assume You), the trust, as the policy owner, handles the policy in the same manner as you would if you owned it—for example, it pays premiums and interest on policy loans. The ILIT can also borrow the cash surrender value, if necessary.

On your death, the trustee of the super trust, as the beneficiary, collects the insurance proceeds. The trustee uses these proceeds as directed by the terms of the trust document. These terms usually provide for a mirror-like reflection of the residuary trust of your will—for example, the use of the income, and principal if necessary, for the care, support, and maintenance of your spouse, and on his/her death, the use of the trust for the benefit of your children.

### The Purpose of a Super Trust

The principal purpose of a super trust is the elimination of federal estate tax on the proceeds of one or more insurance policies on the life of a husband, or wife, or single individual. If the policy is owned by an ILIT, under most circumstances, the proceeds are not includable in the estate of the deceased.

---

## ■ EXAMPLE

Joe set up his estate so that most of his assets, which are protected from the estate tax by the marital deduction, go to his wife. But Joe wants the rest of his estate (about $2,600,000) to go to his son Jeff and Jeff's children. Jeff is already a successful businessman so Joe does not want Jeff's estate unnecessarily increased, but would like to have his estate assets available to Jeff if needed. With an ILIT, Joe can set up a generation-skipping provision. Result: (1) Joe leaves the ILIT assets to his grandchildren; (2) Jeff is provided for should the need arise; and (3) no estate tax is due on the ILIT assets when Joe and Jeff die.

How is the ILIT funded and for how much? The ILIT purchases a life insurance policy equal to the estate tax on the $2,600,000. Joe gifts the premium costs as needed to the trust, which is the beneficiary of the policy. On Joe's death, the trustee collects the policy proceeds and the trust begins to perform the three results listed in the preceding paragraph. When all the smoke clears after Joe and Jeff have passed on, Joe's $2,600,000 estate has transferred its estate tax liability to the insurance company. At what cost? The cost of the premiums.

What about the generation-skipping feature? The generation-skipping tax (see Chapter 1, Part VIII, which comes into play when transfers are made to grandchildren by skipping the children, has exceptions. One of the exceptions is for amounts covered by the gift tax exclusion (Section 2611(a)(1)) So Joe keeps his annual gifts to the ILIT under $20,000 and avoids (1) gift taxes, (2) generation-skipping tax, and (3) estate tax.

---

### The Pyramiding Problem

In addition, the super trust solves the pyramiding problem. Suppose your estate tax bracket is 50 percent and your anticipated estate tax liability is $1 million. You buy $1 million worth of insurance to pay the tax. But since the $1 million is includable in your estate, you have created a new and additional $500,000 estate tax liability. (Assume that you will be unmarried at the time of death.) More insurance? Logic dictates that each additional insurance purchase would only cut the problem in half. As each additional policy pyramids, the problem gets smaller. But with the tax collector a 50-percent partner in the estate-protection-insurance venture, buying more insurance is an extremely questionable approach.

### How Much Can Be Saved?

Since there is no limit to the amount of life insurance that can be owned by an ILIT, there is no limit on the amount of estate taxes that can be saved. The actual tax savings depends on your estate tax bracket. For example, if your estate is likely to be in a 50-percent bracket, a tax savings of 50 cents out of every $1 of life insurance proceeds can be achieved by using an ILIT.

Can you pass all of the assets you own at death to your family without any reduction for estate taxes? Yes, if the ILIT owns enough life insurance to cover the entire estate tax liability.

**ESTATE LESS THAN $600,000.** If the combined estates (including life insurance proceeds) of the husband and wife are likely to be less than $1,200,000, the use of an ILIT may not be necessary. Why? Assume the husband is the insured. If the wife survives him, a proper estate plan will eliminate all estate taxes.

However, if the wife is the first to die, only $600,000 can be protected from estate taxes when the husband dies. In this case, the ILIT would save estate taxes on any life insurance included in an estate of more than $600,000.

■ **PLANNING POINTER:** An ILIT makes sense if either spouse's estate will exceed $600,000 including life insurance.

**ESTATE MORE THAN $600,000.** If either spouse dies with a taxable estate that includes life insurance, the life insurance is taxed, in effect, at the highest bracket of that particular estate. If the unlimited marital deduction is used to escape the estate tax on the death of the first spouse, the decedent's family has won only a temporary victory, but the tax collector will get the tax when the second spouse dies.

For simplicity, assume both the husband and wife are in a 50-percent estate tax bracket. Obviously, every dollar of life insurance proceeds diverted to an ILIT will ultimately save 50 cents in estate taxes.

**WHAT ARE THE POTENTIAL ESTATE-TAX SAVINGS?** Determine how much the insurance proceeds will cost in estate taxes (1) if the husband dies first and (2) if the wife dies first. That number is the potential estate tax savings if an ILIT is used. Also, consider funding the ILIT with a "last-to-die" life insurance policy.

## Planning a Tax Shelter for Wealth

Tax shelters are usually associated with saving income tax. However, a super trust is the perfect tax shelter for accumulating wealth. In order to use the super trust to shelter wealth most effectively, you must:

1. Develop an overall plan to reduce the anticipated estate tax liability as much as possible.
2. Determine the estimated estate tax liability.
3. Obtain life insurance coverage equal to the estimated amount of your estate tax liability. Keep the insurance proceeds out of your estate (and your spouse's estate) by using an ILIT.
4. Pass all the assets in the combined estates of you and your spouse to family (usually your children) without any reduction due to estate taxes.

The following is a summary of the tax results, which are explained in greater detail later in this chapter.

### An Income and Gift Tax Shelter During Life

**INCOME TAX.** Depending on your circumstances (consumer interest is not deductible), you may or may not be able to get an interest deduction on your personal tax return for the cost of interest on loans used to fund the trust.

**GIFT TAX.** Initially, you transfer the policy to the trust, or the trust purchases a new policy. Each year, you make a gift to the trust for the amount of any necessary premiums and interest. When properly done, gift tax consequences can be avoided.

### An Estate Tax Shelter at Death

**YOUR ESTATE.** If you live for three years following the transfer of a policy to the trust, the proceeds of the policy will not be included in your estate. According to some commentators, a policy originally purchased by the trust is not subject to the three-year rule and will not be included in the estate. However, the IRS may attack (see *Kurilark Estate*, 82 TC 4 (1984)). In any event, after three years the proceeds are safe from inclusion in the estate.

**YOUR SPOUSE'S ESTATE.** The proceeds will not be included in your spouse's estate either. A super trust avoids estate tax in both a husband's and wife's estates. No matter who dies first, the result is the same—no estate tax on the insurance proceeds.

Expertise is required, however. Only a properly drafted trust document followed by a number of complex specific procedural steps can accomplish all of the tax goals.

---

**■ CAUTION: AN ILIT IS NOT FOR EVERYONE**

Generally, an ILIT should not be used unless at least $100,000 of life insurance is involved. For this reason, young couples should usually delay implementing an ILIT until the needs of their children and their business or careers are reasonably well defined.

The current estate tax rules, because of the marital-deduction, generally make an ILIT unnecessary for married persons with estates of $1 million ($600,000, if single) or less. Proper estate planning eliminates all estate taxes for both husband and wife (no matter who dies first) when their combined estates (including anticipated life insurance proceeds) will be $1,200,000 or less.

---

## Life Insurance, Estate Planning, and the Super Trust

### The Policy Owner

When life insurance is acquired to fill the liquidity needs of an estate, proper planning dictates a careful analysis of who the owner and beneficiary of each policy should be. Typically, life insurance policies are owned by the insured party, and the insured's spouse is the primary beneficiary. In a small estate, this arrangement is fine. However, as the estate increases in size, this arrangement can turn into a disaster, as shown by the following examples.

## Estate Planning

### ■ EXAMPLE 1—BEFORE BASIC ESTATE PLANNING

**Fact situation:** Donald and Nancy are married and have one child, Dale, age 5. Donald is worth $2 million, including a $500,000 term insurance policy, with Nancy as the beneficiary. Nancy is worth $500,000 on her own. Each has a will providing that all of his/her respective assets will pass to the survivor. After both are gone, all remaining assets go into a trust for the benefit of Dale.

**TAX CONSEQUENCES IF DONALD DIES FIRST.** When Donald dies, his estate will include the life insurance proceeds ($500,000) and the other assets ($2 million). Because of the unlimited marital deduction, no estate taxes will be due at Donald's death.

**TAX CONSEQUENCES AT NANCY'S SUBSEQUENT DEATH.** Nancy dies. Her estate includes the assets from Donald's estate ($2 million, assuming she lived on the income without using principal), the life insurance proceeds ($500,000), plus her own assets ($500,000)—a total of $3 million. The federal estate tax would be $1,275,800. Assuming her full $192,800 unified credit is available, her net estate tax would be $1,083,000.

**WHAT IF NANCY OWNS THE LIFE INSURANCE POLICY?** Even if Nancy owns the policy insuring Donald's life, the tax results would be the same—$1,083,000 due when Nancy dies.

**WHAT IF NANCY DIES FIRST?** The order of death makes no difference. When the survivor dies, the tax bill will be $1,083,000.

**WHAT IF AN ILIT OWNS THE INSURANCE?** If the owner and beneficiary of Donald's policy is an ILIT, the tax results change dramatically. Now the estate tax due after the death of the survivor of Donald and Nancy would be only $833,000—a savings of $250,000.

Another way of looking at the situation is that if Donald or Nancy owns the policy, only $250,000 of the policy proceeds will be available to satisfy cash needs of their estates. Using an ILIT increases the amount available to $500,000.

If Donald dies first, the ILIT allows Nancy to receive the benefit of the income from investing the policy proceeds and even to have limited access to the $500,000 proceeds without jeopardizing the $250,000 tax savings.

As a practical matter, Nancy can enjoy the benefits of the policy almost as if she had been the beneficiary, without any estate tax cost.

SUMMARY OF TAX CONSEQUENCES—AFTER SURVIVOR DIES

| | Donald Owns the Policy | Nancy Owns the Policy | ILIT Owns the Policy |
|---|---|---|---|
| Total estate taxes payable | $1,083,000 | $1,083,000 | $833,000 |
| Net insurance proceeds available | 250,000 | 250,000 | 500,000 |

### ■ EXAMPLE 2—AFTER BASIC ESTATE PLANNING

**Fact Situation:** In Example 1, Donald and Nancy did no estate tax planning. In this example, assume Donald's will provides for a $600,000 credit shelter trust. Otherwise, the facts are the same as in Example 1.

**TAX CONSEQUENCES IF DONALD DIES FIRST.** No estate taxes are due. Donald's estate passes as follows: $600,000 into the credit shelter trust and the $1,900,000 balance to Nancy (either outright or to a trust that qualifies for the unlimited marital deduction).

**TAX CONSEQUENCES AT NANCY'S SUBSEQUENT DEATH.** Nancy's taxable estate will include her assets ($500,000) plus the assets from Donald's estate that were not placed into the credit shelter trust ($1,900,000)—a total of $2,400,000. The estate taxes are $784,000.

**WHAT IF NANCY OWNS THE INSURANCE?** If Nancy owns the policy, no estate taxes are due if Donald dies first. However when Nancy dies, her taxable estate would still be $2,400,000, resulting in the same $784,000 tax.

SUMMARY OF TAX CONSEQUENCES—AFTER SURVIVOR DIES

| | Donald Owns the Policy | Nancy Owns the Policy | ILIT Owns the Policy |
|---|---|---|---|
| Total estate taxes payable | $784,000 | $588,000 | $320,000 |
| Net after-tax insurance proceeds available | 255,000 | 255,000 | 500,000 |
| Tax savings over Example 1 | 299,000 | 495,000 | 513,000 |

■ **OBSERVATION:** Tax planning causes the order of death to become important. Assuming Nancy's will also provides for a credit shelter trust to which the life insurance policy was allocated, no estate taxes would result on Nancy's death. On Donald's subsequent death, his taxable estate would be $2 million, resulting in estate taxes of $588,000.

*Would an ILIT still save estate taxes?* Yes. If Donald dies first, the total estate taxes after both deaths would be $320,000.

## Creating the Super Trust

Creating an ILIT that will achieve the desired estate, gift, and income tax results requires a carefully drafted trust document. The Internal Revenue Code (the Code) contains three sets of obstacles that must be overcome to achieve the estate tax savings:

1. The *three-year rule* must be avoided;
2. The insured must not be a beneficiary of the ILIT or *retain any incidents of ownership* over the policies owned by the ILIT; and
3. The insured must not *retain any controls or powers* over the ILIT.

## The Three-Year Rule

The three-year rule provides that if the grantor-insured dies within three years of the transfer of an insurance policy to the ILIT, the insurance proceeds will be included in his/her estate (Section 2035). The grantor is the person who creates a trust.

### ■ EXAMPLE

John creates an ILIT on January 15, 1993, by transferring a $1-million life insurance policy on his life to an ILIT. If John dies before January 14, 1996 (less than three years), the policy proceeds will be included in his estate.

### ■ PLANNING POINTER

The three-year rule applies only to policies that can be included in the estate of the insured under the incidents of ownership rule (Section 2042). Therefore, a literal reading of Section 2035 should result in the conclusion that the three-year rule does not apply to a transfer of life insurance by a noninsured donor (the person making a gift to the ILIT), such as a spouse. Whether this is the result Congress intended when it amended Section 2035 in 1981 is not entirely clear. The congressional committee reports contain language to the effect that gifts of life insurance by a noninsured donor should also be subject to the three-year rule.

### Avoiding the Three-Year Rule

The three-year rule applies to all policy transfers made within three years of death, not just to transfers to an ILIT. If the insured is the owner of the policy, having him transfer the policy to a third party, such as a child, for the purpose of having the third party transfer the policy to the ILIT, does not help the insured avoid the three-year rule. Furthermore, adverse estate tax consequences could result to the noninsured part (e.g., a spouse) transferring the policy to the ILIT if that person becomes a beneficiary of the ILIT.

### Planning with Spouse-Owned Insurance

The unlimited marital deduction generally makes spousal ownership of insurance unnecessary. However, if the noninsured spouse owns the policy or provides the ILIT with the funds to pay the premiums, the three-year rule can be avoided.

#### ■ EXAMPLE 1

Mary purchases a policy insuring her husband, Bill, and transfers it to an ILIT. Mary is the grantor. In the alternative, Mary could transfer cash to an ILIT, and the trustee could purchase a policy on Bill's life. In either case, the three-year rule should not apply to Bill or Mary.

**PLANNING POINTER:** Although Bill and Mary should be able to avoid the three-year rule, such an approach could result in adverse estate tax consequences to Mary under Section 2036. If Mary is a beneficiary of the ILIT, the trust assets would be included in her estate. This problem may be avoided if someone other than Mary transfers the policy to the ILIT.

■ **EXAMPLE 2**

Mary gifts the policy to her adult son, who in turn transfers the policy to the ILIT. This should avoid the Section 2036 problem because Mary did not make a transfer to the ILIT and did not retain a life estate. Nevertheless, the IRS may seek to invoke the step-transaction doctrine and to characterize the arrangement as if Mary made the transfer to the ILIT, especially if the two transfers took place almost simultaneously as part of a prearranged plan.

**PLANNING POINTER:** If the insured spouse is in reasonably good health, then having him or her transfer the policy is probably a risk worth taking. This is especially true if the noninsured spouse is to be a beneficiary of the ILIT. If the insured spouse doesn't live three years, the policy proceeds will be included in the estate. However, if the ILIT contains a contingent marital deduction clause (leaves the trust assets to his/her spouse), estate taxes can still be avoided in the event the insured dies first.

### Cash Transfer (Gifts) by the Grantor-Insured

Does the three-year rule apply if the insured transfers funds to an ILIT so it can purchase the policy?

Since December 31, 1981, the three-year rule should no longer be a problem because the rule appears to apply only to transfers of policies and not transfers of cash, even though cash is used to purchase policies.

## The Incidents of Ownership Rule

If the grantor-insured of the ILIT retains any incidents of ownership in the policy at the time of his death, the policy proceeds are included in his estate.

The term incidents of ownership relates to the economic benefits of the policy, including the power to change the beneficiary, surrender or cancel the policy, assign the policy, revoke an assignment, pledge the policy for a loan, or obtain from the insurance company a loan against the cash surrender value of the policy (Regulation § 20.2042-1(c)(2)).

Any power over the economic benefits of an insurance policy is considered an incident of ownership as shown by the following cases:

- ☐ The power to change the beneficiary of the policy: *Chase National Bank v. United States*, 278 US 327 (1929)).
- ☐ The power to borrow against the cash surrender value of the policy: *Caldwell v. Jordan*, 119 F. Supp. 66 (ND Ala. 1953)).
- ☐ The power to obtain the cash surrender value of the policy: *Liebmann v. Hassett*, 148 F2d 247 (1st Cir. 1945)).

### Planning to Avoid the Incidents of Ownership Rule

- ☐ *What if the grantor originally owned the policy on his life?* All incidents of ownership in the policy must be transferred to the ILIT.
- ☐ *What if the trustee buys the policy in the first place?* This is a most common method. The trustee (trust) must then be the original applicant, owner, and beneficiary of the policy.

- ☐ *What if the grantor-wife originally owned the policy on her husband's life?* If the wife transfers the policy to an existing ILIT created by her husband and she is a beneficiary, the proceeds will be included in her estate (Sections 2036, 2038).

### Indirect Incidents of Ownership

Even if the incident of ownership is not retained directly by the grantor-insured, the policy may nevertheless be included in his estate if he retains an incident of ownership in a fiduciary capacity (Regulation 20.2042-1(c)(4)).

■ **CAUTION:** There is a split among the courts as to what type of power held in a fiduciary capacity is considered an incident of ownership. Until this uncertainty is settled, do not take any unnecessary risk, do not make the insured a trustee of the ILIT.

## Incidents of Ownership of a Corporation

If a policy is owned by a corporation insuring the life of the controlling shareholder, the incidents of ownership that the corporation has in the policy are attributed to the insured shareholder. If you have a controlling interest in the corporation (more than 50 percent), you have incidents of ownership. (Regulation 20.2042-1(c)(6))

■ **WHAT TO DO:** The insured should transfer the policy out of the corporation into his own name. (This can be accomplished tax-free for income tax purposes.) Then a transfer to an ILIT can beat the estate tax. But remember, the insured must survive for three years after the transfer.

### Adding Flexibility Without Retaining Incidents of Ownership

After the ILIT is created, what can be done if the grantor-insured changes his mind about how the policy proceeds should be used?

To achieve flexibility, the ILIT should contain provisions enabling the trustee, under certain circumstances, to distribute the trust corpus (all assets, including the right to distribute the insurance policies in kind) during the grantor-insured's lifetime. Since the grantor-insured's spouse generally is a beneficiary, such a provision could result in policies being distributed to the spouse, or any other beneficiary of the ILIT.

## Beneficiaries

The following rules concerning the beneficiary can help keep the policy proceeds out of the grantor's estate:

- ☐ The ILIT must be the beneficiary of all insurance policies which it owns.
- ☐ The grantor-insured's estate cannot be a beneficiary, directly or indirectly, of the ILIT.
- ☐ If the ILIT is the beneficiary, the trustee of the ILIT cannot be required to pay the policy proceeds to the grantor-insured's estate. Proceeds that are payable to the grantor-insured's estate are subject to estate tax. (Section 2042(1)).
- ☐ If the proceeds are payable to a beneficiary other than the estate of the grantor-insured, but the beneficiary is obligated to pay the estate's debts or taxes, the

grantor-insured's estate is considered a beneficiary of the ILIT (Regulation 20.2042-1(b)(1)).

## ■ HOW TO WIN INDIRECTLY

Authorizing the ILIT to pay your estate tax is a no-no. The proceeds will be included in your estate. But it is okay to authorize the trustee to loan the amount of the potential estate tax liability to your executor. Now the proceeds will not be included in your estate. Indirect, yes. But this technique gets the job done.

### Planning to Avoid the Beneficiary Rules

Although the estate of the grantor-insured cannot be a beneficiary of the ILIT, it can get the benefit of the policy proceeds without adverse estate tax results. The trustee of the ILIT can be authorized to purchase nonliquid assets from the estate at their fair-market value. (*Old Colony Trust Co.* 39 B.T.A. 871, (1939); Rev. Rul. 77-157, 1977-1 CB 279). This is a variation of loaning money to the estate.

## ■ EXAMPLE

Bob dies with a taxable estate of $2.4 million that consists entirely of commercial real estate. His estate owes $750,000 in estate taxes. Bob created an ILIT five years before he died with an $800,000 life insurance policy insuring his life. The proceeds were paid to the ILIT.

To raise the $750,000 to pay the estate taxes, Bob's estate could (1) sell some of the real estate to the general public, (2) sell some of the real estate to the ILIT, or (3) borrow money from the ILIT or some third party pledging the real estate as collateral.

Selling the real estate to outsiders is not consistent with Bob's wishes as he wants his heirs to own the property. It may not be feasible to obtain a favorable loan from a third party.

What to do? Bob's ILIT to the rescue. It contains the proper language to authorize the trustee to provide the liquidity Bob's estate needs through loans to, or purchases of, assets from his estate without subjecting the insurance proceeds to estate taxes.

### Certain Family Problems

Typically, the beneficiaries of an ILIT are the spouse and children of the grantor-insured. What happens if there is a divorce, or if additional children are born or adopted after the ILIT is established? As a practical matter, the rules offer the grantor-insured a single opportunity—at the time the ILIT is created—to determine the beneficiaries of the ILIT, when distributions can be made, and how much can be distributed to each beneficiary. It is essential that all planning be completed before the ILIT is drafted.

**DIVORCE.** A well-drafted ILIT should contemplate the possibility of divorce. The grantor-insured should define his spouse as that person to whom he is married at (1) the time a lifetime distribution is to be made or (2) at the time of his death, in the event distributions start after his death. Put another way, a husband would define his wife as his "then wife." Although a subsequent divorce or death of the spouse and remarriage change the beneficiaries of the ILIT, such a clause should not be considered a retained power (*Tully v. United States*, 528 F2d 1401 (Ct. LD 1976)).

**CHILDREN.** When children are beneficiaries of an ILIT, it is advisable to designate all children living at the time the ILIT is formed and any children born or adopted later as one class of beneficiaries. The fact that the grantor-insured has the power to have or adopt additional children is not a retained power if the trust document automatically includes after-born or after-adopted children in the one class of beneficiaries (Rev. Rul. 80-255).

Circumstances involving children often change. How can the grantor-insured deal with these changes after an ILIT is created without running afoul of the retained-power prohibition? Although the grantor-insured cannot retain the power to alter the beneficiaries of the ILIT, his spouse can have limited powers to change the beneficiaries without jeopardizing the estate tax savings. Thus the ILIT can authorize the spouse to direct which children will be beneficiaries and what portion of the ILIT each child of the grantor-insured will receive after her death.

#### ■ EXAMPLE 1—VARYING BENEFICIARY PERCENTAGES

Joe creates an ILIT and names his wife Sue and his two sons Bill and Bob beneficiaries. The ILIT provides that the trustee should distribute the trust balance equally to Bill and Bob after Sue's death. Ten years later, Bill is involved in an auto accident and as a result requires constant medical care. A well-drafted ILIT would give Sue the right to alter the 50-50 split originally provided by Joe to provide additional funds to pay Bill's medical bills.

#### ■ EXAMPLE 2—CHANGING BENEFICIARIES

Jimmy creates an ILIT and names his wife Rose and two sons Art and Pete beneficiaries. After Jimmy's death, Art invents a new product that makes him a multimillionaire. Rose might like to have, and could be given, the power to remove Art as a beneficiary or reduce his percentage of the ILIT.

When the surviving spouse is given the powers described in the above examples, the grantor-insured must limit the scope of powers so the funds remaining in the ILIT at the surviving spouse's death are not included in his/her estate. This can be accomplished easily by limiting the surviving spouse's power to changing beneficiaries and percentages among the descendants of the grantor-insured.

## Retained Powers Can Be Fatal

Even if the grantor-insured dots all the i's and crosses all the other t's when creating an ILIT, he can still blow it all if he retains certain rights or powers. What happens? The insurance proceeds will be included in his estate.

### Retaining Right to Income

Insurance proceeds are included in the grantor-insured's estate if he retains, directly or indirectly, the right to receive the ILIT income during his life (Section 2036(a)(1)).

## ■ PLANNING POINTERS

1. If the trust income can be used to discharge the grantor-insured's legal obligations (for example, support of children), he is considered to have retained a life interest in the ILIT. The trap closes even if the income is not used for the support (Regulation § 20.2036-(1)(b)(2)).

2. Since most ILITs are funded solely with life insurance policies, an ILIT generates little or no income during the grantor-insured's life. Therefore, the grantor-insured loses nothing by not using trust income to meet his legal obligations or by not becoming an income beneficiary.

However, it is okay if the ILIT provides for income to be distributed among the grantor-insured's spouse and descendants on a discretionary basis.

### Power to Affect the Beneficial Enjoyment

The grantor-insured, at the time of his death, must not have any power, directly or indirectly, that affects the beneficial enjoyment of trust income or principal (Sections 2036(a)(2), 2038). Section 2038 triggers inclusion of insurance proceeds in the estate if the grantor retains a power "to alter, amend, revoke, or terminate" the enjoyment of the asset transferred. For example, the grantor must not retain the power to:

1. Add or remove beneficiaries of the ILIT;
2. Alter the amounts to be distributed to a beneficiary; or
3. Determine when distributions will be made.

### Grantor As Trustee

The grantor-insured is prohibited from retaining any of the tax-sensitive powers in a fiduciary capacity. Simply put, he cannot be a trustee or co-trustee (*United States v. O'Malley*, 383 US 627 (1966)).

The IRS takes a broad view of the power prohibited under Sections 2036(a)(2) and 2038 (Rev. Rul. 79-353). In this ruling, the grantor-insured retains the power to remove a corporate trustee and replace it with another corporate trustee. The trust document grants the corporate trustee some of the tax-sensitive powers covered by Section 2038. The IRS held that the power to remove and replace the corporate trustee results in a retained power under Section 2038.

## ■ CAUTION

1. *A Third Party as Trustee.* Many estate planners doubt whether the courts would support Rev. Rul. 79-353. Until the ruling is withdrawn or overturned in the courts, powers similar to the power described in the ruling should not be retained. When the trustee of an ILIT is someone other than the grantor-insured, Rev. Rul. 79-353 does not present a problem.

2. *A Spouse as Trustee.* Naming the grantor-insured's spouse trustee or co-trustee could cause the proceeds remaining in the ILIT on the spouse's subsequent death to be included in her estate if the ILIT granted her, as trustee, any tax-sensitive powers.

Your course should be clear: *Neither you nor your spouse should be the trustee of your ILIT.*

## Solving Gift Tax Problems

For the moment, forget about the estate tax and the income tax. Consider only the gift tax problem when dealing with an ILIT. There are two ways an ILIT can acquire life insurance policies:

1. A transfer of an existing policy to the ILIT and
2. A transfer of cash or other assets that the trustee will use to purchase a new policy.

Regardless of the method used, the transfer to the ILIT is considered a gift for gift tax purposes.

### Transferring Existing Policies

When an existing policy is transferred to an ILIT, the amount of the gift is equal to the amount it would have cost to replace the policy on the date of the gift (Regulation 25.2512-6(a)).

**ORDINARY LIFE POLICY.** In the case of a whole life (often called ordinary life) policy, the gift tax value is (1) the interpolated terminal reserve value, usually slightly more than the cash surrender value, (2) plus any unearned portion of the current year's premium and (3) any dividend accumulations, less (4) the amount of any policy loan.

**TERM POLICY.** When a term insurance policy is gifted on a premium due date, the gift tax value is zero. If a term policy is gifted at any other time, the gift tax value should be equal to the unearned premiums on the date of the gift.

### Gifts to Pay Future Premiums

There are four ways in which an ILIT can obtain the funds used to pay premiums on policies it owns.

1. The ILIT is funded with income-producing property, and the resulting income is used to pay premiums.
2. The grantor-insured pays the premiums.
3. The grantor-insured's spouse pays the premiums.
4. The grantor-insured makes annual gifts to the ILIT in amounts sufficient to pay the premiums.

Each method results in a gift.

In the case of a funded trust, the gift results when the trust is funded. If a substantial amount of assets is needed to produce sufficient income to pay the premiums, the gift tax consequences could be onerous. Because of this, ILITs are rarely funded with substantial assets.

Premium payments by the grantor-insured are considered gifts made to the trust beneficiaries. Such gifts may be considered gifts of a future interest (defined immediately following), causing the grantor to lose the annual gift tax exclusion. The same problem exists if the spouse of the grantor-insured pays the premiums; such payments may cause adverse estate tax consequences (Section 2036).

Because of the potential gift tax problems resulting from the first three ways listed, premiums generally are paid in the manner described in No. 4.

### The Annual Gift Tax Exclusion

The first $10,000 (called the annual exclusion) of gifts made each year by the donor (the person making the gift) to each donee (the person receiving the gift) can be gift-tax-free (Section 2503(b)). To gain tax-free treatment, the gift must be a gift of a present interest. A future interest disqualifies the gift from the annual exclusion.

In order to qualify as a gift of a present interest, the beneficiary of the gift must have an unrestricted right to the immediate use, possession, or enjoyment of the property subject to the gift.

#### ■ EXAMPLE 1—PRESENT INTEREST

Bob has three children. Every year Bob gives each child $10,000 in cash. These are gifts of a present interest (the kids can spend, save, or squander the money now) and Bob is entitled to the annual exclusion.

#### ■ EXAMPLE 2—FUTURE INTEREST

The facts are the same as in Example 1, except the cash is given to a trustee with instructions to accumulate the income and give each child everything in the trust in five years (obviously, in the future as opposed to now). There is no annual exclusion. All the gifts are taxable gifts.

## Crummey Power—What Is It? (Caution: Very Technical Stuff)

Generally, to qualify gifts of property to an ILIT as gifts of a present interest requires the inclusion of a so-called Crummey power. From a tax standpoint, a Crummey power is anything but crummy. The name comes from *Crummey v. Comm'r* (397 F2d 82, (9th Cir. 1968)), in which the donors created an irrevocable trust for the benefit of their four children—two minors and two adults. The trust allowed each child to demand annually that the trustee distribute to him the amounts contributed to the trust for his benefit. In order to exercise this power, the child was required to notify the trustee prior to the end of the year in which the gifts were made to the trust. The amount of the demand right was limited to $4,000.

The court held that the annual gifts qualified as gifts of a present interest because the children had the right to demand that the trustee distribute the gifts to them. The court concluded that as long as the donee or holder of the demand power was legally and technically capable of immediately enjoying the property, the gift was a present interest. Under the trust instrument and governing state law, each child had a legal right to demand distribution even though no guardian had been appointed for the minor children.

#### ■ TAX-SAVING IDEA IN ACTION

With the use of Crummey powers, it is generally possible to avoid some and, in certain cases, all gift taxes on the formation and continued operation of an ILIT.

## Scope of the Crummey Power—The 5 and 5 Limitation

Some practitioners recommend that the maximum amount of property subject to a Crummey power for any one beneficiary should not exceed the greater of $5,000 or 5 percent of the value of the trust property (called the 5 and 5 limitation). The limitation results from the provisions of Section 2514(e). The lapse (failure to exercise) of a power, including a Crummey power, in excess of the 5 and 5 limitation results in a gift to the other trust beneficiaries equal to the amount of the excess. The excess is considered a gift because the lapse of the power is considered a general power of appointment. (The holder of the power could have taken the excess.) In effect, by not taking the property, the holder made a gift equal to the amount of the lapsed power.

Under the terms of an ILIT with a demand power so limited, the excess is a gift of a future interest (at the earliest, benefits will not be paid until the insurance proceeds are collected) and does not qualify for the annual gift tax exclusion.

### ■ EXAMPLE 1

If a beneficiary has only a 5 and 5 power, the donor's annual exclusion for gifts to the trust for the beneficiary is limited to:

1. $5,000 until the trust reaches $100,000;
2. Five percent of corpus from $100,000 to $200,000; or
3. The full $10,000 exclusion only when the trust exceeds $200,000.

If the beneficiary has a greater power, its lapse will be a taxable gift unless suitable precautions are taken (see following Planning Pointer).

### ■ EXAMPLE 2

A trust with no other assets grants one beneficiary (Joe) of two equal beneficiaries an $11,000 Crummey power. During the year, the trust receives an $11,000 gift subject to Joe's power. Joe allows the power to lapse. A gift of $6,000 (the excess over $5,000) is considered to have been made by Joe to the other beneficiary.

The tax on the portion of the gift ($6,000 in the above example) that does not qualify for the annual gift tax exclusion probably would be paid by using the beneficiary's unified credit. This may not be a bad result when the beneficiary is a minor child or your adult who probably will have no need for his unified credit for either gift or estate tax purposes for many years.

■ **PLANNING POINTER:** The Crummey powerholder's gift-tax exposure can be eliminated by giving the individual (1) a right to demand up to $20,000 (if the donor is married) and (2) a special power of appointment (which gives the beneficiary the right to appoint the gift among specific beneficiaries) over his trust property in excess of the 5 and 5 limitation (Regulation § 25-2511-2(c)). The existence of such a power when a Crummey power lapses should render the gift incomplete for gift tax purposes (see Priv. Ltr. Ruls. 81011123 and 8229097).

The drawback to granting special powers is that they may be exercised in a fashion that is contrary to the grantor-insured's wishes. An alternative to the use of special powers of appointment is to make certain the ILIT has enough beneficiaries holding Crummey powers so as not to exceed the 5 and 5 limitation.

There is no requirement by law or otherwise that Crummey demand powers be granted it a gift to the ILIT exceeds the 5 and 5 limitation. However, to the extent the excess would be considered a gift of a future interest, the excess would not qualify for the annual gift tax exclusion, even though the resulting gift tax probably would be paid by using the grantor's available unified credit, as opposed to cash. Generally, that is an unacceptable result to older-generation grantors.

## Great News: The Cristofani Case

A new case (Estate of Maria Cristofani, 97 TC 5, 1991) is just what the doctor ordered. *It's significance:* Every grandchild, great-grandchild or other contingent beneficiary opens another $10,000-per-year-annual-*Crummey*-exclusion door ($20,000 if married). Use the opening.

An article from my tax column tells the victory-for-our-side story.

APPLAUSE!...GRANDMA LEADS WAY TO TAX VICTORY

Have children?...grandchildren? And some wealth? Who would you rather see enjoy your wealth? The children and grandchildren?...or the IRS?

When I do tax planning with the owner of a family business, the owner often says, "Irv, what can I do with the assets I own outside of the business?" Well, a recent Tax Court case opens a new tax-saving door to help us whip the IRS.

First some basic gift-tax law: You can give $10,000 per year per donee (the person receiving the gift) free of gift tax. If you're married, double it to $20,000. This is called the "annual exclusion." What most people don't know is that you only get the exclusion if you give a present interest ("Here's $10,000 son. Keep it or spend it as you choose.") Give a future interest ("Here, Mr. Trustee, is $10,000 for the benefit of my son. Use it for his college education.") and you blow the annual exclusion; this $10,000 is a taxable gift. Ouch!

Now that you know the rules, apply them to this real-life tax case (*Cristofani*). You be the judge.

Here are the facts: Maria Cristofani set up a trust for her children, Frank and Lillian. Both could receive income or even principal, for their support, health, maintenance and education (unquestionably, a future interest). At Maria's death, the trust was to be distributed to Frank and Lillian, or if either died before Maria, his or her share was to go to his or her children (Maria's five grandchildren, ages 5-13). In 1984, and again in 1985, Maria transferred $70,000 of property to the trust. Frank, Lillian, and Maria's five grandchildren could each withdraw up to $10,000 from the trust within 15 days after the $70,000 transfer to the trust was made. None of them exercised their right to withdraw, even though the trustees notified the grandchildren of the transfers, as required by the trust.

The IRS allowed the $20,000 exclusion total for Frank and Lillian, but turned thumbs down on the $50,000 exclusion total for the five grandchildren. How do you rule? Does Maria get the $50,000 in exclusions?

If you said "Yes," you agreed with the tax court. This is a big victory for our side. Simply put, you can put money in trust for anyone you choose either as a current beneficiary (like Frank and Lillian) or a contingent beneficiary (like the grandchildren) who absolutely have a future interest. But, get this. By giving them notice and 15 days to take the $10,000, you convert the future interest into a present interest. RESULT: No taxable gift. Sounds logical to me.

■ **ACCOMPLISHING THE GIFT-TAX-FREE GOAL:** With proper planning and effective use of Crummey powers, all gift taxes can usually be eliminated when creating and annually funding an ILIT.

### Notice of the Crummey Power

Almost every policy transferred to or acquired by an ILIT will require future premiums to be paid. Typically, the funds needed from time to time to pay these premiums are gifted by the grantor-insured to the ILIT. Without the use of a Crummey power, these gifts could eat up a substantial portion of the grantor-insured's unified credit. So a well-drafted ILIT normally includes a Crummey power. In actuality, it is hoped that none of the power holders will ever exercise their rights, since the exercise would deprive the ILIT of the funds needed to pay premiums. An obvious way of insuring the nonexercise of the power is to fail to let the power holder know of its existence.

In the Crummey case, the court did not directly address the requirement-of-notice issue. However, the IRS has taken the position that a Crummey power is not effective unless the beneficiary has notice os its existence (Rev. Rul. 83-108; Priv. Ltr. Ruls. 7946007, 7947066).

### Timing the Notice

In Crummey, the power was exercisable at any time through December 31 of the year in which a gift to the trust was made. Since most gifts were made to the trust during the last two weeks of December, the beneficiaries had only about two weeks to exercise their power. But the IRS has refused to rule on the validity of a Crummey power where only 10 days notice is required (Priv. Ltr. Rul. 8111123).

Although no precise guidelines have been established regarding the type and length of notice that must be given, it is suggested that all notices be given in writing at least 30 days before the power expires.

## The Unfunded ILIT and Interest Expense

Except for the life insurance policies owned, most ILITs are unfunded. Generally, an unfunded ILIT produces no taxable income or expense during the life of the insured. Remember, policy dividends are tax free to the extent of premiums paid. But what happens if the trustee borrows against the cash surrender value of the policies owned by the ILIT to pay premiums? Interest must be paid on the loan. Is that interest deductible for income tax purposes, and by whom is it deductible (if at all)?

Policy loans can provide a substantial assist to the grantor in paying life insurance premiums, whether or not loan interest is deductible. As a practical matter, however, the deductibility of interest is a matter of serious concern to most prospective grantors. But like it or not, interest paid on life insurance loans is clearly consumer interest and is not deductible.

## Funding the ILIT

The funds needed by an ILIT to pay premiums usually come from one or more of these sources:

1. Income from assets (other than insurance) transferred to the trust;
2. Annual gifts to the trust; or
3. Systematic borrowing against the cash surrender value of policies owned by the trust.

The income tax results vary depending on the source of the premiums.

---

### ■ A GOOD IDEA

Make gifts to the ILIT and pay premiums to the insurance company annually to reduce trust administration time and costs.

---

### Funding with Income Property

If income-producing assets are transferred to an ILIT, the grantor is treated as the trust owner to the extent income is used to pay premiums on policies insuring the life of the grantor or his spouse (Section 677(a)(3)). Result: Income earned by the trust is taxed to the grantor.

---

### ■ A POTENTIAL TAX TRAP CAN BE A TAX FRIEND

The trust income should not be made available to the grantor under any circumstances even though it may be needed to pay the resulting income taxes. Estate taxes are not avoided if the grantor has access to the trust income.

---

If the grantor is wealthy, the income tax result described in the paragraph above is not all bad. Why? The income not distributed to the grantor is out of his estate. That's good. And the fact that he must pay tax on that income gets more dollars out of his estate. That's good, too. A tax friend.

Funding an ILIT with income property, such as stocks and bonds, generally is not recommended because:

- ☐ A transfer to an ILIT is irrevocable. The grantor is locked out of access to the assets no matter how pressing his financial situation might become.
- ☐ Use of trust income to pay premiums on a policy on the life of the grantor or his spouse causes the income to be taxed to the grantor (Section 677(a)(3)).
- ☐ The trustee is burdened with holding and investing the assets.

---

### ■ AN OFTEN-MISSED INCOME-TAX-SAVING IDEA

Trust income, like personal income, is taxed at graduated rates—the higher the income, the higher the tax rate, until the top bracket is reached. Thus it is important that the ILIT instrument create a separate trust for each donee, wherever practical. While this is of no practical consequence so long as the only trust assets are life insurance policies, it can become critical after the insured's death when the ILIT may generate substantial taxable income. For example, one trust with $90,000 of income would pay much more income tax than the total tax due for three trusts (one for each donee, who would then be three beneficiaries) each with $30,000 of income.

## Important ILIT Planning Questions

*If the grantor is married, does it make any difference if the ILIT policy is carried on his life or his spouse's life?* Yes. Because an ILIT eliminates estate tax on both deaths, whether the husband or wife dies first, the best results are usually obtained by insuring the life of the spouse with the lowest premium cost. It is important to consider such variables as age and ability to obtain the lowest premium due to health requirements. However, if liquidity is needed after the death of one of the spouses, then insure that spouse for the amount of liquidity needed even if the premium cost for that spouse is higher. (If divorce is a possibility, this is probably a bad idea.)

*Can an adult child of the insured be the grantor of the ILIT?* Yes. The adult child could buy the policy on his Dad's life and transfer it to the ILIT. The estate tax bite will be lowered for Mom's and Dad's estates. Ultimately, the proceeds of the ILIT will benefit the adult child directly.

*Can an ILIT be used to provide liquidity for the noninsured spouse and reduce the estate tax for other assets owned by this spouse?* Yes, as shown here:

**■ EXAMPLE**

Suppose the noninsured spouse, Sue, owns a rapidly appreciating asset, like stock in the family business inherited from her husband. Ultimately, she plans to pass the stock on to her children, who are also the ultimate beneficiaries of an ILIT created by her husband, the grantor-insured. At present, the children don't have the cash to buy the stock from her and she is unwilling to gift it to them during her lifetime. Here's the problem: The longer she holds the stock, the larger her estate and the greater her estate tax burden becomes. Her problem can be solved, at least in part, if her husband's ILIT purchases the stock from her with the insurance proceeds following his death. Everyone likes the results:

1. Sue will have the cash needed to pay her living expenses. On her death, the remaining cash can be used to pay her estate taxes and estate expenses.
2. Since Sue no longer owns the appreciating stock, the size of her estate is—in effect—frozen, thus reducing her ultimate estate tax liability. When the ILIT terminates after Sue's death, the stock will go to the children.
3. *Does the stock sale by Sue in the previous example result in taxable income to Her?* Generally no, because (1) Sue will sell her stock to the ILIT at its fair-market value and (2) her basis for income tax purposes would be stepped up to its fair-market value as of the date of her husband's death.

**■ PLANNING POINTER**: Even if the ILIT does not have sufficient liquidity to purchase the stock (or other assets) for cash, consider an installment purchase. The deferred portion of the purchase price could be paid from future earnings of the assets.

But be careful. The purchase of assets by an ILIT must be coordinated with other estate planning objectives and techniques as discussed throughout this book.

## Why You Might Want to Dump the Crummey Power and Other Tax-Saving Ideas

ILITs have been around for a long time. Long enough, in fact, for a sort of "conventional wisdom" to develop among professionals who bless their clients with ILIT goodies. And that's the way the material in this chapter has been written: according to conventional wisdom.

Let's review: In addition to being irrevocable, the ILIT is usually unfunded. Crummey-style demand rights are created to allow the annual contributions to the trust needed to pay premiums to qualify for the annual gift-tax exclusion. Thus, no gift tax is paid on funding the ILIT and the unicredit remains intact.

Okay, consider these reasons for forgetting about any Crummey powers and allowing each gift to the ILIT to be a taxable gift:

1. The value of the unicredit (and the $10,000/$20,000 annual exclusion) is worth less each year due to the ravages of inflation. So the sooner you use it, the more value it has.
2. Congress might change the law by:
   a. reducing the unified credit,
   b. reducing the annual exclusion, or
   c. reducing or eliminating the use of a Crummey power.

   Any or all of these possibilities make the use of a Crummey power questionable for long-term planning.
3. No Crummey power in your ILIT.
   a. eliminates the annual notice hassle.
   b. Allows secrecy. Since the beneficiaries are not required to receive any notice, you have the choice of telling the beneficiaries or not telling them about the ILIT.
4. Now let's get to the most important reason—saving taxes. I'll admit that if available cash is a problem, the Crummey power and conventional wisdom is the way to go. But, what if, in your case, you have the cash to make the premium gifts to the ILIT, you have used up your unicredit, and the gifts to the ILIT each year require you to pay gift tax in cash? Is this necessarily bad?

   Maybe not. It's a fact: The gift tax and the estate tax are not the same. True, they both use the same rate schedule and share the same unicredit, but they are very different. How? For simplicity, let's assume that your gift and estate tax rate and the top rate are the same—50 percent.

   Okay, you make a taxable gift of $10,000 to your ILIT. You must pay $5,000 in gift tax. The tax is levied on the value of the gift. In this case, the tax of $5,000 is exactly 50 percent of the amount gifted (transferred). Now watch this. To produce the same result in your estate—that is, a transfer of $10,000—will cost your estate $10,000. Or look at it this way. For every $20,000 in your estate, which is in the 50-percent bracket, your heirs will net only $10,000.

Let's work out the effective tax rate:

| | Gift Tax | Estate Tax |
|---|---|---|
| a. Amount transferred,, including tax | $15,000 | $20,000 |
| b. Less-Amount of tax | 5,000 | 10,000 |
| c. Net amount to your family | $10,000 | $10,000 |
| d. Effective rate of tax [Line (b) divided by Line (a)] | 33.33% | 50.00% |

As you can clearly see, the top estate tax rate is truly 50 percent, but the top gift tax rate, in reality, is only 33.33 percent.

5. Conventional wisdom says don't fund the trust. Again, assume you are rich and have plenty of cash. Let's say you fund the ILIT with $1,200,000 or more (forcing some current gift tax). Then you invest the funds in the trust and use the income and principal as necessary to pay the premiums on a second-to-die policy.

## ■ THIS IS THE LAW

Where the income of the trust may be used to pay premiums on insurance on the life of the grantor (you) or your spouse, you are treated as owner of the income for income tax purposes. This means that you must account for the income on your personal tax return and pay the taxes (Section 677(a)(3).

This is intentional (of course, the result is the same even if it is unintentional). Violation of the grantor trust rules creates a "defective trust."

Now it should also be mentioned that conventional wisdom dictates avoiding taxable income in the trust by choosing investments which generate tax-exempt income. So once again, let's buck conventional wisdom. Why? Because taxable investments typically have higher yields than tax-exempt investments. A taxable investment gives the trustee, and ultimately the trust beneficiaries, more money. This happens because you, the grantor, pay the tax on the trust income. That's not bad. That's good.

## ■ EXAMPLE

Say Joe gives his ILIT $1,200,000, which is invested at an eight percent taxable yield, or $96,000. The trustee's tax would have been approximately $26,000, leaving the trustee with $70,000 to put toward insurance premiums. But with a defective trust, the trustee pays zero income taxes, leaving the ILIT with the full $96,000. Great! An additional $26,000 is available to pay insurance premiums.

Wait! There's more. In effect, Joe has made an additional $26,000 gift to his ILIT free of any gift tax or subsequent estate tax. Not bad, huh?

### What Happens If You Are Not Insurable?

When dealing with a husband and wife, the perfect circumstances are when both are in good health, and nonsmokers. A second-to-die policy and an ILIT can be combined to pay your estate taxes or increase your wealth at the lowest possible premium cost. If either the husband or wife is uninsurable, but acceptable (meaning that an insurance company will not issue a policy on a certain individual because of that person's poor health, but the company will accept this person as one of the insureds on a second-to-die policy), some benefit can still be obtained from the lower second-to-die premiums.

But what if both the husband and wife are uninsurable (or so old or rated so high that as a practical matter neither or both together are insurable)? Or what if our potential insured is single and uninsurable? Must these people lose a large portion of their estate to taxation and deprive their children and grandchildren of the family wealth? Not really. The children and grandchildren can use the second-to-die/ILIT technique or a variation to reclaim the estate within a single generation.

Here's how. The grandparents make a gift to the grandchildren, who pay the premium on a second-to-die policy for their mom and dad (the children of the uninsurable grandparents). An ILIT is not necessary and the policies could be owned by the grandchildren or a trust for their benefit. Compared to the age of the grandparents, a second-to-die policy purchased by one of their children and his/her spouse should allow the premium cost to be much lower. Of course, when the grandparents die, 50 percent or more of their estate will go down the drain in taxes. But one generation later, when the inevitable occurs, the grandparents' child and his/her spouse will die too. Then, the grandchildren will collect the insurance proceeds, which may be more or less than the taxes paid at the death of grandma and grandpa, depending on various factors (the amount of the gift used to pay premiums, age and health of the insureds, etc.).

If the grandparents gifted the premium money to their children and their spouses, then they would use an ILIT as the tax-free means of getting the insurance proceeds to their children.

## Eliminating the Estate Tax, Creating Wealth—A Summary

Eliminate the estate tax?...Yes, it can be done. No, you can't prevent the IRS from collecting its pound of flesh in the form of an estate tax, but you can shift the burden of paying the tax from your estate to the insurance industry.

This is the game plan:

1. With the help of a professional advisor, develop an overall plan to reduce your anticipated estate tax liability as much as possible.
2. Determine the estimated estate tax liability.
3. Obtain life insurance coverage equal to the estimated amount of estate tax liability. Keep the insurance proceeds out of your estate (and your spouse's estate) by using an ILIT.
4. Pass all the assets in your estate to your family without any reduction due to estate taxes.

■ **YOUR GOAL:** Eliminate any reduction of your estate because of the federal estate tax. Your estate planner must get you through points 1 and 2. After you accomplish point 3, point 4 follows automatically.

### Let's Put It All Together

In a nutshell: In order to make your estate-tax-eliminating plan work, you need an insurance product (to transfer the estate tax burden) and an ILIT (to keep the proceeds out of the tax collector's clutches).

### Creating Wealth Via an ILIT

There is no logical reason to conclude that shifting your estate tax burden to an insurance carrier must be the ceiling for the use of an ILIT.

The identical concept described in this chapter to save all or part of the estate tax can be used to create wealth. Assume you estimated needing $10 million to pay your estate tax. So you acquired $10 million of second-to-die insurance in an ILIT. After 30 years, the second insured dies and it turns out, though you'll never know it, that you overshot the mark by $2 million. As a practical matter you not only paid $8 million in taxes with your ILIT, you did, in fact, create $2 million of wealth unintentionally.

So, what if you did it intentionally? Set your mind to create wealth via an ILIT. It can be done. Read Part V, Chapter Four, "Junk Money," to learn how.

### How Much Does the Insurance Cost?

Probably a question that has no answer. Why? Because you must know such things as what kind of insurance, single payment or annual premiums, and age and health of the insured.

Nevertheless, I thought it would be a great way to end this chapter by giving you an idea of what the premium cost would be at various ages. Then again, I decided it would be more imperative to tell you how much insurance you could buy for a given annual insurance cost.

**AMOUNT OF WHOLE LIFE INSURANCE YOU CAN BUY FOR $10,000 PER YEAR, PAYING PREMIUMS FOR ONLY 10 YEARS (OR TOTAL PREMIUMS OF $100,000)**

| Age | Male | Female | Second-to-Die* |
|---|---|---|---|
| 30 | $1,479,664 | $1,932,714 | $4,324,771 |
| 35 | 1,076,257 | 1,415,101 | 3,005,407 |
| 40 | 796,848 | 1,051,897 | 2,096,281 |
| 45 | 598,835 | 800,734 | 1,475,495 |
| 50 | 460,429 | 621,238 | 1,049,445 |
| 55 | 358,659 | 485,491 | 755,832 |
| 60 | 277,272 | 371,625 | 546,556 |
| 65 | 212,721 | 289,331 | 400,084 |
| 70 | 161,987 | 222,809 | 290,783 |
| 75 | 127,533 | 171,429 | 211,437 |
| 80 | 100,278 | 132,437 | 163,334 |

*Assumes both are same age.

Okay then. This is what the preceding schedule tells you: How much insurance you can buy for a premium of $10,000 per year, assuming you are a preferred risk, a nonsmoker, and buy a whole life policy (as opposed to a universal life policy or a universal life policy with some term mixed in or some other type of insurance) where you pay the premiums for 10 years only (then the policy will self carry), and using current assumptions (that the earnings of the top-rated company selected will continue at the same rate for the life of the policy). The data in the schedule was provided by Rick Nelson of R.K. Nelson & Associates, Inc.

If you need 10 times the amount of the insurance shown, just move the decimal point (For example, for a male, age 45, $598,835 x 10 equals $5,988,350. The premium cost would rise to $100,000 per year). Or, if you need 18 times the amount shown, just multiply the amount shown by 18. For example, for second-to-die, age 60, $546,556 x 18 equals $9,838,008. The premium cost would be $180,000 per year.

Now let's see just how badly we can beat up the estate tax liability or actually create wealth, assuming a top estate-tax bracket of 55 percent, you and your spouse are 55 years old, and you buy a second-to-die policy (in an ILIT, of course) in the various amounts shown.

**AMOUNT OF ESTATE TAX PAID OR WEALTH CREATED WHEN PURCHASING A SECOND-TO-DIE POLICY FOR TWO (HUSBAND AND WIFE) 55-YEAR-OLDS**

**TRANSFER ESTATE TAX LIABILITY TO INSURANCE COMPANY**

| (1) Amount of Estate Subject to 55% Tax (Millions) | (2) Tax on Column (1) (Millions) | (3) Total Premium to Buy Insurance Equal to Column (2)* | To Increase Wealth by 50% (4) 50% of Column (1) (Millions) | (5) Premium Required** |
|---|---|---|---|---|
| $ 1 | $ .55 | $ 67,090 | $ .50 | $ 61,036 |
| 5 | 2.75 | 333,445 | 2.50 | 303,178 |
| 10 | 5.50 | 666,390 | 5.00 | 605,855 |
| 25 | 13.75 | 1,665,226 | 12.50 | 1,513,888 |
| 50 | 27.50 | 3,329,952 | 25.00 | 3,027,275 |
| 100 | 55.00 | 6,659,405 | 50.00 | 6,054,050 |

*Paid at rate of 1/10 of amount shown for 10 years. Then policy self-carries.

**Amount of premium required to purchase insurance equal to amount in column (4); premium paid at rate of 1/10 of amount shown for 10 years.

Understandably, determining the variations and adjustments needed to refine the above schedule so you can tell how it precisely would impact you and your family requires the input of a competent insurance consultant with actual current quotes for premiums and coverage. If you are a stickler for detail, you'll want your professional advisor to consider the time value of money among other factors.

## ■ AN OBSERVATION AND A SUGGESTION

One thing is clear. In the preceding schedule for our two 55-year-olds, an investment, for example, of $605,855 [Column (5)] in premiums will yield $5 million after the second of our two insureds dies. That's a ratio of 8.25 to 1. The ratio stays the same for all amounts on the schedule. Put another way, for every dollar in premium, you get back at least $8.25.

My suggestion. Get your insurance consultant to run the numbers for,

1. You alone,
2. Your spouse alone, and
3. Second-to-die.

Then make your own decision. Remember, an ILIT will always protect the proceeds from the estate tax.

# PART VIII

# Estate Planning

VIII

# INTRODUCTION

## You Ain't Dead Yet

A will is not an estate plan.

A trust is not an estate plan.

Both are not an estate plan. At best, these documents are one part of your death plan.

But wait a minute. *You ain't dead yet.*

Try it this way. This is a psychological test. When I say the words "estate planning," what word do you think of? "Death." Right? Some people say, "Dying." Why? Because to the legal, accounting and insurance professions, the words "estate planning" are synonymous with death planning. That's what they have conveyed to you—their client. They think that way. They practice their professions that way.

Well, I don't. But "why?" you ask. Because 95 percent (or more) of the business owners I consult with are healthy for their ages. So are their spouses. Tell you what. Stop reading for a moment and turn to page 426 in the appendix. Find your life expectancy. Next, your spouse's life expectancy.

For sure, no estate tax is due until you die. Most likely, none will be due until the second of you joins the other in heaven. How many years do you think that might be?

So chances are, we've got a long time to plan for your demise, and probably even more years before the IRS sees penny one in estate taxes from you and your spouse.

That's why *I'm hooked on lifetime planning as the real key to death planning.* Yes, your estate plan should dovetail with your lifetime plan. Of course, your lifetime planning—as you get older and circumstances change—is a moving target. So is your estate planning.

Even when done properly, estate planning is never quite done. It is an ongoing process—a process that should start as soon as possible—and continue, especially for larger estates, until you draw your last breath.

# 1 Basic Estate Planning Concepts

Even though the subject is technical, this chapter is basically nontechnical.

Estate planning is more an art than a science. It may require the input and expertise of a CPA, a lawyer, an insurance agent or broker, a bank trust officer, and an appraiser. Death planning should never be done without doing lifetime planning at the same time. With few exceptions, most estate plans can be changed right up to the moment the taxpayer dies.

## Estate-Planning Preparation

There are four basic steps you should take when preparing an estate plan:

1. List your family and beneficiaries, as well as your assets and liabilities (see Exhibit A)
2. Accumulate all necessary documents (see Exhibit B)
3. List your goals and minimum requirements as if you were going to live to be 120. Then list your goals and requirements as if you were going to die tomorrow.
4. Consult the appropriate professional advisors for help in selecting and implementing the best estate planning devices for your particular circumstances. *You must select one advisor to coordinate the entire plan.*

Among the most popular estate planning devices are:

**INSURANCE TRUST.** This is a revocable trust, often called a living trust, created during life and naming the trustee as the beneficiary of the insurance policies but leaving with the creator of the trust all former rights enjoyed as owner under the insurance policies. A living trust may or may not have insurance involved.

**POUR-OVER WILL.** This is a simple will, generally leaving personal effects to your spouse and then pouring over the balance of the assets into a living trust.

**MARITAL TRUST.** Usually called Trust A or the spousal trust. This is a separate trust established in your will or living trust. It comes to life after your death and holds assets for your spouse, usually for your spouse's life with a right in your spouse to direct the trust upon death. This right is called a general power of appointment. This trust qualifies for a marital deduction under the federal estate tax.

**RESIDUARY TRUST.** Usually called Trust B but sometimes referred to as a residual trust, family trust, or credit shelter trust, this is a second, separate trust that is established by your trust will. It too comes to life after your death and usually holds the balance of your property after funding the marital trust. The provisions usually benefit the surviving spouse during his or her lifetime and the children during and after the spouse's life. This trust is sometimes called a bypass trust because it bypasses the surviving spouse's estate.

**ESTATE TRUST.** This type of trust permits the accumulation of income during your surviving spouse's life but requires the principal and accumulated income to be distributed to your spouse's probate estate. It qualifies for the marital deduction.

**QUALIFIED TERMINABLE INTEREST PROPERTY (QTIP) TRUST.** This type of separate trust holds qualified terminable interest property, and qualifies for the marital deduction. The required characteristics of a QTIP trust are the same as for a life estate power-of-appointment trust (marital trust) except (1) there is no requirement for a general power of appointment and (2) the executor must elect on the estate tax return to have the interest qualify for the marital deduction.

Essentially a QTIP trust is a trust under which the surviving spouse is entitled to all the income for life and no person can appoint any part of the property to anyone other than the surviving spouse during her life. QTIP trust property qualifies for the marital deduction only if the executor of the estate of the decedent spouse elects to claim the marital deduction with respect to the property. If this election is made, the QTIP trust property will be included in the surviving spouse's estate unless she disposes of all or part of her interest income during her lifetime.

■ **A TECHNICAL NOTE:** Survivor annuities are treated as QTIP property under Sections 2056(b)(7)(C) and 2523(f)(6).

## ■ EXHIBIT A: FAMILY/BENEFICIARY AND ASSET/LIABILITY WORK SHEET

Your Name: ______________________________

Date Prepared: ______________________________

### A. FAMILY AND BENEFICIARIES

List your spouse, children, grandchildren, and anyone else you want to receive a portion of your estate, including charities.

| | Name | Birthday | Relationship | Married | Dependents |
|---|---|---|---|---|---|
| 1. | ________ | ________ | ________ | ________ | ________ |
| 2. | ________ | ________ | ________ | ________ | ________ |
| 3. | ________ | ________ | ________ | ________ | ________ |
| 4. | ________ | ________ | ________ | ________ | ________ |
| 5. | ________ | ________ | ________ | ________ | ________ |

Indicate if any beneficiary has (1) any current interests in existing trusts. (2) potential inheritances or other expectancies. (3) any special problems that need attention.

### B. ASSETS AND LIABILITIES (PERSONAL BALANCE SHEET)

| Assets | Date acquired | Tax basis | Value today | Estimated death value |
|---|---|---|---|---|
| 1. Real estate (see Liabilities) | ________ | $ ________ | $ ________ | $ ________ |
| 2. Stocks—marketable | ________ | ________ | ________ | ________ |
| 3. Bonds—marketable | ________ | ________ | ________ | ________ |
| 4. Cash and bank accounts | ________ | ________ | ________ | ________ |
| 5. Life insurance (see Liabilities) | ________ | ________ | ________ | ________ |
| 6. Mortgages, notes, and accounts receivable | ________ | ________ | ________ | ________ |
| 7. Closely held corporations | ________ | ________ | ________ | ________ |
| 8. Partnerships and proprietorships | ________ | ________ | ________ | ________ |
| 9. Profit-sharing and pension plans | ________ | ________ | ________ | ________ |
| 10. Annuities | ________ | ________ | ________ | ________ |
| 11. Tangible property | ________ | ________ | ________ | ________ |
| 12. Residence (see Liabilities) | ________ | ________ | ________ | ________ |
| 13. Joint property | ________ | ________ | ________ | ________ |
| 14. Other property | ________ | ________ | ________ | ________ |
| Total assets | ________ | $ ________ | $ ________ | $ ________ |

| Liabilities | Owned today | Estimated at death |
|---|---|---|
| 1. Mortgages (see Assets) | $______ | $______ |
| 5. Insurance loans (see Assets) | ______ | ______ |
| 12. Mortgages (see Assets) | ______ | ______ |
| 15. Notes and loans | ______ | ______ |
| 16. Taxes | ______ | ______ |
| 17. Other | ______ | ______ |
| Total liabilities | $______ | $______ |
| Net worth at death | ______ | ______ |
| (Total assets minus total liabilities) | $______ | $______ |

**NOTES:**

(1) Your spouse must make an identical list.

(2) Children who have assets over $100,000 should make a list.

(3) For value at death use 10 or 15 years. Try to determine the value of your estate down the road.

(4) Make schedules for each asset and liability when necessary.

(5) The current balance due on any mortgage should not be deducted from the "value today," but listed as a liability.

(6) List all insurance policies on your life.
For each policy list the following: company, policy number, date of policy, type of policy, name of insured, owner, annual premium, face amount, present cash value, policy loans, death value, beneficiary designation, dividend additions, special features, and settlement options.

(7) For closely held corporations and partnerships give a description, percent owned, buy-sell agreements in effect, and special pertinent information (financial statements, all agreements).

(8) For joint property, make a separate schedule showing the joint tenant for each piece of property.

(9) Other property could include an interest in any trust already established, an expectancy of an inheritance, or a general power of appointment.

(10) Indicate if any assets are located outside your state of permanent residence.

## Property Included in a Decedent's Estate

That's what you are called when you die—a decedent. Then the Internal Revenue Code (the Code), via its various sections, determines which items are included in your estate. The following table, intended for your professionals, lists not only the items included, but also the Code section that authorizes their inclusion.

| CODE SECTION | TYPE OF PROPERTY |
|---|---|
| 2031 | All property, real or personal, tangible or intangible, wherever situated |
| 2033 | To the extent of the interest therein of the decedent at the time of his death |
| 2034 | Any interest of dower or curtesy |
| 2035(d) | Gifts made within three years of the donor's death are not included in his estate unless the subject of the gift is life insurance, a retained life estate, a reversionary interest, the right to revoke a prior transfer or a general power of appointment |
| 2035(c) | Gift tax paid or due on gifts made during three years before decedent's death |
| 2036 | Transfers with retained life estate<br>■ **EXAMPLE:** Decedent's estate included a house, which she transferred to her daughter but continued to live in until her death (*Estate of Honigman*). |
| 2037 | Transfers taking effect at death<br>■ **EXAMPLE:** By a trust agreement, decedent, D, gave a life interest to her second husband A of income-producing real property. The property would revert to D if she survived A; but if A survived D (A Did), upon A's death the property would pass to D's child. At D's death, both D and A were 88 years old; the value of the property was $100,000 and the applicable rate was 11.6 percent.<br>Under the terms of the trust, decedent retained a reversionary interest. Whether the property is includable in D's estate depends on whether the reversionary interest exceeds 5 percent—Section 2037(a)(2). Decedent's reversionary interest does exceed 5 percent.<br>The value of the reversionary interest, however, is not the interest includable in D's estate. Section 2037(a) requires the inclusion of the entire interest at its date-of-death value of $100,000, less the value of A's life estate. The valuation tables are now published monthly and are without regard to sex. The interest factor used is 120 percent of the applicable federal midterm rate. The includable interest is the value of the property reduced by the value of A's life estate at age 88 or $37,325 ($100,000 minus [$100,000 x 0.62675]). This interest is determined by using the remainder factor applicable to a person aged 88, as specified in Treasury Regulation § 20.2031-7(f) (see IRS Notice 89-60, 1989-22 IRB). |
| 2038 | Revocable transfer...by trust or otherwise |
| 2039 | The value of an annuity or other payment receivable |
| 2040 | Joint interests |
| 2041 | Powers of appointment |
| 2042 | Proceeds of life insurance |
| 2043 | Gifts—transfer for insufficient consideration |
| 2044 | Certain property for which a marital deduction was previously allowed (QTIP trusts) |
| 2045 | Prior interests |
| 2046 & 2518 | Disclaimers |
| 2001(b) | Taxable gifts made after December 31, 1976, are used to increase the total tax due but are actually not part of the gross estate |

**■ EXHIBIT B: DOCUMENTS AND OTHER INFORMATION NEEDED FOR ESTATE PLANNING**

**A. DOCUMENTS**

- ☐ 1. Your will
- ☐ 2. Spouse's will
- ☐ 3. Wills of other members of family, if pertinent
- ☐ 4. Trust instruments created by you, other trusts in which you have an interest or general power of appointment (marital or other)
- ☐ 5. Leases on property on which you are the lessor or lessee
- ☐ 6. Partnership agreements
- ☐ 7. Financial statements and tax returns for past two years in all business in which you have a substantial interest
- ☐ 8. Personal balance sheet (from Exhibit A)
- ☐ 9. Divorce decrees or separation agreements
- ☐ 10. Antenuptial or postnuptial agreements
- ☐ 11. Close corporation buy-sell agreements
- ☐ 12. Copies of employment contracts
- ☐ 13. Personal income tax returns, federal and state, for the past two years.
- ☐ 14. Gift tax returns (and any revenue agent's report)
- ☐ 15. Documents evidencing current and future interests in employer's qualified plans and other employment benefits
- ☐ 16. Any other documents giving you a right, title, or interest of any kind

**B. ADVISORS**

| | Name | Address | Phone No. |
|---|---|---|---|
| 1. Attorney* | ____________ | ____________ | __________ |
| 2. Accountant* | ____________ | ____________ | __________ |
| 3. Trust officer | ____________ | ____________ | __________ |
| 4. Other bank officer | ____________ | ____________ | __________ |
| 5. Life insurance consultant* | ____________ | ____________ | __________ |
| 6. Investment adviser | ____________ | ____________ | __________ |
| 7. Stock broker | ____________ | ____________ | __________ |
| 8. Tax adviser* | ____________ | ____________ | __________ |
| 9. General insurance broker | ____________ | ____________ | __________ |

*Indicate which advisor is responsible for coordinating the entire effort and has final responsibility.

## A Typical Estate Plan

A typical estate plan might look like Exhibit C. The residuary Trust B (or bypass trust) is used to house at least $600,000 (the amount exempt from estate tax) in assets. Because these assets totally avoid Trust A, that is why Trust B is sometimes called by bypass trust.

## ■ EXHIBIT C: A TYPICAL ESTATE PLAN FOR TAXPAYER T

The life insurance or living trust and pour-over will

A. During T's lifetime.
   1. Trustee is beneficiary of life insurance policies; T is usually trustee if no insurance.

B. Upon T's death.
   1. Assets flow as shown.
   2. During T's spouse's lifetime, Trusts A and B are held for his/her benefit by trustee.
   3. Upon T's spouse's death:
      a. Trust A is used as spouse directs.
      b. Trust B goes to children.

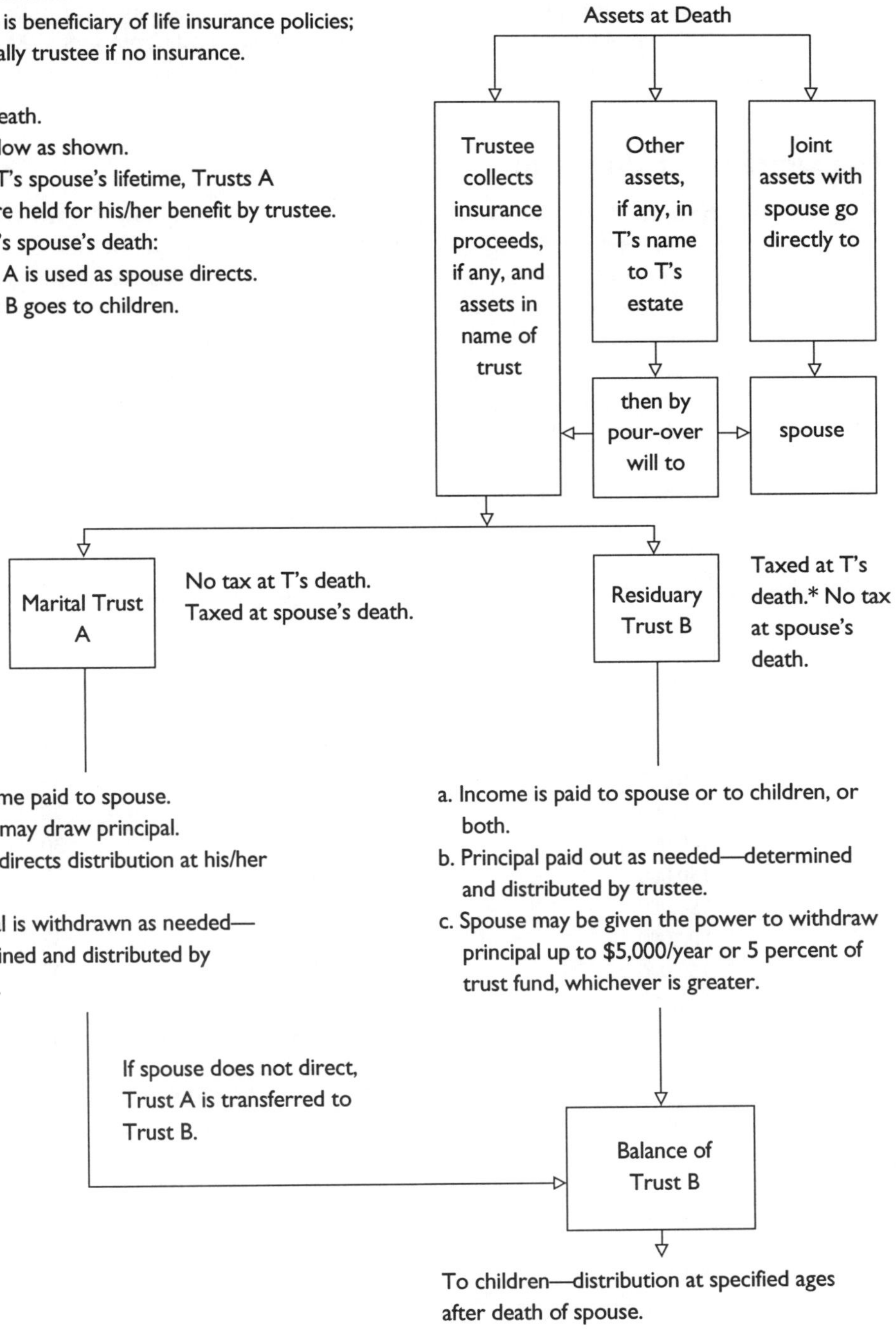


*But would be only $600,000, so although subject to tax would typically escape a cash tax because the unified credit would actually "pay" the tax due.

The residual trust also accepts all other property not taken up by the marital deduction or other dispositions made by the estate plan, including disclaimers.

A QTIP trust may be substituted for marital Trust A, which does not appear in some estate plans. In others, Trust A is used in combination with a QTIP trust. However, outright transfers to a surviving spouse are also common.

Taxpayers commonly use all of the unified credit (it renders $600,000 estate tax free) and then use the unlimited marital deduction to defer all federal estate taxes to the death of the second spouse.

## The Unitax and Unicredit

The unified transfer tax (Unitax) is levied on lifetime gifts and on gifts at death. The unified credit (Unicredit) is $192,800 and actually pays the first $192,800 of your lifetime gift tax bill or estate tax bill. If you made a lifetime taxable gift of $600,000 or died with a taxable estate of $600,000, the Unicredit would pay the entire tax due—$192,800. Put another way, any combination of taxable gifts made during your life and added to your taxable estate are free of tax if the total if $600,000 or less.

The following schedule shows the Unitax rates for up to $1,250,000. The complete rate schedule is in the Appendix.

**■ FEDERAL UNIFIED GIFT AND ESTATE TAX (UNITAX) RATES UP TO $1,250,000**

| Taxable amount | Tax | % on excess |
|---|---|---|
| -0- | -0- | 18% |
| $ 10,000 | $ 1,800 | 20 |
| 20,000 | 3,800 | 22 |
| 40,000 | 8,200 | 24 |
| 60,000 | 13,000 | 26 |
| 80,000 | 18,200 | 28 |
| 100,000 | 23,800 | 30 |
| 150,000 | 38,800 | 32 |
| 250,000 | 70,800 | 34 |
| 500,000 | 155,800 | 37 |
| 750,000 | 248,300 | 39 |
| 1,000,000 | 345,800 | 41 |
| 1,250,000 | 448,300 | 43 |

Okay, let's see how the Unitax is figured on $600,000. You'll see that the result is $192,800—the amount of the Unicredit. Refer to the schedule above.

| | |
|---|---|
| Tax on $500,000 | $155,800 |
| Tax on $100,000 @ 37% | 37,000 |
| Total Tax | $192,800* |

*No cash tax; paid with Unicredit.

Now let's use your new-found expertise to figure the tax on $1,450,000.

| | |
|---|---|
| Tax on $1,250,000 | $448,300 |
| Tax on $200,000 @ 43% | 86,000 |
| Total Tax | 534,300 |
| Less—paid with Unicredit | 192,800 |
| Tax to be paid with real American dollars | $341,500 |

## The Marital Deduction for the Surviving Spouse

The marital deduction became law by virtue of the Revenue Act of 1948. It was designed to extend to residents of all states the same estate-tax advantages that had previously existed only for residents of community property states. Tax savings are so large that the marital deduction is now the heart of most estate plans.

There are at least seven ways of achieving the marital deduction:

1. Bequest or devise outright to surviving spouse.
2. Testamentary trust qualifying for marital deduction (created in will) because it does not violate the terminable interest rule (i.e., has a general power of appointment).
3. Intestate distribution to surviving spouse (property not covered by will, but required to be distributed to the surviving spouse by state law).
4. Life insurance proceeds payable to spouse (decedent owned policy at death).
5. Joint ownership (or tenancy by the entirety) with right of survivorship (when spouse is other tenant).
6. Bequest to a QTIP trust where the executor elects to qualify it for the marital deduction.
7. Surviving spouse is the beneficiary of a retirement plan.

### Determining the Amount of the Marital Deduction

All transfers (except certain terminable interests) between spouses (including community property) are allowed to pass free of gift and estate taxes. Congress makes a husband and wife one economic unit for estate tax and gift tax purposes.

■ **EXAMPLE:** Andy leaves his wife his entire estate—exactly $2,000,000—when he dies. The entire amount is tax-free because of the marital deduction. The result would be the same no matter how large Andy's estate might be.

### The Terminable-Interest Rule (Complicated Stuff)

Assets transferred to a spouse either during lifetime or at death qualify for the gift or estate marital deduction. Any interest in such assets that is not a terminable interest will so qualify. A lifetime interest given to the spouse in trust, together with a general power of appointment to designate the recipient of the principal, is not considered a terminable interest and will qualify for the marital deduction, provided the spouse can designate any recipient desired. The power must be exercisable in favor of the spouse or his/her estate, including creditors. The spouse must have the power alone, although it may be exercisable by will or during life, or both. The spouse must be entitled to the income for life payable at least annually (section 2056(b)).

## ■ EXAMPLES

1. A life estate for the surviving spouse with remainder to another person does not qualify, e.g.: "The income from all my real estate to my wife for life and on her death, the property to my son, John."
2. The surviving spouse must survive for a certain period of time. "To my wife, if she survives me for one year" would not qualify. A period not exceeding six months qualifies if the spouse does not die during that period.
3. A life estate to the surviving spouse with a general power of appointment qualifies. "To my wife for life, but at any time prior to her death or on her death, she may, by will, appoint the property to any person or persons, including her estate as she may designate."

The marital deduction can be easily lost or put in jeopardy by the terminable interest rule. In the *Estate of Blanche T. Fiedler*, 67 TC 21 (1976), a life insurance policy had a marital deduction provision that gave the surviving spouse the right to revoke the designation of contingent beneficiaries and appoint the proceeds to his estate. The surviving spouse elected a settlement option 19 months after his wife's death. The court held the insurance proceeds qualify for the marital deduction, since the policy satisfies the requirements of Section 2056(b)(6).

In the *Estate of David A. Siegel* T.C. Memo 1985-441, joint wills contractually bound spouses to have the estate of survivor pass to agreed-upon beneficiaries. The court disallowed the marital deduction because it was a terminable interest.

A surviving spouse had unrestricted power of appointment under Virginia law where the decedent's will provided her with a life estate, not in trust, and unrestricted power to consume and dispose, with remainder to their children. Rev. Rul. 77-30 holds that the estate gets a marital deduction.

A decedent created what would, in most states, be a life estate with general power of appointment for his surviving spouse (*W*). However, Maryland law requires express provisions allowing her to appoint corpus to herself, her estate and creditors. *W's* power of appointment did not meet the requirements of either Section 2041(b) or 2056(b)(5). Under Rev. Rule. 76-502 the IRS disallowed the marital deduction.

Here's an article from my tax column that shows you how this complex rule can trip up innocent taxpayers.

HOW NOT TO PLAY THE ESTATE TAX GAME

Sometimes the IRS beats up a taxpayer because of a complex tax law. The taxpayer may be technically wrong, but, in my opinion, the complex tax law is what's wrong. Such cases really make me angry. This is the story behind a real case that tripped up a real taxpayer and could affect every married reader of this column.

Here are the facts. Corinne, a Texas resident, had a typical will—she left everything to her husband, Charles, and wanted her estate to go to her two children if Charles died before she did. One clause in her will gave her estate to the kids if Charles should *"predecease me or die before this Will is admitted to probate"* (emphasis added). Re-read those last eight words of the will-slowly. The kids would get the property, instead of Charles, if two things happened: First, Charles had to survive Corinne and, second, Charles had to die before Corinne's will was admitted to probate. This is exactly what happened after Corinne died: Charles survived her; her will was admitted to probate within three weeks of her death, so Charles got Corinne's property, not the kids.

Now, a little lesson in the federal estate tax law. A wonderful rule called the "unlimited marital deduction" allows a husband or wife to make unlimited gifts to each other, during life or at death, free of any estate tax. Hey, that's a good law. But wait. You can blow the marital deduction by giving your spouse a "terminable interest," defined as an interest that will cease after a certain length of time or upon the occurrence of an event.

Okay, now let's apply the law to Corinne's case. The IRS did, and blew away a marital deduction of over $500,000 claimed by Corinne's estate. Is the IRS right? Yes, said the Tax Court. You see, under Texas law, a will can be admitted to probate at any time within four years after death. So what? Well, legally, Charles' interest in the estate could have been terminated up to four years after Corinne died, if the will took that long to get to probate and he had died within that period. Simply put, even though it didn't happen that way, it was a possibility. Result? Charles' interest was terminable. No marital deduction (see Tax Court Memo, 1989-610).

A mistake like this could cost your family thousands, or millions, of dollars depending on the size of your estate. It is, in my opinion, impossible for anyone, except a professional who specializes in this area of the tax law, to recognize the opportunities, traps, and exceptions when planning an estate. How can you protect your family? Use only full-time tax practitioners who are experts in this area. Others can be dangerous to your family's tax and economic health.

## Tax Planning with the Unlimited Marital Deduction

The following points will guide you in getting the maximum benefit from the unlimited marital deduction.

### Deferral of Appreciation

**GROSS ESTATE DEDUCTION.** Because the marital property is deducted from the gross estate of the first spouse to die and is included in the gross estate of the second, taxation of the marital deduction property and any appreciation thereof is deferred to the estate of the surviving spouse.

The marital deduction is disallowed if the surviving spouse is not a U.S. citizen. However, there is an exception if the property is transferred to a qualified domestic trust as provided under Section 2056A.

**NONMARITAL PROPERTY (TRUST B OR BYPASS TRUST).** Property that does not qualify for the marital deduction and that is placed in a nonmarital trust (a marital deduction is not received) for the benefit of the surviving spouse or others, or both, is taxed on the death of the first spouse. That property and any appreciation on it is not subject to the estate tax on the death of the surviving spouse. A portion of that property, however, may be subject to a generation-skipping transfer tax (discussed later in this chapter).

Every estate should have at least $600,000 of nonmarital property to fill up the maximum allowable tax-free cup.

### Control in Surviving Spouse

If the surviving spouse feels a need to control the property, an outright distribution or a life estate-general power of appointment trust (for Trust A) with a right of withdrawal (limited or unlimited) may be indicated.

The surviving spouse can be granted a limited power of appointment for the property in Trust B. This is just one more use of Trust B (bypass trust).

### An Estate Trust for the Wealthy

For a surviving spouse earning substantial income, an estate trust may be desirable. An estate trust gives the trustee discretion to accumulate part or all of the income rather than distribute it to the surviving spouse. Principal and accumulated income must be distributed to the estate at death. An estate trust allows income to be split between the surviving spouse and the trust, which usually results in lower overall income taxes.

---

#### ■ TAX-SAVING IDEA

Remember, both the QTIP trust and a general power of appointment marital trust create taxable income for the surviving spouse because the trust must be a simple trust, which means the trust cannot accumulate any income but must pay all the income to the beneficiary. The spouse has no way of avoiding the high-taxed income. An estate trust solves the problem.

---

### Factors Affecting the Marital Deduction

Since the marital deduction eliminates all tax at the death of the first spouse, there is a tendency to use the marital deduction to the fullest extent possible. This may not produce the lowest overall tax. Several factors should be considered before deciding on the size of the marital deduction to be used.

**INFLATION.** Use the best estimate.

**AGE AND HEALTH OF SPOUSE.** The following life expectancy table should be helpful:

| Age | Males | Females |
|---|---|---|
| 60 | 17.5 | 22.5 |
| 65 | 14.3 | 18.7 |
| 70 | 11.4 | 15.1 |
| 75 | 9.0 | 11.8 |
| 80 | 7.2 | 9.3 |

**EARNINGS ON DEFERRED TAXES.** How much can be earned with the estate tax savings (after income taxes) from the death of the first spouse to the estimated death of the second spouse?

**APPRECIATION.** What is the likelihood of assets not taxed in the first estate appreciating in value—causing a larger tax in the second estate?

### A Must Planning Point for Every Estate

Transfer to the surviving spouse's marital estate—either outright or in trust—assets that will be consumed (cash), that will be subject to income tax (pension accounts and annuities), or that will depreciate in value (personal property). Transfer highly appreciating assets to the credit shelter trust (Trust B). All assets transferred to Trust B will not be included in the gross estate of the second spouse to die.

**GIFTS.** How much might a gift program reduce the size of the second estate?

■ **PLANNING POINTER:** A systematic gifting program should be established in every wealthy person's estate plan, and the sooner the better. The grantor should gift away assets that are likely to appreciate. *Size of the estate:* Probably the most significant factor. Consider the size of your estate, the size of your spouse's estate now, and expectancies (from parents/others) that would increase the size of your spouse's estate).

---

■ **TAX-SAVING IDEA**

Assume both the husband and the wife are elderly and the most-likely surviving spouse already has a large estate: the first spouse to die should leave a life interest only to the surviving spouse. This is a terminable interest and will not qualify for the marital deduction. However, when the second spouse dies, the property is excluded from the second spouse's estate.

Combine this concept with a QTIP trust. To qualify as a QTIP, the trust must met all of the qualifications of Section 2056(b)(7). A QTIP is a terminable interest; however, the executor may elect to qualify it for the marital deduction. The executor may make the election for all or part of the trust property. If the surviving spouse already has a large estate, this gives the executor the flexibility to evaluate the situation and make the QTIP election for whatever portion he so desires to receive the best estate tax benefits.

---

### "Must" Considerations for Large and Small Estates

People with large estates (depending on the age differential and health of the spouses) may find use of the unlimited marital deduction subjects the second estate to a substantially greater tax than would have been paid if less than an unlimited marital deduction had been used.

What about small estates? Remember that the basis of property acquired from a decedent is equal to the amount at which it was included in the decedent's gross estate. Thus, in the case of appreciated property, the beneficiary will receive a step-up in basis and the appreciation will generally escape income taxes. In many smaller estates, better tax results can be attained by keeping appreciated property rather than gifting it to the spouse.

■ **EXAMPLE**

If Sue inherits 1,000 shares of Public Co. left by her husband, Ken, that had a $150,000 value at the date of death, but only cost $70,000, the taxable gain would be only $5,000 if Sue sold the stock for $155,000. On the other hand, if Ken had gifted the stock to Sue many years before his death, the taxable gain on sale would be $85,000 ($155,000 less the $70,000 cost basis).

There is an exception for appreciated gifts received by the decedent within one year of death. Section 1014(e) provides that if that property passes back to the donor, or the spouse of the donor, there will be no step-up in basis. Instead, the basis will be the same basis the decedent had just prior to death. This rule prevents transfers for the expressed purpose of getting a step-up in basis.

■ **EXAMPLE**

Ann, the wife of Joe, who is wealthy, becomes terminally ill. Joe immediately gifts stock to Ann with a $10,000 tax basis and a fair-market value of $500,000. Ann dies six months after the stock gift, and her will bequests the stock to Joe. Joe does not receive a step-up in basis as provided in Section 1014(e), as the gift was made within one year of Ann's death and passes back to Joe, the donor. If Ann had lived more than one year after the gift, the step-up would have been allowed.

If the stock had passed to someone else, say a child, the step-up would have been allowed. Of course, the stock could not get the benefit of the marital deduction, but it could be sheltered by the unified credit.

### Inflexibility of Joint Tenancy

An estate plan that does take advantage of the Unicredit with a bypass trust (Trust B), that moves at least $600,000 tax-free will still have an important weakness if all the property is in joint tenancy with rights of survivorship. Since the jointly owned property passes directly to the spouse by operation of law, it may not be placed into the bypass trust. In some cases there may not be enough nonjoint property to fund the trust. Even when jointly owned property is at a minimum, if the wife dies first she will have nothing to shelter with her Unicredit.

One solution is to make interspousal gifts, sheltered by the unlimited gift tax marital deduction, to assure that each spouse has an estate large (at least $600,000) enough to make full use of the Unicredit.

■ **IMPORTANT:** When the estate plan is done, ask if the first $1,200,000 will pass tax-free. If not, something is wrong. Go back to the drawing board.

Another weakness is that joint tenancies generally cannot be disclaimed by the surviving joint tenant. The IRS has argued that a joint tenancy interest may only be disclaimed within nine months after the creation of the joint interest. However, Illinois law allows a surviving joint tenant to disclaim property. In *Kennedy v. Commissioner*, 804 F2d 1332 (7th Cir. 1986) the Appeals court overruled the regulations for disclaimers of a joint interest.

A third weakness is that Section 2040(b) provides that only one half of the value of a qualified joint interest of a husband and wife be included in the decedent's gross estate. Therefore, only one half of the property's tax basis is stepped-up at the date of death of the first spouse.

## ■ PLANNING POINTER

One of the reasons people place property in joint tenancy is to avoid probate. This does avoid probate but creates other problems such as inflexibility, disclaimer problems, and basis problems. *These traps can easily be overcome by using a revocable living trust.* You can establish the trust during your lifetime. You can retain the right to revoke the trust; the right to all the income; the right to change trustees; and the right to change the beneficiaries. The trust usually provides for the management of assets, although you can be your own trustee. The trust also provides for distribution on death and can ensure privacy. It can help you avoid being placed under a court-appointed guardian in the event of incompetence. The trust can be used as the A-B trust upon death or can pour over into the marital or residual trust. With a revocable living trust, the estate is settled without a court proceeding, as the assets are not frozen on death.

Beneficiaries can disclaim all or part of their interest. Since the full value of the trust assets is included in your gross estate—but not probate estate—the basis of the property is 100 percent stepped-up to fair-market value at your death.

### Order of Death

Tax consequences change depending on who dies first, husband or wife. The final decision on leaving property to the wife should be made only after completing a schedule containing at least the following information.

| A. If husband dies first | His estate | Her estate |
|---|---|---|
| 1. Gross estate | | |
| Own property | $XXXXX | $XXXXX |
| Marital deduction* | –(XXXX) | +XXXX |
| Balance/Total | $XXXX | $XXXXX |
| 2. Tax payable | $XXX | $XXXX |

| B. If wife dies first | His estate | Her estate |
|---|---|---|
| 1. Gross estate | $XXXXX | $XXXXX |
| Assume (1) no marital deduction | - | - |
| or | | |
| (2) marital deduction* | +XXXX | –(XXXX) |
| Balance/Total | $XXXXX | $XXXXX |
| 2. Tax payable | $XXXX | $XXX |

*Can vary from zero to the entire estate.

An analysis of the figures will determine the direction of the estate plan and the various devices to be utilized in implementing the same.

There are several alternatives when leaving property to the wife. It can be left

1. All in trust.
2. All outright.
3. Combination—most men leave at least the residence, an auto and some cash (usually via insurance) outright.

## Step-Up in Basis at Death

Among the most significant estate tax principles is the step-up in basis that a decedent's appreciated property is allowed at death (Section 1014). The amount of taxes saved for a spouse or beneficiaries can be enormous. For example, if the decedent bought stock for $1,000, which, over the course of his lifetime, appreciated to $50,000, he would face a hefty capital gains tax upon sale. If he holds on to the stock until death, however, his spouse, or whoever receives the shares from his estate, gets a stepped-up tax basis. That is, the recipient gets a new tax basis equal to the value the stock had on the decedent's date of death (or, if applicable, the alternate valuation date under Section 2032).

Income in respect of a decedent (IRD) does not receive a step-up (Section 1014(c)), however. These are nonproperty assets that the decedent had a right to at the date of death but had not included in income because of his cash basis method of accounting. Common IRD items include interest, commissions, fees receivable, installment sales, and amounts due from pension or profit-sharing plans and IRAs.

The estate-planning rule for individuals with significant amounts of appreciated assets is simple: Do not sell! This is particularly good advice as the taxpayer gets older. Common sense should always prevail. If an elderly taxpayer has substantially appreciated property and a buyer is in the wings eager to buy, consider the following alternatives to avoid current income tax recognition:

- ☐ Rent the property to the buyer with an option to buy at a fixed price after death.
- ☐ Make a tax-free Section 1031 exchange for like-kind property.
- ☐ If taxpayer is a corporate seller, make a tax-free exchange under Section 368 (reorganizations).
- ☐ If sale involves an involuntary conversion, replace with similar property and elect the Section 1033 nonrecognition provisions.

### ■ INCOME TAX-SAVINGS IDEA

The savings does not affect the federal estate tax. The assets enter the estate at the higher (fair-market) value. If cash is needed to pay the estate taxes and the appreciated assets must be sold, the executor should be the one to sell the appreciated assets after the decedent's death. Otherwise, if the decedent sells before death, the appreciation is subject to income tax. The after-income tax proceeds of sale will be hit with a second tax—the estate tax.

Maximize the available depreciation deductions prior to death. The date-of-death step-up does not result in a recapture.

Assets that have declined in value during the decedent's lifetime will have a step-down in basis at death. That is, the recipient of the assets will take the lower date-of-death fair-market value as his basis. A potential capital loss can be forfeited for these assets. Thus, they should be sold before death.

■ **EXAMPLE:** Joe acquires property that can be depreciated over five years for $100,000 on September 27, 1992. He dies on January 9, 1993 when the property's fair-market value is $97,000. On Joe's 1992 tax return, the election to expense $10,000 could be taken, plus one-half year's depreciation of 20 percent, [20% × $90,000 ($100,000 – $10,000)] × one-half, or $9,000 (a total of $19,000). None of the depreciation is subject to recapture, and the property's basis is stepped-up to $97,000.

# Joint Interests

Joint interest is the most popular form of concurrent ownership (ownership by more than one person). Types of joint ownership include:

- ☐ *Tenancy by the entirety.* A tenancy by the entirety exists only when the co-owners are husband and wife. Upon the death of either co-owner, the survivor becomes the sole owner by right of survivorship. This right of survivorship cannot be destroyed during the lives of the co-owners unless both consent. In some states, this form of ownership can exist only with respect to real property; in other states, it may also exist in the case of personal property. Many states do not provide for this form of ownership.
- ☐ *Joint tenancy with right of survivorship.* Joint tenancy, unlike a tenancy by the entirety, is not limited to husband and wife. However, the two forms of ownership are similar in that the right of survivorship exists in both. There is also a point of difference—in joint tenancy, one co-owner may usually convey an undivided interest in the jointly held property during life. This may not be done, however, by will; on the death of either of two joint tenants, the survivor immediately becomes the sole owner of all the property. The entire joint interest is not subject to probate but is included in the decedent's taxable estate, subject to some exceptions (see "Joint Tenancy" following).
- ☐ *Tenancy in common.* Tenancy in common is not limited to husband and wife, nor is there a right of survivorship. Either co-owner may dispose of his undivided interest in the property during life or on death by will. Only the decedent's interest (not the co-owner's interest) is subject to probate and inclusion in the estate.
- ☐ *Community property.* The features of community property vary in the different states, and the law of the particular state must be examined with respect to an individual owning such property. The states where community property exists are Arizona, California, Idaho, Louisiana, Nevada, New Mexico, Texas, Washington, and Wisconsin.

## Reasons for Using Joint Interests

The most common reason for using joint interests is to avoid probate and assure property passes to the survivor without any intervention. Some states have even established pseudo joint interests.

One form of pseudo joint interest is the institution trust account. Under this method, an individual signs an agreement with a financial institution providing that the funds in the account shall be held in the name of the person opening the account as trustee. One or more persons are named as beneficiaries. The trustee may make additional deposits or withdrawals at any time. The beneficiaries may be changed by the trustee at any time prior to death. At the death of the trustee, the funds become the property of the living beneficiaries, shared equally. There is no probate of the funds.

Under another plan called a payable-upon-death account, an individual signs an agreement with a financial institution providing that on his death the account shall be paid to a designated person or persons. The person establishing the account (holder) may make additional deposits or withdrawals at any time. The holder may change the designated persons at any time. At the death of the holder, the funds become the property of the designated persons. There is no probate of the funds. While it is conceded that joint tenancy may be useful, it in no way deserves the exalted position it holds in the mind of the public. Generally, the estate planner's objective is to convince the client to abandon joint tenancy since, under this method, neither tenant may make an effective testamentary disposition of the property.

### ■ EXAMPLE

In 1992 Husband dies. The only property he owns or has an interest in is $1,200,000 of joint-tenancy property with Wife. There is no tax at his death, but when Wife dies owning only the same $1,200,000 property owned when Husband died (and assuming it has the same value), the tax on Wife's estate will be $235,000.

If Husband had owned the property in his own name or as tenants in common, he could have used up his $192,000 Unicredit, keeping $600,000 worth of property in a bypass trust (Trust B); when Wife died owning the other $600,000 half, she would have had a zero-estate tax, resulting in a $235,000 saving.

### Tax Consequences of Joint Tenancy

When considering a joint tenancy, the taxpayer should look at the consequences this action will have on income, gift, and estate taxes.

**INCOME TAX.** For income-producing property, each tenant must include in his gross income that portion of the income from the property to which he is entitled under local law. The interest increment on Series E bonds is taxable to both joint tenants in proportion to the amount of the purchase price contributed by each.

Assuming no contribution by the surviving joint tenant, the basis of the property to the survivor is the value of the property as reported for estate tax purposes in the estate of the deceased joint tenant. If the joint tenant made a contribution, then only that portion included in the decedent's estate is subject to this rule. However, there is a special rule (discussed later in this chapter) if the sole surviving joint tenant is the decedent's spouse.

### ■ EXAMPLE

George and his son Junior acquire raw land for $100,000 in 1992 in joint tenancy with rights of survivorship. George provides $75,000 of the funds to acquire the land, and Junior provides $25,000. They agree to split the income from the land 75 percent/25 percent. In 1994, George dies when the land's value is $150,000. George would have reported 75 percent of any income from the land up to his date of death. There is no probate of the land as it passes to Junior immediately upon George's death. Junior reports 25 percent of the income up to George's death and 100 percent thereafter. George's gross estate includes 75 percent of the value of the land, or $112,500 (75 percent x $150,000).

This is the proportionate share of his contribution to the purchase of the land. Junior's tax basis in the land is $137,500. This is made up of the $112,500 includable in George's estate plus Junior's $25,000 contribution.

If George's will devised his share of the land to his wife Ann, it would be of no consequence, as the joint ownership, by operation of law, overrides the will. Ann would receive no interest in the land, and it therefore would not qualify for the marital deduction. Also, Ann would have no right to any income from the land. There is no flexibility in testamentary planning.

If George had gifted $25,000 cash to Junior to acquire the land, the full value would have been included in George's estate (Section 2040(a)).

---

■ **MORTGAGED JOINTLY OWNED REAL ESTATE:** If land, for example, is mortgaged, the determination of the value includable in an estate can become difficult. The practitioner must go back to the date of acquisition and come forward, determining who provided the funds, either from income, principal, or otherwise, to reduce the mortgage. It is worth the trouble since it usually reduces the decedent's gross estate and the estate tax.

**GIFT TAX.** For savings or bank accounts, Series E bonds, or stock held in street name (title kept by brokerage house), when a joint tenancy is created with the donor's funds, no gift tax is due at the time the gift is established with the joint tenant. The tax is due when the joint tenant uses the funds or has the property put in his name. For all other types of property, a gift is made when the joint tenancy is created. A joint tenancy is created when a purchaser buys property with his own funds and has the property conveyed to himself and another as joint tenants with right of survivorship. Under some local laws, the recipient may sever the joint tenancy. One half the value of such property is considered a gift, for tax purposes, to the joint tenant who is not the purchaser.

When joint tenancy is created with a spouse, there is a gift. However, there is an unlimited deduction for lifetime gifts to a spouse (Section 2523). No gift tax return is required.

## Unwinding Joint Tenancy

Care must be taken if it is decided to transfer property from joint tenancy to tenants in common. Additional gifts may be created at that point. This is not a major concern if the other joint tenant is a spouse. The severing of joint tenancy results in a gift if each joint tenant does not receive his proportionate share of the property.

### ■ EXAMPLE 1

In 1991, Lou placed land he owned with a fair-market value of $500,000 in joint tenancy with his daughter Sue. Lou filed a gift tax return for the $250,000 gift and used part of his Unicredit. In 1994, Lou's tax adviser suggested that Lou sever the joint tenancy for estate-planning purposes when it's value was $1,200,000. Sue signed the legal documents transferring the land back to Lou. Sue has given up her one-half interest in the land and has therefore made a taxable gift of $600,000 (.5 x $1,200,000) to her father Lou. If one half of the land had been transferred to Lou and one half to Sue as tenants in common, no gift would have resulted.

**■ EXAMPLE 2**

Assume the same facts as in Example 1, except Lou's joint tenant was his wife Mary. The gift in 1991 would get the benefit of being a marital deduction pursuant to Section 2523 and would not require using any of the Unicredit. In 1994, Mary's $600,000 gift to Lou would also be subject to the marital deduction—no gift tax consequences.

**■ EXAMPLE 3**

Assume the same facts as in Example 1, except in this case the property is a savings account. No gift is created when checking, savings, and other bank accounts are placed in joint tenancy. However, if the noncontributing joint tenant utilizes the funds, there is a gift at that time. If a joint bank account is created, even though there is no gift at that time, the noncontributing joint tenant has a legal right to demand one half of the account balance.

**■ A BETTER IDEA THAN JOINT TENANCY:** Instead of joint tenancy to avoid probate, consider a trust arrangement. Revocable (living trusts) and irrevocable trusts are discussed more completely in Chapter 2 of this part.

**ESTATE TAX—SECTION 2040.** The entire value of the jointly held property is includable in the gross estate of the first tenant to die except to the extent the executor is able to show the other tenant's contribution toward the property acquisition (usually called the consideration-furnished test). However, if the other tenant's contribution was received as a gift from the decedent, it will not be treated as the other tenant's contribution, but the decedent's contribution.

The amount of joint property acquired by gift or inheritance includable in the gross estate of the decedent is only that fraction of the property owned by the decedent (i.e., one half if there are two joint tenants).

**EXCEPTION WHEN JOINT TENANTS ARE SPOUSES.** Section 2040(b) provides that a qualified joint interest is treated as if 50 percent were owned by each spouse, regardless of who paid for the property. The rule is simple: one half of all property jointly owned by spouses with right of survivorship is excluded from the estate of the first to die. It makes no difference which spouse paid for the property or how much either contributed. The only requirement is that the surviving spouse and the decedent were the only joint tenants.

**■ AN IMPORTANT DIFFERENCE:** Only one half of the property receives a step-up in basis when the joint-tenant spouse dies. The other one-half retains the old basis.

In this respect, joint-tenancy property is a second-class citizen compared with community property, which receives a stepped-up basis on the entire property even though only one half of the value may be includable in the decedent's gross estate (Section 1014(b)(6) and Rev. Rul. 87-98).

## Grantor Retained-Income Trust (GRIT)

GRITs are a sophisticated estate-planning device which, when properly used, can shelter substantial sums from estate taxes. Under current law, a GRIT, which leaves the remainder interest to a member of your family, can only be used when your residence (it could be up to two residences) is transferred to the GRIT. The term "member of the family" means your spouse, ancestors (i.e., your mom or dad), your descendants (i.e., your children and grandchildren), your brothers and sisters, and the spouses of these family members [Section 2702(e)].

Simply put, GRITS using any kind of property are okay if the remainder interest goes to a person not a member of the family; if the remainder goes to a member of the family, only a residence can be used.

A grantor sets up an irrevocable trust and transfers a residence to it. The terms of the trust provide that the grantor has a right to occupy the residence for a certain term (a fixed number of years). At the end of the term, the remainder vests, generally in the lower generation family members (the children). If the grantor outlives the term of the trust, the property is removed from his estate. In addition, any appreciation from the date of the original gift is also removed.

### Gift Tax Consequences

The grantor is making a gift of a future interest of the remainder interest in the residence. It does not qualify for the $10,000 annual exclusion, but the gift can be split with your spouse, and the Unicredit can be used to reduce the gift tax liability. If the grantor survives the term, any adjusted taxable gift from the GRIT enters into the estate tax computation. However, the value of the remainder interest gift can be reduced to a small amount by extending the term of the retained interest.

#### ■ EXAMPLE 1

A single grantor, Eric, funds a GRIT for his only daughter with his residence that has a fair-market value of $2,000,000. Eric is entitled to possession of the house for 10 years. Eric has never made a previous taxable gift. Assume the value of the gift as determined by IRS tables is $771,086. (See Chapter 2, Part II, for an explanation of how the gift-tax value is determined.)

| | |
|---|---|
| The gift tax is: | |
| Tax on $771,086 | $256,524 |
| (the $10,000 annual exclusion is not allowed) | |
| Less: the Unicredit | 192,800 |
| Gift tax due | $63,724 |

The filing of the gift-tax return and the payment of gift tax starts the three-year statute of limitations.

#### ■ EXAMPLE 2

Assume in Example 1 that Eric (he rented the house for five years) dies 15 years later when the value of the property transferred is $3,000,000 and Eric's marginal estate tax rate is 50 percent. The estate tax savings is $1,243,476.

| | |
|---|---|
| FMV | $3,000,000 |
| Rate of tax | × 50% |
| Total | 1,500,000 |
| Less: gift tax | 256,524 |
| Tax savings | $1,243,476 |

### Estate Tax Consequences

If the grantor dies before the GRIT term expires, the full value of the property is includable in his estate. He is no worse than if he had retained the property. The property is not includable in the grantor's probate estate, saving probate costs and avoiding ancillary administration if the property is located in a state other than the decedent's domicile at death.

Under Section 2001(b), any Unicredit used against a GRIT gift is restored. If a spouse gift-splits a GRIT gift and uses part or all of his or her Unicredit, the non-grantor's unicredit would not be restored.

If the GRIT has been successful, that is, the grantor has outlived the term of years, the IRS may not later successfully argue that the value at the time of the gift was understated. The statute of limitations on a gift-tax return runs three years after the due date of the return. The Service has ruled that the Unicredit must be applied against any gift-tax liability first before any gift tax is paid (see Rev. Rul. 84-11).

### Checklist of GRIT Planning Points

Following are some important planning points when the creation of a GRIT is considered:

**WHAT A GRIT CAN BE FUNDED WITH.** Only your residence, or up to two residences. In such a case, it would be best to use a separate GRIT for each residence.

**TAX BASIS OF THE RESIDENCE TO THE REMAINDERMAN.** There is no step-up in basis if the grantor outlives the term of years because it is not includable in his gross estate. If the residence will be handed down from generation to generation, the basis is immaterial.

Since a gift is involved, as the residence is transferred to the remainderman without consideration, there is a carryover basis.

**WHO SHOULD USE A GRIT.** A GRIT works best for single grantors. It can be used by elderly people; however, the taxable gift portion is generally greater because the terms of years must be shorter. In essence, it works as a substitute for the marital deduction. Of course, married taxpayers can use one, too.

**THE WIN-WIN SITUATION WITH LIFE INSURANCE.** If the grantor is insurable, he can turn the GRIT into a win-win situation by taking out a life insurance policy for a term of years equivalent to the number of years of the retained interest in the trust. The face amount of the policy should be approximately equal to the additional tax cost in the event the grantor dies prior to the termination of the GRIT interest. The life insurance should be kept out of the grantor's estate with an irrevocable life insurance trust.

## The Magnificent Grantor Retained Annuity Trust (GRAT)

A GRAT can be used to transfer almost any income-producing property and has the potential to save huge amounts of estate taxes. For our purposes—business transfer—the typical GRAT is used to transfer stock in a closely held corporation that has elected S corporation status. Our typical goal—transfer of the business to save estate taxes, yet keep control with the owner/founder (let's call him Joe)—requires a two-step process:

1. Recapitalize the S corporation (let's call it Joe S Co.): Voting stock (say 100 shares) and nonvoting stock (say 10,000 shares) replace 100 percent of the old single type of stock, all of which is owned by Joe.
2. Joe transfers all or a portion of the 10,000 shares of nonvoting stock to one or more GRATs.

## A Simplified Explanation

In effect, a GRAT takes one piece of property and divides it into two separate pieces. For example, cutting a bar of gold into two pieces does not increase or decrease the value of the gold; the larger piece simply would be more valuable than the smaller piece. Note that there is only one variable—the size of the two gold pieces (parts).

A GRAT has two separate parts. For example, Joe puts 6,000 shares (valued at $1 million) of the 10,000 shares of Joe S Co. nonvoting stock into a GRAT. The two parts are measured in time (rather than size of the part). The first part, called the "present interest" (or "annuity interest"), is for a fixed term (one year, two years, five years, 10 years or more). The time frame that follows the fixed term is the second part, which is called the "remainder interest." The two parts (in this case, 6,000 shares of Joe S Co. nonvoting stock) are worth a total of $1 million: some of the value allocated to the annuity interest, the balance to the remainder interest.

■ **IMPORTANT:** Joe keeps the annuity interest. He gives away the remainder interest to his children. Only the value of the remainder interest is subject to gift taxes.

Now, let's focus on how the value of the annuity interest is determined based on two distinctly separate variables that you (and you alone) control:

1. *The size of the annuity.* Logic tells you that an annuity of nine percent a year (in this case nine percent of $1 million, or $90,000) is worth more than an annuity of eight percent. A 10-percent annuity would have an even greater value, and so on.
2. *The length of the annuity.* The same kind of logic tells you that an annuity that entitles you to receive, for example, nine percent ($90,000 in this case) for 10 years has more value than receiving a $90,000 annuity for nine years or less.

   ■ **NOTE:** The "applicable federal rates" (explained later in a letter you will read) also impacts the value of the annuity interest, but you have no control over this variable.

Okay, let's apply your new GRAT knowledge. This is the game plan: try to get the value of the annuity interest high; this automatically forces the value of the remainder interest (the part subject to gift tax) to become lower. Suppose, for example, that the remainder interest turns out to have a value of $60,000. This means you have blown $1 million of current value out of your estate while only using up $60,000 worth of your unified credit.

■ **REMEMBER:** Since the remainder interest is a future interest, as opposed to a present interest, you are not entitled to get any annual $10,000 exclusions and are forced to use your unified credit when creating a GRAT.

The above example shows you the power of a GRAT. Your $600,000 unified credit can go a long way. The lower you make the value of the remainder interest, the farther your unified credit can go to remove millions of dollars of S corporation stock from your estate. Of course, your spouse can join in the fun by using his/her unified credit to support his/her own GRAT. For example, Joe could transfer half (or more or less) of his nonvoting stock to his wife Sue, and Sue could create her own GRAT.

Keep the above in mind as you read the material about GRATs that follows immediately.

## GRATs: A More Comprehensive Explanation

The following material contains excerpts from a letter about GRATs (slightly edited) written by an attorney friend of mine (Howard Denenberg, who specializes in estate planning and practices in Chicago). He sends it to clients he thinks might benefit from a GRAT.

Howard suggests a series of short-term GRATs as a hedge against dying before the end of a long-term GRAT's final day. A good idea.

Another way of hedging this dying-too-soon bet is to purchase a life insurance policy (to be owned by an irrevocable life insurance trust), which would replace the estate tax due because of the grantor's early death. At the end of the GRAT's term, the policy could be dropped (if term insurance) or cashed in (if ordinary life). But chances are the extra insurance will be welcomed at the end of the GRAT's term to fund the additional estate taxes anticipated because of the growth in value of the grantor's other assets.

> WHAT IS A GRAT?
>
> A GRAT is an irrevocable trust established by a person (referred to as the "Grantor") for a designated period of years (the "trust term"). During the trust term, the Grantor reserves the right to receive a designated dollar amount in installments payable at least annually or more frequently (an "annuity interest"). During the trust term, the Grantor could serve as the Trustee of the GRAT and thus retain the control of the assets transferred to the GRAT. At the expiration of the trust term, the annuity interest terminates and the trust assets, whatever their value, are then distributed to or held in further trust for the benefit of beneficiaries named in the trust instrument. These beneficiaries are typically the Grantor's family, perhaps the Grantor's spouse for life, and then the Grantor's children.
>
> GRAT TRANSFERS ARE GIFTS
>
> The funding of the GRAT constitutes a gift under the federal transfer tax system. However, the amount of this gift is not equal to the value of the assets transferred to the trust. Rather, the value of the annuity interest retained by the Grantor serves to offset the value of the property transferred to the trust and reduce the amount of the taxable gift. The value of the retained annuity interest is based on the amount of the annuity payable each year and on the duration of the annuity. The greater the amount of the annuity, and the longer the annuity payout period, the more valuable this retained interest is. Accordingly, by adjusting the amount and duration of the annuity, it is possible to

transfer assets to a GRAT with little or no gift tax consequences. In addition to reducing or eliminating the gift tax, a GRAT removes all appreciation in the transferred assets from the Grantor's estate without additional transfer tax.

The Internal Revenue Service has issued tables which must be used to value the retained annuity interest. These tables, which are based on the Applicable Federal Rate and on the payout period, provide a multiplier. The annuity amount is then multiplied by this multiplier to arrive at the value of the annuity interest for gift tax purposes. The lower the Applicable Federal Rate, the greater the present value of the annuity interest and the smaller the amount of the taxable gift. All other things being equal, an Applicable Federal Rate of 7% produces a higher value for the retained annuity interest (and a lower resultant taxable gift) than an Applicable Federal Rate of 10%.

TRANSFER TAX SAVINGS

By adjusting the annuity amount and trust term, it is possible to structure an annuity interest with a value exactly equal to the value of the property transferred into the GRAT. This results in gift tax being eliminated altogether. Such a GRAT is referred to as a Zero-Out GRAT, since the gift to the trust is completely offset by the retained annuity interest. If the Applicable Federal Rate is 7% and assets currently valued at $1,000,000 are transferred to a Zero-Out GRAT, the following table shows some of the variations in structure which will result in the retained annuity interest having a value of $1,000,000, *thereby eliminating any gift tax*. (Actually, the GRAT does not totally zero-out. Some value, though small, must be left.)

| Trust Term | Amount of Annuity | Percentage |
|---|---|---|
| 2 years | $555,000/year | 55.50% |
| 3 years | $385,000/year | 38.50% |
| 5 years | $245,000/year | 24.50% |
| 7 years | $190,000/year | 19.00% |
| 10 years | $145,000/year | 14.50% |
| 15 years | $111,000/year | 11.00% |
| 20 years | $ 95,000/year | 9.50% |

To the extent the income from the trust assets is insufficient to pay the annual annuity amount, the trust assets must be used. Any time trust corpus is used to satisfy a portion of the annuity obligation, there will be a valuation needed. If the trust assets consist of stock of a closely held corporation, it may be necessary to obtain an appraisal of the stock value if the stock is to be distributed. If the appraisal indicates appreciation in the value of the stock, then a smaller portion of the stock would be required to be distributed.

A Zero-Out GRAT only generates a transfer tax savings if the annual after-tax yield on the trust funds (both income and appreciation) during the trust term exceeds the Applicable Federal Rate published at the date of creation of the GRAT. When the Applicable Federal Rate was 10%, the GRAT would only be effective if the yield exceeded 10%. Currently, the yield must exceed 7%, since the published rate is 7%.

If the yield does not exceed the Applicable Federal Rate, then the trust principal will be fully consumed to pay the annuity. If the annual yield exceeds the Applicable Federal Rate, there will be a savings of transfer tax only on the amount of yield in excess of the Applicable Federal Rate (the "net yield"), plus appreciation thereon. The original contribution to the trust, plus yield at the Applicable Federal Rate, will be repaid to the Grantor in the form of an annuity.

Suppose, for example, you transfer $1,000,000 of closely held stock yielding an after-tax return of 15% to a 10-year GRAT. The annual annuity payment needed to zero-out the 10-year GRAT so that no gift tax would be paid is $145,000, or 14%. (See the foregoing table.) However, the 15% return yields annual income of $150,000. Thus, no portion of the principal need be expended to pay the annuity—it would be funded entirely from income. If you survived the 10-year term, the entire initial contribution of $1,000,000, plus appreciation, as well as the accumulated income in excess of the annuity amount ($5,000—$150,000 - $145,000) for the 10 years, will escape transfer taxation (both gift and estate).

If you reduce the term of the GRAT from 10 years to 5 years, then part of the principal of the GRAT will be returned to you in order to fund the annual annuity payment of $245,000, since the earnings are only $150,000 at 15%. However, approximately $360,000, plus appreciation, will still escape transfer tax, which amount is computed as follows:

| | |
|---|---|
| $1,000,000 | initial contribution |
| 150,000 | 15% earnings |
| (245,000) | annuity pay. |
| 905,000 | end of 1st year |
| 135,750 | earnings |
| (245,000) | annuity pay. |
| 795,750 | end of 2nd year. |
| 119,363 | earnings |
| (245,000) | annuity pay. |
| 670,113 | end of 3rd year. |
| 100,517 | earnings |
| (245,000) | annuity pay. |
| 525,630 | end of 4th year. |
| 78,845 | earnings |
| (245,000) | annuity pay. |
| $ 359,475 | end of 5th year. |

DISCOUNT

When closely held stock (as opposed to marketable securities or other types of securities) is contributed to the GRAT, additional leverage is created for transfer tax purposes by being able to utilize a minority discount for valuation purposes. The discount allowed for a minority interest gift of nonmarketable securities could be as high as 40%...

HOW LONG A GRAT PERIOD

A 5-year Zero-Out GRAT funded with $1,000,000 requires an annuity payout of $245,000 per year (24.50% of the original trust corpus). If the trust were to last for 10 years, the annuity need only be $145,000 per year (14.50%). Finally, if the term of the GRAT were 20 years, the annuity payout would be $95,000 per year (9.50%). As these numbers indicate, the longer the trust term, the smaller the annuity payment required each year to Zero-Out...

QUERY

Another issue that remains unresolved is the consequences of the Grantor paying the income tax on undistributed income. For example, if a 10-year GRAT term is selected so that the annual income of $150,000 exceeds the required annuity payment of $145,000, will the Grantor be deemed to be making additional gifts of the income tax paid on the $5,000 that is accumulated for the ultimate beneficiaries of the GRAT? From an estate planning standpoint, it is better to accumulate the extra $5,000 of income rather than paying it to the Grantor and increasing his or her estate, although that could be done. (Note that no additional transfer tax savings are attained by distributing to the Grantor income in excess of the required annuity payout.) In fact, from an estate planning standpoint, it is advantageous to deplete the Grantor's estate by the amount of income tax paid on unreceived income. This income tax result occurs because the GRAT is deemed to be a Grantor-type trust, that is, all income is taxed to the Grantor whether distributed or not. It would seem that paying the income tax obligations imposed by the Internal Revenue Code would not be an additional gift. The Internal Revenue Code and regulations are silent on this point.

DOWNSIDE

There is a downside to using a series of short-term Zero-Out GRATs, however. In addition to the obvious increased setup costs and accounting fees, the government may change the tax laws, in which case a longer-term Zero-Out GRAT may afford "grandfather" protection. Moreover, the Applicable Federal Rate may increase in the future, thereby reducing the effectiveness of subsequent GRATs.

Further, the assets transferred to Zero-Out GRATs retain a "carry over" basis for income tax purposes (as opposed to getting a "step-up" in basis if held until death).

■ **NOTE:** The term "Zero-Out GRAT" cannot be taken literally. The IRS requires that some value be attributed to the gift, even if the value is minimal. This requires adjusting the GRAT's term and yield (rate) so the gift has some value, thus requiring a small amount of gift tax (as opposed to zero).

## Generation-Skipping Tax

The IRS is never happy when the guys on your side—the taxpayers—figure out a way to beat the tax machine. Before the generation-skipping tax (GST), our side did indeed have the IRS beat. This is how we did it.

■ **EXAMPLE**

Joe Elder was loaded. So much so that Joe knew his two kids—Curley and Shirley—could never spend all that money. Besides, if he left everything to Curley and Shirley, the IRS would get 50 percent, plus more when his kids died. What to do?...Easy. Leave a portion of his wealth—$5 million—in trust for the benefit of Curley and Shirley for life, with the remainder to their kids (Joe's grandchildren—Ann and Andy).

Let's see how the above plan worked out. Joe died. His executor paid the tax on the $5 million put into the trust from other assets in Joe's estate. After 38 years, the second of Curley and Shirley died. By that time, the trust was worth $20 million. This was true even though Curley and Shirley used some of the income to maintain their lifestyles. (Remember, this is a rich family, and Curley and Shirley had other funds.)

How much did the IRS get out of that $20 million? Not one penny. Why? Estate taxes on this trust fund had been paid by Joe's estate when the trust was created. The $20 million, which was split 38 years later by Ann and Andy, had come, not from Curley and Shirley, but from Joe.

As a result, no estate tax was due when Curley and Shirley died. Of course, when Ann and Andy die (assuming there is no marital deduction), the IRS will finally get its pound of flesh.

Quite simply, Joe's family had skipped the estate tax for a full generation. Nice!

---

The IRS did not like the estate tax results of tax plans such as Joe's; neither did Congress. As a result, the GST rules were passed by Congress.

Take heart! In a nutshell, the same trick Joe pulled off is still available. But only $1 million ($2 million if Joe is married and splits the gift) can be transferred by Joe to his grandchildren. Any excess is subject to a GST tax (explained in the material that follows).

*The GST material, that follows is complex.*

### Planning Generation-Skipping Transfers and Direct Skips

The GST Rules, via Section 2611-2613, limit the benefits on estate tax savings by the use of generation-skipping trusts or direct skips.

The law attempts to prevent a testator from placing property in trust, with income payable to middle (second) generations, remainder to lower (third) generations, and at the same time excluding the value from the gross estate of the middle (second) generation.

The GST Rules are complex. This discussion covers only the basics. Planning revolves around using the exclusions and exemptions.

**GENERATION-SKIPPING TRANSFERS.** A generation skipping transfer includes a taxable distribution, a taxable termination, and a direct skip. It also covers transfers during life, at death, release of powers, lapses of time, and other transfers whether in trust or not.

A taxable distribution is any distribution from a trust to a skip person which is not treated as a direct skip or a taxable termination (Section 2612(b)). This includes distributions of income. For example, if the B Trust sprays income to the grandchildren, this is a generation-skipping transfer.

A taxable termination refers to termination by death, lapse of time, release of power, or otherwise of an interest in property held in trust unless immediately after such termination a nonskip person has an interest in such property. At no time after such termination may a distribution (including distributions on termination) be made from such trust to a skip person (Section 2612(a)(1)). Accordingly, any termination of a present interest in a trust will be a taxable termination unless one of the specified exceptions applies. The B Trust (credit shelter trust) generally is not a skip trust, as the remainder generally goes to the children.

A direct skip is a transfer of an interest in property to a skip person. A direct skip may be made to a vested trust for a grandchild under Section 2503(b).

A trust includes not only express trusts by any arrangement (other than an estate) that has substantially the same effect as a trust (Section 2652(b)(1)). For example, such arrangements as life estates and remainders, estates for years, and insurance and annuity contracts are specifically listed in Section 2652(b)(3).

A person has an interest in property held in trust if he is currently entitled to receive distributions of income or corpus or is a permissible recipient of such distributions (Section 2652(c)(1)). Accordingly, the mere possibility of receiving a current distribution is generally sufficient to cause a person to be treated as having such an interest.

## Exclusions

Certain transfers receive the benefit of special exclusion rules and avoid being labeled generation-skipping transfers. Section 2611(b)(1) provides that if any transfer would not be a taxable gift by reason of Section 2503(e), which pertains to certain transfers for educational or medical expenses, if made *inter vivos* by an individual, such transfer will not be a generation-skipping transfer.

A transfer will not constitute a generation-skipping transfer to the extent the transferred property was previously subjected to a generation-skipping transfer tax, and the transferee in the prior transfer was assigned to the same generation as (or a lower generation than) the transferee in the current transfer (Section 2611(b)(2)). This exclusion is only applicable if the transfers do not have the effect of avoiding generation-skipping transfer tax.

Section 2642(c)(1) effectively provides that there will be no generation-skipping tax on a direct-skip transfer if it is a nontaxable gift. A nontaxable gift is any transfer of property to the extent the transfer is not treated as a taxable gift because of the application of the $10,000 annual gift tax exclusion, or the gift tax exclusion for payment of certain education or medical expenses (Section 2642(c)(3)). However, Section 2642(c) provides that for transfers to a trust that are $10,000 or less, will only be excludable if no portion of the trust income or corpus could be distributed to a person other than the individual benefitted by the gift (Sections 2642(c)(2) and (c)(3)). This creates a problem when there is a Crummey power used with a life insurance trust.

■ **PLANNING POINTER:** Combine this provision with an irrevocable life insurance trust with a "Crummey" withdrawal power. If it is a Section 2503(b) trust, and all gifts are below the exclusion amount, there will never be a GST. However, the Crummey power should never lapse, and any income therefrom should be distributable solely to the power holder.

## Exemptions

**$1 MILLION GST EXEMPTION.** Each individual is allowed a $1,000,000 GST exemption with respect to property for which such individual is treated as transferor. (Section 2631(a)). The individual or his executor is entitled to allocate this $1,000,000 exemption among such property, but once such a voluntary allocation is made, it becomes irrevocable (Section 2631(b)). The allocation of the GST exemption has a direct bearing on the computation of the generation-skipping transfer tax because of its effect on the applicable fraction; thus the inclusion ratio. This is important because the transferred property often bears the tax cost. Also, once a transfer, or portion of a transfer, is designated as exempt, all subsequent appreciation in value of exempt property is also exempt from generation-skipping transfer tax. This is important from a planning viewpoint.

The GST exemption is automatically allocated to any direct skips made by an individual during his lifetime unless the individual affirmatively elects not to have such an allocation made (Section 2632(b)(3)).

A married couple has in the aggregate $2 million worth of GST exemption. This can be utilized from separate property or through gift splitting. A special effort is required to take full advantage of the entire $2 million. In effect, full utilization requires either the prepayment of some transfer tax or the use of a specialized qualified terminable interest property (QTIP) trust. To take full advantage of a GST exemption, a person must be the transferor with respect to the property. Since $1 million exceeds the $600,000 exemption equivalent, the necessary $1 million transfer will generate a gift or estate tax unless it qualifies for a marital deduction. With one exception, however, transfers that qualify for the marital deduction cause the transferee or donee spouse (not the transferring or donor spouse) to be treated as the transferor of the transferred property from that point forward. This single exception is for QTIP property as to which a special generation-skipping transfer tax election was made.

**QTIP TRUSTS.** A special QTIP election involves electing to treat all property as to which a standard QTIP election will be made as though no such election had been made (Section 2652(a)(3)). It only applies for GST purposes, and the effect is to override Section 2044(c), which states that the surviving spouse or donee spouse shall be considered to be the transferor of property covered by the standard QTIP election.

## Skip Persons and Nonskip Persons

There are two types of skip persons: certain natural individuals and certain trusts. An individual skip person is a person assigned to a generation that is at least two generations below the generational assignment of the transferor (Section 2613(a)(1)). For example, the testator-grantor's grandchild is a skip person. A trust also is a skip person if all interests in such trust are held by skip persons or there is no person holding an interest in the trust, and if, at no time after the transfer to the trust, may a distribution from the trust be made to a nonskip person (Section 2613(a)(2)). Section 2612(c)(2) provides a special rule, however, that no direct skip occurs on a transfer to a grandchild where the grandchild's parent, who is a descendant of the transferor, is deceased.

A nonskip person is a person who is not a skip person (Section 2613(b)). The testator-grantor's spouse and children are nonskip persons. Accordingly, any trust in which a nonskip person holds an interest is a nonskip person. Charities are also nonskip persons.

Critical in determining who are the skip persons and nonskip persons are the rules governing the generational assignment of persons other than the transferor.

**LINEAL DESCENDANTS.** The generation assignment of any lineal descendant of any grandparent of the transferor is determined by comparing the number of generations between the transferor and the transferor's grandparent with the number of generations between the individual and that grandparent and the descendant (Section 2651(b)(1)). The same concept applies to the spouse's (or former spouse) side of the family (Section 2651(b)(2)). For example, Tom's parents and their brothers and sisters and Tom's first cousins are in the same generation. On the spouse's side, the generation assignment of a lineal descendant of a grandparent of the transferor's spouse is determined by comparing the number of generations between the spouse and the spouse's grandparent with the number of generations between such grandparent and the descendant (Section 2651(b)(2)). For example, Tom's mother-in-law and father-in-law and their brothers and sisters are one generation above Tom's brothers-in-law and sisters-in-law and their cousins are in the same generation as Tom. Adopted persons and persons related by the half-blood are considered to be blood relatives (Section 2651(b)(3)).

**SPOUSES.** An individual who has been married to the transferor at any time is assigned to the transferor's generation (Section 2651(c)(1)). It makes no difference how old the spouse is. If Pop, age 70, marries a woman age 25, she is treated as being of the transferor's (Pop's) generation. Moreover, an individual who has at any time been married to a lineal descendant (see preceding paragraph) is assigned to the same generation as the descendant (Section 2651(c)(2)).

**OTHER INDIVIDUALS.** An individual not covered by the lineal descendant rule or the spousal rule is assigned to a generation on the basis of comparing the date of birth of such individual with that of the transferor (Section 2651(d)). A person born not more than 12 1/2 years after the transferor is assigned to the transferor's generation. A person born more than 12 1/2 years but less than 37 1/2 years after the transferor is assigned to the first generation below the transferor. There is a new generation for each additional 25 years from the transferor's date of birth.

## Direct Skips

The taxable amount is the value of the property received by the transferor (Section 2623). Direct skips are taxed at a much more favorable effective tax rate than other generation-skipping transfers.

This favorable taxation is the result of the tax exclusion manner in which the taxable amount is determined. For taxable terminations and taxable distributions, this determination is made on a tax inclusive basis, that is, the amount paid to the government as generation-skipping transfer tax is itself subject to generation-skipping transfer taxation (Sections 2641(a) and 2621(b)). This is similar to the current rules on computing estate tax—that is, the amount paid as estate tax is itself subject to estate tax. On the other hand, tax exclusive merely means the amount subjected to tax is the amount remaining after the tax itself is paid. The amount paid to the government as generation-skipping transfer tax on a direct skip is not itself subject to generation-skipping transfer. For example, a $3 million direct skip made produces a $1 million generation-skipping tax (assuming that tax is to be paid out of the $3 million of transferred property). The taxable amount is the $2 million remaining after paying the $1 million tax. The tax is simply 50 percent of that $2 million taxable amount. On the other hand, a $3 million taxable termination or taxable distribution generates a $1.5 million generation-skipping transfer tax. This makes the effective rate on a direct skip lower than on the other types of generation-skipping transfers. The value of the property received is to be determined at the time of the generation-skipping transfer (Section 2624(a)).

The GST on a direct skip is determined by multiplying the highest federal estate tax (FET) rate times an inclusion ratio (Section 2641(a)).

GST = taxable amount x maximum FET rate x inclusion ratio

The inclusion ratio is determined by subtracting the applicable fraction from 1 (Section 2642(a)(1)). In determining the applicable fraction for a direct skip or a trust skip, the numerator is the amount of the GST exemption allocated to the direct skip (or to the trust), and the denominator is the value of the property involved in the direct skip or a trust skip, reduced by any charitable gift or estate tax deduction allowed with respect to such property (Section 2642(a)(2)).

The denominator amount is net of any FET state death taxes chargeable to the property involved in the direct skip or trust skip (Section 2642(a)(2)(B)(ii)). For direct skips constituting taxable gifts, this is generally the value for federal gift tax purposes (Section 2642(b)(1)). However, this general rule only applies if either a voluntary allocation of the GST exemption was made to the taxable gift on a timely filed federal gift tax return, or a deemed allocation of such exemption was made to that gift pursuant to Section 2632(b). If the transferor initially elected not to have that deemed allocation made, the denominator is computed based on the value of the transferred property at the time the voluntary allocation is filed (Section 2642(b)(3)). The effect of this provision is to prevent a taxpayer from delaying the GST exemption allocation decision in order to determine whether or not the transferred property will appreciate.

For direct skips occurring under a transferor's will, this will be the FET value (Section 2642(b)(2)(A)). The transferor's estate tax value, not the value at the time of the surviving spouse's death, is also used with respect to any QTIP included in the spouse's gross estate, but only to the extent that property was the subject of the special QTIP election provided for in Section 2652(a)(3) (the reverse QTIP election) Section 2642(b)(4)). All qualified terminable interest property not subject to this special QTIP election is valued at the surviving spouse's FET value, which makes sense since the surviving spouse is the transferor.

## Checklist of GST Planning Pointers

The GST is capable of saving substantial tax dollars. The following list will help plan saving those dollars.

- ☐ Generation skip by fully utilizing the $10,000 (or $20,000 if gift-splitting) annual exclusion per donee.
- ☐ Fully use the $1 million GST exemption.
- ☐ Split-gift to fully utilize a spouse's GST exemption, which results in a husband and wife getting a $2 million GST exemption.
- ☐ Consider making direct skips as opposed to a taxable termination or distribution.
- ☐ Keep all gifts under the $10,000 annual exclusion amount and use an irrevocable life insurance trust (ILIT) with a *Crummey* power qualifying under Section 2503(b). (No part of the gift will at any time pass to any other person, but only to the person exercising the power).
- ☐ Instead of using an ILIT, gift $10,000 to each grandchild and let each grandchild use the funds to buy insurance on your life with each grandchild as beneficiary.
- ☐ Wise use of the $1 million exemption allows future appreciation to be transferred tax free. If the assets of the trust are valued at $1 million when the trust is created and the exemption is applied to this trust, there is no generation-skipping transfer tax due, even though the trust may be worth $5 million when the grantor dies.

# 2 Everything You Ought to Know about Trusts

The start of this chapter is nontechnical; then it gets technical.

Trusts are unquestionably the most underused estate planning tool. The uses are limited only by the imagination of the grantor and the estate planner.

A trust is simply a manner of holding property in which title is held by one person or entity for the benefit of another. For all practical purposes today, a trust must be set out in writing and can be as short as one sentence or as long as hundreds of pages.

The trust document is nothing more than a statement telling the trustee how the property in trust is to be administered and, on termination, to whom (the beneficiary or beneficiaries) the property is to go. Trust documents should always be prepared by an attorney.

All estates in excess of a certain dollar amount, depending on local law, must be probated. Whether the will creates a testamentary trust or not, the probate process must be suffered through.

## Probate

Probate administration is a court proceeding whereby a decedent's will is formally validated and his estate is inventoried, administered, and distributed.

An executor or administrator is appointed—an executor if the taxpayer dies with a will and an administrator if he dies without one. The executor or administrator is required to file an inventory with the court; pay uncontested claims or claims allowed by the court; file the required federal and state tax returns and pay the taxes due; invest assets; distribute assets as provided in the will or by law; and render a final accounting to the court.

All assets of a decedent are subject to probate except:

1. The proceeds of life insurance or other death benefit contracts such as pension and profit-sharing plans, which are payable to anyone other than the estate of the decedent. Such proceeds pass, pursuant to the insurance policy or other contract.

2. Joint tenancy assets.
3. Assets held in a trust. These pass pursuant to the trust agreement.
4. Paid-on-death accounts to a beneficiary designated by the depositor in a form furnished by the depositary.
5. Totten trust accounts. These are paid to the beneficiary of the so-called trust account, who is designated by the depositor in a form furnished by the depositary.

A will is effective only with regard to assets that are subject to probate. The five types of assets listed previously, when owned by the decedent, will be included in his/her estate for estate tax purposes even though they are not included in the probate estate.

### Probate Strategies

Does probating an estate ever make sense? The answer is a loud yes. The reason is claims against your estate after you die. The probate process allows claims to be filed against your estate. The identical claims could be filed against your living, or *inter vivos*, trust, which becomes irrevocable on the instant of your death.

So why probate? Because once the time for filing claims against the estate has passed (usually four to six months), the estate and its assets are safe from all claims that could have been made against you when you were alive. Those same claims could have been filed against your living trust's assets until the statute of limitations had run (usually up to seven years, depending on local law).

In our litigious society, it is important to close the litigation-claim door once you die. This is particularly important for business owners because claimants often try to pierce the corporate veil.

Is it possible that you (or your estate) could be liable for any environmental claims? If so, probate is a must. A living trust can still be used, but make sure to leave enough assets out of trust to require probate.

*This gives you the best of all worlds: Your living trust gives you all of the advantages of having a living trust, yet the probate of a small portion of your assets slams the claims door after a short time frame.* Then all of your assets—the estate assets as well as the bulk of your assets owned by the trust—are protected from late claims.

## Types of Trusts

Although overlapping, the tax and nontax purposes for using trusts fall into two categories—testamentary and *inter vivos.*

### Testamentary Trust

A testamentary trust is set up as part of your will whereby property passing through the will goes to the trustee of the trust for the benefit of others (beneficiaries). Typical testamentary trusts are marital trusts, QTIP trusts, residual (credit shelter) trusts, and charitable trusts.

For nontax purposes, a grantor might use a testamentary trust to:

- ☐ Overcome civil disabilities of minors by avoiding the appointment of a general guardian by the court and the necessity for court appearances.

- ☐ Free the beneficiary against financial worry and responsibility.
- ☐ Protect the beneficiary against financial inexperience by providing professional management of assets.
- ☐ Protect funds against future spouse of widow or child.
- ☐ Protect the beneficiary, and possibly the grantor, against creditors.
- ☐ Assist in overcoming limitations of an elderly, ill, disabled, or incompetent beneficiary.
- ☐ Permit unified control and management of business interest.
- ☐ Conserve assets that are not needed for the support of the beneficiaries.
- ☐ Avoid probate of all or a portion of the decedent's estate.
- ☐ Provide privacy with respect to assets transferred.
- ☐ Permit selection of the particular local law that will govern the administration of the assets transferred.

The tax reasons for choosing a testamentary trust might include:

- ☐ Reducing overall income taxes for the family unit.
- ☐ Reducing overall family estate tax.
- ☐ Excluding principal from the gross estate of a beneficiary for estate tax purposes (a generation-skipping trust).

### *Inter Vivos* (Living) Trust

An *inter vivos* trust is set up during a person's lifetime and may or may not terminate on that person's death.

The nontax reasons for establishing an *inter vivos* trust include all nontax items listed under testamentary purposes, plus:

- ☐ Being able to change or cancel at any time.
- ☐ Freeing grantor from burden of managing finances.
- ☐ Arranging for continuity of management before as well as after death.
- ☐ Avoiding probate/reducing probate and administration expenses.
- ☐ Avoiding publicity arising out of probate.
- ☐ Permitting uninterrupted management of the grantor's assets.
- ☐ Reducing likelihood of contests from disgruntled heirs.
- ☐ Allowing your heirs to enjoy the property in the trust quickly, as opposed to probate delays.
- ☐ Avoiding problems of joint ownership.
- ☐ Providing prenuptial protection.
- ☐ Permitting grantor to see his estate plan in operation during his life, that is, the performance of his fiduciaries.
- ☐ Receiving proceeds from insurance, employee benefits (pension and profit-sharing plans), and pour-over wills.

The main tax reasons for choosing an *inter vivos* trust are:

- ☐ Reducing the overall family unit tax impact by reducing income tax during life as well as after death and reducing estate tax via lifetime planning.

- ☐ Dividing family income via irrevocable (nongrantor) trusts and multiple trusts.

This list indicates the many advantages and flexibility of using a testamentary or living trust. The list should be reviewed each time either type of trust is to be written.

## Taxation of Trusts

For income tax purposes, the grantor or creator of the trust is treated as the trust owner (except as stated for Section 678) if his situation falls within even one of the Internal Revenue Code (the Code) sections in the following table:

| SECTION | RULE |
|---|---|
| 673 | Grantor retains a reversion—any interest in either corpus or income that may reasonably be expected to take effect within 10 years except on reversion at the death of the income beneficiary whose life expectancy was less than 10 years when the property was placed in trust. |
| 674 | General rule—if a grantor or nonadverse party, or both, can exercise a power of beneficial enjoyment of either trust income or corpus without the approval or consent of any adverse party. Exceptions to the general rule are specified. An adverse party has a substantial beneficial interest that would be affected by the exercise or nonexercise of his power. Usually, a nonadverse party is someone other than a beneficiary. |
| 675 | Grantor or nonadverse party retains any of four enumerated and prohibited administrative controls. |
| 676 | Grantor or nonadverse party retains the power to revoke the trust or revest the grantor with title of the trust assets. |
| 677 | Grantor or nonadverse party, without the approval of an adverse party, may deal with trust income as it concerns either the grantor or the grantor's spouse: (1) Distribute it (the income). (2) Hold or accumulate it for future distribution. (3) Apply it to the payment of premiums on life insurance policies on the life of either (except if such insurance is irrevocably payable to charity). |

### ■ TAX-SAVING IDEA

Use simple trusts for minors who have already attained age 14. All income is taxable to the child even though it is not distributed. The child receives his/her standard deduction, and the balance is usually taxed at a low rate because the kiddie tax does not apply.

### ■ EXAMPLE

| PROVISION IN TRUST | | TYPE OF TRUST |
|---|---|---|
| a. | Accumulate income until beneficiary,, B,, attains age 21; then | Complex |
| b. | pay out the income currently until B attains age 25; ther | Simple |
| c. | distribute the corpus | Complex |

In any year in which a trust is actually allowed a charitable deduction, the trust is a complex trust. If the fiduciary is required to keep the corpus intact (that is, to fund depreciation with current income rather than distribute it), it is a simple trust.

For the income of a complex trust, the fiduciary is taxed on income earned and retained in the trust. The beneficiaries are taxed on income earned by the trust and distributed to them or required to be distributed to them.

### Distributable Net Income

Distributions of distributable net income (DNI) are deductible by the trust (estate) and taxable to the beneficiary who receives all or any portion of it. Section 643 and the Regulations detail the DNI rules.

Except for special provisions for foreign trusts, capital gains are excluded from DNI by Treasury Regulation 1.643(a)-3, unless they are:

1. Allocated to income under the trust instrument or local law.
2. Allocated to corpus and actually distributed during the year.
3. Utilized (pursuant to the governing instrument or by a practice followed by the fiduciary) in determining the amount distributed.

The following table summarizes the 643(a) DNI rules.

| Item | Used to determine DNI |
|---|---|
| Personal exemption | No |
| Capital gains and losses | Generally, no |
| Deduction allowed trust or estate for amounts paid, credited, or required to be distributed | No |
| Dividends allocable to corpus—extraordinary and taxable stock dividends | Simple trust, no; complex trust, allocated to corpus actually distributed during the year. |
| Tax-exempt interest | Yes |
| Income of foreign trust | Yes; special rules (Section 643(a)(6)) |

■ **EXAMPLE:**

Regulation 1.643(d)-2 offers the following example:

| | | |
|---|---|---|
| Dividends (from domestic corporations) | | $30,000 |
| Dividends (allocated to corpus by the trustee in good faith)—$20,000 | | – |
| Taxable interest | | $10,000 |
| Nontaxable interest | $10,000 | |
| Less allocable expenses | 1,000 | 9,000 |
| Long-term capital gains—$10,000 | | – |
| Total | | $49,000 |
| Less expenses (trustee's fees) | $ 5,000 | |
| Less expenses allocable to tax-exempt interest | 1,000 | 4,000 |
| Distributable net income | | $45,000 |

Section 642(b) provides an exemption of $600 for an estate; $300 for a trust that is required to distribute all of its income currently, whether the trust is simple or complex; and $100 for all other trusts.

### The Throwback and Multiple-Trust Rules

First of all, what's a throwback? When a complex trust has income it does not distribute to its beneficiaries, the trust pays tax on this income. When the trust distributes this accumulated income in a future year, the beneficiaries under certain circumstances must pay tax on these prior-year accumulations under the throwback rules.

The Tax Reform Act of 1976 amended Sections 665-668 as follows:

- ☐ The throwback rules no longer apply to capital gains.
- ☐ An accumulation distribution does not include amounts accumulated either before a beneficiary is born or before the beneficiary attains age 21 (Section 665(b)), except in multiple-trust situations.

  ■ **TAX-SAVING IDEA:** It is worthwhile to accumulate income before birth and have the new-born child taxed at trust rates without threat of throwback upon distribution.
- ☐ Distributions from a complex trust that exceed DNI are subject to the throwback rules if the trust has undistributed net income (Section 665(a)). However, distributions in excess of DNI are not accumulation distributions as long as they do not exceed the trust income for the year as defined in the trust document (Section 665(b)).

  ■ **NOTE:** The throwback rules do not apply to estates. So, accumulate income in the estate to take advantage of the lower tax brackets every year.

## Additional Trust Considerations

### Special Tax on Transfers of Appreciated Property to Trusts

If a trust sells property within two years or less of the transfer, any gain recognized by the trust (up to the amount of the unrealized appreciation of the property at the time of the original transfer) is taxed to the trust at the grantor's tax rates (Sections 644(a) and (d)). Such gains are simply treated as if the grantor had recognized the gain and then transferred the net proceeds (sales price less tax) to the trust. Any gain recognized by the trust in excess of unrealized appreciation at the time of transfer is taxed to the trust under the normal capital gains rules.

The special tax does not apply to property transferred to a charitable remainder trust, pooled income funds, or a trust from a decedent (testamentary trust). Nor does the tax apply to gains that are otherwise not recognized under the Code. An example might be an involuntary conversion or a tax-free reorganization.

### Education Trusts for Children of Different Ages

You should consider not dividing a simple trust for the benefit of two or more of your children for education and support until the youngest child has completed his/her education or has reached a particular age when such child is likely to have completed his/her education. To do otherwise could mean the younger children would have to be educated and supported from their separate shares while the older children would have received a greater share by the pure accident of earlier birth (having already received support and education from their parents). That, coupled with the rising cost of education, makes it unfair to the younger children. They receive the same education but it is more costly because of inflation. In addition, some schools are more expensive than others. Cash flow can be impaired, and it puts pressure on the trustee to be fair to each child. Instead, you might consider using a discretionary (complex) trust. This gives the trustee discretion to pay for reasonable education for each beneficiary.

## ■ PLANNING POINTER: HOW TO DEDUCT YOUR CHILD'S COLLEGE EDUCATION

A gift of fully depreciated business equipment works well. The grantor gifts the equipment to an irrevocable trust with an independent trustee. The grantor's business (sole proprietorship, partnership, or corporation) leases the equipment with an arms-length option to buy at the end of the lease term. The lease will usually terminate near the end of the child's senior year in school. When the trust terminates, the remaining proceeds from the equipment buy-back becomes the child's graduation gift. Options to renew the lease could be included in the event the child goes to graduate school. The grantor receives a tax deduction for the lease payments and never loses control over the equipment.

### Planning with Powers of Appointment

Section 2041 details the rules for inclusion or exclusion of a power of appointment in the estate for estate tax purposes. There are three types of powers—general, limited or special, and a power protecting against a failure to exercise.

**GENERAL.** A person with a general power can direct property to anyone, as per Section 2041(b)(1). As a result, for tax purposes, the property is included in the estate of the person with the general power, whether or not the power is ever exercised.

**LIMITED OR SPECIAL.** A person with limited or special power can direct property only to certain people. For example, a husband's will might state that property is to be directed to his wife for life and then to his children in amounts the wife directs. For tax purposes, this property is not included in the estate of the person (here, the wife) with the limited power.

## ■ EXAMPLE

Ben has three children. One marries an extremely wealthy spouse, one is mentally retarded, and one is moderately well off. Ben can leave part of his estate to a trust, giving his wife limited power to make provisions in her will to treat his children according to their respective needs and avoid loading the estate of his wealthy child with further assets at high income and estate-tax levels. This is not a general power of appointment and does not qualify for the marital deduction.

| SECTION | RULE |
|---|---|
| 678 | The grantor will not be treated as the owner when another person had a power exercisable solely by that other person to vest the corpus or income in himself; the other person will be treated as owner. |
| 679 | (added to eliminate trafficking in foreign trusts) Any portion of a foreign trust into which a United States grantor transfers property when there is a United States beneficiary of that portion of the trust.<br>Section 671 is a one-paragraph section covering trust income, deductions and credits; and Section 672 covers definitions and rules. |

## Income Taxable to a Trust or Trustee

Unlike a corporation, a trust's income is taxed only once, either to the beneficiary or the trust. Whether income is taxed to the trust or to the beneficiaries depends on whether the trust is a grantor trust, a simple trust, or a complex trust.

**GRANTOR TRUST.** A grantor trust is a specific type of trust for tax purposes (distinct from a simple or complex trust) created under six basic rules in Sections 673-677. If the grantor falls within even one rule, than to compute his own taxable income he must take into account all income, deductions, and credits of such portion of the trust of which he is considered owner. The net effect is that, for income tax purposes, the trust is ignored.

**SIMPLE TRUST.** A simple trust is a trust that is required to distribute all of its income currently, is not allowed a deduction for a charitable contribution, and makes no distributions except of current income.

**COMPLEX TRUST.** Of necessity, any trust that is neither a grantor trust nor a simple trust is a complex trust. Such a trust does one or more of the following: accumulate income; distribute corpus; take a charitable deduction.

Income of a grantor trust is taxed to the grantor currently. Income of a simple trust, whether distributed or not, is taxable to the beneficiaries under Section 651. Such income will have the same character in the hands of the beneficiary as in the trust (Section 652). It is possible for a trust to be classified as simple one year and as complex another year.

# 3 Tax Planning with Gifts

This chapter is mostly nontechnical.

Gifts represent a major tax-planning strategy. They can move income within the family unit, remove income from your estate, and provide money for the education of future generations. Charitable gifts can create both current and future tax deductions.

Gifts can help divide family income by taking advantage of the zero or low tax bracket of one or more family members. This thrust accomplishes two sure savings: (1) income tax—from the high bracket of the donor to the low bracket of the donee, and (2) estate tax—although a portion of the asset in some circumstances comes back to the donor's estate for inclusion in the tax computation, the income it produced after the date the gift is given is excluded from the donor's estate.

Current law still provides these advantages: (1) the $10,000 annual exclusion per donee, and (2) gift splitting by spouses for gifts made by either spouse to third persons removes one half of the gift from the donor's estate. The consenting spouse must ultimately pick up this half in his or her estate. Even so, this spouse has a separate estate with which to utilize the Unicredit and start at the bottom of the Unitax bracket table.

The grossing up concept does not include the gift tax paid (except for gifts made within three years before death) from the estate of the donor, thus saving the donor an amount approximately equal to his highest estate-tax bracket times the gift tax.

**■ EXAMPLE**

Don, a widower, makes an $810,000 gift in equal shares to his six children and pays a gift tax of $55,500. Don dies two years later, leaving a $1-million equivalent taxable estate. Considering only the facts given, the overall tax savings are as follows:

| | | TAX | |
|---|---|---|---|
| | | No gift | With gift |
| Potential taxable estate | | $1,865,500 | $1,865,500 |
| LESS | | | |
| Six exclusions at $10,000 | | | (60,000) |
| Taxable gift ($810,000 – $60,000) | | (750,000) | |
| Tax paid on $750,000 taxable gift | | | |
| Tax on $750,000 | $248,300 | | |
| Less Unicredit | (192,800) | | (55,500) |
| Total | | | (865,500) |
| Actual taxable estate | | $1,865,500 | $1,000,000 |
| Estate tax | | | |
| Taxable estate | | $1,865,500 | $1,000,000 |
| Add adjusted taxable gifts | | 0 | 750,000 |
| Amount subject to tax | | $1,865,500 | $1,750,000 |
| Tentative tax | | $720,275 | $668,300 |
| LESS | | | |
| Gift tax paid | | 0 | (55,500) |
| Unicredit | | (192,800) | (192,800) |
| Balance due | | $527,475 | $420,000 |
| Savings [$527,475 – ($420,000) + $55,500)] | | | $51,975 |

Primarily, the savings come from two sources: (1) removing from the estate the $60,000 ($10,000 annual exclusion per donee) and (2) the gift tax paid more than three years prior to death. There are also savings from removing future appreciation on the gifted property and the income from the property.

Gifts are also advantageous planning tools because all gifts to the donee/spouse, due to the unlimited marital deduction (requiring no cash gift tax outlay), effectively remove the postgift income produced by the gift assets from the donor's estate. Gifts reduce probate and other estate costs. Gifts can also provide independence and security for donees.

## Methods of Making Gifts

There are various ways a gift can be made for tax purposes.

### Outright

You must make sure the gift is completed. How? By giving possession of the property to the donee, transferring title to the property, and reading and applying the rules in Treas. Reg. 25.2511-2 if the property is in trust or if there are any strings attached to the gift. If you do not complete the gift, it will probably be included in your estate.

A gift given close to year-end can cause problems (loss of the $10,000 or $20,000 exclusion). Rev. Rul. 67-396 states a gift is deemed completed only after the donor has no power to change the disposition of the property. A gift is not consummated by the mere delivery of the donor's own check or note. The gift of a check does not become complete until it is paid, certified, or accepted by the drawee, or is negotiated for value to a third person.

### In Trust

There are three ways to give a gift in trust:

1. Term of years—gives only income for fixed period (must be for a period over 31 years)
2. Irrevocable—gives principal and income forever
3. Multiple trusts (more than one trust)—additional low tax brackets

### Under Uniform Gifts to Minors Act

For minor children or grandchildren, gifts under the Uniform Gifts to Minors Act (UGMA) in custodianship are commonplace. This eliminates the expense of a trust. Gifts under the UGMA generally include money, securities (including closely held stock or debentures), and life insurance or annuity contracts. Some states, such as New York, allow custodial gifts of real property, personal property, and intangibles. Custodial gifts are irrevocable, and the property must be distributed to the child upon reaching majority (generally 18). If you are the grantor, you should not be the custodian; but your spouse can be. If you are the custodian and die prior to the minor child's or grandchild's reaching majority, the value of the property is includable in your estate.

**DIVIDING FAMILY INCOME THROUGH BUSINESS ARRANGEMENTS.** Form a family partnership. Or provide income to family members by stock ownership by means of common stock and S corporation earnings, or preferred stock and dividends (on preferred only). You might also lease property from a family member, or give a family member the money to buy the property or give the property to the family member, and then lease the property.

**INTEREST-FREE LOANS.** The tax court in a 1977 decision (*Lester Crown*, 585 F2d 234) held that use of money interest-free was not a gift. The amount of the loan, of course, is included in the estate of the lender. This case opened the door to unlimited interest-free loans. However, Congress substantially limited this technique by enacting Section 7872. But planning opportunities still exist. Let's see how.

All gift loans are treated as demand loans. Therefore, any below-market loan (below the applicable federal rate) is a gift. The income is imputed to the donor. However, two important exceptions apply: (1) a gift loan not to exceed $10,000 (Section 7872(c)(2), as long as the loans are not used to directly purchase income-producing assets; and (2) a gift loan not to exceed $100,000, as long as the borrower's net investment income does not exceed $1,000 (Section 7872(d)). Therefore, a $90,000 loan to a child to buy a home would not have imputed interest (it would be a gift), as long as the child's investment income does not exceed $1,000. This loan could be partially forgiven ($10,000, or $20,000 if married) each year.

If the donee does have net investment income in excess of $1,000, the imputed interest to the donor is the lesser of the imputed (or forgone) interest, or the donee's net investment income. If a loan not exceeding $100,000 is made for the principal purpose of tax avoidance, interest is fully imputed to the donor (Section 7872(d)(1)(B)).

**■ EXAMPLE 1**

Lou makes an interest-free demand loan of $10,000 to each of his four children to purchase personal automobiles. These are de minimis loans and no interest is imputed.

**■ EXAMPLE 2**

Ben loans his daughter Jen $100,000 interest-free to buy a personal residence. This was not motivated by tax avoidance. The loan is to be repaid over 25 years. Assume the short-term applicable federal rate is seven percent (all gift loans are treated as demand loans). Jen's net investment income for the year is $400. The $7,000 ($100,000 × 7%) of imputed interest is not required to be recognized by Ben because the exception under Section 7872(d) is met. The $7,000 gift is a present-interest gift that is nontaxable because of the $10,000 annual exclusion.

**TRANSFERRING PROPERTY WORTH MORE THAN $10,000.** Sometimes, the property to be transferred is worth more than $10,000 (or $20,000 for split gifts). Several techniques are available to avoid a taxable gift and maximize the exclusion.

You can gift a part (fractional) interest in the property annually. You might also loan money or make an installment sale to the donee, taking back notes due over a period of years. Cancel the notes as they fall due. There is no income if the cancellation is made with donative intent (*American Dental Co.*, 68 S Ct. 577 (1943)) on the date of the forgiveness. Here, the donor did not have a donative intent on the date of the gift.

Another option is to mortgage the property before making the gift, then pay off the mortgage annually.

## Choosing Property to Gift

Because the tax law attacks the gift and estate tax as a unit problem, the selection of the right property to give or to retain has great significance.

If liquidity is a problem, you should not give cash, marketable securities, life insurance (although this may be very advantageous to give if you can assure availability of proceeds as loan, or to purchase assets of the estate, to help pay estate tax), benefits from qualified employee plans, or assets that can be sold to raise cash.

**■ TAX-SAVING IDEA:** If you are reluctant to give cash or marketable securities, create a new S corporation (this corporation owns the cash, securities, etc.) and gift stock in the corporation. The result is that your estate is reduced tax-free, while the donee receives stock in the S corporation, yet you control it.

Or, gift a home; tangible personal property, such as jewelry or a car; or stock in a closely held corporation.

For appreciated property, make the gift immediately prior to any sale. The donee would then take your tax basis and holding period, and the sale would result in a capital gain to the low-bracket donee.

For depreciated (loss) property, the property should be sold first. You take the tax loss and then gift the proceeds to the donee. However, you should not sell to a related person; the loss is disallowed.

When gifting money and property, the money should be gifted first, then the property. A portion of the gift tax may be added to the basis of the property but never to the basis of cash (Section 1015(d)).

Assuming there is no liquidity problem, insurance is the perfect gift property. It has a low gift value (term insurance has none), and yet it removes a great deal from the estate.

## Giving Property Expected to Appreciate

When you want to reduce your estate, a gift of property that is likely to appreciate over time is usually the best gift. For example, a gift of a $10,000 bond today that retains the same value over time only ultimately removes $10,000 from the estate. A $10,000 gift of stock that grows to a worth of $100,000 by the time you die does the job of removing value from your estate magnificently. For most people, stock in a closely held corporation is the most likely candidate for gifts of property expected to appreciate.

## Giving Property Already Appreciated

Generally, assets that have not yet greatly appreciated should be given away. Assets that have greatly appreciated should, if possible, be held until death. The step-up in basis to the date-of-death value allows a complete escape from the income tax on the appreciation.

**APPRECIATION AFTER THE GIFT.** Under Section 2035(d), any gift is valued at the date of the gift, and if the gift later appreciates in value, such appreciation is not included in your estate. In addition to removing the tax on appreciation, the rule automatically removes the annual exclusion taken at the time of the gift from your estate.

The amount of the gift, less the $10,000 exclusion, is still included in the estate's taxable base and so affects the ultimate estate tax. Section 2035(c) provides that any gift tax paid within three years of death is estate-includable.

## Giving Stock in a Closely Held Corporation

A gift of stock in a closely held corporation usually accomplishes several objectives:

- ☐ It removes property expected to appreciate from your estate.
- ☐ It removes property that you do not want to convert to cash from your estate.
- ☐ It transfers some ownership and possibly control of your business to younger members of the family.

■ **CAUTION:** If qualification for a Section 303 redemption and/or Section 6166 deferred estate tax payments is desirable, you should retain enough closely held stock to satisfy the required percentages.

**RETENTION OF VOTING RIGHTS BY DONOR.** Section 2036(a) is a legislative reversal of the *Byrum* case. This section prevents you from escaping estate taxes by transferring the stock of closely held companies directly or in trust while retaining voting rights. Section 2036(b) adds that only those transfers of stock in controlled corporations where you (after the transfer and during the three-year period ending at death) owned or could vote 20 percent or more of the stock causes such stock to be included in your estate. The attribution rules of Section 318 apply. A transfer with retained voting rights may, in some cases, still follow the *Byrum* rule and escape inclusion in your estate.

### Gift in Joint Tenancy to a Spouse

Present interest gifts to spouses qualify for an unlimited gift-tax marital deduction. Because such gifts are exempt from gift tax, it does not matter for gift-tax purposes whether the creation of a joint interest in property between spouses constitutes a gift. Under Section 2040(b), when the first spouse dies, half of the value of the qualifying joint interest is automatically included in the decedent's gross estate. Only half of the basis is stepped up.

### Gift of Mortgaged Property to a Trust or to a Family Member

If you own property that has a low tax basis with a high mortgage on it, the difference will be taxable income to you when you dispose of it by gift (see *Beulah B. Crane v Commissioner*, 67 SCt. 1047, and Treas. Reg. 1.1001-2(a)(1)).

■ **EXAMPLE**

If Ben owns property with a tax basis of $4,000, a market value of $15,000, and a $10,000 mortgage, and that property is gifted to an irrevocable trust, the excess of the mortgage over the tax basis (or $6,000) is taxable income to Ben.

■ **STRATEGY:** Mortgage the property for any amount that does not exceed its tax basis. Pocket the cash tax free. Then give the property subject to the mortgage to a low-bracket family member, who pays off the loan using the income from the property.

### Low-Basis Property

Generally, low-basis property is the better choice for a gift—the donee probably is in a lower tax bracket than the donor. Of course, if the donor can wait and hold the property until death, it will get a step-up in basis. The appreciation escapes the income tax forever.

## The Gift Tax

The gift tax is not imposed on the receipt of the property by the donee, nor is it necessarily determined by the measure of enrichment resulting to the donee from the transfer, nor is it conditioned upon ability to identify the donee at the time of the transfer. On the contrary, the tax is a primary and personal liability of the donor, is an excise tax on his act of making the transfer, is measured by the value of the property passing from the donor, and attaches regardless of the fact that the identity of the donee may not then be known or ascertainable (Treas. Reg. 25.2511-2).

## Unitax, Unicredit, and Lifetime Gifts

The federal Unified Gift and Estate Tax (Unitax) and Unified Credit Against Gift and Estate Tax (Unicredit) attempt to treat taxpayers who make substantial lifetime gifts and taxpayers who retain their assets until death the same. The rates are progressive; they are thus computed on the basis of cumulative lifetime transfers, and at death the lifetime transfers form the base to which the death transfers are added before determining the tax due.

Even though the law provides for a unified transfer system, it is still advantageous to make lifetime gifts, since gifts up to $10,000 per donee, or $20,000 if there is gift splitting, escape the transfer tax altogether. This excludable amount is not subject to gift tax, and is not added to the base for calculating the estate tax.

Future appreciation on the property gifted is completely removed from the donor's estate as only the value at the time of the gift is includable in the base for calculating the estate tax. However, the donor's tax basis carries over to the donee on a gift. This loss of the step-up in basis upon death should be considered in every gifting situation.

### ■ EXAMPLE 1

Meg, a widow, gifted real estate with a fair-market value of $110,000 and a tax basis of $50,000 to her daughter, Peg. Meg died 10 years later when the value of the real estate was $300,000. The taxable gift is $100,000 ($110,000 less the $10,000 exclusion). In computing Meg's estate tax, the adjusted taxable gift includable in the tax base is $100,000, not $300,000. Therefore, Meg was successful in removing $200,000 from her estate. However, Peg's tax basis is the same as Meg's tax basis: $50,000, not $100,000 or $300,000.

In a situation where gift tax must actually be paid in cash, not only is future appreciation removed from your estate but so is the gift tax paid, if you live three years after the date of the gift.

### ■ EXAMPLE 2

Lou made no lifetime gifts and died single with a $10-million taxable estate. The net proceeds available to his family is calculated as follows:

| | |
|---|---|
| Gross Estate | $10,000,000 |
| Less estate tax (average 49%) | 4,948,000 |
| Net to family | $5,052,000 |

### ■ EXAMPLE 3

Lou gifts $6,800,000 to his family, pays the gift tax and lives for three years. The net after-tax proceeds transferred to Lou's family are increased by approximately $1,800,000:

| | |
|---|---|
| Gross estate | $10,000,000* |
| Less gift tax on $6,800,000 | 3,188,000 |
| Net to family | $6,812,000 |

*The $10 million (rounded) is made up of the $6,800,000 gift plus the $3,188,000 tax paid.

Interspousal gifts may avoid wasting the unified credit in the event the spouse without an estate predeceases the spouse with a large estate.

**■ EXAMPLE 4**

Peg, the wife of a wealthy taxpayer (Greg), died prematurely. However, her estate consisted of only $100,000. In this case, Peg's Unicredit is mostly wasted. This could have been avoided if Greg had gifted $500,000 of additional cash or property to Peg. Her will should then leave Greg a life interest only in her property, keeping it out of his estate. The entire $600,000 would have been fully sheltered by Peg's Unicredit.

### Educational and Medical Expenses

Current law allows an unlimited exclusion for qualifying transfers for amounts paid for a donee's medical expenses or school tuition (Section 2503(e)). Technically, such transfers are not treated as gifts. Qualifying transfers are amounts paid on behalf of any individual to (1) an educational institution as tuition for such individual, or (2) any person or entity providing medical care with respect to such individual.

There is no requirement that the person receiving the benefits be related to the donor. However, the payments must not be reimbursements to the donee, but must be made directly to the service provider. Also, medical expenses that are later reimbursed by insurance do not qualify.

The statutory language refers to tuition. There is no further definition. The Committee Report indicates that the exclusion applies to tuition for both full- and part-time students. But it is limited to direct tuition costs. No exclusion is provided for books, supplies, dormitory fees, or other support costs. Rev. Rul. 82-98, reviews this subject in detail.

### Gifts of a Present Interest

When the donee of a gift may presently possess or enjoy the property, the gift is a present interest and qualifies for the annual $10,000 gift-tax exclusion. Conversely, the exclusion does not apply to gifts of a future interest (Section 2503(b)).

**■ EXAMPLE**

Lou puts a $100,000 bond into trust, saying "the income to myself for life, then the $100,000 to my son John upon my death."

John has received a gift—a gift of the remainder interest in the property. However, John received a future interest—no $10,000-annual exclusion. He does not have present possession or enjoyment (the income) of the property.

A gift in trust for a minor is not considered a gift of a future interest if the property and the income therefrom (1) may be expended by, or for the benefit of, the donee before attaining the age of 21, and (2) will to the extent not so expended pass to the donee on attaining the age of 21. In the event the donee dies before the age of 21, the interest must be payable to (1) the estate of the donee or (2) as the donee appoints under a general power of appointment (Section 2503(c)).

Over time, the IRS has attempted to broaden the definition of future interest.

**INCOME PORTION WHEN CORPUS IS A GIFT OF A FUTURE INTEREST.** The words "present interest" have been defined as the "present power of possession and enjoyment of the gift" (*Stephen F. Heringer*, 235 F2d 149 (1956)). The power to accumulate income until the minor reaches 21 doesn't make the interest a future interest. The exclusion is allowed for the income interest, but not for the corpus because of the fact that it is payable after 21 (*Arlean I. Herr*, 303 F2d 780 (1962)).

The rule for income to age 21 is clear, but now suppose the income to age 21 qualifies in every respect with Section 2503(c) and the income after age 21 will continue to be paid for life. The IRS, in *Samuel LeVine*, 50 TC 422 (1968), contended these two income interests should be separated. The court allowed the full exclusion, holding the two components are one whole and qualify as a present interest.

**TRUST CONTINUES AFTER AGE 21.** A gift to a minor in trust that gives him the right, at age 21, to compel immediate distribution of the trust property is a gift of a present interest and thus qualifies for the exclusion. If the minor does not compel immediate distribution at age 21 and the trust by its terms continues for a fixed period thereafter (during which time the donee cannot compel distribution), the result is the same; it is a gift of present interest. The IRS finally revoked its old automatic termination requirement in Rev. Rul. 74-43.

### Statute of Limitations

The statute of limitations begins to run under Section 6501 after the gift-tax return is filed. The statute runs in three years, unless there has been fraud or an omission in excess of 25 percent of the total amount of gifts (Section 2504(c)). This blocks the IRS from making an assessment on the return itself.

Section 6075 instructs when to file a gift-tax return—annually on April 15 of the year following the year in which the gift was made. However, if the only gifts made qualify fully for the (1) marital deduction, (2) annual exclusion, or (3) educational or medical expense exclusion, no return is required.

If the statute has run, but the value of a gift was shown as $10,000 on the prior year's gift-tax return, and an IRS agent is contending 10 years later that the value of the gift should have been $50,000, can the agent affect the current gift-tax return under examination? No! The IRS has agreed that for gift-tax purposes, a gift cannot be revalued once the three-year statute of limitations has run out.

However, the following article from my tax column shows you the IRS can reopen the valuation door after you die.

> IRS VICTORY AFFECTS EVERY GIFT OF CLOSELY HELD STOCK—PAST AND FUTURE
>
> Have you ever made a gift of stock of your closely held business? Thinking of doing so? Then this is must reading. A new Tax Court case (*Smith vs. Commissioner*, 94 TC 55, 6/13/90) is sending out ominous shock waves. In a nutshell, this case allows the IRS to revalue your lifetime gifts after you die. Your estate can get ripped with more tax on those old gifts. This is a terrible blow to a basic time-honored method of transferring family businesses: the founder gifting stock to his children.
>
> Here's the story. The decedent (Smith) made taxable gifts of corporate stock in 1982, filed a gift-tax return in 1983 and paid the gift tax due in a timely

manner. Smith died in 1984. The time for the IRS to assess a gift-tax deficiency expired after three years on April 15, 1986. Put another way, the statute of limitations ran out against the IRS and blocked it from getting any additional gift tax on the 1982 stock gift. Sounds like that should be the end of the story.

Unfortunately for every family owned business in the country, it's only the beginning of the story. In 1988, the IRS went after Smith's estate, claiming that the value of the stock gifted in 1982 was $400,000 more on the date of the gift than the amount reported on the gift tax return. Get *them* apples. Here it is, six years later, and the IRS wants to revalue the gift for estate purposes. Remember, the IRS was out of luck for gift-tax purposes because the statute of limitations had run out against them. No way could the IRS pull off such a caper—right? Wrong! The Tax Court agreed with the IRS, allowing the revaluation.

What's the impact of the court's decision? It keeps the IRS' revaluation book open on lifetime gifts until after you die. It could be five years or 50 or more years, but time will never run out on the IRS. Wow!

What should you do? All gifts of closely held business stock you make from this day forward must be backed up by a valuation done by a qualified expert. Retain the valuation report with the related gift-tax return. If you didn't file a gift-tax return, because the value of the stock was less than $10,000 per donee, keep the valuation report with your will.

What about prior stock gifts—whether or not a gift-tax return was filed? Get a proper valuation done now to back up the old gift. Don't backdate the valuation. Backdating for a tax advantage could be criminal fraud.

## Year-End Gifts

A portion of one of my tax columns explains how to cope with this annual problem.

THE RIGHT WAY TO MAKE A YEAR-END GIFT

Every year as New Year's Eve approaches, loving parents and grandparents slip checks to the young'uns. Back on December 24, 1980, Elizabeth Dillingham wanted to play this year-end game. She delivered six checks for $3,000 (the magic number before the boost to $10,000) to six donees. On January 28, 1981, Elizabeth delivered another set of $3,000 checks to the same six donees. All 12 of the checks were cashed in 1981.

Almost 10 years later, the court lowered the boom on Elizabeth's 1980 gifts (Estate of Elizabeth Dillingham, 5/14/90, CA-10). The court ruled that the 1980 checks were not unconditionally delivered and that Elizabeth still had control over the checks because she could have stopped payment on them.

What can you do to protect your year-end cash gifts made by check? Either make sure the donees cash the checks in the year they are given or, better yet, have the checks certified before delivering them to the donees.

## Donees

Donees fall into three natural categories; minors (usually the donor's children and grandchildren); spouse (usually the wife); and others, who are usually family members and charities.

### Vehicles for Holding Minor's Interest

A minor's interest in property may be held outright by the minor (to be avoided), by a custodian for the benefit of a minor, in trust, or in limited partnership. The nature of the property usually dictates the choice.

**CUSTODIANSHIP.** A useful and practical method of making gifts to minors is by means of custodianship arrangements under the Uniform Gifts to Minors Act (UGMA). A gift made in this fashion is relatively simple to accomplish. Gifts of securities, money, life or endowment insurance, and annuity contracts may be made under this act. The donor can be custodian, may resign, or may designate any adult as successor custodian. Married donors have the right under Section 2513 to treat such gifts as made half by the husband and half by the wife.

The income earned is taxable to the donee/minor, not to the donor. The property—including accumulations of income—held by the custodian is not included in the donor's estate for estate-tax purposes.

■ **NOTE:** You should not become the custodian; the gift property will be included in your estate. Use an adult child, or some other adult relative or friend. The IRS says Section 2038 triggers inclusion (*Stuit*, 452 F2d 190 (1971)). The IRS extends this rule in Rev. Rul. 70-348, holding that even if the decedent was not originally appointed custodian but is acting as successor custodian at the time of his/her death, the property is includable.

There is an exception. In this actual case, the donor/husband was the original custodian; he resigned, appointing his wife, W, successor custodian; she died. At the time of the gift, W had consented to a Section 2513 split gift. The IRS has ruled in Rev. Rul. 74-556, that no part of the custodial property was includable in W's estate. Section 2038 doesn't apply. Under Section 2513, the consenting spouse is merely considered a donor for gift-tax purposes, while the spouse who owned the property is the real donor.

### Making a Gift Under the Uniform Gifts to Minors Act

If the gift is a security in registered form, register it in the name of the donor, another adult, or a trust company, followed in substance by the words "as custodian for (name of minor) under the (state) Uniform Gifts to Minors Act." If the gift is not in registered form, the securities must be delivered to the custodian together with a statement, signed by the donor, similar to the above.

If the subject of the gift is money, pay it or deliver it to a broker or domestic financial institution for credit to an account in the name of the donor, another adult, or a trust company, followed in substance by the words "as custodian for (name of minor) under the (state) Uniform Gifts to Minors Act."

If the subject of the gift is a life or endowment insurance policy or annuity contract, cause the ownership of the policy or contract to be registered with the issuing insurance company in the name of the donor, another adult, or a trust company, followed in substance by the words "as custodian for (name of minor) under the (state) Uniform Gifts to Minors Act."

For property that isn't recorded by deed, title, or in registered form, documentation should be prepared indicating the transfer of the property by gift. A sample document follows.

## ■ SAMPLE TRANSFER OF PROPERTY BY GIFT

**GIFT**

KNOW ALL MEN BY THESE PRESENTS, that I, the undersigned, Thomas T. Jones, of Chicago, Illinois, in consideration of natural love and affection, give to my son, Robert M. Jones, of Chicago, Illinois $33,000 of the inventory of the business known as Jones Hardware in Chicago, Illinois, effective January 1, 19__, the value of which is $33,000.

Dated ________, 19_

Thomas T. Jones

### Trusts for Minors Qualifying for $10,000 Exclusion

**SECTION 2503(C) TRUSTS—TRANSFER FOR THE BENEFIT OF A MINOR.** A technique that combines the advantages of a trust and still qualifies for the annual $10,000 gift exclusion is referred to as a Section 2503(c) trust. There are no restrictions on the type of property that can be transferred to, or subsequently acquired by, the trustee. Section 2503(c) has three requirements:

1. The principal and income may be expended by or for the benefit of the donee while the donee is less than age 21.
2. All accumulated principal and income must be distributed at age 21.
3. If the donee dies before age 21, all income and principal must be paid either to the donee's estate or to the donee's appointee pursuant to a general power of appointment.

It is possible to delay the termination of the trust beyond age 21 if the donee has the right to compel the immediate distribution of the trust principal at age 21 by written notice to the trustee (Rev. Rul. 74-43).

**SECTION 2503(B) TRUSTS—EXCLUSIONS FROM GIFTS.** A variation on the Section 2503(c) trust is the Section 2503(b) trust, which provides an annual exclusion for the present income interest (to age 21), but not for the future remainder interest (beyond age 21). In a Section 2503(b) trust, the trust income must be paid to the donee; in a Section 2503(c) trust, the trust income may be either paid to the donee or accumulated.

**CRUMMEY TRUST.** Another variation of the Section 2503 trust is the so-called *Crummey* (397 F2d 82 (9th Cir. 1968)) trust.

The *Crummey* trust is used to create a trust for a minor (or for the benefit of several minors) where the power to terminate the trust at age 21 is not given to the minor beneficiary. A clause is inserted in the trust providing that the beneficiary has the right to withdraw $10,000 ($20,000 if there is a spouse to split the gifts) from the trust principal during the year of the gift. This qualifies the gift, which is entitled to an annual exclusion. The trust generally terminates at a later age. For *Crummey* trusts, the IRS takes the position that the beneficiary must be informed of his right to demand distribution and have enough time to exercise that right (Ltr. Rul. 7946007).

### Gifts to a Spouse

The size of the spouse's estimated estate is, of course, the key to how much one spouse should give to the other. Every time a gift by one spouse to the other is contemplated, it is essential to work out the arithmetic for the potential estate tax, assuming (1) the husband dies first and (2) the wife dies first.

If the wife or husband has a small estate, use of the unlimited marital deduction is a no-lose situation. To the extent one spouse does not have a taxable estate of $600,000 (the full amount that is estate-tax-free), gifts from the other spouse should be considered. Also, the postgift income and appreciation is out of the wealthier spouse's estate.

Whether the donee-spouse survives or does not survive the donor-spouse, the donee will be able to make generation-skipping transfers to the grandchildren.

## Basis of Gift Property

Section 1015 governs the basis of gift property to a donee. If the donee has a gain on sale, the donee's basis is the same as the donor's basis. If the donee has a loss on sale, the donee's basis is either the donor's basis or the value at the date of gift, whichever will result in the smaller loss.

**■ EXAMPLE 1**

| Donor's Basis | Value at Time of Gift | Gift Tax Paid | Donee's Selling Price | Taxable Gain | Deductible Loss |
|---|---|---|---|---|---|
| $10,000 | $40,000 | $5,000 | $20,000 | $6,250* | – |
| 10,000 | 8,000 | 600 | 6,000 | – | $2,000 |
| 10,000 | 4,000 | None | 6,000 | None | None |
| 10,000 | 15,000 | 3,000 | 5,000 | – | 6,000† |

*New basis = $10,000 + $3,750 (75% x $5,000) = $13,750; $20,000 (selling price) – $13,750 = $6,250.

†New basis = $10,000 + $1,000 (1/3 x $3,000) = $11,000; $5,000 (selling price) – $11,000 = ($6,000).

The basis is also increased by a portion of the gift tax paid, if any, if the property has appreciated. The portion that may be added is computed by dividing the net appreciation in the value of the gift by the value of the gift.

■ **EXAMPLE 2**

Lenny gives his daughter securities worth $100,000 that cost him $20,000 and pays $15,000 gift tax on the transfer. The daughter's basis becomes $32,000, computed as follows:

| | |
|---|---|
| Donor's carryover basis | $20,000 |
| Gift tax added to the basis: | |
| $80,000/$100,000 × $15,000 | 12,000 |
| Daughter's basis | $32,000 |

## Gifts Within Three Years of Death

Section 2035(d) eliminates the gift-in-contemplation-of-death rules on most transfers by decedents. Accordingly, gifts made within three years of death are excluded from the decedent's gross estate. However, there is a tradeoff—the donee will be denied a step-up in basis. The donee's basis will be determined under the usual rules.

Interests in property otherwise includable in the gross estate (under Section 2036, 2037, 2038, 2041, or 2042; or which would have been included had the interest been retained by the decedent) are still included in the gross estate if transferred within three years of death.

Insurance is not a beneficiary of the rules—it is still included in the estate under Section 2042 if gifted within three years of death. It is the most important exception.

The other exceptions are:

| SECTION | SUBJECT |
|---|---|
| 2036 | Retained life estate |
| 2037 | Transfer effective at death |
| 2038 | Revocable transfers |
| 2041 | Powers of appointment |

In addition, transfers made within three years of death (other than gifts qualifying for the $10,000 annual gift tax exclusion) are includable in the gross estate for purposes of determining the estate's qualification for special use valuation, deferral of estate taxes and stock redemptions under Section 303.

The revocable transfers exception applies in two types of circumstances.

■ **EXAMPLE**

*T* makes a revocable transfer to a trust and retains the right to revoke at his death. The entire trust is included in his estate, regardless of the date of the initial transfer. If *T* relinquished the power to revoke, the trust is still included in his estate if the relinquishment was within three years of his death.

Gift tax paid on transfers made during the three-year period preceding death are includable in the estate. There is no gain because the donor's basis, which is higher than the selling price, is used. There is no loss because the fair-market value at the time of the gift (used as basis for loss, since it is lower than the donor's basis) is lower than the selling price.

### Basis of Gift Property Acquired from a Decedent

The tax law curbs a potential abuse when a donor might try to transfer low-basis property to a potential decedent just before death to acquire a step-up in basis and avoid income taxes on the appreciation when the property is sold. With an unlimited marital deduction, the step-up could be tax-free in the case of a deathbed transfer to a spouse.

#### ■ EXAMPLE

*H* gives his dying spouse *W*, highly appreciated property. No gift tax is imposed, thanks to the unlimited marital deduction. At *W*'s death, the property returns to *H* with a stepped-up basis. Again, no transfer tax is imposed. This does not work if the gift took place within one year of *W*'s death.

Section 1014(e) stops such maneuvers. It provides a special carryover basis rule for appreciated property received by a decedent by way of gift within one year of a decedent's death, where the property passes back to the original donor or donor's spouse. The basis of such property in the hands of the original donor or his spouse is the basis to the decedent immediately prior to death, rather than its fair-market value on the date of death.

The result is the same if the donor or his spouse has the right to receive sales proceeds from the estate rather than the property itself. However, if, in the previous example, the property passed to the children of *H* and *W*, rather than back to *H*, Section 1014(e) would not apply. Also, if the decedent lived more than one year after the transfer, the step-up is allowed.

# 4 Postmortem Estate Planning Ideas and Checklists

This is basically a technical chapter.

Although the basic estate plan is fixed by decisions made and documents executed before death, there is room for much estate planning after death, as well. The following checklist provides, as a starting point, a summary of the most used tools in the area. The list is developed approximately in the order in which these tools should be considered for use.

## The First Set of Decisions for All Estates

Most estates find that there is more than one way to handle a particular item or situation for tax purposes. The wrong choice can cause an expensive tax error.

**DECEDENT'S FINAL INCOME TAX RETURN—JOINT OR SEPARATE.** Provided the decedent's spouse has not remarried, the estate may file a joint return with such spouse or may file a separate return for the decedent (Sections 6013(a)(2), 6013(a)(3)).

**MEDICAL EXPENSES.** Medical expenses paid out of the estate within one year after death may be deducted on the decedent's final Form 1040 or on Form 706 (the Estate Tax Return), but not both (Section 213(c)).

Where all or a large portion of the medical expense will be lost on Form 1040 because of the 7.5-percent adjusted gross income (AGI) limitation, all the medical expense should be deducted on Form 706.

If the medical deduction is taken on Form 1040, a statement should be attached to the return waiving the deduction under Section 2053. The portion of the deduction on Form 1040 reduced by the 7.5- percent limitation may not be deducted on Form 706 (Section 213(c)(2)).

If the estate is not subject to estate tax because of the marital deduction or the unicredit, the medical expenses should be deducted on Form 1040.

**ACCRUED INTEREST ON SERIES E OR EE BONDS.** Interest accrued on Series E or EE bonds owned by the decedent may be treated as income on decedent's final return (Section 454(c) election), as income on a beneficiary's return, or as income on estate income tax return (Rev. Rul. 68-145). This election gives the executor an opportunity to increase retroactively the gross income on a decedent's final individual or joint return.

■ **PLANNING POINTER:** Before making the election, the executor should weigh the effect of losing the Section 691(c) deduction of the estate tax attributable to income in respect of a decedent. The deduction is available to the estate or to a beneficiary and is not subject to the two percent limitation on miscellaneous itemized deductions (Section 67(b)(8)).

**DEDUCTIONS IN RESPECT OF A DECEDENT.** Deductions in respect of a decedent (DRD) are deductible expenses incurred by the decedent while living but not deducted because of his cash method of accounting. This includes both business and personal deductions and includes commonly accrued business expenses (Section 162), interest (Section 163), taxes (Section 164), and miscellaneous expenses incurred for the production of income, tax preparation, and so on (Section 212). These are double deductions that properly can be claimed on both the estate tax return and the income tax return (Section 691(b)).

**ADMINISTRATION EXPENSES, CASUALTY LOSSES, AND SELLING EXPENSES.** Executors' commissions, legal fees, accounting fees, and other administration expenses can be deducted on the estate tax return under Section 2053(a)(2) or on the estate's fiduciary income tax returns (Form 1041) under Section 212 but not on both. It is also proper to split these deductions between these two returns. If any amount is deducted on Form 1041, a statement should be attached to the return waiving the deduction under Section 2053.

■ **A GOOD TAX TECHNIQUE:** Some practitioners deduct these expenses on both returns without filing a waiver. They decide ultimately where to claim the expenses when the return is audited and the marginal estate and income tax brackets are finally determined. If there is no audit, an amended return must be filed.

If the estate is not subject to estate tax, the deductions should be taken on Form 1041 in a year when it will offset taxable income. If no fiduciary income tax return is required, the beneficiaries may take the deduction as a miscellaneous itemized deduction on their Form 1040, subject to the two percent limitation.

If there is a required fiduciary income tax return and the income is not sufficient to absorb these expenses, timing is very important to salvage tax benefits. The deduction for excess administrative expenses is allowed only in the year of termination of the estate or trust. Then they pass through and are deductible by the beneficiaries.

If an estate or trust has a net operating loss (NOL) or a nondeductible capital loss, unlike excess deductions, it may be carried forward to the next year. Any unused NOL or capital loss carryover passes through to the beneficiary upon termination of the estate or trust.

**EXAMPLE**

An estate not subject to estate tax has the following income and expenses:

| | 1992 | 1993 (terminated) |
|---|---|---|
| Business income | $20,000 | $45,000 |
| Business deductions | (30,000) | 0 |
| Administrative expenses | (50,000) | 0 |

The estate will have no income tax liability in 1992, but the $50,000 in administrative expenses is wasted.

The 1992 NOL is $10,000 ($20,000 - $30,000), as the administrative expenses are treated as itemized deductions. In 1993, the fiduciary will have taxable income of $35,000, which will pass through to the beneficiaries, as the $10,000 NOL can be carried forward but not the excess deductions. If the administrative expenses had been delayed and paid in 1993, instead of $35,000 of income, the beneficiaries would have had an excess deduction of $15,000.

| | |
|---|---|
| Business income | $45,000 |
| Less: NOL carryover | (10,000) |
| Net | 35,000 |
| Less: administrative expenses | (50,000) |
| Excess deductions | $(15,000) |

Casualty losses to property included in the gross estate are deductible to the extent not compensated by insurance on either the estate tax return under Section 2054 or the estate income tax return under Section 165(c).

Selling expenses can be deducted by an estate for estate tax purposes or used to reduce the amount realized for income tax purposes on a sale of the property.

■ **PLANNING POINTER:** A double deduction is not allowed. The executor must select where to deduct such expenses.

**FEES TO BENEFICIARY.** If a fiduciary is also a beneficiary, determine whether executor's fees should be taken. Determine if the overall tax impact will be reduced by timely waiving of all fees. If the executor desires to waive his fee, a waiver should be filed within nine months after the date of death to avoid a gift to other beneficiaries.

**SUBCHAPTER S ELECTION.** Determine if an S corporation election should continue in force. If the decedent's closely held corporation is a Subchapter C corporation, consideration should be given to making an S election.

**WIDOW'S ALLOWANCE.** The allowance is income to the widow to the extent of the distributable net income of the estate; it is a debt of the estate for probate purposes, thus reducing the estate tax liability by way of a marital deduction; it is a deduction for estate income tax purposes (Sections 661, 662).

Under Section 643(c), the term beneficiary is not limited solely to heirs, legatees, and devisees. Therefore, the allowance is a distribution of income to the widow (Rev. Rul. 75-124).

**DISCLAIMER OF BEQUESTS AND DEVISES.** This can, and often should, be done by a wealthy wife, well-off children, or other beneficiaries whose after-tax financial position may in fact be worsened by a bequest. The effect of a disclaimer is to have property pass as if the disclaimant had predeceased the decedent.

Sections 2046 (estates) and 2518 (gifts) provide definitive rules for disclaimers of property interests. Once a qualified disclaimer by a disclaimant is made within the statute, he/she is treated as if the disclaimed property interest had never been transferred to him/her. A qualified disclaimer must be made in writing and received by the transferor, his legal representative, or the holder of legal title no later than nine months after the later of creation of the interest or the attainment of age 21 by the disclaimant. The disclaimant must not accept the interest or any of its benefits. Receipt of any consideration for disclaiming constitutes an acceptance. The interest must pass to another person as a result of the disclaimer. However, an individual may disclaim in his/her capacity as executor even if the property passes to him/her as an individual (Priv. Ltr. Rul. 8015013).

A timely transfer of property to the person who would have received it under a disclaimer, which is valid under local law, is considered an effective disclaimer for federal estate and gift tax purposes. However, all other federal disclaimer requirements must be met (Section 2518(c)).

## PLANNING POINTERS

1. Spouses can provide in their wills that the surviving spouse receives all the property and, to the extent that the survivor disclaims any of the property, it will go into a trust for the children. This gives the survivor nine months after the spouse's death to decide how best to divide up the estate for tax purposes.

   This disclaimer trust can provide that all income be paid to the surviving spouse for life, and can include an ascertainable standard of living clause. If it is a discretionary trust with the survivor as a discretionary beneficiary, this provides tremendous planning flexibility.

2. You should consider four testamentary trusts under your will: (1) marital trust with a general power of appointment, (2) the credit shelter trust, (3) a QTIP trust, and (4) a disclaimer trust.

An otherwise valid disclaimer qualifies when a surviving spouse disclaims the property and it passes to a trust in which the spouse has an income interest. This is the situation in many estate plans—the disclaimed property passes to the residual trust that names the surviving spouse as a required or potential income beneficiary (Section 2518(b)(4)). This provision makes disclaimers a more attractive estate-planning device, because a surviving spouse will not lose all benefits from disclaimed property. The survivor can receive income from the residual trust.

**THE ALTERNATE VALUATION DATE.** Section 2032(c) provides that the alternate valuation date (the option to value the property in a decedent's estate at the date of death or six months after death) can only be used if it decreases both the gross estate and the estate tax.

Section 2032(d) allows an alternate valuation election on an amended or delinquent return as long as the election is made no later than one year after the original due date of the return, including extensions.

The alternate valuation election can affect marital and charitable deductions, the percentage requirements for Section 303 redemptions, and the Section 6166 installment payment elections.

**FUND TESTAMENTARY TRUSTS EARLY.** Not only is the estate a separate taxable entity, but the beneficiaries of trusts (as well as the trusts themselves in certain cases) are also taxable entities.

Funding the trusts (Trust A and Trust B or QTIP trust) early sets up the use of all potential taxable entities: the estate, the trusts, each beneficiary.

**SELECT THE BEST FISCAL YEAR END FOR THE ESTATE.** All trusts must use a calendar year, but estates may still use a fiscal year.

■ **PLANNING POINTER:** For an estate, consider a January yearend for deferral purposes. An estate beneficiary includes income from an estate in the year the estate ends—not in the year received. Distributions received in February through December will not be taxed until the next calendar year. That's an 11-month deferral. Do it.

**LEARN HOW TO PLAY THE TRUST A, TRUST B GAME.** The marital trust (Trust A) is taxed only after the death of the surviving spouse; the QTIP trust is taxed in the same way, except a disposition of any part of the qualified property during the life of the surviving spouse is considered a taxable gift. The residuary trust (B or bypass trust) is taxed at the death of the first spouse to die and it is a tax-paid trust.

■ **PLANNING POINTER:** Try to use up Trust A and the QTIP trust, or both, during the surviving spouse's lifetime. Direct income-producing property to these trusts; let the surviving spouse make withdrawals, then make cash gifts to the children.

In Trust B, make the investment objective growth to beat inflation. Direct growth property to this trust; no estate tax is due (no matter how high the value) when distributed to the children. When the executor divides the estate property pursuant to a pecuniary bequest, Trusts A, B, and QTIP trust must each share pro rata on distribution (Rev. Proc. 64-19). But you can beat this rule by bequeathing to Trust B specific property that is likely to appreciate rapidly.

## Checklist for a QTIP Trust

If your estate plan contains a QTIP trust, your executor must make the election to receive the benefits of the marital deduction under the QTIP provisions. For most estates with a surviving spouse, this will probably be the most important postmortem estate-planning decision. The election must be made on the estate tax return.

The following checklist outlines the executor's options:

- ☐ Elect to treat the entire life-income interest as a qualifying interest. The result would be no estate tax on this interest at this time, but tax would be due at your spouse's death.
- ☐ Elect nothing. The result would be tax is due now, but none would be due at your spouse's death.
- ☐ A combination of the two preceding choices: Pay tax on a portion now; defer a portion.

Before making a choice, your executor should consider:

- ☐ Size of your estate
- ☐ Size of your spouse's estate
- ☐ Tax rate of estates—yours and your spouse's
- ☐ Possible after-tax yield on estate tax saved on death of first spouse
- ☐ Length of the deferral (when will the surviving spouse die?). The longer the surviving spouse lives, the more can be earned with the estate tax saved on the first death, and the more $10,000 annual exclusions are available for each donee, each year
- ☐ Rate of inflation
- ☐ Other sources of income and principal of surviving spouse. The surviving spouse may have enough income without the additional income that would flow from accepting the QTIP life-income interest. High income taxes on this QTIP income might be counterproductive taxwise.

## Paying Estate Tax in Installments

Section 6166 provides that if the stock or other closely held business interest is 35 percent of the decedent's adjusted gross estate, the tax attributable to the interest can be paid over a 15-year period as follows: interest only for the first four years; 10 equal payments of principal and interest thereafter with interest at four percent on the unpaid portion of the deferred tax (to a maximum tax of $345,800); and the current rate on the balance Section 6601(i)). In the case of farm or other Section 2032A closely held property, the four percent rate applies to the estate tax attributable to the first $1 million.

In either case, the estate may deduct the interest it pays on the deferral from the gross estate (Priv. Ltr. Rul. 791206). An amended Form 706 is required. Section 6161 allows the IRS to grant an extra 12 months to pay a Section 6166 installment if there is reasonable cause for the extension.

The stock or other closely held business interest must be either a proprietorship, a 20 percent or more capital interest in a partnership, or 20 percent or more in value of the voting stock of a closely held corporation. A partnership or corporate interest qualifies if either has no more than 15 partners or shareholders. If the decedent had an interest in two or more businesses (if each separate interest is more than 20 percent of the total value of such business), they are aggregated and treated as an interest in one closely held business decedent or by any member of his family shall be treated as owned by the decedent. The term family means only the decedent's brothers and sisters (whether by the whole or half blood), spouse, ancestors (grandparents), and lineal descendants (children and grandchildren). This is referred to as the "Gallo Wine Amendment" because the Gallo family lobbied so hard for its passage.

---

### ■ PLANNING POINTER

Spread the stock of the family-held corporation around among as many family members as possible to use everyone's unicredit. By creating minority interests in each decedent's estate, the stock can be discounted for valuation purposes.

---

## Final Decisions on Termination of Estate

The date of termination of an estate (or trust) is extremely important and should be considered in relation to the interests of the beneficiaries. Actually, on termination, all the rules should be reviewed.

The executor should maximize the use of taxable entities, considering the tax bracket of the beneficiaries, the taxable year in which the distribution is made, and the type of distribution—cash or property.

The executor should also consider estate termination immediately after the fiscal year-end to obtain use of the estate $600 exemption for the preceding taxable year, avoid the throwback rule, have undistributed income of the preceding year taxed in the estate's low bracket, and maximize use of Section 642(h).

Under Section 642(h), the excess of deductions over income in the year of termination of the estate can be taken by the beneficiaries succeeding to the property of the estate (the remaindermen) as deductions on their individual income tax returns. And remaindermen love it. Do it.

### What to Do

An excess of deductions over income in any taxable year other than the year of termination cannot be utilized by the estate or any beneficiary. It is wasted, forever. As a result, tax logic dictates that the administration expenses should not be paid until the year of termination. Make this final year a short year—only long enough to pay the deductions and realize minimal income. High-income-tax- bracket beneficiaries thus get the benefit of estate-paid deductions. In addition, this opportunity is also available to *trusts*.

■ **NOTE:** When an estate or trust terminates, Section 642(h) also allows the beneficiaries to utilize an NOL carryover or a capital-loss carryover on their personal tax returns.

5

# Other Estate Planning Concepts and Checklists

This chapter is interspersed with technical and nontechnical material.

## Annuities in Lifetime Planning

There are four basic annuity approaches that should be considered in lifetime planning:

1. Annuities from a qualified employer plan (see Part IX, Chapter 4).
2. Private family annuities (this chapter).
3. Charitable remainder trust (this chapter).
4. Current commercial annuities (presently being paid).

All annuity approaches are important; all are useful tools, yet each serves different purposes and is usually used separately under distinct fact patterns to accomplish specific objectives.

### General Rule—Section 2039

Annuities in which you have an interest at the date of your death are includable in your gross estate. This includes annuities presently in the pay status or where you had a right to receive payment at your death. However, if all rights to receive payment terminate on death (for example, a life annuity with no survivorship provisions), nothing is includable in the estate.

Annuities generally come in one of four forms: (1) an amount payable in a lump sum, (2) an annuity payable over a term of years certain (i.e., 10 years), (3) an annuity payable for life, and (4) joint life annuities (joint and survivor).

### Private Family Annuities

A private family annuity may be defined generally as one in which the obligor is an entity other than an insurance company or a bank (*Lloyd*, 33 BTA 903 (1936)).

The person receiving the annuity is called the annuitant. The person paying the annuity is called the obligor.

**USING A PRIVATE ANNUITY TO SELL (TRANSFER) YOUR BUSINESS.** A private annuity exists when a business owner (you) sells stock (all or some of it) in return for the buyer's (usually one of your children) promise to make periodic payments in fixed amounts for your life. When structured properly, the annuity has no value at your death. Result: There is no estate tax due on the annuity or the stock sold. The amount of the annuity payments is determined by the value of the stock, your life expectancy (as determined in IRS tables), and prevailing interest rates. The interest rate used to compute the annuity must be 120 percent of the current midterm federal applicable rate (published monthly by the IRS). There is no gift tax on the sale, as long as the value of the stock transferred does not exceed the present value of the annuity. The annuity payments cannot be the same as or limited to the income generated by the stock, and the buyer must be personally liable for the payments. Part of each payment received by the seller is tax-free return of principal, part is capital gain, and part is interest income.

Private annuities offer unique planning opportunities. They can be used between family members or between shareholders and their closely held corporations.

The mechanics of a private annuity are simple even though the tax-planning considerations are complex. The seller (the annuitant) sells the property to the buyer (the obligor) at fair-market value (FMV) in return for the unsecured promise of the obligor to pay the annuitant a certain annual sum for the life of the annuitant. At the death of the annuitant, payments cease. Since no payments are due to the estate or any beneficiaries, nothing is includable in the annuitant's gross estate.

There is no gift if the sale price is at an arms-length FMV, that is, when the present value of the annuity payments equals the value of the property transferred. Treasury Regulation 25.2512-5(f) is used to value the gift, if any.

Future appreciation is removed from the annuitant's (your) estate. At your death, since the annuity terminates and there is no retained security interest, the property is not includable in your estate.

## ■ PLANNING POINTER

A formal independent appraisal is a must. The annuitant's health must also be considered. A written health report is highly desirable.

The gain on the sale during your life is reported over time, similar to an installment sale. The annuity rules of Section 72 apply (see Rev. Rul. 69-74). You report each payment as part tax-free return of capital until your basis is recovered, part capital gain, and part ordinary income (the interest factor).

The transfer avoids probate at your death. The buyer's basis is stepped up to FMV based on the actuarial value of future payments by applying Table A of Treas. Reg. § 20.2031-7. If it is depreciable property, the value is depreciated accordingly. When you die and the actual payments made can be determined, the basis is adjusted accordingly. If you live beyond your life expectancy, the additional payments are capitalized and subject to depreciation.

Even though there is interest built into the annuity payments, the buyer-obligor cannot deduct any interest.

---

## ■ EXAMPLE

Frank owns a piece of income-producing real estate. He agrees to sell it to Sid, his son, for a promise by Sid to pay him $2,400 a month for as long as Frank lives. Assume this promise is equal to the FMV of the real estate based on Frank's health and age.

As a result, there is no gift tax due since the price is at FMV. For income-tax purposes, Sid can depreciate the property at the new raised basis equal to the FMV. Sid's tax basis is adjusted when Frank dies. Sid cannot deduct the payments to Frank as they are made (Rev. Rul. 55-119).

For Frank, the sale is income-tax-free at the time of sale. Each year, one portion of the payments received is tax-free; one portion is ordinary income; and one portion is capital gain (Rev. Rul. 69-74).

The property is excluded from Frank's estate (*Cain*, 37 TC 185 (1961) because Sid's obligation to continue payments ceases when Frank dies.

---

The example raises additional problems, and different rules must be addressed. If you live beyond your life expectancy, the extra payments made to you are taxed at the same rate as earlier payments. When the capital gains run out, all the income is ordinary income.

Under Section 72(b)(3), if you die prior to recovering your entire investment, the unrecovered investment is an ordinary deduction on your final income tax return, filed on Form 1040.

For gift-tax purposes, if the consideration received by you is less than FMV, the difference between the FMV and such consideration is a gift.

If you retain too many strings, the property may be included in your estate. Among factors the IRS considers strings are the right to use the property as security for the payments; eliminating the obligor's right to mortgage or otherwise encumber the property during your lifetime; and, an intention that the transfer actually take place at your death (for example, retention of controlling interest by you when corporate stock or partnership interest is transferred).

---

## ■ PLANNING POINTER

To avoid the strings and still meet your financial-planning needs, insure the obligor (buyer) to guarantee future annuity payments to you in the event of the obligor's premature death. However, no mention should be made of the insurance in the private annuity agreement. If it is mentioned, the IRS may treat the annuity as secured, which results in immediate recognition of all the gain to you. There will be estate tax implications, as well.

You could also be insured. To keep the insurance proceeds out of your estate, the obligor would take out the policy on your life. You would gift cash to the obligor each year, often from the annuity proceeds, to make the insurance premium payments. This helps mitigate the lack of interest deductions by the obligor. The gifts further reduce your gross estate.

---

**WHEN TO USE A PRIVATE FAMILY ANNUITY.** A private family annuity works well with rapidly appreciating, closely held stock. If the younger generation family member is on the company's payroll, his/her salary can possibly be increased to cover all or a portion of the annuity payments, but beware of unreasonable compensation.

An S election is usually a smart move. The corporation's profits are withdrawn by the younger member and used to make the annuity payments.

## Charitable Gifts

It is better to give than to receive, and it is even better to give if the gift means you can save income taxes and estate taxes.

Two reasons are usually given for making lifetime charitable gifts.

First, you receive gratification from making the gift. Often the gift is publicized in the community. Second, a current income-tax deduction is received, saving more wealth that can pass to the charity or other noncharitable beneficiaries at your death.

### Life Insurance as a Charitable Gift

Life insurance is a good method for providing for charities without impairing your personal cash flow too severely while living. The charity receives a large sum of money when you die. However, you may not retain any significant rights that may amount to a partial interest. If you do, no charitable deduction is allowed (Section 170(f)(3)).

**Life Insurance/Charity Checklist**

1. Buy a new policy for a charity; make the charity beneficiary. The premium payments are deductible. There must be an insurable interest based on marriage, blood, or financial considerations. Therefore, the charity should not be applicant, nor should the donor (you) apply for the policy in the charity's name.
2. Gift an existing policy to a charity, and pay the premiums. A life insurance policy is not a capital asset. Therefore, any cash value buildup, which is untaxed ordinary income, is not deductible if gifted to a charity. The current deduction is limited to your tax basis: premiums paid less dividends received. Any future payments made on the policy are deductible when paid.
3. Gift an existing paid-up policy to a charity. The tax basis is deductible.
4. Change the beneficiaries on an existing policy to a charity, or make the charity a fractional beneficiary if it won't significantly affect surviving family members. There is no current income-tax deduction.
5. Buy life insurance on another person if the grantor is not insurable, and gift it to the charity. There must be an insurable interest.
6. Gift a policy to a charity in return for a life annuity for the donor's spouse. In the agreement with the charity, the annuity amount may vary but will often be equivalent to the earnings from the insurance proceeds. The charity receives the remainder interest.
7. Assign the life insurance dividends to charity. The taxpayer gets a charitable deduction for the dividends, which are not taxable to the insured. The dividends are a tax-free return of premiums.

8. Sell an existing policy to a charity at cost. This will be treated as part sale and part gift under Section 1011(b).
9. Use life insurance in a charitable remainder trust or charitable lead trust.

---

**■ EXAMPLE**

Moses sells a $100,000 life insurance policy to a charity for $15,000. The policy has a FMV (cash surrender value) of $25,000 and a tax basis of $15,000 (premiums paid less dividends received).

| | |
|---|---|
| Sale price | $15,000 |
| Basis proration: | |
| $\$15{,}000 \times \dfrac{\$15{,}000}{\$25{,}000}$ | 9,000 |
| Gain recognized | $6,000 |

The donor is allowed a charitable deduction, subject to the charitable-deduction limitations, of $6,000 (the amount of the gain). If the charity doesn't have the cash, it can borrow against the cash value. This doesn't affect the part sale/part gift.

Section 2035(d)(2) requires life insurance gifted within three years of death to be included in the donor's estate. However, if death should occur, an offsetting charitable deduction is generally allowed.

---

### Charitable-Remainder Trusts

A useful planning tool, particularly for the charitably minded taxpayer, is the charitable-remainder trust. It is essentially a device used to provide a lifetime benefit to a noncharitable beneficiary—for example, self, wife, or child—and to give the property (remainder) to a charitable organization. The payments that may be made to the individual beneficiary are rigidly prescribed by the tax law.

Section 2055(e)(2)(A) disallows an estate-tax deduction for any charitable-remainder trust except one of these three:

- ☐ *Annuity trust.* The beneficiary receives, for life, annual distributions of five percent or more based on the value of the assets at the inception of the trust; the remainder passes to charity at the beneficiary's death (Section 664(d)(1)).
- ☐ *Unitrust.* The beneficiary receives, for life, annual distributions of five percent or more based on the value of the trust assets each year; the remainder passes to charity at the beneficiary's death (Section 664(d)(2)).
- ☐ *Pooled-income funds.* The fund is set up by a public charity, and all contributions are pooled for the benefit of all beneficiaries. The beneficiary receives annual distributions equal to the income of the entire fund allocable to the contribution made, and the remainder passes to the public charity itself at the time of the beneficiary's death (Section 642(c)(5)).

Immediate needs of a family member can be estimated with some certainty; estimated future needs are, at best, approximations. A fixed-dollar annuity may prove insufficient because of inflation; unitrust payments may vary drastically from year to year due to market-value fluctuations. These problems cannot be solved by either of these trusts.

A pooled-income fund is a better approach to solving market fluctuation and inflation problems. This is true because the yield from diversified investments in stocks and bonds is not likely to fluctuate as severely as the market, and, in the long run, may at least have a chance of compensating for inflation.

**USES OF CHARITABLE-REMAINDER TRUSTS.** A charitable-remainder trust can solve a multitude of problems because of its many available uses. You realize immediate income- tax savings by means of a charitable deduction. Low-yield securities in a trust produce the double benefits of an immediate tax deduction and an increase in your personal income for life through an increased yield available from the trust. Capital gains taxes are avoided when appreciated securities are contributed.

■ **PLANNING POINTER:** The appreciation on capital assets donated to charity is a tax preference item (Section 57(a)(6)). This must be considered if you are in an alternative minimum tax situation.

When you do not need the income, it can be diverted to a low-tax-bracket family member, for example, "To granddaughter, Pricy, for 20 years, then to X Charity." If a pooled-income fund is selected, diversification and professional management are provided.

Lifetime gifts also eliminate estate tax equal to the charitable remainder, unless a life estate for a person other than you is inserted after your death. The value of such person's interest is taxed upon your death.

■ **EXAMPLE**

Donor *D*, creates a trust "To *D* for life, then to *S*, his son, for life, then to the *X* Charity." *D* dies; *S* survives. The value of *S*'s interest is included in *D*'s estate.

For testamentary gifts, the value of the charitable remainder escapes the estate tax.

## The Tax Consequences

**INCOME TAXES—THE DONOR.** In the year the gift is made, the donor (you) receives an income-tax deduction equal to the value of the remainder interest that passes to the charity (Section 170(f)(2)(A)), subject to the usual 50 percent and 30 percent of adjusted gross income limitations. Thus, the amount of the deduction varies, depending on the life expectancy of the income beneficiary or beneficiaries (generally not more than two) and the expected rate of return selected on investment. The regulations present a series of tables to be used to determine the value of the charitable remainder.

| Type of annuity | Regulation |
|---|---|
| Annuity | 20.2031-7(f) |
| Unitrust | 1.664-4 |
| Pooled-income fund | 1.642(c)-6(d) |

## ■ EXAMPLE

Dave, age 70, transfers $10,000 worth of ABC stock to an annuity trust that will pay him five percent annually. Assume the tables at Treas. Reg. 20.2031-7(f) value the remainder for a 70-year-old beneficiary at .39478 (these tables are revised monthly). Dave's income-tax deduction is $3,948 ($10,000 × .39478).

Also assume the ABC stock cost Dave $2,000. The $8,000 potential capital gain is avoided forever, unless the alternative minimum tax applies.

## ■ A NEAT IDEA: SAVE TAXES, INCREASE INCOME

Use an irrevocable life insurance trust to replace the money going to charity. The life insurance can be removed from the estate along with the cash that you gift to the trust (or the children if they own the policies directly) to pay the premiums. The estate tax-free policy proceeds can then be used to provide income for your family after your death. Result: Increased income for you during your life; increased income for your family after you are gone.

An exception to the rules is a residence or farm. If you retain a life interest in a personal residence or farm devised to a charity, your estate is entitled to a charitable deduction for the value of the remainder interest (Section 2055(e)(2)). If the remainder interest is other than a personal residence, it must be a charitable-remainder annuity trust, a charitable-remainder unitrust, or a pooled-income fund to qualify.

Rev. Rul. 77-169 holds that, for the estate to receive a charitable deduction, the will must provide for the residence itself to be turned over to a charity, not the proceeds of sale.

If gifted during your lifetime, a current income-tax deduction is allowed (Section 170(f)(3)(B)).

### ■ EXAMPLE 1

Tom transfers his personal residence to a charity when it has a fair-market value of $200,000. He includes in the deed on transfer the right for him to reside there for the remainder of his life. Tom is allowed an income-tax deduction for the remainder interest. Nine years later, when the house is worth $300,000, Tom dies. The value of the house is included in his gross estate, under Section 2035 (retained life interests). The estate receives an offsetting charitable deduction under Section 2055(a).

### ■ EXAMPLE 2

Assume in Example 1 that Tom also retained the right for his daughter to live in the house for her life. Generally, the estate- tax deduction is not allowed for a remainder interest unless it is a qualifying annuity trust, unitrust or pooled-income fund. However, there is an exception for remainder interests in a personal residence or condominium (Treas. Reg. 1.170A-7(b)(3)).

## Requirements to Receive Benefits

In order to receive the benefits of an annuity trust, unitrust or pooled-income trust, specific requirements must be met.

**Annuity Trust Primary Requirements**

- ☐ A fixed amount, or percentage (annuity), of the initial value of the trust must be payable to the noncharitable beneficiary.
- ☐ The annual annuity payments must not be less than an amount equal to five percent of the initial market value of all the property transferred to the trust.
- ☐ The annuity must be paid at least annually to the beneficiary out of income and corpus. If income is not high enough, corpus must be invaded to pay the required annuity amount.
- ☐ The trust must be irrevocable; a power held by the donor, the trustee, or the beneficiary to invade, alter, or amend the trust is prohibited. Once established, no further contributions can be made to the trust (Treas. Reg. 1.664-2(b)).
- ☐ The trust must name as beneficiary one or more individuals living at the time the property is transferred to the trust.
- ☐ The noncharitable beneficiary interest must be for a term not exceeding 20 years or for life.

**Unitrust Principal Requirements**

- ☐ A fixed percentage of the net FMV of the principal, as revalued annually, must be paid to the noncharitable beneficiary.
- ☐ The percentage to be paid cannot be less than five percent of the annual value.
- ☐ The unitrust can provide some flexibility for the noncharitable beneficiary, who can receive the lesser of a specific fixed percentage or the trust income for the year, plus any excess income to the extent of any deficiency in the prior years because the distribution was limited to the amount of trust income in such years.
- ☐ The trust must be irrevocable; a power held by the donor, the trustee, or the beneficiary to invade, alter, or amend the trust is prohibited.
- ☐ The noncharitable beneficiary interest must be for a term not exceeding 20 years or for life.
- ☐ Additional contributions may be made (Treas. Reg. 1.664-3(b) and Rev. Rul. 74-149).
- ☐ All, not a portion, of the remainder must go to charity.

Unlike the charitable-remainder annuity trust, no payment to the noncharitable beneficiary may be made out of principal. However, any excess trust income in a current year may be used to make up a prior year's deficiency.

---

■ **EXAMPLE**

Under his will, Alex bequeaths $100,000 to a trustee who will annually pay to Bob, for life, an amount equal to the lesser of five percent of the value of the trust property or the net income of the trust for each year. Any deficiency below the stated percentage in any year is to be made up from prior years' excess income, if any. If, in Year 1, the trust had income of $4,000, only that amount would be distributed to Bob, instead of the required payment of $5,000 (5 percent x $100,000). If, in Year 2, the trust income amounted to $8,500 and the required payment was $5,500 (5 percent x $110,000, the increased FMV of the principal), Bob would be entitled to $6,500—the current payment of $5,500 plus the Year 1 deficiency of $1,000. The $2,000 of undistributed income ($8,500 - $6,500) would be held to be used, if needed, to make up for income deficiencies in future years.

---

### Pooled-Income Fund Requirements

- ☐ The donor must contribute an irrevocable and vested remainder interest to the charity that creates and maintains it.
- ☐ The property gifted by the donor must be commingled with the property gifted by others.
- ☐ The fund is prohibited from investing in tax-exempt securities.
- ☐ The donor must retain for himself, or one or more other named beneficiaries, a life-income interest.
- ☐ Each life beneficiary must be entitled to, and receive, a *pro rata* share of the income annually based on the actual earnings of the fund.

The cost to create and maintain the trust is borne by the charity. This is a significant factor when the contemplated gift is small.

When you own stock in a closely held corporation that has significantly appreciated, gifting all or a portion of the stock to a charitable remainder unitrust is a smart tax move. The corporation then redeems the stock—it must not be prearranged or required to do so. You cannot do this with S corporation stock because as soon as the stock is transferred to the charity, the S election will be terminated.

#### ■ EXAMPLE 1

Moe owns 100 percent of Success Co. He gifts $100,000 of the stock, with a tax basis of $2,000, to a charitable-remainder unitrust. One month later, Success Co. redeems the stock. Moe takes a current deduction based on the value of the remainder interest. He will receive at least $5,000 per year from the trust, unless the actual income is lower, which is unlikely. Moe is not subject to capital gains tax on the $95,000 gain, but could be subject to alternative minimum tax (AMT).

This concept can be taken a step further by multiple owners who want to buy life insurance to fund a buyout. They could use the annual income from the trust to pay the premiums.

#### ■ EXAMPLE 2

Assume, as in Example 1, two equal shareholders establish charitable-remainder trusts transferring $100,000 each in stock. The business is valued at $2 million after the redemptions. Each shareholder takes out life insurance of $1 million on the other to fund the buyout using a cross-purchase agreement.

The income from the unitrust provides the funds to pay the premiums.

The cash can come from the corporation tax-free (actually partially deductible by the shareholders). The life insurance proceeds are not trapped in the corporation to become part of E & P. The life insurance is not paid to the corporation, causing a potential alternative minimum tax (AMT to the corporation), because book income exceeds taxable income.

There is no loss in the step-up in basis as the survivor's basis in the stock purchased from the decedent's estate is cost (also FMV). The estate has no income-tax consequences because of the step-up in basis at decedent's death.

The cross-purchase agreement fixes the value and guarantees the decedent's survivors estate liquidity. The surviving stockholder is not saddled with undesirable owners.

### Charitable Bailout

This article from my tax column tells you how this concept works.

HOW TO RECEIVE BY GIVING

One cardinal rule of saving taxes is easy to state and easy to understand: *When you pay, deduct all.* Here's a tax idea that goes even a step further: You get a full deduction for what *someone else* pays.

First, some basics. When you give property to a charity, you get a deduction equal to its fair-market value on the date of the gift. Your cost or how you acquired the property is immaterial. An example is the easiest way to explain the wonderful tax consequences.

*Example:* Years ago, when you started Success Co., the stock was worth 10 cents a share. You owned 100 percent then, and still do today. But, today it's worth $100 per share. If you sold 100 shares for $10,000, the capital- gains tax would be about $2,800. But, if you donate the stock to your favorite charity, the capital-gains tax is ignored and you get the full $10,000 deduction. In the 28-percent tax bracket, that means you would pocket $2,800.

This little tax ploy is known as a "charitable bailout." It's one of the answers to the age-old problem of how to get money out of a closely held corporation. It's not so easy to find a buyer for your stock when you want to sell only a few shares. In fact, you may have trouble trying to give it away because the charity won't be able to sell it either.

This is where the bailout comes in. You arrange to have your corporation buy the stock from the charity at its full value. *Result*: You unlock $10,000 from the corporation. *Caution*: Be careful about the deal you make with the charity. You lose your tax benefits if the charity is obliged to sell the stock to the corporation. It's okay to nix sales to anyone else, but the charity must at least have the option of keeping the stock. Chances are they'll want to cash it in faster than you want it back, but caution, you won't avoid the capital-gains tax if you make the donation contingent upon the charity selling the stock back to the corporation.

When the smoke clears, Success Co. has, in fact, paid for your $10,000 charitable deduction. And who still owns 100 percent of Success Co? You do. A great tax deal all around. One more caution: Gifts of appreciated property may be subject to the Alternative Minimum Tax.

## Section 303 Redemption

A Section 303 Redemption is a buyout plan where the corporation purchases from the estate of a deceased shareholder an amount of stock equal to the sum of all death taxes (federal and state) and the cost of funeral and administrative expenses.

The purpose of the 303 plan is to enable an estate to sell stock back to a corporation as a capital exchange. No gain is realized by the estate on the sale because the basis of the stock is "stepped up" to the value of the shares on the date of the decedent's death. The proceeds from the sale may be used for liquidity needs of the estate or for any other purpose.

A 303 redemption is only available to an estate possessing a closely held business interest that constitutes more than 35 percent of the value of the adjusted gross estate.

### Funding the Redemption

The most common way to guarantee that the corporation will have cash to pay for the stock is through life insurance. Generally, the corporation is the owner and beneficiary of a policy on the shareholder's life. Upon death, the corporation receives the policy proceeds income-tax-free and uses the funds to purchase the stock.

In my view, Section 303 is a mistake. I never plan toward a Section 303 redemption; instead, I use the other techniques described in this book.

The above is a classical description of a 303 redemption. But readers of this book know insurance does not belong in a corporation. Better to have the insurance owned by an irrevocable life insurance trust and paid to the trust.

Do we ever use a 303 redemption in our office? Yes, when we do post-mortem estate planning on a matter where we did not do the planning and the corporation is the only place to find the liquidity needed for estate taxes. Put another way, someone made a mistake. (Probably by making the corporation the beneficiary of life insurance.)

A Section 303 redemption is a nice way to get money out of the corporation tax-free when it has excess cash that could only be removed otherwise as a taxable dividend. But this nice way should be used as a bonus, not as a major estate-planning technique.

## Commonly Overlooked Estate Tax-Saving Devices

Estate tax-saving devices, which should be used more often, are overlooked in many cases. Following is a short checklist of estate tax-saving devices that are commonly missed in practice, even by experienced practitioners.

**SPRINKLE OR ACCUMULATE TRUST B INCOME.** The surviving spouse often does not need the income from Trust B. This income added to Trust A income or QTIP trust income (a must to receive the marital deduction) and other income puts the Trust B income in the surviving spouse's highest tax bracket.

To save your heirs income taxes, authorize the trustee to sprinkle the income among your heirs (usually your children or grandchildren who are in low income-tax brackets).

**TRUST B AS BENEFICIARY OF INTEREST IN A QUALIFIED PLAN.** Distributions from a qualified deferred compensation plan (i.e., pension) are fully subject to income tax. By making Trust B the beneficiary, the sprinkle/accumulation income-tax advantage is available, and upon the death of the beneficiaries of Trust B (usually your wife and children), the property in the trust will pass free of estate tax to the beneficiary receiving the final distribution. This is because Trust B is a tax-paid trust, having paid its estate-tax dues upon your death.

Normally, Trust B is the perfect place to put assets that are likely to appreciate rapidly after your death. If you don't own such assets, making Trust B the beneficiary of your qualified plan or IRA is the next best bet.

**DUAL SAFE DEPOSIT BOXES.** This is actually not a tax-saving device, but rather a convenient and practical idea. In most states a person's safe deposit box is sealed at death and can be opened only after certain legal procedures. This can cause delay. You can avoid this problem by having two safe deposit boxes, one in the name of each spouse. The wife can keep in her vault important documents that will be needed in the event of her husband's death; the husband can keep those documents he will need if his wife dies.

## Estate and Gift Planning Checklist

A complete planning list for the subject matter covered in this chapter is probably impossible. Whether you are just beginning to plan your estate or gift program or are completing the task, a checklist is almost always a must. The following list covers most of the points that might come up in real-life situations.

| Applicable | N/A | Consider Further | Technique |
|---|---|---|---|
| | | | INCOME TAX PLANNING |
| ☐ | ☐ | ☐ | 1. Consider gifting cash to a custodial account for a minor. **CAVEAT**: The donor should not be the custodian of the account. |
| ☐ | ☐ | ☐ | 2. Consider gifting income-producing assets to an irrevocable simple trust or in custodianship. **CAVEAT**: The income should not be used to satisfy the support obligation of the grantor; otherwise, the income will be taxed to the grantor. |
| ☐ | ☐ | ☐ | 3. Consider using an accumulation trust for irrevocable gifts to minors. **CAVEAT**: Satisfy Section 2503(c) or use a Crummey-type power to qualify as a present-interest gift. Also, the grantor should not be the trustee. |
| ☐ | ☐ | ☐ | 4. Consider using a reversionary trust (Clifford type) to shift income to lower-bracket family members, i.e., grandparents, parents or children. **CAVEAT**: The property generally may not revert to the grantor for over 31 years. |
| ☐ | ☐ | ☐ | 5. Consider interest-free loans or low-interest loans to lower-bracket family members. **CAVEAT**: Be sure to satisfy the safe-harbor limits of Section 7872. |
| ☐ | ☐ | ☐ | 6. Consider an interest-bearing loan by a low-bracket family member to a high-bracket family member. |
| ☐ | ☐ | ☐ | 7. Consider a family partnership to split income among family members. |
| ☐ | ☐ | ☐ | 8. Consider gifting S corporation stock to a low-bracket family member. A qualified S corporation trust may be applicable. Non-voting common stock may be gifted. |

| Applicable | N/A | Consider Further | Technique |
|---|---|---|---|
| | | | INCOME TAX PLANNING |
| ☐ | ☐ | ☐ | 9. Gift appreciated property before sale, or zero-basis property such as grain or livestock. **CAVEAT**: Transfers in trust where property is sold within two years will be taxed to the grantor (Code Section 644). For gifts of grain or livestock, make the gift in the year following production to avoid disallowance of related expenses. |
| ☐ | ☐ | ☐ | 10. Make a bargain sale to a family member (part-sale/part-gift). This gives the donor some cash while avoiding part or all of the taxable gain. |
| ☐ | ☐ | ☐ | 11. Sell business or investment assets whose values are below their tax basis before death to avoid a step-down in basis. |
| ☐ | ☐ | ☐ | 12. Lease depreciable property to a family member. |
| ☐ | ☐ | ☐ | 13. Plan to avoid loss of tax carryovers on death; i.e., capital loss, net operating loss, investment credit, etc. |
| ☐ | ☐ | ☐ | 14. Consider gift and leaseback of business property. |
| ☐ | ☐ | ☐ | 15. Consider sale and leaseback of business property using an installment sale. |
| ☐ | ☐ | ☐ | 16. Consider employing a child, grandchild or other family member. |
| | | | COMPENSATION PLANNING |
| ☐ | ☐ | ☐ | 17. Utilize qualified retirement plans. |
| ☐ | ☐ | ☐ | 18. Utilize individual retirement accounts for husband and wife. |
| ☐ | ☐ | ☐ | 19. Take full advantage of corporate fringe benefits. |
| ☐ | ☐ | ☐ | 20. Consider an unfunded or funded (Rabbi Trust) nonqualified deferred compensation plan. **CAVEAT**: Avoid constructive receipt. |
| ☐ | ☐ | ☐ | 21. Provide for the $5,000 death-benefit exclusion. |
| | | | GIFT PLANNING |
| ☐ | ☐ | ☐ | 22. Make present-interest gifts annually to utilize the $10,000 annual exclusion. Avoid gifts of a future interest. |
| ☐ | ☐ | ☐ | 23. Utilize the provisions of gift-splitting for married individuals. **CAVEAT**: Gift-splitting election must be made on a timely filed return. |
| ☐ | ☐ | ☐ | 24. Make gifts of appreciating property to remove future appreciation from the estate. |
| ☐ | ☐ | ☐ | 25. Make gifts even though a gift tax is incurred. Future appreciation is removed and the donor's estate is reduced by the gift tax paid (except gifts within three years of death) and the gift tax is imposed at the lower marginal rates at the time of the gift. |

| Appli-cable | N/A | Consider Further | Technique<br>GIFT TAX PLANNING |
|---|---|---|---|
| ☐ | ☐ | ☐ | 26. Consider gifting property subject to a mortgage to reduce the net gift. |
| ☐ | ☐ | ☐ | 27. Consider a partial gift of property subject to a mortgage just prior to sale with a wraparound mortgage. |
| ☐ | ☐ | ☐ | 28. Gift life insurance policies (other than to the spouse) or make someone else the owner other than the insured when the policy is taken out. Avoid incidents of ownership. **CAVEAT**: Gifts of life insurance by the donor/insured within three years of death are included in that insured's gross estate. |
| ☐ | ☐ | ☐ | 29. Consider an irrevocable unfunded (no income-producing assets) life insurance trust. Include a Crummey power. **CAVEAT**: The insured should not pay the premiums directly. |
| ☐ | ☐ | ☐ | 30. Consider an irrevocable funded life insurance trust. Include a Crummey power. **CAVEAT**: The insured will be taxed on any income even though he has no incidents of ownership. |
| ☐ | ☐ | ☐ | 31. Consider split-dollar life insurance for gifting purposes. **CAVEAT**: The retention of the corporation's right to borrow against the cash surrender value will cause the proceeds to be includable in the insured's estate if the corporation is controlled by the insured. |
| ☐ | ☐ | ☐ | 32. Consider borrowing against a life insurance policy just prior to gifting to reduce the amount of gift. |
| ☐ | ☐ | ☐ | 33. Consider forgiveness of debt as a gifting technique. **CAVEAT**: Be aware of the part-gift, part-sale concept. |
| ☐ | ☐ | ☐ | 34. Avoid incomplete transfers, i.e., retention of life estates, revocable transfers, reversionary interests and certain powers. |
| ☐ | ☐ | ☐ | 35. Avoid gifts where there will be a loss in the step-up in basis at the date of death. |
| ☐ | ☐ | ☐ | 36. Consider gifts to the spouse with a smaller estate to avoid the possibility of losing the spouse's unified tax credit (exemption equivalent). The spouse with the smaller estate generally will leave a life estate to the spouse with the larger estate. |
| ☐ | ☐ | ☐ | 37. Consider gifts to the spouse with a smaller estate to balance the estates which will split the marginal estate tax rates. |
| ☐ | ☐ | ☐ | 38. Consider lifetime marital transfers to a qualified terminable interest property trust. Note: The QTIP election must be made on a timely filed Form 709. |
| ☐ | ☐ | ☐ | 39. Utilize the gift exclusion for qualified transfers (tuition and medical care). |

| Appli-cable | N/A | Consider Further | | Technique |
|---|---|---|---|---|
| | | | | GIFT TAX PLANNING |
| ☐ | ☐ | ☐ | 40. | Consider making *inter vivos* charitable gifts of cash or appreciated property to receive the income-tax benefits as well as remove the property from the estate. **CAVEAT**: Consider any potential alternative minimum tax effect. Note: A private foundation could be utilized to avoid loss of control of certain property. |
| ☐ | ☐ | ☐ | 41. | Consider an *inter vivos* qualified charitable remainder annuity trust or unitrust. **CAVEAT**: The trust must comply with Code Section 664. |
| ☐ | ☐ | ☐ | 42. | Consider nontrust charitable remainder gifts of a principal residence or farm. |
| ☐ | ☐ | ☐ | 43. | Consider an *inter vivos* charitable remainder trust where the surviving spouse is the only noncharitable beneficiary. |
| ☐ | ☐ | ☐ | 44. | Consider a charitable lead trust. **CAVEAT**: The trust is subject to the private foundation rules. |
| ☐ | ☐ | ☐ | 45. | Consider severing joint-tenancy property with a spouse to provide flexibility and avoid over-funding of the marital deduction and the loss of the step-up in basis on one-half of the property. |
| ☐ | ☐ | ☐ | 46. | Consider making a net gift when there is a gift-tax liability. **CAVEAT**: If the gift-tax liability exceeds the basis of the gifted property, there will be a taxable gain. |
| ☐ | ☐ | ☐ | 47. | Consider gifting your personal residence. **CAVEAT**: There cannot be an implied agreement that the donor is to live on the property. |
| | | | | OTHER PLANNING TECHNIQUES |
| ☐ | ☐ | ☐ | 48. | Utilize the unlimited testamentary marital deduction, but do not overfund the marital deduction so as to waste your exemption equivalent. |
| ☐ | ☐ | ☐ | 49. | Consider an estate equalization clause. |
| ☐ | ☐ | ☐ | 50. | Consider a testamentary qualified terminable interest property trust for marital deduction purposes. NOTE: The QTIP election must be made on a timely filed Form 706. |
| ☐ | ☐ | ☐ | 51. | Avoid nonqualifying, nondeductible terminable interest transfers to a surviving spouse. |
| ☐ | ☐ | ☐ | 52. | In large estates, spouses should avoid large joint-tenancy holdings because it limits flexibility, overfunds the marital deduction by not utilizing the exemption equivalent, and does not receive a step-up in basis on one-half of the joint-tenancy property. |
| ☐ | ☐ | ☐ | 53. | Where the surviving spouse already has a large estate, consider leaving a life interest only. |

| Applicable | N/A | Consider Further | Technique<br>OTHER PLANNING TECHNIQUES |
|---|---|---|---|
| ☐ | ☐ | ☐ | 54. When you own life insurance policies on your spouse, they should be bequested to lower-generation family members. |
| ☐ | ☐ | ☐ | 55. Allocate, to the extent possible, items which will decrease in value to the marital bequest, i.e., wasting assets and cash that will be spent or gifted. |
| ☐ | ☐ | ☐ | 56. Consider allocating IRD (income in respect of a decedent) items to the surviving spouse so that the income-tax liability reduces the surviving spouse's gross estate. |
| ☐ | ☐ | ☐ | 57. Consider spreading IRD items among several taxpayers, i.e., surviving spouse, children, trusts, etc. |
| ☐ | ☐ | ☐ | 58. Consider including a power limited by an ascertainable standard relating to the health, education, support or maintenance of the surviving spouse in the residuary family trust. |
| ☐ | ☐ | ☐ | 59. Consider giving the surviving spouse limited powers of appointment in the residuary family trust. |
| ☐ | ☐ | ☐ | 60. Consider giving the surviving spouse the power to withdraw the greater of $5,000 or five percent of the value of the residuary family trust. **CAVEAT**: The value of this power will be includable in the survivor's estate. |
| ☐ | ☐ | ☐ | 61. Consider a family estate trust. |
| ☐ | ☐ | ☐ | 62. Consider having the residuary family trust be a discretionary (complex) trust to sprinkle and spray income among family members. |
| ☐ | ☐ | ☐ | 63. Consider inter-family installment sales to freeze the estate. |
| ☐ | ☐ | ☐ | 64. Consider a like-kind exchange of rapidly appreciating assets with lower-generation family members. **CAVEAT**: Neither property should be sold within two years. |
| ☐ | ☐ | ☐ | 65. Consider an inter-family installment sale with a cancellation of debt clause in the event of death. **CAVEAT**: It must be a *bona fide* sale for full and adequate consideration. |
| ☐ | ☐ | ☐ | 66. Consider a family split-purchase, i.e., the older generation acquires the life interest in the property and the younger generation acquires the remainder interest. |
| ☐ | ☐ | ☐ | 67. Consider a grantor annuity trust or grantor retained income trust (GRIT). |
| ☐ | ☐ | ☐ | 68. Where a life income interest only is owned, consider a sale of the life interest to the remaindermen or a lower-bracket family member. |
| ☐ | ☐ | ☐ | 69. Consider a private annuity with a family member. |

| Appli-cable | N/A | Consider Further | | Technique<br>OTHER PLANNING TECHNIQUES |
|---|---|---|---|---|
| | | | | Consider a private annuity redemption with a closely-held corporation. **CAVEAT**: A waiver of family attribution will generally have to be filed. |
| ☐ | ☐ | ☐ | 70. | Provide for qualified disclaimers and appropriate disposition of disclaimed property. |
| ☐ | ☐ | ☐ | 71. | Consider as many as four testamentary trusts, i.e., (1) marital deduction trust with a general power of appointment, (2) a family trust to shelter the exemption equivalent, (3) a QTIP trust, and (4) a disclaimer trust. |
| ☐ | ☐ | ☐ | 72. | Consider withdrawing retirement funds over a joint and survivor annuity. |
| ☐ | ☐ | ☐ | 73. | Plan to qualify for 5-year or 10-year averaging of a lump-sum retirement distribution. Note: The taxpayer must have attained the age of 50 by January 1, 1986 to qualify for 10-year averaging. |
| ☐ | ☐ | ☐ | 74. | Consider incorporating an unincorporated business for ease of transferability and possible discounting for valuation purposes. |
| ☐ | ☐ | ☐ | 75. | Create multiple corporate entities for discounting purposes. |
| ☐ | ☐ | ☐ | 76. | Create minority interests in corporations for discounting purposes. |
| ☐ | ☐ | ☐ | 77. | Consider a personal holding company. |
| ☐ | ☐ | ☐ | 78. | Consider bequesting stock in a family corporation to the working children and bequest corporate debentures or other assets to the children not working in the business. |
| ☐ | ☐ | ☐ | 79. | Consider a corporate estate freeze by recapitalizing the corporation. **CAVEAT**: This technique has been severely limited by Chapter 14. |
| ☐ | ☐ | ☐ | 80. | Utilize buy-sell agreements, stock-redemption agreements, rights of first refusal, and other stock restrictions for purpose of fixing the value of closely held stock. But, note that a mandatory buy-sell or redemption will disqualify the stock for Section 6166 tax deferral. Also, see Section 2703. |
| ☐ | ☐ | ☐ | 81. | Consider blockage discounts of corporate stock. |
| ☐ | ☐ | ☐ | 82. | Consider a partnership estate freeze. **CAVEAT**: This technique has been severely limited by Chapter 14. |
| ☐ | ☐ | ☐ | 83. | Consider whether a partnership should terminate on death or provide for a successor in interest. |
| ☐ | ☐ | ☐ | 84. | Create fractional interests in multiple trusts for discounting purposes. |
| ☐ | ☐ | ☐ | 85. | Create undivided interests in real estate or fractional interest in land trusts for discounting purposes. **CAVEAT**: This technique has been successfully challenged by the IRS in certain jurisdictions. |

| Applicable | N/A | Consider Further | | Technique<br>OTHER PLANNING TECHNIQUES |
|---|---|---|---|---|
| ☐ | ☐ | ☐ | 86. | Make long-term, low-interest loans to family members for discounting purposes. **CAVEAT**: The value cannot be discounted if the loan is canceled at death. |
| ☐ | ☐ | ☐ | 87. | Plan to qualify for special use valuation of farmland. |
| ☐ | ☐ | ☐ | 88. | Consider testamentary charitable dispositions. |
| ☐ | ☐ | ☐ | 89. | Consider a testamentary qualified charitable remainder annuity trust or unitrust. **CAVEAT**: The trust must comply with Code Section 664. |
| ☐ | ☐ | ☐ | 90. | Consider a testamentary charitable remainder trust where the spouse is the only noncharitable beneficiary. |
| ☐ | ☐ | ☐ | 91. | Consider utilizing the special $1,000,000 per grantor generation-skipping tax exemption. |
| ☐ | ☐ | ☐ | 92. | Consider the purchase of flower bonds. **CAVEAT**: Flower bonds are valued at par in the gross estate if they can be used to pay estate taxes whether or not they are actually so used. |
| ☐ | ☐ | ☐ | 93. | Consider creating illiquidity in an estate to qualify for deferred installment payments of estate tax. |
| ☐ | ☐ | ☐ | 94. | Plan to qualify for deferred installment payments under Code Section 6166 and take maximum advantage of the four percent interest rate on deferred estate taxes. (Section 6601(j)). Consider gifting nonbusiness property as soon as possible (more than three years before death to qualify). |
| ☐ | ☐ | ☐ | 95. | Plan to qualify for a Section 303 stock redemption. Consider gifting nonbusiness property as soon as possible (more than three years before death to qualify). |
| ☐ | ☐ | ☐ | 96. | Plan for a complete redemption of closely held corporate stock. **CAVEAT**: Be aware of the waiver of family attribution rules. |
| ☐ | ☐ | ☐ | 97. | Consider simultaneous (common disaster) death clauses for married taxpayers to assure a marital deduction and an equalizing of estates. |
| ☐ | ☐ | ☐ | 98. | Where both spouses have very large estates, consider a survivorship clause in the marital bequest, not to exceed six months. **CAVEAT**: This clause can be disastrous where there is a great imbalance in the estates. |
| ☐ | ☐ | ☐ | 99. | Consider a revocable living trust to avoid probate. |
| ☐ | ☐ | ☐ | 100. | Consider a standby trust in the event of disability or incompetence. |
| ☐ | ☐ | ☐ | 101. | Consider a waiver of a bonding requirement where the executor is also the primary beneficiary. |
| ☐ | ☐ | ☐ | 102. | Consider having the estate tax, inheritance taxes, funeral and administrative expenses paid out of the residuary estate (generally the credit shelter, or B trust) so as not to reduce the marital deduction. |

| Appli-cable | N/A | Consider Further | | Technique<br>OTHER PLANNING TECHNIQUES |
|---|---|---|---|---|
| ☐ | ☐ | ☐ | 103. | If you have excess accumulated retirement funds (subject to 15-percent excise tax) payable solely to your surviving spouse, consider making the Section 4980A(d)(5) election to have the special tax apply to your surviving spouse. |
| ☐ | ☐ | ☐ | 104. | Consider last-to-die life insurance to pay estate and inheritance taxes. Use an irrevocable life insurance trust to keep the proceeds out of the estates of the two people, usually spouses, insured. |

# PART IX

# IRD: How to Turn $350,000 into $1 Million (or More)

IX

# INTRODUCTION

## Your Profit-Sharing/Pension Plan Ain't Worth What You Think It Is

This is a painful subject. One of the best, yet simplest and most terrifying (you'll understand why this word fits in a moment), explanations I have ever heard (on a tape, not in person) on the subject was in a speech given by Jonathan Blattmachr to the Million Dollar Round Table (successful insurance consultants). Here's what Jonathan, a brilliant New York estate planning lawyer, said:

> "...what I'm going to talk about now is the most heavily taxed receipt in estate planning. I see it in every estate I plan for and I see it in every estate I administer.
>
> "It is called income in respect of a decedent, typically known by its initials IRD. Now it's a technical tax term. Basically it means taxing income to which you were entitled at the time you died that is not on your final [income tax] return. It includes, for example, every bit of deferred compensation you have or your clients have.
>
> "I could tell you the story about the physician who came to me with $8 million in IRAs and pension plans. Within a year after he died without planning, his estate had been whittled down to under $800,000. So all of you who think you're building up big money or your clients are building up big money in pension plans, IRAs, rabbi trusts, secular trusts, all of that is income in respect of a decedent and subject not only to estate tax but income tax as well. And you will pay at least an 80 percent effective rate of taxation if you're from a high tax jurisdiction like Massachusetts, California, Oregon, or New York, the land of taxes...In New York, if you do it wrong, the amount of tax can exceed the amount subject to tax. And life insurance is an ideal asset...to break the vicious cycle of IRD.
>
> "...all of you in this room have...income in respect of a decedent...and everybody you know in your neighborhood, the lawyers, the doctors and dentists,

are loaded up with income in respect of a decedent..."

And add closely held business owners to the list of those who can get clobbered by IRD. As a matter of fact, anyone who has accumulated even a small amount of dollars in a qualified retirement plan (or nonqualified plan for that matter) is an IRD disease carrier.

The IRD disease eats pension and profit-sharing plan dollars. The interesting thing about this disease is that it never afflicts the carrier, only those who survive the carrier.

Typically, the disease leaves only $350,000 (or less) for each $1 million of IRD. Can the disease be cured? Yes. Read on.

1

# An Introduction to the Biggest Tax Horror Story in the Law

This chapter is not technical.

Exactly what is this animal called "income in respect of a decedent" (IRD)?

Quite simply, IRD is your right to receive funds (money) that would have been income to you if you had lived to receive them. But you died before receiving them. What's the tax result? Such funds are taxable for income tax purposes to the person (your heirs or your estate) who receives them in your stead.

The short definition: The recipient of the decedent's income, for income tax purposes, steps into the decedent's shoes.

### ■ EXAMPLE 1

Payday is Friday. Joe earns $2,000 per week, or $400 per day. Joe dies on a Thursday night. His paycheck for $1,600 (4 days times $400) is paid to Joe's estate. That $1,600 is IRD.

Say Joe's widow, Jane, gets the $1,600. She must pay income tax on it when she files her income tax return as if she, not Joe, had earned the $1,600.

Now let's take a look at how IRD does its thing—extracts two taxes from the same chunk of income. At the same time, let's take a look at why it happens.

What you are about to read is deceptively simple, but it explains the when, how and why of IRD. First, the income tax taxes income. Second, the estate tax taxes the fair-market value of the assets you own at your death. Nothing new here. But enter IRD, which uses both taxes, at the same time, to attack each dollar of income. Simply put, the same dollar is taxed twice.

### ■ EXAMPLE 2

Sam, who is single, owns a $100,000 bond due in five years. The bond has a fair-market value of $100,000 and pays six percent interest semiannually. The next interest payment is due June 30. Sam dies on June 29. The $3,000 interest is paid to his estate, which makes no distributions to any of Sam's heirs during its first year of existence. The estate must pay income tax on the entire $3,000 (actually one day's interest—June 30—is not IRD because the interest for that day was earned after Joe died). Okay, that's tax number one.

Next, the estate tax. The fair-market value of the bond is $100,000. The accrued interest on June 29 was $3,000 and has an FMV of $3,000 (less one day's interest). So, add 'em up. The fair-market value of the bond on the day Joe died was $103,000. That's the amount on which Joe's estate must pay estate tax. The $100,000 is taxed once. But the $3,000 is hit with two taxes—income and estate.

■ WHAT'S THE RESULT?

A confiscatory tax. Burn it into your mind. If your estate is large enough to be subject to estate tax, IRD is bad. Always! The only good thing about it is it will never strike you personally. Why? Because while you are alive, IRD is harmless. But when you die, IRD is born and can...and will...ravish your heirs.

## The Secret Tax

What's amazing about IRD is that it's practically a secret tax. Many professionals (including lawyers and insurance consultants) have never heard of it. And I have yet to meet a client who has heard of it before we explain the horror.

Worse yet, it is a rare professional (even those practicing in the estate planning area) who knows what to do to avoid the robbery-like-yet-legal tax results of IRD.

2

# A Technical Explanation of Income in Respect to a Decedent

This entire chapter is technical.

This book is not intended to be a technical treatise in any sense of the word. But in all fairness to the professional tax practitioners who must wrestle with IRD, this chapter gives a more detailed and technical explanation of IRD.

No, you won't make me feel bad if you decide to skip all or a portion of this chapter and leave it for your professional tax advisors. Ready? Here comes the technical stuff.

IRD is not specifically defined in the Internal Revenue Code or Regulations, but, in general, it includes most items of income, unpaid at death and not reported in taxable income in a cash basis, to which a decedent had a legal or equitable right before death and to which such right survives the decedent. In effect, IRD causes a double tax on such items by requiring their inclusion in both the decedent's estate tax return and the recipient's income tax return.

Even though some relief is given through an income tax deduction for the estate tax paid on these items, the deduction can never be as great as the income required to be included. Exhibit I, which follows, demonstrates how the tax law affects IRD.

## ■ EXHIBIT I: IRD AND THE INTERNAL REVENUE CODE

| Section | Law |
|---|---|
| 691(a)(1) | **Inclusion in income**<br>All items of gross income that would have been includable in a decedent's income had he lived will be income when received by:<br>1. The decedent's estate.<br>2. The person who received the right to the income if not included in the decedent's estate.<br>3. The person who acquires such right after distribution from the decedent's estate. |

**691(a)(2) Sale of right**

Any transfer of the right by either the estate or the person owning the right will trigger immediate taxability to the transferor for the full amount of the IRD plus any additional consideration received.

**691(a)(3) Character of income**

The character of the income (ordinary or capital gain) will be same to the recipient as it would have been to the decedent if he had lived and received it.

**691(a)(4) Installment obligations**

Any installment obligation that the decedent elected to report under Section 453 will be treated in the hands of the holder of that obligation in the same manner as such obligation would have been treated by the decedent had he lived and collected all or a portion of it.

**691(b) Allowance of deduction and credit**

Any (1) item of interest, taxes, or a then deductible expense, (2) right to depletion, or (3) credit for foreign taxes that would have been allowed to the decedent had he lived will be allowed to the estate or person paying it.

**691(c) Deduction for estate tax**

Anyone required to include IRD can reduce his gross income by a deduction. The deduction is equal to the difference between the actual estate tax and what the tax would have been had there been no IRD. This deduction may be claimed pro rata by each recipient of IRD at the time he reports the IRD.

A special adjustment is required for generation-skipping transfers involving a deemed transferor (IRC§691(c)(3).

**1014(c) Basis for IRD**

Even though Section 2033 requires IRD items to be included in the estate at fair market value, Section 1014(c) prevents any change in basis on death of the decedent. For installment obligations, the basis of an IRD item in the hands of the estate and its beneficiaries is determined under Section 453. Also, Section 691(a)(5) provides an amount equal to the excess of the face value of the obligation over the decedent's basis shall be considered as IRD.

## Types of IRD

Actually, a complete list of types of IRD would be endless, but several types are more common than others.

**COMPENSATION.** Compensation includes earnings not in the last paycheck, accrued vacations, accrued bonuses or commissions, and sick pay to the extent not excluded from income under Section 105. Discretionary bonuses paid after death are also IRD, even though the decedent has no enforceable right to them prior to death. For self-employed individuals, compensation includes accounts receivable, fees and commissions receivable, and so on.

For farmers, compensation may or may not include grain, raised animals, and other zero-basis property items. If the farmer was materially participating in the farm operations at the date of death, a step-up is allowed. However, the IRS states that if the decedent was a nonparticipating farmer, no step-up is allowed (see Rev. Rul. 58-436 and Rev. Rul. 64-289).

**INTEREST, DIVIDENDS, AND DISCOUNTS.** Generally, interest and dividends are IRD to the extent that they were receivable (due) or accrued on the date of decedent's death. Dividends are IRD if the decedent was alive and a shareholder on the record date. A dividend is not IRD if it was declared prior to death on stock held of record after death. IRD includes the discount from the face amount of an obligation receivable by the decedent to the extent that the discount was earned prior to death.

■ **EXAMPLE:** Don acquired a $10,000 bond with 10 years to maturity for $8,000 on January 1, 1986. He died on September 30, 1993. The discount earned per annum is $200 (1/10 of $2,000). IRD is $150 (9/12 of $200).

**PERIOD PAYMENTS.** Rents, royalties, and other periodic payments are IRD to the extent they are earned prior to death but not collected.

**SALES IN GENERAL (NONINSTALLMENT).** Sales consummated by the decedent and collected after death are IRD.

**PARTNERSHIPS.** If the partnership taxable year is ended by the death of the partner, the decedent's final return would include his share of the partnership income to the date of death. There is no IRD.

If the year was not ended, the successor would report the decedent partner's share of income to the extent it was earned prior to death. This income is IRD. This is true even if the decedent partner had withdrawn funds prior to death.

■ **EXAMPLE:** Paul died on September 30, 1993. He was a partner of a partnership on a calendar year basis that was not terminated by Paul's death. Paul withdrew $90,000 on June 30, 1993. His share of 1993 earnings was $60,000; $40,000 was earned prior to September 30, 1993. Paul's successor will report taxable income of $60,000, but only $40,000 will be IRD.

Payments for unrealized receivables, as well as payments attributable to substantially appreciated inventory, are IRD. Payments under Section 736(a) in liquidation of a partnership interest fall into both categories. Guaranteed payments and goodwill that is treated as ordinary income are IRD. Goodwill not to be treated as ordinary income (as provided in the partnership agreement) is not IRD.

**SUBCHAPTER S.** If the executor continues the S status and if undistributed profits of the corporation for the fiscal year ended during which the death occurred are taxed to the estate as deemed dividends, there is no IRD. Except for the deemed dividends for undistributed profits at year end, the rules are the same as for dividends for regular corporations, whether S status continues or not. If the S corporation sustains a loss, there is no IRD. The S corporation must issue two K-1s for the year: one in the decedent's name up to the date of death and one to the estate for the remainder of the year.

**PAYMENTS FROM QUALIFIED PLANS.** To the extent payments are includable in the estate and subject to the estate tax, IRD exists.

If there is distribution of employer securities (the appreciation on such securities is not taxed until the recipient sells them), which are worth more at the time of distribution than the cost to the plan trustee at the time acquired, the untaxed appreciation is IRD (See Rev. Rul. 75-125).

**OTHER EMPLOYER PAYMENTS.** Death benefits qualifying for the $5,000 exclusion provided by Section 101(b)(1), and gifts (nontaxable as income to widow or family) are not IRD.

**INSTALLMENT SALES—CAPITAL GAINS PORTION.** It is firmly established that installment sales that are owned by and survive the decedent produce IRD that is ordinary income for the interest and capital gain (either long or short, assuming no recapture) for the balance.

Also, if the obligation is disposed of at less than face value, the proceeds are compared to decedent's basis, rather than estate tax value, to determine gain or loss. This gain is also IRD.

■ **EXAMPLE:** Dudley, at the time of his death, owned an installment receivable with a $70,000 basis and a $100,000 face, resulting in a 30 percent gross-profit percentage. If Dudley had lived, 30 percent of each principal collection would have resulted in long-term capital gain. Two transactions were completed by his estate after Dudley's death: $20,000 was collected—30 percent thereof, or $6,000, would be a capital gain to the estate and IRD. The $80,000 remaining face value was sold for $70,000; $14,000 is a long-term capital gain and IRD ($70,000 - $56,000 ($80,000 x 70 percent) equals $14,000).

## Deductions and Credits of a Decedent

**DEDUCTIONS.** Section 691(b) creates deductions in respect of a decedent (DRD). DRDs are debts of the decedent that reduce the gross estate and that would have been deductible for income tax purposes had the decedent lived. Items of DRD are allowable as income tax deductions by the successor who is liable for and makes payment for the corresponding income. If the DRD should exceed the IRD, there is no requirement that they be reduced because of the double benefit they create. There is no negative estate tax in respect of a decedent.

### ■ EXAMPLE

Dora died owning a $10,000 note receivable with $800 or accrued interest, a house with $1,200 due in real estate taxes, and $200 of interest due on the mortgage.

| DRD | |
|---|---|
| Real estate taxes | $1,200 |
| Mortgage interest | 200 |
| Total DRD | 1,400 |
| IRD—Interest on bond | 800 |
| Net DRD | $ 600 |

## The Section 691(c) Computation

The 691(c) computation is actually two computations—one for the estate tax return as filed and the other as a recomputation of the way the estate return would have been filed if there had been no net IRD (IRD minus DRD). The difference between the tax due on the actual return and the imaginary return is the deduction. The deduction is then apportioned among the recipients of the IRD.

### ■ EXAMPLE

Assume that there are three IRD items (a total of $12,000 as shown), that the estate tax return as actually filed shows a tax liability of $45,000 and that the recomputed (imaginary) return shows a liability of $40,000. Also assume there are no DRD items. The estate tax attributable to IRD is then $5,000 and is apportioned as follows:

| IRD items | Amount | Percentage | Apportionment |
|---|---|---|---|
| Salary | $ 9,000 | 75% | $3,750 |
| Interest | 500 | 4 | 200 |
| Dividends | 2,500 | 21 | 1,050 |
| Total | $12,000 | 100% | $5,000 |

## IRD and DRD Planning

Planning in the IRD area actually has two meanings: avoiding IRD items, since they carry a double tax, and seeking out DRD items, since they carry a double benefit. When the IRD is long-term capital gain, the executor should consider Sections 441 (select fiscal year) and 443(a)(2) (short-year return for first year) and elect the most beneficial tax year for the estate. The objective would be to avoid bunching all the IRD items into the estate's income in one year.

The executor should also consider combining fiscal-year selection with executor's power to distribute income among beneficiaries. The executor can spread the tax burden to different years and different beneficiaries to minimize taxes.

It is almost always wiser not to sell appreciated property if the taxpayer is elderly. At death, the step-up in basis erases the potential capital gain.

## The 15-Percent Excess Tax

Section 4980A creates a nightmare of complex rules that are designed to extract an extra 15-percent excise tax out of your qualified plan distributions. The basic rules follow:

**DISTRIBUTIONS MADE OVER MORE THAN ONE YEAR.** If the distributions, during life or after death, from any qualified retirement plans and individual retirement accounts (IRAs) exceed the greater of (1) $150,000, or (2) $112,500 as indexed for inflation, per year, the excess is taxed at 15 percent.

**LUMP-SUM DISTRIBUTION.** A lump-sum distribution is subject to an excise tax equal to 15 percent of the distribution in excess of $750,000. Examples of both types of distributions, and how the distributions are taxed, are shown in the next chapter.

# 3 How IRD Destroys the Value of Your Retirement Plans

This chapter gets a bit technical but is must reading.

By now you know that IRD is the work of the Devil. In this case, the Devil is Congress, and the Devil's target is qualified employee retirement plans.

## A Bit of History

In the good old days (after World War II), qualified deferred compensation plans (mostly pension plans and profit-sharing plans, because 401(k) plans, ESOPs, and IRAs were not yet even a gleam in Congress' eyes) were great. During life. Even at death.

Qualified plans were a great deal then and still are a great deal today. Their features and benefits include these tax goodies:

1. A deduction for contributions to a plan trust by the employer.
2. No tax to the employee when the funds are received by the trust.
3. No tax to the employee while the funds and accumulated earnings on the funds stay in the trust.
4. Favorable tax treatment when the funds come out of the trust.

### The Grim Reaper Reaps an Ever-Larger Tax Toll

When qualified plans first appeared, the law clearly excluded any amounts in the plans from estate taxes...Great! Then Congress changed the law: Only the first $100,000 escaped estate tax...Still not too bad. Then, another change: Every penny in all your plans is subject to estate tax...ALL is IRD...A tax travesty!

Wait, there's more. In 1986, Congress passed what is often called "the success tax": Basically a 15 percent excise tax on plan fund accumulations in excess of $750,000 (see Chapter 2, this part). Not only 100 percent IRD, but a 15 percent kick in the shins to boot.

## How Qualified Plan Benefits Are Taxed

Let's make it clear at this point that we are talking about all qualified plans: defined benefit (pension) plans, money purchase pension plans, profit-sharing plans, 401(k) plans, ESOPs, Keogh plans, and all types of IRAs. For the purpose of computing the 15 percent excise tax, you add up the amounts in each plan and wind up with a single total.

The precise manner in which every type of distribution from a qualified plan is taxed, or all the rules and exceptions, are not covered in this book. Our purpose is to convey concepts. So for simplicity, the following assumptions are used in all the examples that follow:

| | |
|---|---|
| Income tax bracket | 30%* |
| Estate tax bracket | 50%* |
| Excise tax amount | 15%** |

*Can change depending on various factors, including 5-year or 10-year averaging and a rate hike by Congress.

**Accurate under current law.

■ **NOTE:** When you have a real-life situation, of course, substitute the actual tax rates. Also, the cost of state income tax and inheritance tax must be considered.

## The Problem

My usual explanation of IRD to a client, "The IRS gets 65 percent or more, and your family gets 35 percent or less," has a predictable response—ranging from a look of horror to an expletive utterance. When the IRD potential is in a qualified plan—the most common situation, almost every client asks, "What happens if I take it out before I die?" Good question. Here's the answer.

### The Tax Impact on a Lump-Sum Distribution from a Qualified Plan During Life

The following computations assume the distributions (one for $750,000, which does not incur the 15 percent excise tax; one for $1,750,000, which does incur this tax) are taken during life and held until death.

**THE FIRST TAX DURING LIFE**

| | No Excise Tax | Excise Tax: Next $1 Million | Excise Tax: Total Distribution |
|---|---|---|---|
| Amount of Distribution from Plan | $750,000 | $1,000,000 | $1,750,000 |
| Less | | | |
| Excise Tax, 15% | - | 150,000 | 150,000 |
| Income Tax, 30% | 225,000 | 300,000 | 525,000 |
| Total Tax | 225,000 | 450,000 | 675,000 |
| Balance after Income and Excise Tax | $525,000 | $ 550,000 | $1,075,000 |
| Effective Rate of Both Taxes | 30% | 45% | 38.57% |

**THE SECOND TAX AT DEATH**

| | No Excise Tax | Excise Tax Next $1 Million | Excise Tax Total Distribution |
|---|---|---|---|
| Balance from Above | $525,000 | $550,000 | $1,075,000 |
| Less - Estate Tax, 50% | 262,500 | 275,000 | 537,500 |
| Balance for Family after Estate Tax | $262,500 | $275,000 | $ 537,500 |
| Amount Received by IRS | $487,500 | $725,000 | $1,212,500 |
| **PERCENT OF DISTRIBUTION RECEIVED BY:** | | | |
| Family | 35% | 27.5% | 30.71% |
| IRS | 65% | 72.5% | 69.29% |

■ **IMPORTANT:** The point of the above computation is to graphically demonstrate that *you can't beat the IRD-qualified plan game by taking distributions during life.*

The percentage received by the IRS creeps higher as the amount distributed rises and, of course, is even higher when you break into the 55 percent estate tax bracket.

Installment distributions (as opposed to a lump-sum distribution) suffer the same high-tax fate, but the computation is more complicated.

## The Tax Impact (IRD) on Funds in a Qualified Plan at Death

This is when IRD does its dirty work.

The computations that follow use the same assumptions as before in the lifetime distributions. A 55 percent estate tax illustration accompanies the 50 percent example. The decedent is assumed to be 70 years old.

**THE IRD COMPUTATION WHEN ALL FUNDS TOTAL $750,000 OR LESS**

| | Estate Tax Rate 50% | Estate Tax Rate 55% |
|---|---|---|
| **ESTATE TAX** | | |
| Total Funds Accumulated in all Qualified Plans | $750,000 | $750,000 |
| Estate Tax, 50%/55% | $375,000 | $412,500 |
| **INCOME TAX** | | |
| Total Funds | $750,000 | $750,000 |
| Less—Estate Tax, Section 691(c) Deduction | 375,000 | 412,500 |
| Balance | 375,000 | 337,500 |
| Income Tax, 30% | $112,500 | $101,250 |

| | | |
|---|---|---|
| **SUMMARY** | | |
| Total Funds | $750,000 | $750,000 |
| Less Tax— | | |
| Estate | 375,000 | 412,500 |
| Income | 112,500 | 101,250 |
| Total Taxes | 487,500 | 513,750 |
| Amount to Family | $262,500 | $236,250 |
| Percent to: | | |
| Family | 35% | 31.5% |
| IRS | 65% | 68.5% |

## THE IRD COMPUTATION WHEN ALL FUNDS TOTAL MORE THAN $750,000

The computation is made in the order shown in the following schedules: excise tax, estate tax and income tax.

**Schedule A**

Excise Tax

| | |
|---|---|
| **Step #1** | |
| Factor used for a 70 year old (Section 7520), assuming interest rate of 8 percent; actuarial values, Alpha Volume* | 7.219 |
| Threshold Amount** | $ 150,000 |
| Present Value of Hypothetical Life Annuity (7.219 x $150,000) | $1,082,850 |
| **Step #2** | |
| Total Funds at Death | $1,750,000 |
| Less—Present Value of Hypothetical Life Annuity | 1,082,850 |
| Excess Accumulation | $ 667,150 |
| Excise Tax, 15% (To Schedule B) | $ 100,073 |

*Interest rate assumptions. The present value of the life annuity must be calculated using the interest rate and mortality assumptions in Regulations 20.2031-7 in effect on the date of death.

**Greater of $150,000 or indexed based on $112,500. For 1993, the indexed amount is $144,551.

**Schedule B**

| | Estate Tax Rate | |
|---|---|---|
| | 50% | 55% |
| **ESTATE TAX** | | |
| Total Funds | $1,750,000 | $1,750,000 |
| Less—Excise Tax Deduction from Schedule A (Section 4980A(d)(2) and Section (c)(1)(B)) | 100,073 | 100,073 |
| Taxable Estate | 1,649,927 | 1,649,927 |
| Estate Tax, 50%/55% | $824,964 | $907,460 |

| | | |
|---|---|---|
| **INCOME TAX** | | |
| Total Funds | $1,750,000 | $1,750,000 |
| Less—Estate Tax, Section 691(c) Deduction | 824,964 | 907,460 |
| Balance | 925,036 | 842,540 |
| Income Tax, 30% | $277,511 | $252,762 |
| **SUMMARY** | | |
| Total Funds | $1,750,000 | $1,750,000 |
| Less Tax — | | |
| Excise | 100,073 | 100,073 |
| Estate | 824,964 | 907,460 |
| Income | 277,511 | 252,762 |
| Total Taxes | 1,202,548 | 1,260,295 |
| Amount to Family | $547,452 | $489,705 |
| Percent to: | | |
| Family | 31.28% | 27.98% |
| IRS | 68.72% | 72.02% |

## Must Reading

Based on the preceding computations of tax, can qualified plans ever be a good tax investment? The answer can be a loud *YES*. Or a loud *NO*.

For most people the answer is YES, including owners of closely held businesses. This is true for two reasons:

1. The funds in the plan will actually be used for retirement purposes because no other funds are available, and
2. The owner's estate is less than $1.2 million, which means that the combination of the unlimited marital deduction and the unified credit eliminates the estate tax.

For such Yes people, qualified plans have been, still are, and will continue to be one of the best tax games in town.

But beware. Yes people can easily become No people. How? Once your estate grows in size so it is no longer protected from estate tax by the unified credit, any funds in your qualified plans—whether taken as a distribution during your life or left to the IRD tax-eating machine—makes you a No person. What should you do if your company still has one or more qualified plans that are making contributions for your benefit and you're the 100 percent (if you own less, you must make some computations) owner of the company? You should consider waiving out of the plan for all future contributions for your benefit.

*When should you waive out of the plan?* If you think you might use the funds in the plan, plus additional contributions and earnings, for your retirement, keep contributing to the plan. But if logic tells you that you're accumulating more junk money (as defined in Chapter 4 of Part V), stop making contributions for yourself or your spouse.

What should you do if you are a No person and have funds inside of a qualified plan? Read the next chapter.

But first take a look at Schedule C. The amount of tax is scary.

## ■ SCHEDULE C—ILLUSTRATION OF TAX CONFISCATION

H, a widower, has accumulated $3,000,000 in a Pension Plan. H dies in 1995 at age 75 leaving children. H leaves the $3,000,000 *in trust* to his *grandchildren*. H had received required minimum distributions since age 70 1/2. H's remaining Grandfathered Amount is $1,300,000, which is greater than his $112,500 Threshold which had increased to $175,000 by 1995 ($175,000 x 5.2149 = $912,607).

Furthermore, federal and state income tax rates have increased to 40% by 1995. H's estate is sufficiently large to place him and his family in the highest income, estate, generation-skipping, etc. tax brackets after applying all available exemptions, exclusions, deductions and credits (without regard to tax surcharges).

| | |
|---|---|
| Value of Plan | $3,000,000 |
| Federal Estate Tax @ 55% | (1,650,000) |
| Balance | $1,350,000 |
| Generation Skipping Tax (55% rate) | (742,500) |
| Balance | 607,550 |
| 15% Excise Tax on $1,700,000 ($3,000,000 - $1,300,000, which is the amount grandfathered) | (255,000)* |
| Balance | 352,500 |
| Federal and State income tax @ 40% | (141,000) |
| BALANCE TO GRANDCHILDREN (about 7¢/$1.00 | $211,500 |

*Assumes the excise tax is allowable as a Deduction in Respect of a Decedent under Section 691(c). *If it is not* the grandchildren get $109,500 ($352,500 - (40% x 607,500) or 3.6¢/$1.00.)

# 4 How to Turn $350,000 into $1 Million (or More)

Except for a few technical points, this chapter is a breeze.

Now you know the problem—every dollar in your qualified plans at your death enriches the IRS by 65 cents or more. Your family gets only 35 cents. Usually less.

This chapter shows you how to turn the tables. The IRS gets zero; your family gets 100 percent. Probably more than 100 percent. Much more.

*Now STOP! Don't read another word of this chapter unless you (1) have already read Chapter 4 ("Junk Money...How to Multiply Your Wealth") of Part V and (2) clearly remember the principles enunciated there.* The concepts presented in that chapter are utilized in this chapter.

However, there is one significant difference. In the earlier chapter, the funds used to buy the annuities are your funds and all income tax has been paid. The IRS has no claim on the funds, directly or indirectly.

In this chapter, once again we want to start our tax-saving process by purchasing an annuity. But there's a major problem. The funds to be used are inside a qualified employee benefit plan—usually a pension plan or a profit-sharing plan. These funds, although they unquestionably belong to you as a plan participant, are subject to a mountain of rules. Some of the rules may be imposed by the terms of the plan document; some by the IRS.

One rule is certain: If you want to put all or a part of your share of the plan funds in your pocket—either in a lump-sum or over a period of time—you must pay a heavy price. Income tax. And maybe excise tax.

■ **NOTE:** From this point on, this chapter could become a maze of technical rules, citing Code Sections and Treasury Regulations. I'm skipping all of that with the caveat that the reader must be aware that the complexity of the law in the distribution of funds from a qualified plan cannot be ignored. It will be worth your while to consult an expert.

The balance of this chapter covers the common situations you encounter in practice.

■ **IMPORTANT:** In every case, you must read plan documents to determine that the methods described in this chapter are permitted under the plan documents. If not permitted, the documents must be amended. But caution, amending documents to accomplish one particular purpose can create other problems because of the peculiarity of the qualified plan rules. *Always get a second opinion from an expert in the pension law area.*

## The IRD-Avoidance Concept in a Nutshell

Although complex to implement, the concept can be explained as a simple three-step process:

| | |
|---|---|
| **STEP #1** | **TAX RESULT** |
| The plan participant (let's call him Ben) takes his distribution in the form of an annuity payable for life. | a) Income tax: Tax-free.<br>b) Estate tax: No value at death, so no estate tax. |
| **STEP #2** | |
| Ben collects the annuity payments | a) Income tax: Taxable as ordinary income.<br>b) 15 percent excise tax: Subject to tax if payments are large enough. |
| **STEP #3** | |
| Ben causes an irrevocable life insurance trust (ILIT) to purchase a life insurance policy, using the after-tax balance of the annuity payments to pay the premiums. | Estate tax: Insurance proceeds are estate tax free. |

■ **IMPORTANT:** This concept mimics the junk-money concept presented in Part V, Chapter 4. Only the variations required to utilize and expand the concept as originally presented are discussed in this chapter.

### Dollar Amount Required for IRD-Avoidance Concept to Be Effective

The *IRD-avoidance concept* was originally designed to avoid the tax devastation created by large amounts of IRD in large estates. But interestingly, after reviewing the first proposal that dealt with the concept, which was submitted to me by an insurance consultant, a light went on: The concept works well even if the amount in the qualified plan is small, the estate is small, or both. Like discovering gold when none is expected.

Let's look at that first proposal. (Nothing is changed except the names. Let's call the client Ben Elder.) First, a little background. Ben's son, a 55-year-old business owner named Joe, was consulting with me to put his transfer/estate plan into place.

During our first planning telephone conference, Joe told me his Dad's (Ben's) story. (Only the facts pertinent to our subject matter are given.)

Ben, the founder of the business and 80 years old, married his second wife, Jane, 20 years ago. Ben felt an obligation to provide for Jane if he died first. Believe it or not, Ben was still working but finally was going to retire. He had $825,000 in a profit-sharing plan; Jane was the beneficiary. Ben planned to take a lump-sum distribution from the plan and invest the after-tax proceeds in tax-free municipal bonds to be held in joint tenancy with Jane. Of course, if Ben died first, the Elder children (including Joe) would not receive the bonds as part of their inheritance. Except for Ben and Jane's residence, the balance of Ben's estate would go to the Elder children.

Joe asked me for a second opinion.

Following is the memo sent to me by Ben and Joe's insurance consultant, whom I'll call Ken. My comments are in parentheses.

A. Current Tax Situation of Pension Assets

| | |
|---|---|
| $825,000 | Pension Assets |
| 9,520 | Less Excise Tax |
| 815,480 | Amount Subject to 10-year Forwarding Average Tax |
| 235,130 | Less Income Tax |
| 580,350 | Amount Available for Investing at 6 Percent in Tax-Free Bonds |
| .06 | Investment Rate |
| $34,821 | Tax-Free Income |

AT DEATH

| | |
|---|---|
| $580,350 | Amount Included in Gross Estate |
| 290,175 | Less Estate Tax |
| $290,175 | Left to Family |

B. Tax Situation Using Annuity & Life Insurance

Life Annuity for Male Age 80 of $825,000 will provide income of:

| | |
|---|---|
| $133,536 | Annual Annuity |
| 41,396 | Less Income Tax |
| 92,140 | Spendable Cash |
| 53,112 | Less Premium for Life Insurance |
| $39,028 | Net Cash |

**AT DEATH**

Under Annuity & Life Insurance, at Ben's death the annuity stops, but $825,000 is paid as the death benefit to an irrevocable life insurance trust (ILIT) to provide income of $49,500 per year (to Jane for life) at 6 percent tax-free.

When Mrs. Elder dies, $825,000 is left to the family estate tax-free using an irrevocable trust.

SUMMARY

At Ben's Death
$290,000 left to Elder Family without Annuity & Life Insurance.
$825,000 left to Elder Family with Annuity & Life Insurance. (A $535,000 increase. Actually, the Elder Family would have received zero under Ben's original plan, as the qualified plan distribution would have gone to Jane.)

During Ben's Life—Current Income
$34,821 without Annuity & Life Insurance.
$39,028 with Annuity & Life Insurance (a $4,207 increase).
(After Ben's death, Jane receives $49,500 [$825,000 times 6 percent] instead of $34,821, an increase of $14,679.)

Ken's memo says it all. But for the purpose of this exercise, assume Ben's estate is in a zero estate tax bracket (less than $1,200,000), and he is in a low income tax bracket. Substitute any numbers of rates you like in Ken's memo. The result is always the same. *The concept increases current income and eliminates the estate tax.*

---

■ **NOTE:**

1. If interest rates rise significantly after the annuity is purchased, the concept could result in a lower lifetime income.
2. In a small estate (where the unified credit for a single participant or the unified credit and marital deduction for a married participant eliminates the estate tax), an ILIT is not necessary.

---

## A Closer Look at Qualified Plan Annuities

As a general rule, when the trustee of a qualified plan distributes all or part of the funds to a participant of the plan, the distribution is subject to tax: income tax for sure and possibly the 15 percent excise tax.

There is an exception to the general rule: When the trustee buys an annuity from an insurance carrier, the purchase of the annuity for the participant's benefit is not a taxable transaction. There are basically two types of annuities for our purposes:

1. *Single-life annuity.* The participant receives annuity payments (usually monthly or quarterly) for as long as he/she lives. When the participant dies, the payments stop.
2. *Joint and survivor annuity.* The participant receives payments for life, but if he/she dies before his/her spouse, the spouse receives 50 percent of the amount paid to the participant for as long as the spouse lives. This is the typical joint and survivor annuity (let's call it a "50-percent joint and survivor annuity") offered in most plans. Also, the plan could provide that the same amount be paid to the spouse after the participant's death: a 100-percent joint and survivor annuity.

■ **NOTE:** The amount of each payment is fixed and will not vary over time.
Let's translate the various types of annuities into cost and benefits received. Assume that the cost of the annuity is $1,000,000 (because that's the amount of money in

the qualified plan accumulated for your benefit). How much would your monthly benefit be? Here are the factors that would determine the amount of your monthly benefit:

1. *Interest rate*; higher rates mean higher benefits.
2. *The insurance carrier*; you must shop.
3. *Your age*; the older you are the greater your monthly annuity benefit.
4. *The type of annuity*:
    a. A single-life annuity with a $1-million cost for a participant of any age yields a higher benefit than a joint and survivor annuity with a $1-million cost.
    b. A 50-percent joint and survivor annuity with a $1-million cost pays the participant more than a 100-percent joint and survivor annuity with the same cost.

Here are a few more rules you should know when dealing in this area.

1. If the participant is married, a joint and survivor annuity must be taken by the participant, unless the spouse waives his/her rights.

    ■ **NOTE:** For our purposes, a single-life annuity makes the most sense (the benefit is highest) when the intent is to buy a single-life insurance policy in the ILIT.

    On the other hand, if the intent is to buy a second-to-die policy in the ILIT, a joint and survivor annuity makes the most sense. Why? To provide the surviving spouse the funds with which to pay the continuing premiums.

    However, if the wife is wealthy in her own right, you should take a look at a combination of a) a single-life annuity, b) a second-to-die policy in the ILIT, and c) the spouse using his/her own funds to pay premiums if the participant dies first. This combination probably will give you the biggest bang for your buck.

2. In a defined benefit plan (the typical pension plan), if the plan was funded to provide a 100-percent joint and survivor annuity (and you're the boss), you might as well take the joint and survivor annuity. You could take the single-life annuity, but because a single-life annuity costs less than a joint and survivor annuity, you'll be leaving behind some of the funds accumulated for your benefit in the plan.
3. The amount of the annuity benefit paid to a female participant cannot be reduced even though her actuarial life expectancy is greater than her male counterpart.

■ **ACKNOWLEDGEMENT:** Thanks to Ralph J. Wood Jr. of Gerwoud Pension Organization, Inc., Chicago, and Gerald Goldstein of Advance Benefits Systems Corporation, Thousand Oaks, Calif., for giving me a simple explanation of the very complex rules in this area.

### Putting It All Together

Now let's see what happens in practice when a participant (let's call her Pearl) gets ready to retire and wants to take her plan benefits in the form of an annuity. The plan administrator (or trustee) would determine the amount of Pearl's annuity using unisex tables provided by the IRS. Based on Pearl's age (65), the administrator would determine the lump-sum amount (say $500,000) available to buy an annuity for Pearl. Then the administrator would go to the commercial insurance marketplace to see how much of an annuity that $500,000 will buy. At this point the unisex tables are out of the window. The insurance company determines the amount of the annuity payments based on male/female statistics.

Actually, the process is a bit different depending on the type of plan—defined contribution plan or defined benefit plan—in which Pearl is a participant. Let's look at both.

**DEFINED CONTRIBUTION PLAN.** Typically, this would be a profit-sharing plan. Pearl's plan allows for a single-life annuity or a 50-percent joint and survivor annuity (as well as other distribution options of no interest to us). Pearl selects a single-life annuity.

The administrator starts with a fixed amount of money: The balance in Pearl's account ($500,000). The question then becomes how much will the annuity (monthly, quarterly, annually) payments be when buying a $500,000 single-life annuity for a 65-year-old female? Work with an insurance consultant to search the marketplace and get quotes from various insurance companies for the answers.

**DEFINED BENEFIT PLAN.** Typically, this would be a pension plan that defines Pearl's benefit (say $4,000 per month starting at age 65 and payable for life). In this case, the administrator starts with the amount of the pension as opposed to a fixed amount (in a defined contribution plan). That pension amount is converted to another kind of pension (using the unisex tables) based on what the plan document says: The plan document would have the necessary language to make the conversion based on "actuarial equivalency."

In order for the administrator to buy a commercial annuity, the plan must provide by its terms to have a "lump-sum equivalent." If the plan does, fine. If it does not, the plan should be amended. This lump-sum equivalent is the amount the administrator would use to buy a commercial annuity.

■ **NOTE:** A defined benefit plan by definition is set up to provide periodic retirement payments. As such, it is not necessary to purchase a commercial annuity. The administrator can make the annuity payments from the plan trust (instead of buying a commercial annuity). Just hire an actuarial firm to do the calculations.

## Crunching the Numbers

The numbers (quotes) that follow were provided by two experienced insurance consultants: David Greenspahn of Assured Enterprises, Ltd., Chicago, and Rick Knut Nelson of R.K. Nelson & Associates, Inc., Northbrook, Illinois. Thanks David! Thanks Rick!

I told David and Rick exactly the same thing, explaining the *what* and *why* of the needed information. They made a few suggestions, and the quotes were an improvement over my anticipated results. So following are the data (Schedule I and Schedule II) selected from the two proposals that give the "best" results in the series of computation schedules (Schedules A-1, A-2, and A-3) that follow the data. Were this a real-life situation, I would have used the proposals (both the annuity and the life insurance quotes) that would have produced the best results for the client. David and Rick would have shared the business.

### ■ SCHEDULE I

**IMMEDIATE ANNUITY**
**$1,000,000 PURCHASE PRICE**
**LIFETIME BENEFIT—MONTHLY**

| Type of Annuity | Age 60 | Age 65 | Age 70 |
|---|---|---|---|
| Single-Life— | | | |
| Male | $7,198 | $8,047 | $9,286 |
| Female | 6,598 | 7,248 | 7,888 |
| 100-Percent Joint and Survivor* | 6,138 | 6,518 | 7,068 |

*Husband and wife assumed to be same age

### ■ SCHEDULE II

**$1,000,000 LIFE INSURANCE**
**15 YEARS OF PREMIUM**
**PAYMENTS TO VANISH**

| Type of Annuity | Age 60 | Age 65 | Age 70 |
|---|---|---|---|
| Single-Life— | | | |
| Male | $26,002 | $34,403 | $46,244 |
| Female | 19,190 | 24,802 | 32,610 |
| Second-to-die* | 12,709 | 17,391 | 24,073 |

*Husband and wife assumed to be same age

■ **CAUTION:** The volatility of interest rates and other factors will cause the above quotes to change. Accept them only as an example. Always get your own quotes.

### Using the Data to Develop an IRD-Avoidance Proposal

Look back at Schedule A and Schedule B in Chapter 3 of this Part. Using the format of Schedules A and B, the data from the above Schedules I and II are used to develop three IRD-avoidance proposals (for ages 60, 65, and 70).

All the proposals assume:

1. There is exactly $1 million in a profit-sharing plan for the benefit of the participant (Pete).
2. Pete is the age shown and his wife (Patsie) is the same age.
3. Pete is in a 50-percent estate tax bracket.

4. The profit-sharing plan has language that allows the type of annuity selected.
5. The entire $1 million is used to buy an annuity and the entire after-tax annual annuity amount is used to buy life insurance in an ILIT.

## SCHEDULE A-1

### PROPOSALS FOR SINGLE-LIFE ANNUITY AND SINGLE-LIFE INSURANCE POLICY

| | | Age | |
|---|---|---|---|
| Annuity Computation | 60 | 65 | 70 |
| Monthly Benefit - Single-Life Annuity, Male; Cost of Annuity, $1 Million | $ 7,198 | $ 8,047 | $ 9,286 |
| Annual Amount (Monthly Benefit Times 12) | $ 86,376 | $ 96,564 | $ 111,432 |
| Less—Current Tax | | | |
| Excise Tax, 15%** | – | – | – |
| Income Tax, 30% | 25,913 | 28,969 | 33,430 |
| Total Current Tax | 25,913 | 28,969 | 33,430 |
| After-Tax Balance | $ 60,463 | $ 67,595 | $ 78,002 |
| Insurance Computation | | | |
| Premium per $1 Million of Single-Life Insurance Policy, Male | $ 26,002 | $ 34,403 | $ 46,244 |
| Amount of Insurance* (to Schedule A-3) | $2,325,321 | $1,964,800 | $1,686,749 |

*"Premium per $1 million" divided by "After-tax balance"; for example, for age 60, $60,463 divided by $26,002 equals 2.325321 (or $2,325,321 in insurance).

**There is no excise tax because the amount of the annual annuity is less than the $150,000 threshold amount. But if at the time of the individual's death the value of the annuity is more than $750,000, the excess is subject to the excise tax; this is true even if the decedent's spouse continues to receive payments under a joint and survivor annuity. The life expectancy of the person who died (the plan participant) is used to determine the excise tax. The excise tax is not affected by the marital deduction.

## ■ SCHEDULE A-2

### PROPOSALS FOR JOINT AND SURVIVOR ANNUITY AND SECOND-TO-DIE POLICY

| | Age | | |
|---|---|---|---|
| Annuity Computation | 60 | 65 | 70 |
| Monthly Benefit - Joint and Survivor Annuity; Cost of Annuity, $1 Million | $ 6,138 | $ 6,518 | $ 7,068 |
| Annual Amount (Monthly Benefit Times 12) | $ 73,656 | $ 78,216 | $ 84,816 |
| Less—Current Tax | | | |
| Excise Tax, 15% | - | - | - |
| Income Tax, 30% | 22,097 | 23,465 | 25,445 |
| Total Current Tax | 22,097 | 23,465 | 25,445 |
| After-Tax Balance | $ 51,559 | $ 54,751 | $ 59,371 |
| Insurance Computation | | | |
| Premium per $1 Million of Second-to-Die Insurance | $ 12,709 | $ 17,391 | $ 24,073 |
| Amount of Insurance* (to Schedule A-3) | $4,056,889 | $3,148,238 | $2,466,290 |

*"Premium per $1 million" divided by "After-tax balance"; for example, for age 60, $51,559 divided by $12,709 equals 4.056889 (or $4,056,889 in insurance).

■ **SCHEDULE A-3**

## SUMMARY OF COMPUTATIONS

| | $350,000 Turns Into* | |
|---|---|---|
| | Start With Single-Life Annuity | Start With 100 Percent Joint and Survivor Annuity |
| End with Single-Life Insurance Policy (from Schedule A-1) for Amount Shown | | |
| Male Age: | | |
| 60 | $2,325,321 | – |
| 65 | 1,964,800 | – |
| 70 | 1,686,749 | – |
| End with Second-to-Die Insurance Policy (From Schedule A-2) for Amount Shown | | |
| Husband and Wife Both Age: | | |
| 60 | – | $4,056,889 |
| 65 | – | 3,148,238 |
| 70 | – | 2,466,290 |

*As the computations in Chapter Three of this part show, in a 50% estate tax bracket, the family gets 35 percent ($350,000 out of $1 million) or less.

### What the Summary Shows

For example, for a husband and wife, both age 65, a 100-percent joint and survivor annuity with a cost of $1 million can be used to fund the premium for a $3,148,238 second-to-die policy. Using the assumptions in the various schedules, this means that instead of Pete and Patsie's family getting only $350,000, the family will get $3,148,238 after both Pete and Patsie pass on. Put another way, $350,000 after taxes turns into $3,148,238 after taxes.

■ **ACKNOWLEDGEMENT:** Paul Lau, a senior tax manager at Blackman Kallick, was a mountain of knowledge and information and helped in many ways to make this part of the book happen. Paul conducted much research and analysis of the law and regulations to determine how the various tax computations should be made. Thanks Paul!

■ **NOTE:** The preceding proposals and computations show the power of the IRD-avoidance concept. Of course, the possible variations using this IRD-avoidance concept could create a paper blizzard.

Only the very rich would use the entire amount of the after-tax annuity to purchase life insurance. *In most cases, the participant would split the after-tax annuity amount between current income and life insurance premiums that would pay for a policy in the amount equal to the funds being held for his/her benefit in the qualified plan.* For example, $1 million in the plan would be replaced by $1 million of insurance in the ILIT; the balance of after-tax annuity dollars and premium payments would be used to maintain lifestyle.

## Other Ways to Beat IRD

As I struggled to accumulate data, write, and rewrite this chapter, many good friends in my lawyer and insurance consultant network suggested other methods of beating up the IRD monster.

Various types of charitable gifts of your interest in a qualified plan were suggested often. If you are charitably inclined, a great idea.

### The Good News Rules

If IRD items are used to satisfy a testamentary charitable bequest, the estate receives an estate tax charitable deduction and an income tax charitable deduction for any of the income paid to charity. The charity does not pay any tax on the income.

For example, in Letter Ruling 9237020, Mom creates a testamentary charitable remainder unitrust for the benefit of Son by naming the trust the beneficiary of her qualified plan. The IRS rules that (1) the trust would qualify for an estate tax charitable deduction equal to the value of the remainder interest and (2) the trust will not be taxed on the IRD. And finally, the payments made to Son in satisfaction of annual unitrust amounts will be taxed to him under the rules of Section 664(b), as would any other unitrust payments.

Also, the use of a subtrust, combined with a split-dollar plan, surfaced several times. I like it, but I don't know if it will fly with the IRS. If the IRS rules the subtrust concept is okay, it must be seriously considered as an alternative to the IRD-avoidance concept presented in this book.

### And Finally

I welcome comments, criticism, and ideas to build on the IRD-avoidance concept. Send them to me.

And to all readers, a warning: The IRD-avoidance concept is a lot more complicated that it appears in these pages. Make sure you work with qualified professionals.

# PART X

# Real-Life Transfers

(From my private files.)

# X INTRODUCTION

## Yes—You, Too, Can Do Transfer/Succession/Estate Planning

This part of the book could fill several volumes if we emptied the Blackman Kallick transfer/succession/estate planning files into these pages.

Instead, this part of the book shows you how to combine the human factors (the first four parts of the book) with the technical aspects (the rest of the book), so you, too, can walk in the footsteps of the Blackman Kallick professionals who do transfer/succession/estate planning.

What follows are materials illustrating the Blackman Kallick approach to planning. Properly executed, this methodology produces superior results.

Let's review the planning process starting with the point in time when we're engaged by the client (almost always by phone):

### Step #1—The Data

We ask the client to send four items (called a "consulting package"):

1. *For the business.* The last year-end tax return and year-end financial statements.
2. *Personal.* The last personal tax return and a personal financial statement (a simple listing of assets at current value and liabilities, including a list of all life insurance on the client's life and on his/her spouse).
3. *A family tree.*
4. *Estate documents.* Wills and trusts.

If other important data exists—such as buy-sell agreements and prenuptial agreements—get it.

### Step #2—Examining the Consulting Package

We examine the package to prepare the best possible agenda. We also call the client to clear up any questions or to request more data.

■ **COMMENT**: Experience and knowledge of tax law is a must for the professional advisor. Establish a network of professionals to help you. Your network will grow along with your knowledge.

### Step #3—Prepare Agenda

A good agenda makes for a good consulting conference. (See the samples that follow.) The agenda is identical whether the conference will be by phone or in person. If by phone, the agenda is faxed to the client.

### Step #4—The Planning Conference

The purpose of the planning conference is twofold: to establish the client's objectives (as explained in Part I) and to explain the technical material as required (limit your explanations to what is necessary; too much information leads to confusion and procrastination).

■ **COMMENT:** Remember—you want information. Listen more than you speak.

### Step #5—Write Report

See the samples that follow. With the client's permission, provide report copies to appropriate professional advisors.

### Step #6—Coordinate

This is where the rubber meets the road. Your job is to coordinate (quarterback) the efforts of the client and his/her professionals (e.g. lawyer, insurance consultant and accountant).

Remember, you are a consultant. An invited guest. Don't overstay your welcome. Let the client's regular advisors take the lead. Tell them, "Part of my job is to help you get rid of me." And mean it.

### Step #7—Follow-Up

Your follow-up has two phases: First, see that the final plan is implemented as agreed upon (or as modified). Second, even after the plan is in place, inform the client of any changes in the law or new techniques that would help him/her improve the original plan.

## And Finally

No doubt others who read this and learn the process will find ways to improve the process. I'll be the first to applaud.

# 1 An Overview

This article from my tax column gives a good overview of the process.

HAVING TROUBLE COMPLETING YOUR TRANSFER/ESTATE PLAN?...READ THIS

George, age 68, and the owner of a successful family business in Ohio, answered my question—"What are your goals?"—with a torrent of words. "Have the business continue forever...stay involved...but on a part-time basis...more in a consulting capacity than active management...spend most of my business time staying in touch with old customers...make sure that George, Jr. eventually owns the business...take care of my wife and two daughters when I pass on...but keep them out of the business."

George's 35-year-old-son, George, Jr., nodded his agreement. The three of us were having a typical "transfer-of-ownership/estate-tax planning consultation" in my Chicago office. The two Georges had been working on a transfer/estate plan for three years. They had come to see me for a second opinion. After looking at old tax returns, financial statements, and a number of other documents, I had prepared a discussion agenda. This led to lots of questions. Lots of answers. Lots of discussion. A few problems and some sore spots were exposed. I took lots of notes. Almost three hours later, something interesting happened: Both George and his son said that for the first time, they knew what they wanted to do and why they wanted to do it.

It happens all the time. A frank, open discussion, mixed with the choices available, gets most—rarely all—of the family/business/human (you know, the emotional stuff) problems solved, and let's a tax-saving plan shine through. The decisions reached at this meeting will fit most of the business owner/readers (particularly those who have one or more kids in their business and one or more who are not in the business) of this column like a glove.

Here's a brief outline of some of the important decisions the two Georges are implementing and why:

1. The corporation will be recapitalized and have two types of stock—voting and non-voting. (This will give George [Dad] the tools to retain control and transfer the corporation to George, Jr.)
2. Dad will immediately gift 49% of the voting stock, worth about $20,000, to George, Jr. (This will give Dad voting control for as long as he lives.)
3. Every year, Dad will gift $20,000 of non-voting stock to George, Jr. (This will transfer the business to George, Jr. over time and reduce Dad's estate-tax liability by about $10,000 with each annual gift.)
4. Upon Dad's death, all of his remaining stock—voting and non-voting—will be bequeathed to George, Jr. Any estate tax that is due on this transfer will be paid solely by George, Jr. (This gives George, Jr. the entire business at little or no cost. All of George's other assets, including his life insurance, will be left in trust for George's wife—an estate-tax-free maneuver.
5. During George's life, he will continue to receive a small salary of about $12,000 for services actually rendered. (This will allow George to continue to receive his customary fringe benefits, including his all-important health insurance.)

2

# The Agenda

Here is a typical "Discussion Agenda." Only the names have been changed. The agenda was faxed to the client in Arizona two days before the telephone conference.

---

**DISCUSSION AGENDA: TAX PLANNING**
**ABC INDUSTRIES, INC.—JAY CLIENT**
**NOVEMBER 12, 199_**

I. Objectives (short-term, long-term).
  A. Personal.
  B. Business.
  C. Family.
  D. Retirement.

II. Family tree (see my Schedule A in Appendix).

III. Business.
  A. Outlook.
  B. FMV (fair-market value) of fixed assets.
  C. Rental of plant/equipment.
    1. Lease of plant (see my Schedule B)—Fair rental?
    2. Equipment—Discuss.
      a. Raised basis.
      b. Converts business property to nonbusiness property for nonbusiness kids.
  D. Eyeball value.

IV. Stock ownership.
  A. Now.
  B. Intent.

1. During life.
2. At death.

V. Transfer to kids.
   A. Voting control-discuss recapitalization.
   B. Gift program.
   C. Stock bonus to son (discuss danger of community property).
   D. Buy-sell agreement—need:
      1. For keeping stock in family.
      2. If son is to be ultimate owner.
   E. Use of GRAT after 4/30/9_ (next year-end) after become S corporation.

VI. Personal financial statement (see my Schedule B).
   A. Profit-sharing plan.
      1. Make no further contributions for yourself.
      2. Make beneficiary of account living trust.
   B. Transfer title of assets to living trust, except:
      1. Day-to-day bank account.
      2. Nontitled personal property.
      Reason: To avoid probate

VII. Other points to discuss.
   A. Life insurance.
      1. Still need details on $300,000 policy owned by ABC. (This is only existing policy on your life—right?)
      2. Discuss proposals from Ken Insurance Consultant.
         a. Received.
         b. Additional to be sent.
      3. All policies will be removed from estate; to be owned by:
         a. Children, or
         b. Irrevocable life insurance trust (ILIT).
      4. Make sure to maximize use of annual exclusions (not counting in-laws, appears to be 11) each year starting in 199_, via:
         a. Crummey powers in ILIT.
         b. Gifts of ABC stock to kids.
   B. Professional valuation needed if gifts of stock (or stock bonus).
   C. Amend living trust so qualified to hold S corporation stock.
   D. Will/trust.
      1. Replace Joe Friend as executor/trustee?
      2. If so, with whom?
   E. Estimate estate-tax liability.
   F. Follow-up.
      1. Attorney to draft documents.
      2. Who to do what and when.

Following are excerpts from other discussion agendas to show you various styles and how various subjects and facts are shown:

**EXAMPLE #1**

III. Business.
    D. Eyeball value. Consider if any adjustment to income is necessary before applying multiple.
    E. Other points from Success, Inc. financial statements.
        1. Compensation to family.
            a. How determined?
            b. When taken (salary/bonus)?
        2. Dividends of $15,000 paid for Y/E 12/31/9_. Why?
        3. Profit-sharing plan. Financial statements for plan for Y/E 12/31/9_.
            a. Discuss $200,000 aggregation rule (see my Schedule B).
            b. Impact on:
                1. Plan.
                2. Reasonable compensation (see my Schedule H, 199_ Form 1040, "Wage Income").
            c. Consider:
                1. IRD (discuss in VI). May waive out of future contributions.
                2. If stay in plan:
                    a. Integrate with Social Security.
                    b. Age-weighted/target benefit plan.
                4. Discuss leasing for new equipment acquisitions.

VI. Personal financial statement (see my Schedule G).
    A. Discuss joint tenancy.
    B. Raised basis concept.
    C. Failure of wills.
        1. Joint property.
        2. Pension plan.
        3. Insurance.
    D. Discuss changing titles.
    E. About $850,000 in IRD and growing.
        1. Explain how taxed.
        2. Consider waiving out of future contributions.
            a. Aggregation rules.
            b. IRD.

VII. S corporation.
    A. Advantages.
        1. In general.
        2. GRAT.
    B. Disadvantages.
        1. Fringe benefits (except qualified plan).
        2. 10-year rule. Need to merge two subsidiaries before Y/E 12/31/9_.

VIII. Life insurance (see my Schedule D).
    A. Take split-dollar policies out of corporation.
        1. Avoid PS 58 equivalent.
        2. Put into irrevocable life insurance trust (ILIT) or
        3. Give to kids.

- B. Frances—Prudential policies.
  - 1. $100,000 (looks like some type of whole life—need details).
  - 2. $250,000 (term)—need premium run for next 30 years (consider dropping depending on run into).
  - 3. If keep:
    - a. Put in ILIT, or
    - b. Give to kids.
- C. Implement ILIT (W. Lawyer has done draft—see my Schedule E).
  - 1. Current policies.
  - 2. New policies?
    - a. Funds from:
      - 1. Present and new assets.
      - 2. Profit-sharing plan.
      - 3. Possible purchase of single premium life annuity from (1), (2) or both to get premium dollars.
    - b. Get quotes:
      - 1. Single life.
        - a. Dad.
        - b. Mom.
      - 2. Second-to-die.

IX. Estate planning.

- A. Wills.
  - 1. Execute draft (Dad and Mom—see my Schedule F) or
  - 2. Discuss use of living trust.
    - a. Why to do or not to do.
    - b. Even if use living trusts, still leave enough assets to probate so can get rid of claims.
- B. Estimate estate tax liability (including insurance—see my Schedule G, Page 1).
- C. How to reduce liability.
  - 1. Full use of unified credit.
  - 2. Gift program.
  - 3. Death benefit agreement (George Sr.) to children.
  - 4. Irrevocable life insurance trust.
    - a. Current policies.
    - b. Consider new policies (transfer remaining estate tax liability—all or in part to insurance carrier).
- D. Attorney to draft or complete documents as required.
  - 1. Wills.
  - 2. Living trust.
  - 3. ILIT.
  - 4. Buy-sell agreement.
  - 5. Death benefit.
  - 6. Recapitalization plan if decide on voting/nonvoting stock.
  - 7. GRAT.
  - 8. Family limited partnership (for nonbusiness assets).

X. Plan follow-up.

**EXAMPLE #2**

IV. Stock ownership (see my Schedule B).

**NOTE:** TRUSTS—FOR THREE CHILDREN and a corporation do not qualify for S corporation election (also, do not know nature of Joan (5 shares) and AB Company (2,000 shares) trusts).

**FACTS:**

1. 41 shareholders
2. Controlled by Dan

| Owned By | Shares | % |
|---|---|---|
| Dad | 16,438 | 16.8* |
| Dad as trustee for 3 children's trusts | 33,000 | 33.6* |
| Mom | 11,056 | 11.3 |
| Total | | 61.7 |

*Dad has control (50.4%) without Mom's shares.

**QUESTION:** Won't Dad lose control without Mom's shares when stock options vest (per schedule of 11,536 shares—Note 5, 3/31/9_ Financial Statements)?

**OBJECTIVE:** Dad wants to stay in control.

**CONSIDER:** Recapitalization. Voting/nonvoting stock—

1. Only nonvoting stock used for stock options.
2. Then could redeem nonvoting stock (see Schedule B Form 1040 for redemption tax as dividend) if need cash personally without losing voting control.

**PROBLEM:** How do children (or other shareholders) turn their interest in corporation into income-producing investment or cash? Now? Down the road? (See V. and VI.B.)

VI. Succession planning.

A. Who? How?...run after Dan?

B. Discuss ESOP.

1. Organized way to buy out stockholders.
2. Various tax advantages.
3. Dan can keep control.
4. Consider:
   a. Feasibility study.
   b. Discuss with ESOP attorney.

■ **COMMENT:** Aside from the obvious, the agenda should be altered to fit the personality, sophistication and circumstances of the individual client.

Also, it is a wonderful aid to your memory when you have many transfer/succession/estate plans pending.

# 3 The Conference

Reread Part I, Chapter 1.

During the conference, take good notes, either on the agenda (my preference), a note pad, or both. It's easier to write when you are listening (what you should be doing most of the time). Your notes are the basis for your report and follow-up.

---

**■ EXAMPLE**

*Distinctive facts:* Business kids ready to take over from Father (54). A Florida business.

[The "I. BACKGROUND" AND "II. OBJECTIVES" start almost every report for two reasons: First, to let the client know we have the facts straight, and second, as an aid to our memory when we pick up the report months (sometimes even years) later.]

---

# 4 The Report/Follow-up

The only tangible evidence of the final work product is the report (or memo). Make it good. No fluff. Before the process was well-developed, we, too (like almost every estate planner we have ever seen), would pump out a big report with charts, graphs, comparisons, tax savings, and the like. But no more.

We tell the client what he/she needs to know. We bend the report to fit the client—length, complexity of language, size of the estate, value to the client of the particular issues, and so on.

The following examples are intended to illustrate the more typical transfer/succession/estate plans and the most common issues that come up. All are from my private files and are presented verbatim.

Of course, all names have been changed. Following is the cast of characters for all of the examples:

| Part Played | Name |
|---|---|
| Owner/Founder | Father Client |
| Father's wife and mother of their children | Mother |
| Father's (second, third, etc.) wife,, but not the mother of his children | Wife |
| Children: | |
| In the business | Son #1, #2, etc. |
| (business children) | Daughter #1, #2, etc. |
| Too young to be in the business | Kid #1, #2, etc. |
| Father's main business | Co. #1 |
| Father's other businesses | Co. #2, #3, etc. |

My comments to help explain the facts or some other point are shown in parentheses [————] or are preceded by the word "COMMENT."

## ■ EXAMPLE #1 [ON BLACKMAN KALLICK LETTERHEAD]

TO Father Client

DATE November 6, 199_

FROM Brian Whitlock and Irv Blackman

SUBJECT Transfer/Estate Planning

The purpose of this memorandum is to review the topics discussed in our meeting of November 5, 199_.

### I. BACKGROUND

Father Client (54) and his wife Mother (51) own 70 percent of the stock of two subchapter S corporations, Co. #1 and Co. #2. Co. #1 is a metal fabricator located in Littletown, Florida. Co. #2 markets a (special) tool that was designed by Father and is manufactured by Co. #1.

### II. OBJECTIVES

1. Father would like to reduce his current income taxes.
2. Father would like to provide himself with a stream of income as he changes his business focus from the day-to-day operations of Co. #1 to other interests.
3. Father would like to transfer ownership of Co. #1 to his three sons: Son #1 (2), Son #2 (26), and Son #3 (23).
4. Father has a key employee (Tom) to whom he would like to transfer stock.
5. Father would like to receive $200,000 a year for the rest of his life, be removed from all Co. #1 loan guarantees, be repaid his current loan to Co. #1 of $391,000 plus interest at 10%, continue to receive rent on the building, and continue to receive health insurance coverage as well as the use of his automobile.
6. Father could care less about the amount of death taxes he pays.

### III. INCOME TAX ISSUES

#### Wages Paid to Mother

The continuation of wages to Mother does not make economic sense. The wages that are currently paid to Mother add to the corporation's payroll costs (through higher Social Security taxes, unemployment taxes, and workmen's compensation costs) without any increase in your future Social Security benefits.

The wages paid to Mother are not large enough to entitle her to collect a separate Social Security check that would be larger than the combined check she could collect with Father. If her wages were added to Father's wages, the result would reduce payroll costs and increase the combined Social Security benefits at retirement.

**RECOMMENDATION:** Discontinue paying Mother any salary from the corporation.

### S Corporations and FICA Tax

It is important that the corporation continue to pay its officers and shareholders a reasonable salary, so long as they continue to actively work for the corporation. The Tax Court has held that it is improper for an S corporation to pay little or no FICA wages while making S corporation distributions. The wages of the officers should not be reduced down to the minimum required for unemployment tax purposes ($7,000). As discussed during our meeting, the Internal Revenue Service computer automatically sends notices to any S corporation that makes distributions to shareholders while at the same time paying little or no wages to its officers.

**RECOMMENDATION:** Father should be receiving at least $50,000 to $60,000 in salary. Son #1, Son #2, and Son #3 should also be drawing salaries of at least $20,000.

### C Corporation vs. S Corporation

Both Co. #1 and Co. #2 operate as S corporations. Being an S corporation is not always desirable. If a corporation is generating less than $200,000 of taxable income, the impact of the lower tax brackets available to C corporations (i.e., 15 percent on the first $50,000 of income) should not be ignored. In addition, if you are receiving substantial fringe benefits, such as medical insurance through the company, the C corporation status provides you with additional tax savings. S corporations are not allowed to deduct fringe benefits paid for the benefit of any shareholder who owns more than two percent of the stock of the corporation. Short term, and while you are young and in good health, C corporation status is preferred for corporations with modest amounts of taxable income.

**RECOMMENDATION:** Co. #2 should be converted to a C corporation. All of Father's fringe benefits should be provided through Co. #2.

### Common Paymaster

You currently perform services for more than one corporation at the same time. All of your compensation is currently paid out of Co. #1. Even after you become an employee of only Co. #2, the Internal Revenue Service could argue that both of the corporations to which you provide services should be paying FICA tax on your salary.

**RECOMMENDATION:** The minutes of Co. #2 and Co. #1 should authorize Co. #2 to act as the common paymaster for both corporations as regards Father's salary.

### Miscellaneous Income-Tax Rules

I will contact your accountant in order to discuss the following items of concern:

1. The amount of depreciation shown on your Form 1040 for your building appears to be low;
2. The applicability of Section 263A to Co. #1's inventory method of accounting;
3. The reporting of built-in gains and C corporation earnings on the face of your corporate income tax return; and
4. Necessary estimated tax payments for 199_ in order to cover your subchapter S income and avoid penalties.

## IV. ESTATE-TAX ISSUES

### Utilization of the Credit Shelter Equivalent

The transfer tax laws seek to impose a tax upon all gratuitous transfers of property which occur either during one's life or upon death. The federal transfer tax laws are "unified" in their focus, so that the same tax rates are imposed whether the transfer is subject to gift tax, during life, or estate tax, at death. Each time property changes hands from one generation to the next, either gift tax or estate tax is imposed.

The Internal Revenue Code allows individuals to transfer limited amounts, both during life and at death, free of either transfer tax. The Internal Revenue Code currently provides each taxpayer a tax credit which allows him or her to shelter the equivalent of $600,000 of transfers to persons other than a spouse (the "Credit Shelter Equivalent"). NOTE: *The Internal Revenue Code allows for unlimited transfers to your spouse via the "Unlimited Marital Deduction."*

If *both* husband and wife effectively utilize their maximum Credit Shelter Equivalent of $600,000, together they can transfer $1,200,000 ($600,000 + $600,000) free of tax. If either spouse fails to use his/her $600,000 Credit Shelter Equivalent, then *he/she loses it.*

### Taking Advantage of the Credit Shelter Equivalent

In order to take advantage of the Credit Shelter Equivalent upon the first spouse's death, both Father's and Mother's estate-planning documents (regardless of whether they are drafted in the form of a will or a revocable living trust) should look alike. The documents should divide the property of the first spouse to die into two shares.

The first share would pass to the surviving spouse as part of the Unlimited Marital Deduction. If the surviving spouse needs help managing investments, this share can be held by a professional trustee or held with a co-trustee (e.g., one or more of your children). The second share would utilize the Credit Shelter Equivalent by transferring $600,000 worth of assets to the Credit Shelter Trust. We like to refer to the Credit Shelter Trust as the "family cookie jar." The family cookie jar is filled on the first death and is available for the primary benefit of the surviving spouse. Provisions can also be added to allow income to be distributed directly to the children, if you so choose. Under most circumstances, the surviving spouse can serve as the sole trustee during his/her lifetime. NOTE: Father's and Mother's wills are both properly designed to take advantage of the Credit Shelter Equivalent (i.e., the family cookie jar).

### The Magic of the Family Cookie Jar

The spouse can be entitled to receive either all of the income or only as much of the income and principal of the family cookie jar as he/she needs during his/her lifetime.

This is where the magic of compounding comes in. Whatever assets remain in the family cookie jar at the time of the surviving spouse's death will pass to the children, free of any death tax. Thus, even though the surviving spouse has access to the family cookie jar, if she doesn't need the income and she can afford to let the income grow and accumulate year after year, then the family cookie jar will grow. There is no tax limit imposed on the growth of this trust. Thus, if by the time of the surviving spouse's death, the balance held in the family cookie jar has grown in value to, say, $2 million, the entire amount would still pass to the children free of any death tax.

Once the family cookie jar is filled, it is free from death tax upon the death of the surviving spouse. Only the surviving spouse's assets that are held outside of the family cookie jar are subject to death tax at the second death.

Father's and Mother's wills both require the trustee to distribute all of the trust income each year. This language inhibits the growth of the trust.

**RECOMMENDATION:** Both Father's and Mother's wills should be revised in order to allow the trustee to accumulate income and thus foster growth of the family cookie jar.

### Title to Assets —Joint Tenancy & Beneficiary Designations

The effectiveness of your will can also be limited by the manner in which you hold title to your property, for example, if the title to your assets is currently listed in "Joint Tenancy." Joint Tenancy's full name is "Joint Tenancy with Rights of Survivorship." At death, a transfer via Joint Tenancy is accomplished without referring to your will, trust, or any other document. In other words, the title designation controls the disposition of the property, not your will. Your will only controls assets held in your name alone.

The exact title of your assets is, therefore, extremely important. All titles should be inspected to insure that they work with, rather than against, your estate-planning documents. Even if your will contains all of the proper language, it will be rendered useless if you do not hold title to your assets in the proper form.

Father's and Mother's cash accounts, marketable securities, and home are all held in Joint Tenancy. In addition, Mother is named the beneficiary of Father's life insurance, IRA, and profit-sharing account. Like Joint Tenancy, the beneficiary designation, not the will, controls the distribution of these assets. These beneficiary designations should be changed to dovetail with your estate-plan objectives.

Father currently owns 35 percent of the stock in his name alone. Mother owns 35 percent of the stock in her name alone. The value of these assets is in excess of $600,000. As a result, no matter who dies first, Father and Mother will both effectively utilize their full Credit Shelter Equivalent.

The effective utilization of *each* spouse's Credit Shelter Equivalent amount of $600,000 will enable Father and Mother to transfer $1,200,000 to the children free of death tax after the second spouse's death.

### Raised Basis

Property owned by a decedent at death receives a "raised basis" (a new purchase price) for income-tax purposes which is equal to the property's fair-market value at the date of death. In other words, if before death you held an asset with a large gain in it, the capital gain would disappear at death. In addition, if the property is depreciable rental property, then the survivor will receive an income-tax advantage. The survivor will be able to depreciate the property and shelter rental income.

Obviously, if we knew who was going to die first, we could avoid all capital gains for the survivor by making sure the spouse who died first held all the appreciated property. The spouse who was likely to survive would own all the cash equivalents, property without appreciation (e.g., typically bonds), and property which would not be sold during the survivor's lifetime.

We are not so lucky as to own a crystal ball. Rather, we should apply those facts that reasonably exist and then still hedge our bet somewhat. In selecting the assets to be transferred in order to assure the full utilization of both Credit Shelter Equivalents, we will consider the basis of each asset and the most likely order of death.

**RECOMMENDATION:** In deciding which property to transfer, you should consider the potential advantage available under the raised basis rules. The stock and the business real estate should be titled solely in Father's name (trust) in order to wipe out gains and phantom capital-gains income. The personal real estate, the high-basis liquid assets and the Co. #1 promissory note should be titled in Mother's name (trust).

### The Probate Process and Revocable Living Trusts

A will acts to transfer only that property which is held in the name of the decedent. The process by which this property transfer is effected is called "probate." Probate is the court procedure in which the claims of the decedent's creditors are heard and the decedent's property is transferred pursuant to the terms of his will. In the absence of a valid will, the court will transfer the property remaining after the satisfaction of all claims to the decedent's closest living relatives.

Probate is extremely beneficial in providing certainty to the family of an active business person like Father or Mother. Probate allows the family to reduce the claims period generally from three (3) years (without probate) to six (6) months.

However, probate has some negative aspects as well. The Probate Court is a public forum. All of the assets of the decedent and all of the provisions of his will are open for general public inspection. In addition, the executor or administrator must make formal public disclosure to the court and/or to the decedent's family and the legatees under the will. As a result, people often feel as if they have lost a certain element of control.

In some jurisdictions, a large estate is very expensive to administer in Probate Court. As a result, people often attempt to utilize mechanisms which will allow them to avoid or reduce the expense and delays of probate without losing the advantages. Lifetime trusts often serve as such a mechanism.

A lifetime trust merely means that it is created and funded during the grantor's life. The trust actively owns property in its name and is managed by the trustee(s).

Lifetime trusts can be adapted to many different uses. Lifetime trusts can be created to hold assets for you or for your children. Trusts are often created to control assets during a child's minority and perhaps even to shelter some property from income taxes. Other lifetime trusts such as the "revocable living trust" are created to hold assets for the grantor.

The revocable living trust is a very flexible and efficient vehicle. It can be changed at any time during the grantor's lifetime. The grantor can serve as the only trustee during his lifetime, thus retaining complete control of the property held in the trust's name. All of the trust assets continue to be listed in the grantor's Social Security number during the grantor's lifetime.

A "revocable living trust" is a lifetime trust designed to reduce the impact of probate on your estate; *it does not save any income or estate taxes*. A revocable living trust is similar to a closely held corporation. The corporation is governed by its articles of incorporation and bylaws. A trust is governed by a trust agreement. The shareholders of a corporation select the board of directors and the corporate officers; the grantor of the trust selects the trustee. If a shareholder of the corporation dies, his interest in the corporation (i.e., his shares of stock) transfers, but the corporation remains intact. The reins of power pass to the new shareholder(s), and the corporation survives. If the grantor of the trust dies, his interest in the trust (i.e., as a beneficiary) terminates, but the trust survives. The reins of power pass to the successor trustee(s) designated in the trust agreement, but the trust remains intact. The assets only leave the trust at the time designated in the trust agreement. As a result, the trust and the assets held in it are not subject to the jurisdiction of the Probate Court.

It is important to remember that a lifetime trust acts to transfer only that property which has been registered in the name of the trust. The trust will not affect property which is not registered in the trust's name. Additionally, the trust only reduces the expense of probate; it does not necessarily eliminate probate. Remember, for an active businessperson, certain aspects of probate are beneficial and should be preserved.

**RECOMMENDATION:** Both Father and Mother should consider creating revocable living trusts as the core documents in their respective estate plans. The trusts would hold title to all of their significant assets and thus reduce probate. The same persons whom they have named to carry out the terms of Father's and Mother's wills could be named in the trust to serve as successor trustees.

## V. BUSINESS TRANSFER ISSUES

Father is willing to transfer the ownership of Co. #1 to his sons. Father's sons want some assurances regarding their ability to control the corporation.

### Buy-Sell Agreements

The creation of a buy-sell agreement can be beneficial to both you and the children. A buy-sell agreement may be used to address some of the concerns facing both Father and the kids. First, the agreement can assure Father control of the family business during his lifetime. Second, the agreement will provide assurances to the children that Father will not transfer the stock to a third party outside the family. Finally, the agreement will provide a mechanism for retaining peace within the family by establishing some guidelines in the event that one of the other shareholders wishes to sell his or her stock.

So long as Father is "in control," many questions will not surface because he alone controls the answers. However, over time and especially after his death, conflict may begin to surface.

If one family member dies, Father may wish to preclude others (i.e., your child's spouse) from acquiring the decedent's stock of the business, either through a death-related transfer under the deceased shareholder's will or via a sale to a nonfamily member. If one of the children becomes disabled or dies, the child's family may need to liquidate his or her interest in the company in order to provide for their welfare.

A buy-sell agreement or a stock redemption agreement can provide answers for these contingencies.

**CAUTION:** IF YOU FIX A PRICE IN THE BUY-SELL AGREEMENT, WHICH MAY AFFECT THE FUTURE RIGHTS OF THE CHILDREN, YOU SHOULD OBTAIN A PROFESSIONALLY PREPARED APPRAISAL OF YOUR BUSINESS.

**RECOMMENDATION:** The agreement should be structured to allow either the corporation or the other shareholders to purchase the stock of any nonemployee shareholder.

### Control

Father wants to keep control at least as long as necessary to complete the funding of the financial requirements. In order to preserve control over the corporation, Father should keep enough shares of voting common stock to constitute a voting majority of the voting stock for all matters for as long as he and Mother live. Generally, Father should keep at least 2/3 of the voting shares in order to control such matters as sale or liquidation. This would limit Father's and Mother's transfers to only three percent of the remaining voting stock.

Greater flexibility in making transfers is available to Father if the corporation authorizes the creation of both voting and nonvoting common stock. The corporation can create, for example, 100 times more nonvoting shares than voting. Father can keep the voting stock and thus retain control, while Father and Mother transfer a large portion of the corporation's equity.

**RECOMMENDATION:** Co. #1 should amend its articles of incorporation in order to authorize additional shares of nonvoting common stock. A stock dividend of the nonvoting common stock (100 for 1) would be declared to the benefit of the current shareholders. Both Father and Mother could then begin to transfer the nonvoting stock to each of their children.

### Deferred Compensation Plans

Father is willing to transfer the ownership of Co. #1 only if he can be provided with financial security. Father is currently receiving his income through salary and S corporation earnings. Short-term, Father could receive income via salary from either Co. #1 or Co. #2 and from increased rents.

We need to plan ahead for Father's future income through some type of deferred-compensation program.

#### Qualified Plans

If we have the financial ability to begin setting aside funds now, and if we want to provide a benefit to *all* employees, we can start a qualified plan: pension, profit sharing, 401(k), etc.

#### Nonqualified Plans

If we want to restrict the plan to only the owner, or if we lack the cash necessary to fund the plan, we can consider a nonqualified plan. A nonqualified plan can be nothing more than an unfunded promise on the part of the corporation to pay future compensation in exchange for the owner's (key employee's) promise to continue working after "early retirement age." If the program is started early enough, the corporation's promise can be of significant value, maybe close to 100 percent of average salary over the last five years. The limit that will be imposed on the plan will be reasonable compensation, but the relevant timeframe is the employee's time commitment when the plan is adopted. If the deferred compensation is earned and accrued currently during years in which the owner is compensated at a level in excess of the FICA wage limit, then it will be free of FICA tax when paid as deferred compensation after retirement. Not only will that save over 15 percent in payroll taxes, but it will allow the owner to draw his full Social Security benefits before age 70 without reduction for earned income.

**RECOMMENDATION:** Co. #1 should create a nonqualified deferred compensation plan for Father. The plan should provide for an annual income benefit beginning at age 65 and extending until the death of the survivor of Mother and Father. The size of the benefit will depend upon the amount of compensation that will be deemed reasonable under the circumstances.

Co. #1 could also create a similar plan for Tom (the key employee) in lieu of stock. A phantom stock plan or a deferred-compensation plan tied to corporate growth may represent an acceptable alternative for both Tom and Co. #1. If Tom buys stock of Co. #1, it will require a large investment with little short-term reward. A deferred-compensation plan will allow Tom to participate in earnings and growth without the up-front dollar investment.

### Grantor Retained Annuity Trust (GRAT)

Father could also receive future income from his stock by utilizing a GRAT. A GRAT is an irrevocable trust that allows the grantor (you) to retain a stream of income in the form of an annuity for a selected term of years with the remainder of the trust passing to your children at the end of the term. Because your children must wait until the end of the term to receive the gift, you are only deemed to have given (for gift-tax purposes) the present value of the right to receive the gifts in the future. The leveraging that is available via a GRAT is significant. Let's look at its application for you.

1. Co. #1 recapitalizes with both voting and nonvoting common stock and declares a 100-to-1 stock dividend to all shareholders of record, leaving Father with 1,000 shares of voting common stock and 100,000 shares of nonvoting common stock. (All stock would be transferred to Father's name alone, per the "raised basis" discussion.)
2. Father transfers, for example, all 100,000 shares of his nonvoting stock or 90 percent of Co. #1 to a 15-percent, nine-year GRAT. The GRAT's share of the $350,000 annual S corporation income would be $247,000. If, for discussion purposes, the gift (the 71,300 nonvoting shares) is valued at $1,400,000, the trust would be required to pay an annuity to Father of $210,000 (15 percent of $1,400,000) per year for nine years. The annuity would be exempt from FICA and payroll taxes. The remaining S corporation income would be retained in the trust and could offset potential declines in S corporation income. The taxable gift to the children in this example would be valued, according to IRS regulations, at only $39,070. Even assuming no appreciation in the real estate, the potential estate tax savings is nearly $885,000.

**NOTE:** The 15-percent, nine-year GRAT is an example only. The percentage rate could be higher or lower (within limits) and the term could be longer or shorter. Any change affects the $39,070 value.

**CAVEATS:**

1. Since the GRAT is a "grantor type" trust for income-tax purposes, Father would pay income tax on the trust's full share of the corporation's annual income of $247,000, even though the annuity payment would only be $210,000. The cash difference would pass to the kids tax-free when the trust terminates at the end of nine years.
2. Since the annuity of $210,000 per year would end after nine years, this stream of income may need to be replaced.
3. If Father dies before the end of the ninth year, the then current value of the stock (instead of the $39,070 in our example) would be included in his estate. We can protect against the loss of this estate-tax savings by purchasing insurance on Father's life alone. The insurance proceeds, which would be estate-tax free (because it would be owned by an irrevocable life insurance trust—explained later in this memo), would pay the estate tax due because the GRAT stock came back into Father's estate.

If you are reluctant to make large transfers of stock to the children, other strategies may be explored.

### Stock Bonus to Employees

Additional nonvoting common stock can be transferred directly by the corporation to the management employees through additional taxable compensation in the form of a stock bonus. The stock bonuses will act to dilute the relative interests in the shareholders and will ultimately save at least 55 percent in estate- and/or gift-tax cost.

The stock bonus represents a current expense to the corporation equal to the value of the stock. The corporation claims this deduction as part of the compensation expense. This expense reduces the net income of the corporation and thus lowers the current income tax payable by the shareholders. As a result, even though the management employees might be paying additional income tax upon the receipt of the bonus, the corporate shareholders would indirectly pay less income tax as a result of the indirect deduction. In summary, the net income-tax cost to the family is zero, but the estate-tax savings are twofold: the current fair-market value of the bonus is removed from the estate, and the future growth of the bonus is also removed.

**RECOMMENDATION:** Father should consider bonusing stock to his sons and Tom in lieu of cash bonuses or cash payments for the stock if he chooses to issue actual stock in lieu of phantom stock.

### Tandem Corporations

Rather than transfer a large portion of your business, it may be possible for you to create a new business, which can be operated in tandem with the existing business. At the time the new corporation is established, the children would own 100 percent of the equity and thus 100 percent of the future growth in the new business. As new products, markets or opportunities arose in your industry which the family wanted to pursue, the new tandem corporation could enter into that new business. Over time, the new business would grow, while the existing business would remain level and potentially decline.

Work could initially be subcontracted between the new corporation and the old corporation, since the new corporation would have limited capital and production facilities of its own. Each corporation would need to work on a reasonable profit margin under the circumstances in order to avoid income reallocation by the Internal Revenue Service.

The creation of tandem corporations provides multiple benefits. First, it gives the boys full short-term control over a portion of the business. Second, the creation of new entities may be beneficial at a later date in the distribution of your estate. There often comes a point in time when one family member may wish to separate from his brothers. The more entities (assets) held in different corporations (or partnerships), the easier it will be to divide assets among your children tax-free.

### Irrevocable Life Insurance Trusts

Life insurance is an illusory asset within an estate plan. Prior to death, the insurance is worth no more than its cash surrender value. (In the case of term insurance, the only value is one year's paid premium.) However, if the insured is the owner of the policy, or if he retains the right to name the beneficiary of the policy, then the full face value of the insurance will be includable in the taxable estate of the owner at death. The family is caught in a dilemma of keeping the policy and paying tax on the proceeds or saving the tax by sacrificing access to the policy proceeds.

An irrevocable life insurance trust allows us the best of both worlds. The family is allowed to receive the use of the proceeds, within limits, without causing the proceeds to be taxed in the estate of either spouse.

The mechanics of an irrevocable life insurance trust are relatively simple, but they must be followed carefully. The policies must be transferred to the trustee as owner and beneficiary. Each year, gifts of cash are made, usually by the insured, to the trustee to pay the premiums. At death, the proceeds are not includable in the estate of the insured, but they are used for the benefit of the insured's loved ones. For example, the insurance proceeds on Father's policies could be used to provide a flow of income to Mother.

If the policy proceeds will not be necessary to provide funds for Mother if Father should die first, you should consider purchasing insurance that will only pay upon the death of the second spouse. The proceeds on a second-to-die policy are available at the time when they are needed the most, upon the second death, when estate taxes are due and when distributions will be made to the children.

If family needs change during the insured's lifetime, and the life insurance is no longer appropriate, the trust can be indirectly terminated. For example, the insured can discontinue making the annual gifts which afford the trustee the ability to pay the premium. Obviously, if the premiums remain unpaid, the policy will lapse, and the trust will be eliminated. In the case of term life insurance, no residual value (i.e., "cash surrender value") would be lost upon termination of the policy. In the case of permanent insurance (i.e., "whole life" or "universal life"), the residual value may be retained in the trust, or the trustee may use it to carry reduced coverage until the residual value is exhausted.

**RECOMMENDATION:** Father will obtain insurance quotes from at least two sources on two types of policies—a policy on his life and a second-to-die policy (his life and Mother's life). The insurance on Father's life would hedge a GRAT. The second-to-die policy would act to create additional nonbusiness assets. Any new life insurance will be purchased by an irrevocable life insurance trust. The quotes should be for $1 million of insurance. The amount of insurance actually purchased may be lower or higher, but the numbers are easily divisible.

### Action List

1. Discontinue Mother's salary; add it to Father's.
2. Check Father's estimated tax payments and withholding in order to avoid penalties.
3. Pay Father at least $50,000 of salary in 199_ from Co. #2.
4. Convert Co. #2 into a C corporation after S corporation earnings are distributed. Brian will discuss with Andy [Father's accountant].
5. Authorize Co. #2 to be the common paymaster for Co. #1 and Co. #2 (for Father's salary). Brian will discuss with Nick [Father's new estate-specialist lawyer].
6. Revise your wills in order to permit the trustee of the credit shelter trust to accumulate income. Brian will discuss with Nick.
7. Discuss utilizing living trusts with your attorney. Brian will discuss with Nick.

8. Transfer the Co. #1 building into Father's name. Transfer the promissory notes and the residence to Mother.
9. Enter into a buy-sell agreement with the boys.
10. Recapitalize Co. #1 with voting and nonvoting common stock.
11. Consider a GRAT in order to provide short-term income to Father (i.e., to age 65).
12. Implement a deferred-compensation plan to begin at or near the termination of the GRAT.
13. Father will obtain a printout from his insurance agent showing the projected performance of his current insurance to age 95. Father will also obtain a quote from his insurance agent for $1 million of new permanent insurance on his life and $1 million of second-to-die insurance.

**COMMENT:** The "ACTION LIST" not only summarizes *what* remains to be done, but often *who* is to do it. The list, in practice, is our follow-up roadmap.

## ■ EXAMPLE #2

[This is a follow-up memo to our file on the matter in Example #1. A copy was sent to Father Client and his attorney, Nick.]

| | |
|---|---|
| TO | File of Father Client |
| FROM | Brian Whitlock |
| DATE | December 4, 199_ |
| SUBJECT | Follow-up |

I had a conference call with Father Client and Nick Lawyer, on Friday, December 4, 199_, for the purpose of formalizing our action plan. As a result of our discussion, the following actions will be undertaken:

1. Nick will prepare a common paymaster authorization for the minute books of both Co. #1 and Co. #1.
2. Nick will contact Rob (Father's old lawyer) regarding the preparation of a codicil to Father's will and Mother's will. The codicils will authorize the trustee of the credit shelter trusts to accumulate income. No action will be taken regarding living trusts at this time.
3. Nick will prepare a deed transferring the title of the Co. #1 building from Mother's name to Father's name.
4. Nick will prepare a formal promissory note from Co. #1 to Father dated December 4, 199_ in the amount of $391,227.34. This note will bear interest at the rate of 9 percent per annum.
5. Mother and Father will transfer their mutual funds into Mother's name in order to raise her separate holding to more than $600,000.
6. Nick will prepare a draft of a cross-purchase, buy-sell agreement covering the stock of Co. #1 only. The buy-sell agreement will allow the boys a first option regarding the purchase of any nonvoting shareholders' stock. The agreement will provide voting shareholders with a first option for the purchase of any voting stock, the nonvoting shareholders with a second option regarding the purchase of voting stock, and the corporation with a third option regarding the purchase of the voting stock.

7. Nick will recapitalize Co. #1 by amending the articles of incorporation in order to create 100 shares of nonvoting common stock for every one share of voting common stock.

8. Nick will prepare an authorization from the minutes to declare a stock dividend of 100 shares of nonvoting stock for every one share of outstanding voting stock.

9. Nick will draft a phantom stock plan as part of an employment agreement for Tom [a key employee not related to Father or Mother]. The phantom stock plan will grant Tom a right to receive a bonus equal to 3 1/2 percent of the net income of the corporation earned in calendar year 199_ (Year 1), 6 2/3 percent of the income earned by the corporation in calendar year 199_ (Year 2), and 10 percent of the net income of the corporation earned in calendar year 199_ (Year 3) and thereafter, provided he is then employed by the corporation at such time. In addition, Tom will receive stock appreciation rights based upon the increase in the value of the stock from the date of grant, November 1, (Year 1), November 1, (Year 2), and November 1, (Year 3), provided he is employed at each of those dates. The stock valuation will be based on a manner consistent with the appraisal to be performed by Blackman Kallick Bartelstein.

10. Nick will create a grantor retained annuity trust (GRAT) that will provide a stream of income to Father for 11 years. At the end of the 11th year, the trust will terminate and the stock held by the trust will be transferred in equal shares to Son #1, Son #2, and Son #3. The GRAT will contain a reversionary right to Father's estate if Father should die during the term of the 11-year GRAT. The GRAT will pay an annuity equal to 13 percent each year to Father in quarterly installments throughout the 11-year period, at the end of each quarter.

11. Nick will prepare an employment agreement between Co. #1, Co. #2 and Father providing for approximately $70,000 per year of annual compensation, plus a deferred-compensation plan to begin when Father reaches age 65. The deferred compensation will be equal to $200,000 a year for life. If Father should die, the deferred compensation of $200,000 per year will continue for the remainder of Mother's life.

    Mike Dorman (a Blackman Kallick valuation department specialist) will contact Father on Monday, December 7 in order to begin getting the necessary information to appraise the stock of Co. #1. Nick Lawyer will begin drafting the documents and will hopefully have a rough draft by the end of the week. Father would like to sign the agreements on December 23.

## ■ EXAMPLE #3

*Distinctive facts:* Daughter #1 (41) runs the business, except for major policy decisions, which are made by Father (64). Father is married to Wife (48). Daughter #1 and Wife have a sort-of-armed-truce relationship. There are two adult (34 and 37) nonbusiness children.

This memo followed a one-on-one conference with Father. All three parties were present at two earlier conferences. A Chicago business.

**[On Blackman Kallick letterhead]**

**MEMORANDUM**

TO: Father Client (Chicago)
FROM: Irv Blackman
DATE: February 14, 199_
RE: Summary of February 7, 199_ meeting

The purpose of this memo is to summarize specific points relating to your lifetime tax plan that would dovetail with your estate plan, all as discussed at our February 7th meeting.

Although we discussed many things, the following only sets forth those items where we 1) reached a decision; and 2) if the decisions are implemented, will accomplish your objectives as detailed below.

## I. TIME FRAME

For the purpose of this memo, your plan is divided into two time frames—lifetime and estate (after death).

A. LIFETIME PLAN

*The balance of your life* - The assumption is that for the balance of your life, you and you alone will control what, when, and how you will spend your time and money. However, there is a window of opportunity because Co. #1 [the only business] lost money for the year ended December 31, 199_. This lowers the value of the company significantly for both gift-tax and estate-tax purposes (but only for the near term for estate-tax purposes).

B. ESTATE PLAN

*Disposition of your assets after death* - For the purpose of the estate plan that we discussed, your wealth is divided into two specific segments: (1) the business assets; and (2) all other assets.

1. Business Assets

The business portion consists of all of the stock you own (both voting and nonvoting) in Co. #1. [Recapitalized at our suggestion after first conference.]

2. Other Assets

These assets include everything else that you own or have an interest in—i.e., home, IRA, qualified plan, etc. These assets total approximately $2,000,000 (See schedule on Page Five)

The division indicated above has no real meaning during your life...recognizing that as long as you are alive, you control your own destiny. But you indicated that after your death, you have four significant objectives you would like accomplished:

a) Pass the business to Daughter #1.

b) Provide for your wife so that she can maintain the standard of living to which she has become accustomed during the course of your life.

c) Have your other two children share in your wealth.

d) Keep peace in the family.

Following is a step-by-step outline of how the above objectives can be accomplished.

## II. COMBINED LIFETIME/ESTATE PLAN

A. Business Part (more specifically, the stock you own in Co. #1.)

Step 1 - Make a large gift to LB-M of nonvoting stock of BE—about $1,000,000.

Important - This will remove not only $1,000,000 (more or less) from your estate, but will also remove the anticipated future growth (value ) of Co. #1 when business conditions turn around.

Step 2 - Create a revocable trust to hold title to your Co. #1 stock.

**NOTE:** This will allow not only this asset, but the assets in B below, to flow more conveniently into your trust and avoid probate of your estate.

Step 3 - We will continue the annual stock-transfer program to Daughter #1 [started at our suggestion]

1. $20,000 gift of stock (nonvoting)
2. Stock Bonus (nonvoting)

Step 4 - An option would be to also make $20,000 gifts of nonvoting stock to your other two children.

If we were to initiate this option, which would continue year after year, it would be essential that a buy-sell agreement be entered into among all the children. This would give Daughter #1 an opportunity to purchase the stock of your other two children while these children would then be able to turn the nonspendable stock certificates into cash. This would leave Daughter #1 owning all of the stock after your death.

Step 5 - Upon your death, you would leave all of the nonvoting stock you then owned in Co. #1 to your three children; all of the voting stock to Daughter #1.

If the buy-sell agreement were in effect, all of these shares would become subject to this agreement. If the buy-sell agreement were not in effect, we would have appropriate language in the trust to make sure that all of the children received their appropriate shares of your wealth.

**NOTE:** I recommend giving some stock to your other two children and then entering into the buy-sell agreement.

Let's summarize what the above does during the course of your life.

A. In terms of your current lifestyle and ability to do what you darn please—NOTHING.

B. What then is the purpose? The purpose is two-fold.

1. Remove as much of the current value of Co. #1 stock from your estate, while you retain control, during your life. Here is an important added bonus: The appreciation in the stock gifted would also be excluded from your estate.

   In summary, you will save substantial estate taxes.

2. To involve your other children in the plan during your life. This sets up the conditions necessary for you to accomplish two of your specific objectives:

   a) Pass the business to Daughter #1, and

   b) Have your other children share in your wealth.

**NOTE:** There is a price to pay for leaving the Co. #1 stock to the children [instead of wife]: estate taxes are due upon your death. This tax can be paid over a period of 15 years with interest at four percent on about the first $350,000 of tax due and market rate of interest on the balance.

C. All of your other assets.

Following is a list of the assets and the values attributable to them from the November 15, 199_ estate-planning projections we prepared for you. The exact figures are not important, but the principle is.

| | |
|---|---|
| 1. Marketable Securities | $200,000 |
| 2. Qualified Retirement Plan | 300,000 |
| 3. Nonqualified Retirement Plan | 200,000 |
| 4. Individual Retirement Account | 20,000 |
| 5. Life Insurance | 380,000 |
| 6. Personal Residence | 1,200,000 |
| TOTAL | $2,300,000 |

Here are the important steps that would be taken.

Step 1 - Your home, which is now held in joint tenancy with Wife, would be transferred to Father who would in turn transfer it to his new trust.

Benefit - This would allow the home to go into the trust and escape not only estate taxes, but income taxes as well when sold after your death.

Step 2 - The beneficiaries of the following would be changed to the trust.

1. Life insurance
2. Qualified Retirement Plan
3. Nonqualified Retirement Plan
4. IRA

**POINT:** This allows us to continue gathering all of the assets that will become available at your death and have them controlled by your trustee.

Step 3 - Make appropriate provisions in your trust and will so that all of your other assets would be held by the trust and dealt with as follows:

1. All of the income from the trust would be payable to Wife for as long as she lives.

   **NOTE:** It is assumed that the residence would be sold (tax-free) and the proceeds would become income-producing property inside the trust.

2. Upon Wife's death, any remaining balance in the trust would be distributed as follows:
   a) Pay the estate tax due (Wife's death would trigger estate-tax liability at that time).
   b) The balance in the trust to your children.

Let's summarize what the above accomplishes.

1. We are able to maximize the amount of income available for the benefit of Wife for as long as she lives and eliminate any estate-tax liability until her death.

2. The business would not be intermingled with your other assets, allowing Daughter #1 to control the business and Wife to have her separate pool of funds to provide for her.
3. Hopefully, this would accomplish the last objective as stated above—keep peace in the family.

We concluded that the next steps would work somewhat as follows:

1. Make sure that the above memo correctly reflects your thinking and, if not, make the appropriate changes.
2. Then discuss the memo and what we would like to accomplish with each of Daughter #1 and Wife, separately.
3. Then meet with your attorneys to draft the necessary documents.

   **NOTE:** We should recognize that Wife has certain rights under Illinois law to renounce your will. This problem must be faced straight up.

I tried to limit this memo to only the most important points. As a result I purposely did not try to cover every possible nuance and detail. No doubt, you will have questions.

Please give me a call as soon as you have had an opportunity to read and digest the above.

cc: Brian Whitlock

## ■ EXAMPLE #4

*Starting with this example, only portions of the report (memo) are shown (in order to eliminate portions similar to the material in the earlier examples).*
*Distinctive facts:* Father (38) is much younger than the typical owner who does transfer/estate planning. His business has the potential to make him an eight-figure multimillionaire before he sees 50. Excluding life insurance, his present wealth exceeds $2 million. A Missouri business.

### I. BACKGROUND

Father (38) owns 100 percent of the stock of Co. #1, located in Smalltown, Missouri. Father formed Co. #1 in 1983. Co. #1 operated as a C corporation until 1990, when it elected S corporation status. Mother (36) also works in the business and handles payroll and cost accounting. Mother and Father have two adopted children, Kid #1 (9) and Kid #2 (1).

### II. OBJECTIVES

*Father's Objectives*

1. Would like to reduce his current income taxes.
2. Would like Co. #1 to continue to grow in the future. Co. #1 has limited exposure in the automotive industry. Father would like to develop more business in that area.
3. Would like to reduce his estate-tax exposure.
4. Would like to protect his family.

### V. OPPORTUNITIES FOR EQUALIZATION

Co. #1 represents a disproportionately large share of Mother's and Father's combined estate. If all of their children do not enter the business, it becomes increasingly difficult to distribute business assets to the business children and equal amounts of nonbusiness assets to the nonbusiness children.

Methods of creating nonbusiness assets need to be explored in order to plan for the possibility that one of the children may not enter the business.

### The S Corporation Nest Egg

If Father only distributed enough cash to meet his income-tax requirements, then the balance of Co. #1's earnings could accumulate as a nest egg within the corporation. This nest egg could be drawn in the future and gifted to nonbusiness children.

**NOTE:** As Mother and Father make gifts of stock, they reduce their *pro rata* share of both the current earnings and the past accumulations of earnings (i.e., the "nest egg").

**RECOMMENDATION:** If Father wants to preserve the nest egg, he could distribute the current earnings of the corporation each year. He could then lend the corporation enough cash to cover its working capital needs. Once the nest egg is converted from an accumulated earnings account to a note payable, it is no longer diluted by future gifts.

### Rental Property

The Co. #1 building (owned by Father), as a rental property, represents a second method of drawing money from the corporation for many years to come. In addition, the commercial (nonbusiness) property represents an asset that could be left to any child who does not enter the business. The nonbusiness child's ownership of the building would not interfere with the management of the business, so long as there is a long-term lease in place.

**RECOMMENDATION:** A long-term lease should be written for the Co. #1 building. A fair-market rent should be charged from the outset, and rent escalation factors should be built into the lease.

### Transfer Issues

The balance of this memo will discuss some of the tax-advantaged vehicles of transfer available to the children.

### Utilization of Annual Exclusion Gifts

In addition to the credit shelter equivalent ($600,000 each) discussed above, each individual taxpayer is allowed to make nontaxable gifts in the amount of $10,000 per person per year. In other words, Father can give $10,000 each calendar year to each child, and Mother can give $10,000 each calendar year to each child (a total of $20,000).

By making regular annual gifts of $10,000 to $20,000 per child per year, over a long period of time, you could significantly reduce the ultimate size of your combined estates.

### Can You Afford to Make Gifts?

Mother and Father have both made gifts to their children from time to time in the past; however, their current finances do not permit them the luxury of being able to make extensive cash gifts to their children. Both must be concerned about their need to have enough liquid assets for their retirement years. Therefore, cash or cash-like property should not be gifted. In fact, cash is *rarely* the best kind of property to gift.

### What Kind of Property Should Be Gifted?

Assets which are not spendable and which do not diminish your lifestyle represent excellent choices for gifts. Illiquid noncash gifts neither deplete your cash, nor do they become a temptation for your children to spend. In addition, many noncash gifts (i.e., stock in the family business) have a greater potential for future appreciation than cash.

**RECOMMENDATION:** Gifts of nonvoting stock of Co. #1 to each of the children would be one choice for future gifts.

### Action List

1. Father and Mother will update their wills. They will discuss the creation of revocable living trusts with their attorney to avoid probate.
2. Their personal residence should be titled in Mother's name alone (or in the name of her revocable trust).
3. The Co. #1 corporate stock should be registered in Father's name alone (or Father's revocable trust).
4. Mother should remove herself from the payroll or significantly reduce her compensation in order to save FICA taxes and payroll expenses.
5. Co. #1 should recapitalize by authorizing the creation of nonvoting common stock and declaring a stock dividend of the nonvoting shares.
6. Father should update the Co. #1 lease and raise the rent to a market rate.
7. Father and Mother should begin gifting nonvoting Co. #1 stock to Child #1 and Child #2.
8. Father and Mother will enter into a buy-sell agreement that will restrict any stock that is transferred to the children.
9. Father and Mother should consider making a large gift of all of the Co. #1 nonvoting stock to a GRAT for the children.
10. Father should remove the life insurance from Co. #1.
11. Father will obtain insurance quotes for $1 million of insurance on his life alone and $1 million of second-to-die insurance. Since the intention is to buy significantly more than $1 million of coverage, the quotes are to determine the range of the premium cost.

## ■ EXAMPLE #5

*Distinctive facts:* Father (64), a nationally recognized leader in his industry, owns 71 percent of Co. #1's common stock. Co. #2 owns 25 percent of this stock and Son #1 owns the balance, four percent. A family trust (created when Father's dad died) owns $225,000 of preferred stock.

Co. #2 owns real estate and is developing a computer service for Co. #1's industry. Father and Mother own 70 percent of the stock. The balance of the stock is owned equally by Son #1 (35) (active in Co. #1), Daughter #1 (32) (active in Co. #2), and Child #1 (25) (employed by an international company). A Michigan business.

### Continuing Needs for Income During Life

Retirement does not reduce our continuing need for income. When we were younger, we probably thought we would spend less after we retired, but we do not. We may spend less money on our children, but now we spend it on our grandchildren. We may spend less on education, but now we spend more on travel, entertainment, or other activities. As a result, we usually spend just as much money during our post-retirement years as we always have, only the reasons change.

The Internal Revenue Code only allows you a corporate income-tax deduction for that portion of your salary (wages) that is reasonable compensation for the work performed. This amount rarely becomes an issue while you are actively employed. However, we are forced to reduce and ultimately cut off our compensation as we reduce our active involvement in the business. If you cannot reasonably draw a salary after your retirement (or worse yet, disability), then you must find ways of replacing that income stream during your retirement years. You could always declare dividends in order to withdraw current and accumulated income, but dividends from a closely held C corporation are subject to double taxation: first, to a corporate-level income tax and, second, to an individual income tax.

**HOW TO SOLVE THE PROBLEM:** S corporation status gives you access to the corporation's earning power at the cost of only one level of income tax.

### S Corporation Status

Section 1361 of the Internal Revenue Code allows a corporation to elect to be taxed on its income in the same way a sole proprietor or partner is taxed on income derived from the business, at individual rates. An S corporation does not pay income tax on the income it earns. Rather, the shareholders include such income on their individual income-tax returns at the same percentage in which they own stock in the company. Once the shareholders have paid tax on this income, the corporation may distribute the income to the shareholders (via a dividend) without incurring any additional income tax.

**KEY TO YOUR FUTURE INCOME STREAM:** As shareholders of an S corporation, Father and Mother will be entitled to their percentage share (currently 70 percent) of Co. #1's net income. Better yet, S-corporation status will give you access to the corporation's stream of income, even after retirement.

### Regular Income-Tax Savings

The highest individual income-tax rate is currently 31 percent, and the highest corporate income-tax rate is currently 34 percent. If the corporation is regularly generating income in excess of $250,000, you would save income tax by operating as an S corporation.

Being an S corporation is not always desirable. If the corporation is generating less than $50,000 of taxable income, the impact of the lowest corporate tax bracket—15 percent—should not be ignored. In addition, if you are receiving substantial fringe benefits such as medical insurance through the company, C-corporation status provides you with additional tax savings. While you are young and in good health, C-corporation status is preferred for corporations with modest amounts of taxable income.

The true test of whether you should operate as an S corporation or a C corporation becomes the long-term need for access to corporate income. While Father is actively employed by the company, he can always draw reasonable compensation from the company. However, if he becomes disabled or does, in fact, retire out of state, he must find alternate ways to withdraw money from the corporation. His receipt of S-corporation distributions would not impair his ability to claim Social Security benefits. (NOTE: The Social Security Administration insists on strict compliance; however, since you physically live over 1,000 miles away from the plant, it should be easy to establish that you, in fact, are retired.)

### Additional Income-Tax Savings

Even if the corporations earn only modest amounts of income, S corporation-status may be useful in the short term because it will allow you to avoid four other problem areas: (a) the underutilization of passive losses, (b) the corporate Alternative Minimum Tax (AMT), (c) the Accumulated Earnings Tax, and (d) the double taxation on gains of appreciated assets.

(a) Co. #2 had $54,000 of nondeductible passive losses in 1991. If Co. #1 had been an S corporation in 199_, these losses would have been deductible against Co. #1's rental income.

(b) Co. #1 paid over $35,000 of AMT in 199_.

(c) The tax code penalizes C corporations that do not pay out dividends and unnecessarily retain earnings by requiring that they pay a tax on accumulated earnings. Co. #2 must currently monitor its accumulations, whereas S corporations are not subject to the Accumulated Earnings Tax.

(d) Co. #2 owns appreciated real estate. Father would have to pay two levels of tax in order to utilize any of the proceeds personally. After Co. #2 is an S corporation for 10 years, one level of tax will be completely eliminated. The second level of income tax could also be partially eliminated under the raised basis rules (discussed later) if Co. #2 is an S corporation at the time of your death.

### Impediments to S-Corporation Status for Co. #2

In order to maintain S-corporation status, Co. #2 must generate 75 percent of its gross receipts from active sources. Active sources could include management fees and jobs associated with the tool-and-die business. Interest, rents, and capital gains are all treated as sources of passive income.

Careful planning may be required in the future in order to assure that the 75 percent test is not violated. It may be necessary to increase the management fees marginally or create new sources of active income (i.e., tool-and-die business) in order to assure compliance with these rules.

In addition, Co. #2 may need to convert its fiscal yearend to December 31 in order to elect S-corporation status. The possible ramifications of this election should be considered.

**RECOMMENDATION:** Co. #2 should elect S-corporation status effective October 1, 199_.

**NOTE:** Co. #1 would not be allowed to elect S-corporation status unless the preferred stock is retired and Co. #2 stock owned by Co. #1 is redeemed. We are not currently recommending S-corporation status for Co. #1, in light of the significant capital demands involved.

### Equitable Treatment of the Children

So long as all the children receive an equal number of shares of stock as gifts, we can achieve Father's objective to treat all of the children equally. Since Child #1 is young and unmarried, there remains the possibility that she may wish to enter the business. A gift of stock to each child will keep the door of the business open to all of them.

**CAVEAT:** As Father knows, however, someday the business kids(s) will have to buy out the nonbusiness kid(s). Although the buy-sell agreement can set a price and a timetable, the business still must have the cash flow necessary to redeem the stock of the nonbusiness kids(s).

### Handling the Business vs. Nonbusiness Children

The above recommendation attempts to address one of the key concerns that most business parents have when they have some kids in the business and some kids outside of the business. By gifting stock of Co. #1 to Son #1 and stock of Co. #2 to Daughter #1 and Child #1, Father and Mother can separate the nonbusiness children from the business children during their lives. This could aid in avoiding future conflicts among the children after both Father and Mother have passed away.

This division of assets is not always acceptable to parents, particularly where it is difficult to agree upon valuation methods for both the business assets (Co. #1) and the nonbusiness assets (the real estate inside of Co. #2).

### Equalization of the Business vs. Nonbusiness Property

A disproportionate share of Father and Mother's net worth is tied up in the stock of Co. #1. In order to preserve equity between the business children and the nonbusiness children, additional nonbusiness assets must be created. Some methods for accomplishing this are discussed below.

### Removing Life Insurance

Co. #1 currently owns three Home Life life insurance policies on Father's life inside the corporation. The corporation is the beneficiary of two policies. Mother is the beneficiary of the third policy. This current insurance structure presents two problems:

1. Since Co. #1 is a regular C corporation, the insurance would be subject to an Alternative Minimum Tax.
2. Since Father controls the corporation and, thus, has the ability to change the beneficiary, the insurance proceeds are potentially includable in Father's estate at death. This could result in double estate taxation.

**RECOMMENDATIONS:**

1. If the insurance proceeds are not necessary to replace Father as a key employee, then these policies should either be terminated or removed from the corporation. If these policies are worth retaining, then Father should purchase them from the corporation.
2. Insurance owned outside the corporation is a nonbusiness asset that can be left to the nonbusiness kids.
3. In order to evaluate the insurance, we should get more information regarding the ownership, the applicant, the type of insurance, the beneficiary, the cash surrender value and how the insurance company projects each policy will perform over the next 30 years at a six percent assured rate of return.

## ■ EXAMPLE #6

*Distinctive facts:* Father (50) and Mother (51) are worth in excess of $35 million; $25 million in stock in Co. #1, a public company, which Father manages. A midwest business.

### Qualified Personal Residence Trust

The Internal Revenue Code continues to allow individuals to create grantor retained income trusts (GRIT) in favor of their children so long as the trust assets consist only of residential real estate or tangible personal property.

Similar to its cousin, the GRAT, a GRIT allows a discount for the present value of the right to receive the residential real estate upon the termination of the trust. In addition, the GRIT would be eligible for an additional discount if the trust provides that the corpus will revert to Mother should she die within the term of the GRIT.

**RECOMMENDATION:** Mother could create a 20-year GRIT that would hold her Nantucket real estate. This irrevocable trust would provide that should Mother live the full 20 years, the real estate would pass to your children or to a trust for their benefit. Additionally, should Mother die during the 20-year term of the trust, the entire principal would revert to her estate. The likelihood of the reversion would be measured using standard Internal Revenue Service tables that attempt to measure this event in the same way that an insurance company measures the risk of death through its mortality tables.

Utilizing the current applicable federal interest rate of 8.4 percent, at age 51, Mother could create a 20-year GRIT with a reversionary feature that would allow her to transfer all of the Nantucket real estate estimated to be worth $1,300,000. In doing so she will exhaust only $188,370 of her $600,000 credit equivalent amount.

### Transfers of Co. #1 [A Publicly Held Company] to Charity

As a result of various restrictions imposed upon key individuals as part of a public offering, Father will be unable to make any transfers of his Co. #1 stock until 199_ at the earliest. Father and Mother have expressed an interest to ultimately transfer *all* of their Co. #1 stock to charity. This transfer can certainly be accomplished on a post-death basis by transferring their entire interest to either qualified charitable interests or a private (family) foundation. [The shares of Co. #1 owned by Father and Mother are worth $25 million with a good possibility of doubling in value every 8 to 10 years.]

**RECOMMENDATION:** Father and Mother should consider making transfers of Co. #1 stock during their lifetime in order to obtain charitable income-tax deductions in addition to estate-tax deductions.

There are a number of vehicles available to you in order to make deferred gifts of Co. #1 stock to charity.

### Charitable Remainder Trusts

A charitable remainder trust is an irrevocable trust in which you (plus one other member of your family) may receive a stream of income (either for both lifetimes or for a selected number of years). At the end of the income period, the then balance of the trust property is transferred to a private foundation or qualified public charity. The charitable remainder trust in effect allows you to keep the income from the property, retain control of the principal during your lifetime, obtain a current income-tax deduction and ensure that the principal will pass to charity.

Since the trust is irrevocable, you are entitled to receive an income-tax deduction in the first year of the trust for the present value of the property that the charity will likely receive upon termination of the trust. The longer the charity must wait in order to receive the property, the smaller the current income-tax deduction.

There are two vehicles that allow you to make a deferred taxable gift and retain control over the principal: a charitable remainder annuity trust (CRAT) and a charitable remainder unitrust (CRUT).

### Charitable Remainder Annuity Trust (CRAT)

The charitable remainder annuity trust allows you to demand a fixed payout from the trust regardless of its investment performance. This fixed annuity may not be less that five percent, nor may it exceed 8.25 percent currently.

Any monies earned in excess of the payout rate are retained by the trust and will ultimately benefit *only* the charity. If the trust earns less than the selected payout rate over an extended period of time, the trust will be forced to sell off its principal assets and the trust will exhaust itself.

#### Advantages

1. Capital-gains tax is avoided upon the transfer of Co. #1 stock.
2. You may control the trustee and the investment advisor.
3. The current income-tax deduction may be utilized to offset any gains from installment sales or any other income that you receive during the current year.
4. The stream of income may be utilized to purchase a second-to-die life insurance policy on Mother and Father that will escape estate taxation.

#### Disadvantages

1. If the annuity rate is greater than Co. #1's dividend rate, it will be necessary to sell off a portion of the stock each year in order to meet the mandatory pay-out rate.
2. You cannot contribute more stock to the same CRAT in later years. Instead you must create a new CRAT to receive additional contributions.
3. Your current income tax-deduction will be limited to 20 percent of your annual adjusted gross income. In addition, gifts of appreciated property will potentially impact your alternative minimum taxable income during the year of the contribution.

### Charitable Remainder Unitrust (CRUT)

Rather than select a fixed payout that will never vary over the income period of the trust (i.e., a CRAT), you may select a payout equal to a percentage of the fluctuating fair-market value of the trust, from time to time. As the trust grows in value, your required payout will also grow. However, if the trust fund shrinks in value, your required payout will decrease each year.

#### Advantages

1. Capital-gains tax is avoided on the transfer of Co. #1 stock.
2. You may control the trustee and the investment advisor.
3. The trust may contain provisions that allow the trustee to avoid selling the Co. #1 stock when the dividend is less than the current year payout rate. The income shortfall may be thus deferred and taken in a later year. This would allow the trust to realize the full potential appreciation from the Co. #1 stock gifted to the trust.
4. Your annual potential fixed payout will grow as the value of the fund grows.
5. You may contribute additional property to the same CRUT in later years, without the need for creating a separate CRUT.
6. The current income-tax deduction may be utilized to offset earned income.
7. The income stream may be utilized to purchase a second-to-die life insurance policy that would pass free of estate tax to the children.

### Disadvantages

1. The CRUT generates a smaller income-tax deduction than the CRAT, as a result of the greater income potential to you.
2. Your current income-tax deduction will be limited to 20 percent of your annual adjusted gross income. In addition, gifts of appreciated property will potentially impact your alternative minimum taxable income during the year of the contribution.

**RECOMMENDATION:** Once the stock-transfer restrictions have been lifted, you should create a CRUT and begin making transfers of stock to the trust during your lifetime.

## Irrevocable Life Insurance Trust

Life insurance is an illusory asset within an estate plan...

**RECOMMENDATION:** An irrevocable life insurance trust should be created to purchase enough second-to-die coverage to transfer all or a portion of your projected estate-tax liability to the insurance carrier.

## Family Limited Partnership

Father is interested in purchasing commercial real estate for investment purposes. If these activities are carried on in Father's name personally, they will cause a significant increase in his estate as the properties appreciate in value. Father would like to retain control over this activity but avoid the estate taxes that may be due as a result.

**RECOMMENDATION:** Father could create a family limited partnership for the purpose of engaging in his real-estate investment activities. Father's interest could be held either by him personally or in the form of a corporation in order to further provide insulation from liability. The children could invest the funds that they currently maintain in cash and marketable securities in exchange for limited partnership interests. Father and Mother may also wish to utilize some of their liquid assets by purchasing limited partnership units. These limited partnership units could be transferred to other members of Father's family (three nonbusiness children) by gift at a later date.

### Advantages

1. A family limited partnership allows Father and Mother to retain control over the investment activities while at the same time utilizing *their* family assets for investment purposes.
2. The family limited partnership vehicle allows the family to insulate itself from liabilities that might arise from the ownership of commercial real estate.
3. The limited partnership units are transferred more easily than an interest in a trust.
4. The income-tax rules available to partnerships holding real estate continue to be more favorable than the income rules available to S corporations and C corporations.

### Disadvantages

1. Although short-sighted, some people view the creation of one more entity or one more tax return as an unnecessary complication or expense.

## ■ EXAMPLE #7

*Distinctive facts:* Father (72) still works in the business half days about six months (the warm months) a year. Son #1 (46) runs the business; his sister (48), child #1, has never been in the business. A Chicago suburban business.

### TRANSFER ISSUES

#### Valuation

Father (72) would like his estate to be distributed to his children equally. It was agreed by all of the family members that even though Son #1 is the only family member currently involved in the business, thus responsible for its growth or shrinkage, the time for valuing all of the assets for the purposes of the division would be deferred until the death of the survivor of Father and Mother. As a result of this reluctance to currently divide the assets, it was decided to continue to make gifts of nonvoting common stock with a value of $20,000 per year per child.

**COMMENT:** Father, based on our experience, made an unusual decision. Normally, Father, after turning the business reins over to one of his children, allows that child to benefit from future success and growth or suffer the detriment of a business reversal.

### GENERATION-SKIPPING TRANSFERS

We additionally discussed whether gifts should be made to the grandchildren in order to utilize all the annual exclusions available to John, Sr. and Pauline.

#### Overview

Each time property changes hands, from one generation to the next, either the gift tax or estate tax is imposed.

One of the goals of effective estate planning is to minimize the amount of transfer taxes that will be imposed upon a family. One way to minimize the total amount of tax upon all generations of one family is to limit the number of times it could be imposed. In other words, limit the number of "transfers."

Historically, one method by which people have limited the number of transfers was by creating "generation-skipping" trusts. Property would be transferred into a trust for the benefit of future multiple generations. The first generation, your children, would have the right to receive the income from the trust property. In addition, the trustee may be able to make other distributions which are necessary to provide for the health, support and welfare of the child and his/her dependents. In theory, if the child does not have control over the trust but only possesses limited rights for life (i.e., "a life estate"), then the property is not taxed as a transfer upon the termination of the child's life estate. If multiple successive life estates are strung together, property may skip from generation to generation without any transfer tax being imposed.

This may be an attractive option for the benefit of those children who themselves will have significant wealth and significant estate tax exposure of their own, such as Child #1 and Son #1.

The Tax Reform Act of 1986 attempts to diffuse the effectiveness of the generation-skipping trust with the imposition of the "Generation-Skipping Tax" (GST). The GST is imposed at the highest federal estate-tax rate of 55 percent on the value of any property transferred as a result of a "direct skip," a "taxable termination" or a "taxable distribution." The net effect of the preceding terms is to block multiple, successive transfers. However, GST rules do provide two significant exclusions:

a. Annual gifts under $10,000 are exempt from both the gift tax and the GST; and

b. Each person is granted an exemption for up to $1,000,000 of transfers, which are subject to estate or gift tax, but exempt from GST.

**RECOMMENDATION:** It was agreed that the gifts made to the grandchildren should not be in the form of either stock or spendable assets. In order to sufficiently restrict any stock of the corporation, transfers would need to be made in trust. It was generally agreed that the trusts and the distributions of income by the S corporation, via the trust to the individuals in order to pay tax on the S corporation income would be difficult to manage on an ongoing basis. In order to keep the gifting process simple, it was generally agreed that the parties should limit gifts to the grandchildren to assets other than stock of Co. #1. (except as noted in item 3 under "Buy-Sell Agreement").

## ■ EXAMPLE #8

*Distinctive facts:* This is a disaster looking for a place to happen. Son #1 (who hired us) runs the business with Son #2. Child #2 (inactive) and Father (retired) round out the family. Each of the children owns 30 percent of the stock of Co. #1; Father owns 10 percent.

These people believe in insurance. Son has a $2-million policy on his life. Co. #1 owns $6.1 million in insurance on each of the children, which funds their buy-sell agreement, and it also owns $1.3 million on Father (not subject to any kind of an agreement).

The following contains excerpts from a preliminary report. A Southern Illinois business.

[On Blackman Kallick letterhead]
Dear Son #1:

...we are...waiting for new policy runs from your insurance man before we can complete our analysis...

Typically, we do not issue a written report until our analysis is complete. However, in order to address your concerns..., we are issuing this limited report.

### Irrevocable Life Insurance Trust

You currently have an irrevocable life insurance trust dated July 17, 199_ that holds a $2-million second-to-die life insurance policy. This policy was acquired in order to assist your estate in paying any estate taxes due upon your death.

This trust was incorrectly drafted. Article II, Paragraph A of the trust currently *requires* the trustee to use the insurance proceeds to "pay any estate-tax obligation which may arise by reason of the death of the second of us to die." This language will result in the proceeds of this trust being included in your taxable estate. Assuming you are in a 55 percent estate-tax bracket, the $2 million of life insurance will be subject to $1.1 million of additional tax. As a result, only $900,000 of net proceeds will be available to pay death taxes.

You can exclude the full proceeds of an irrevocable life insurance trust from your taxable estate with a properly worded trust document. The trust document should not "require" or allow the trustee to directly pay estate taxes for you or your spouse. Rather, the trustee should be permitted to lend assets of the irrevocable trust to your executor - an arm's-length loan. As an alternative, the trustee of the irrevocable trust could be permitted to purchase assets from your taxable estate, thus substituting the insurance proceeds for an otherwise illiquid asset. Cash which has been acquired either through a loan arrangement or a purchase could then be available to your executor for the purpose of paying your estate taxes.

By permitting your insurance proceeds to be used on an indirect basis for the payment of estate taxes, you will save $1.1 million. This insurance arrangement should be restructured at your earliest opportunity.

## Buy-Sell Agreement

Your current buy-sell agreement is structured as a "stock redemption" rather than a "cross-purchase" arrangement. Under a stock redemption arrangement, the corporation is obligated to purchase and thus retire the shares of a departing shareholder. You have currently provided for such purchase by purchasing life insurance on each of the key shareholders. The corporation currently maintains over $6 million of life insurance on the lives of its three key shareholders for the purpose of meeting this obligation upon death.

The purchase price called for in the agreement is the book value adjusted for the fair-market value of the real estate and inventory, discounted by 25 percent. In the event of death, the purchase price shall be the greater of the adjusted book value or the life insurance proceeds. This could easily result in unnecessary income tax being due by the estate of the deceased shareholder.

For example, assume that the adjusted book value of the corporation is $18 million. Each shareholder's one-third interest in the corporation would thus be worth $6 million. This amount would then be discounted by 25 percent, resulting in an individual adjusted book value of $4.5 million. Of the life insurance proceeds, 90 percent would be equal to roughly $5.49 million for each shareholder. The insurance proceeds exceed the adjusted book value by $990,000. This amount would be subject to capital-gains tax and Illinois income tax that would result in over $330,000 of income taxes.

This entire income tax could be avoided by eliminating the differential based upon life-insurance proceeds, or by lowering the amount of life insurance coverage. In no case should the 90 percent of life insurance coverage exceed the discounted, adjusted book value of each shareholder's holdings of the corporation.

Life insurance proceeds in excess of the purchase price held inside of the corporation do not create income which may be withdrawn from the corporation as part of its accumulated adjustments account. In addition, life-insurance proceeds utilized for the stock-purchase redemption of a deceased shareholder will not create income-tax basis for the remaining shareholders if structured as part of a stock-redemption agreement.

The shareholders would have the benefit of both tax-free cash and S-corporation stock basis, if the buy-sell agreement were restructured as a cross-purchase agreement rather than a stock- redemption agreement. A cross-purchase agreement would provide that the remaining shareholders, rather than the corporation, would be the purchasers of the decedent's stock. This could be accomplished through an escrow arrangement, whereby the life insurance on each of the shareholders would be held by an escrow trustee rather than by the S corporation.

Upon the death of any individual shareholder, the life-insurance proceeds would be utilized by the escrow trustee to buy the deceased shareholder's stock. The escrow trustee would then contribute its acquired stock to the remaining shareholders. As a result, the remaining shareholders would receive not only cash in excess of the purchase price but also new shares with an adjusted basis equal to the full purchase price.

### Dad's Life Insurance

The corporation currently owns $1.3 million of life insurance on the life of Father. The proceeds of this life-insurance policy will currently add to the corporation's value upon his death. An attempt should be made to remove the proceeds of this life insurance from the corporation tax-free, thus reducing the value of the corporation and any estate taxes that may be attributable to such life insurance upon the death of either Father or any of the shareholders.

The family should consider transferring the life-insurance policies to an irrevocable life insurance trust that will provide for generation-skipping tax in favor of Father's children and grandchildren. As an alternative, a death-benefit agreement could be structured with the company that would require the corporation to pay a death benefit to a trust for the benefit of Father's children and grandchildren. Death-benefit-only agreements have been held by the courts to be exempt from estate taxation...

**COMMENT:** It is amazing how often life insurance is just not handled "right" in an estate plan. Fortunately, few are as bad as this example. But yes, it is rare that the life insurance of a closely held business owner does not have something wrong, or put another way, something that can be changed that will save thousands or millions of dollars (as in this case).

## ■ EXAMPLE #9

*Distinctive facts:* Two common errors are: (1) taking an officer's bonus at the tail-end of the year to clear profits out of a C corporation, and (2) having the corporation buy new equipment when the correct thing to do taxwise is to have the assets purchased outside of the corporation and leased to the corporation. An Indiana business.

### Avoiding Issues of Unreasonable Compensation

Father's salary has periodically fluctuated along with the corporation's cash flow (ability to pay). As a result, he has historically taken a large bonus at the end of the year in order to avoid putting strains on the company's cash flow.

**RECOMMENDATION:** A statement should be inserted in the corporate minute book authorizing Father to draw a salary of approximately $4,000 per week. In addition, the minutes should state that due to cash-flow requirements, if he chooses to draw any amount less than $4,000 during any weekly pay period, then this amount may be made up during the same fiscal year or any subsequent fiscal year in which cash-flow availability improves. The inclusion of such a statement in the minute book on a prospective basis would greatly aid in avoiding issues involving unreasonable compensation.

Although Father does not intend to retire in the near future, he is concerned that he and his wife should have a stream of income for as long as they live. The corporation does not have any employee-benefit plans in place for any of its employees.

**RECOMMENDATION:** In order to alleviate this concern, the corporation should enter into a nonqualified deferred-compensation arrangement with Father. This agreement would provide a guarantee of income to Father on salary continuation basis should he become disabled. The deferred-compensation agreement should also provide an inducement for Father to continue his employment until age 65 or later, by offering to pay continuing compensation to him (and Mother if Father should die) at a reduced rate after age 65.

**NOTE:** The creation of this deferred-compensation arrangement will result in a new liability upon the books of Co. #1 and may affect the value of the corporation in the future as Father approaches age 65.

### Creating Alternate Streams of Income—Equipment Leasing

Father expressed a desire to buy a new piece of equipment, which when installed would cost approximately $475,000. He believes that the addition of this equipment will increase his sales by approximately 10 percent.

**RECOMMENDATION:** Rather than buying this equipment inside of Co. #1, Father should consider financing and purchasing the equipment personally. The equipment could be leased to the company at a rate which would satisfy his debt obligation. As the debt obligation is paid off, the asset would continue to generate a stream of income to Father and Mother (via rents) that would be independent of the time necessary to justify a continuing salary from Co. #1. NOTE:...Father's ownership of this equipment outside of the corporation will be eligible for raised-basis benefits, and it will create a nonbusiness asset that may be left to his nonbusiness children subject to a long-term lease that would preclude their interference with the operation of the business. Also, rent is one way of getting money out of the corporation that is not subject to Social Security Tax.

## ■ EXAMPLE #10

*Distinctive facts:* Following is the first *junk-money* proposal prepared for me by an insurance consultant. My client, Ralph Client (78), sold his business many years ago and is retired. His wife, Miriam, is 76. Ralph was earning five percent after tax on his $1 million of junk money. A Florida client.

### SUMMARY

| | Income During Life | | To Children After Second Death |
|---|---|---|---|
| | Ralph* | Miriam** | |
| Proposed plan | $60,000 | $ 40,000 | $800,000 |
| Present plan | 50,000 | 50,000 | 500,000 |
| Increase (Decrease) | $10,000 | $(10,000) | $300,000 |

*For as long as Ralph lives.
**For as long as Miriam lives if Ralph dies first.
Prepared for Irving Blackman by F.H. Stitt, CLU

ANALYSIS OF MARGINAL v $1,000,000 OF ESTATE UTILITY OF INCOME AND ASSETS TO CHILDREN

**PRESENT PLAN**

**INCOME**

$1,000,000 at 5% after tax = $50,000/year

**ASSETS TO CHILDREN**

$1,000,000 in Taxable Estate
Marginal Tax Rate for amounts in excess of $2,500,000 - 50%
Assumed Estate Tax - $500,000
Net Assets to Children - $500,000

**PROPOSED PLAN**

**INCOME**

$600,000 Single Premium Joint and Survivor Annuity provides $60,000/year after tax (at 35%) as long as Mr. Client lives
and $40,000/year after tax as long as Mrs. Client survives Mr. Client.

**ASSETS TO CHILDREN**

$400,000, gift to Irrevocable
Trust, and used as a One-Time Premium provides $1,000,000 of initial life insurance, varying in amount and payable at the second to die of Mr. and Mrs. Client.

If the second death occurs in 12 years:

| | |
|---|---|
| Assumed Estate Tax (50% of gift) | $200,000 |
| Net Assets of Children | $800,000 |

■ **EXAMPLE #11**

*Distinctive facts:* My client, Richard (79), still works part-time in the business, is single, and has $1,250,000 in a qualified pension plan. Following are excerpts from a proposal, prepared by an insurance consultant, that tells the rest of the story and how to whip the IRD monster. An Illinois client.

**THIS LEADS TO SOME INTERESTING TAX-SAVING SITUATIONS**

Let us illustrate:

A. Estate of Richard (Single, Age 79)

Present Estate:

| | |
|---|---|
| 1. Residence | $ 350,000 |
| 2. Florida residence | 250,000 |
| 3. Business | 2,000,000 |
| 4. Cash | 200,000 |

| | |
|---|---|
| 5. Pension | 1,250,000 |
| 6. TE Bonds | 400,000 |
| 7. Insurance | 100,000 |
| 8. HHF | 240,000 |
| 9. Miscellaneous | 50,000 |
| Total Estate | $4,840,000 |

B. Estate Tax $2,110,000 with IRD

| | | |
|---|---|---|
| $4,840,000 | | |
| (3,000,000) | = | $1,290,800 |
| $1,840,000 x 55% | = | 1,012,000 |
| 1. Total | | $2,302,800 |
| 2. Less Credit | | 192,800 |
| 3. Net Estate Tax | | $2,110,000 |

C. Estate tax $1,422,500 without IRD

| | | |
|---|---|---|
| 1. Gross Estate | | $4,840,000 |
| 2. Less IRD Pension | | 1,250,000 |
| 3. Net Estate | | 3,590,000 |
| $3,590,000 | | |
| 4. (3,000,000) | = | $1,290,800 |
| 5. $590,000 x 55% | = | 324,500 |
| 6. Total | | 1,615,300 |
| 7. Less Credit | | 192,800 |
| 8. Net Estate Tax | | $1,422,500 |

D.

| | |
|---|---|
| 1. IRD Estate Tax | $2,110,000 |
| 2. Without IRD Estate Tax | (1,422,500) |
| 3. Difference | $687,500 |

**NOTE:** This becomes an income-tax deduction for the Estate.

E. The income taxes on IRD are:
31% (Federal) + 3% (State); 34% of IRD = $425,000

F. 1. However let us assume that Richard took his pension account as a lifetime annuity of $15,505 per month or $186,609 per year. What would have been his situation?

2. Answer - the pension is not in his estate for estate-tax purposes*and* his family would save $687,500 in estate taxes.

3. Let us assume he bought, at the same time, a life insurance policy of *$1,250,000* at an annual premium of $115,961, *for 10 years* in a trust outside his estate. He would have given his children $1,250,000 outside his estate and not taxed.

**NOTE:**: This could be achieved by three children and 10 grandchildren equals 13 gifts of $10,000 per year, or $130,000, with no gift-tax problems.

4. Richard would now have:
   a. Annuity Income $186,069
   b. Less Income Tax 57,681
   c. Net $128,388
   d. Less:
      (1) Insurance (10-pay) $115,961 or (2) Universal life (pay for life) $79,764
   e. Leaves spending money of $12,427 or $48,624
5. Thus, Richard can:
   a. Avoid IRD
   b. Avoid estate taxes
   c. Pass his entire pension to his children without tax
   d. All on a guaranteed basis
   e. Avoid some probate costs
   f. Have some "fun" money left over
6. This report does not cover excise taxes of excess distribution. That calculation is:

| | | |
|---|---|---|
| a. | 1992 Grandfathered Benefit Limit | ($140,276) |
| b. | Annuity | 186,069 |
| c. | Difference | $45,793 |
| d. | Subject to excise tax of | 15% |
| e. | Additional excise tax paid | $6,868 |

7. Thus, on a universal life basis, Richard would:

| | | |
|---|---|---|
| a. | Receive annuity | $186,069 |
| b. | Less insurance | ($79,764) |
| c. | Less income tax | ($57,681) |
| d. | Less excise tax | ($6,868) |
| e. | "Fun Money left" | $41,756 |

Presented by: Ralph J. Wood, Jr.

# Appendix

To me the appendix always means *odds 'n ends*. Stuff that did not fit elsewhere. This appendix contains special odds 'n ends—items that others (business owners and their advisors) on a rather regular/irregular basis ask me, such as, "Irv, where can I find...?" or "What is..." or the like. My bet is that if you do even one transfer/succession/estate plan, you'll use this appendix; do more and it will become an old friend.

## Contents

**SUMMARY OF TAX DIFFERENCES BETWEEN PARTNERSHIPS, C CORPORATIONS, S CORPORATIONS AND SOLE PROPRIETORSHIPS***

| Points to Consider | S Corporations | C Corporations | Partnerships | Sole Proprietorship |
|---|---|---|---|---|
| Transfers of Interest | Readily and easily marketable by transfer of certificate of stock. Sales of shares of partnership, corporation, certain trusts, or non-resident alien terminates election. Buy-sell agreement may prevent. | Same as S corporation with no restriction on eligibility to own shares.Part V, chapter 3, table #3 | Addition of new partners or transfer of partner's interest often requires consent of other partners. Special restrictions apply to publicly traded partnerships. | No restrictions. |
| Non-Loan Capital Sources | Sale of only one class of stock to no more than 35 eligible shareholders. Differences in voting rights permitted. | Sale of multiple classes of stock or other securities to unlimited number of individuals, corporations, or partnerships. | Contribution by general or limited partners with unlimited number of partners permitted. | Contributions by proprietor only. |
| Ownership Limitations | 35 shareholder limit and generally limited to U.S. Citizens and qualified trusts. | No limit on number of class of shareholders. | No limit on number of partners. Special restrictions apply to publicly traded partnerships. | No limit. |
| Liability Exposure | Except in rare circumstances, shareholders are only liable for capital contributions. | Except in rare circumstances, shareholders are only liable for capital contributions. | General partners are personally, jointly and severally liable for partnership obligations. Limited partners liable for capital contributions only. | Proprietor is personally, jointly, and severally liable for everything. |

| Points to Consider | S Corporations | C Corporations | Partnerships | Sole Proprietorship |
|---|---|---|---|---|
| Treatment of Income and Loss | Corporate income determined at entity level and passed through to each shareholder and taxed at individual rates. S corporation's with prior year C corporation E & P may pay tax on certain capital gains, "built-in gains," and "excess net passive income." Income and loss items that affect a shareholders's tax liability are separately stated - e.g., charitable contributions, depletion. | All corporate income taxed at corporate level and again taxed at shareholder level when distributed as dividends. Some C corporations taxed as personal holding companies can be taxed on excess accumulated income. | Same as S corporation, except no partnership capital gains tax on "built-in gains," or tax on passive income. | No tax at entity level but proprietor pays tax at individual rates. |
| Net Operating Losses | Losses pass through to shareholders and are deductible to the extent of their stock and debt basis. Losses suspended until basis created. | Deductible only by the corporation in a year in which it has offsetting income. Losses may be carried back or forward. | Similar passthrough rules as S corporation. | Losses pass through to proprietor and are deductible. |
| Tax-Exempt Income | Tax-exempt income of corporation retains its character when passed through to the shareholders. It increases shareholders' stock bases. | Tax-exempt income increases corporate earnings and profits and it not taxed at corporate level. If distributed to shareholders as dividends, it is subject to tax. | Same passthrough rule as S corporation. | No effect on entity. Taxed at proprietor level. |

| Points to Consider | S Corporations | C Corporations | Partnerships | Sole Proprietorship |
|---|---|---|---|---|
| Capital Gains | Capital and IRC Section 1231 gains pass through to shareholders and retain their character at shareholder level. Rules for taxing S corporations on capital gains depend on whether S corporation election was made after 1986 or before 1987. | Capital and IRC Section 1231 gains taxed at regular corporate rate or a maximum rate of 34%. | Same rule as S corporation. | No effect on entity. Taxed at proprietor level. |
| Capital Losses | Capital losses pass through to shareholders and retain their character at the shareholder level. Losses offset capital gains and then up to $3,000 of ordinary income. May be carried forward indefinitely. | Capital losses deducted at corporate level only to the extent of capital gains. Losses may be carried back 3 years or forward 5 years. | Same rule as S corporation. | No effect on entity. Taxed at proprietor level. |
| Loan Collateralization | Shares may be used as collateral. | Shares may be used as collateral. | Partnership interests cannot serve as loan collateral. | Interest cannot serve as loan collateral. |
| Ownership/Management Responsibility | No requirement for shareholder participation in management. | No requirement for shareholder participation in management. | All general partners participate in management and share joint responsibility. Limited partners do not participate in management. | Proprietor has management responsibility. |

| Points to Consider | S Corporations | C Corporations | Partnerships | Sole Proprietorship |
|---|---|---|---|---|
| Tax Year | S corporation generally must use a calendar year unless business purpose shown for a fiscal year. S corporations can elect to use a tax year other than a required year if they follow the procedure established under IRS Sections 444 and 7519. Under those procedures, electing S corporations are required to make payments ("required payments") to the federal government that are intended to represent the value of the tax deferral obtained by the shareholders through the use of a tax year different from the required tax year. | Calendar or fiscal year permitted. Tax year does not have to match shareholders' tax years. | Must generally use same tax year as majority-interest partners (principal partners if majority partners don't have same tax year; or year resulting in least income deferral if principal partners don't have same tax year) unless business purpose shown for a different tax year. Partnership can elect to use a tax year other than a required year if they follow the procedures established under IRS Sections 444 and 7519. Under those procedures, electing partnerships are required to make payments ("required payments") to the federal government that are intended to represent the value of the tax deferral obtained by the partners through the use of a tax year different from the required tax year. | Tax year must match the proprietor's year end. |
| Federal Tax Return | Form 1120-S, Information return. May have to file estimated tax return. | Form 1120, Corporate income tax return. Usually file estimated tax returns. | Form 1065, Information return. | Schedule C along with Form 1040. |

| Points to Consider | S Corporations | C Corporations | Partnerships | Sole Proprietorship |
|---|---|---|---|---|
| Alternative Minimum Tax | Applies only at shareholder level. No ACE adjustments. | Applies at corporate level. ACE adjustments apply. | Applies only at partner level. No ACE adjustment. | Applies only at proprietor level. No ACE adjustment. |
| Liquidation of Business | No tax at corporate level (except for built-in gains). | "Double tax" on corporate and shareholder levels. | No tax at partnership level. | No tax at entity level but proprietor pays tax on liquidation. |
| Redemption of Ownership Interest | Taxable to the extent proceeds exceed basis of ownership interest. Corporate level gain recognized on in-kinds distribution. | Taxable to the extent proceeds exceed basis of ownership interest. Double tax occurs on in-kind distributions of appreciated property. | Partially deductible to partnership. No tax at partnership level. | Same as liquidation of business. |
| Accumulated Earnings | All income is passed through and taxed at shareholder level. S corporations with carryover C corporation earnings and profits are subject to corporate tax on excess passive income and distributions of accumulated earnings and profits taxed as dividend income. | Corporations may accumulate income for reasonable business needs. Up to $150,000 for personal service corporations and $250,000 for other C corporations may be accumulated without question. Unreasonable accumulation subject to tax. | All income taxed to partners whether distributed or not. | All income taxed to proprietor whether distributed or not. |

| Points to Consider | S Corporations | C Corporations | Partnerships | Sole Proprietorship |
|---|---|---|---|---|
| Distributions and Income allocations | Distributions are taxed to the extent they exceed a shareholder's basis in income. Corporation recognizes gain on distribution of appreciated property. Income may only be allocated in proportion to shareholdings. | Distributions taxed as ordinary income and allocated on basis of shareholders. C corporation will generally recognize gain on sale of distribution of appreciated property. | Distributions taxed to the extent they exceed partner's basis in investment and share of partnership liabilities. Distributive income shares may be allocated by agreement of the partners if they have substantial economic effect. Partnership does not recognize gain on distribution of appreciated property. | No effect on entity or proprietor. |
| Fringe Benefits | Owner of more than 2% of S corporation shares cannot receive tax-free certain fringe benefits including, employer-provided health care, meals and lodging and life insurance. | Shareholder-employees may receive tax qualified fringe benefits without restrictions. | All partners not eligible for tax-free fringes. | Proprietor not eligible for tax-free fringes. |
| Retirement Plans | Although generally the same rules and limitations apply to S corporations as to C corporations, an S corporation can't have a retirement plan that holds its own stock in trust for employees and loans to shareholders are prohibited. | C corporation can provide a broad variety of defined benefit and defined-contribution plans, including those involving the corporation's own stock. | Keogh plans are generally subject to the same limits on contributions and benefits that apply to qualified corporate retirement plans, but Keogh plans can't involve employer stock since there isn't any. | Keogh plans and simplified employee pensions are generally subject to the same contributions and benefits that apply to C corporation plans. |
| Loans From Retirement Plans | Prohibited transaction. | Loans permitted, within limits. | Same as S corporations. | Not permitted. |

| Points to Consider | S Corporations | C Corporations | Partnerships | Sole Proprietorship |
|---|---|---|---|---|
| Investment Interest Deduction | Shareholder deducts his share of the S corporation's investment interest to the extent of his net investment income limitation. No transferability. | No limitation. | Partner may deduct his share of partnership's interest up to the extent of his net investment income limitation. | Proprietor may deduct interest expense up to the extent of his net investment income limitation. |
| FICA Taxes | Tax payable by the corporation and the employees. | Tax payable by the corporation and the employees. | Self-employment tax applies to salary and income from reimbursement. | Self-employment tax applies to salary and income from proprietorship. |
| FUTA and SUTA Taxes | Tax payable by the corporation. | Tax payable by the corporation. | Not applicable to the partners. | No applicable to the proprietor. |
| Investment Income | If investment income exceeds 25 percent of gross receipts and the S corporation has accumulated earnings and profits from C corporation years, an additional passive income tax may apply. | If investment income exceeds 60 percent of gross receipts, the company may be subject to the personal holding company tax. | No restrictions. | No restrictions. |
| Tax Free Receipt of $5,000 Death Benefit | Generally available. | Generally available. | Limited to distributions from retirement plans. | Limited to distributions from retirement plans. |
| Family Tax Planning | Ability to allocate income to lower bracket taxpayers. Ability to transfer value from parents estate to childrens through gifts of stock. | Ability to transfer value from parents estate to childrens through gifts of stock. | Ability to allocate income to lower bracket taxpayers. Ability to transfer value from parents estate to childrens through gifts of partnership interests. | No transferability. |

| Points to Consider | S Corporations | C Corporations | Partnerships | Sole Proprietorship |
|---|---|---|---|---|
| Worthlessness of Investment | Opportunity of ordinary loss if stock is 1244 stock. If not, then capital loss. | Opportunity of ordinary loss if stock is 1244 stock. If not, then capital loss. | Capital loss only on investment. | Depending upon how loss is characterized, could be ordinary or capital loss. |

*Prepared by:
Greg Andresen - Tax Partner
Gary Landau - Audit Partner
Bud Eichner - Director
Blackman Kallick Bartelstein

## HOW ESTATE TAX IS CALCULATED

**TOTAL FAIR MARKET VALUE OF ALL ASSETS**

**—MINUS—**

**DEBTS AND CERTAIN ESTATE EXPENSES, CHARITABLE BEQUESTS, AND BEQUEST TO SURVIVING SPOUSE**

**—EQUALS—**

**TAXABLE ESTATE X ESTATE TAX RATE(S)**

**—EQUALS—**

**GROSS ESTATE TAX - UNIFIED CREDIT***

**—EQUALS—**

**TAX DUE**

Calculations are based on the information in the following chart:

| Taxable Estate | Gross Tax | Less: Unified Credit | Tax Due | Rate On Next $1 of Estate |
|---|---|---|---|---|
| $ 600,000 | $ 192,800 | $(192,800) | -0- | 37% |
| 1,000,000 | 345,800 | (192,800) | $ 153,000 | 41 |
| 1,500,000 | 555,800 | (192,800) | 363,000 | 45 |
| 2,000,000 | 780,800 | (192,800) | 588,000 | 49 |
| 2,500,000 | 1,025,000 | (192,800) | 833,000 | 50 |
| 3,000,000 | 1,290,800 | (192,800) | 1,098,000 | 55 |
| 10,000,000 | 5,140,800 | (192,800) | 4,948,000 | 60 |
| 21,040,000 | 11,764,800 | (192,800) | 11,572,000 | 55 |

*Unified Credit = $192,800, the tax on $600,000 of assets.

■ **NOTE:** The above rates are for years before 1993. After 1992, the top rate is scheduled to be 50 percent. (But I have a sneaking suspicion that Congress may extend the old rates.)

The benefits of the graduated rates and the unified credit are phased out for estates over $10,000,000, but not over $21,040,000. After 1992, substitute $18,340,000 for the $21,040,000.

**P.S. 58 TABLE**

| Age | Rate | Age | Rate | Age | Rate |
|---|---|---|---|---|---|
| 15 | $1.27 | 37 | $3.63 | 59 | $19.08 |
| 16 | 1.38 | 38 | 3.87 | 60 | 20.73 |
| 17 | 1.48 | 39 | 4.14 | 61 | 22.53 |
| 18 | 1.52 | 40 | 4.42 | 62 | 24.50 |
| 19 | 1.56 | 41 | 4.73 | 63 | 26.63 |
| 20 | 1.61 | 42 | 5.07 | 64 | 28.98 |
| 21 | 1.67 | 43 | 5.44 | 65 | 31.51 |
| 22 | 1.73 | 44 | 5.85 | 66 | 34.28 |
| 23 | 1.79 | 45 | 6.30 | 67 | 37.31 |
| 24 | 1.86 | 46 | 6.78 | 68 | 40.59 |
| 25 | 1.93 | 47 | 7.32 | 69 | 44.17 |
| 26 | 2.02 | 48 | 7.89 | 70 | 48.06 |
| 27 | 2.11 | 49 | 8.53 | 71 | 52.29 |
| 28 | 2.20 | 50 | 9.22 | 72 | 56.89 |
| 29 | 2.31 | 51 | 9.97 | 73 | 61.89 |
| 30 | 2.43 | 52 | 10.79 | 74 | 67.33 |
| 31 | 2.57 | 53 | 11.69 | 75 | 73.23 |
| 32 | 2.70 | 54 | 12.67 | 76 | 79.63 |
| 33 | 2.86 | 55 | 13.74 | 77 | 86.57 |
| 34 | 3.02 | 56 | 14.91 | 78 | 94.09 |
| 35 | 3.21 | 57 | 16.18 | 79 | 102.23 |
| 36 | 3.41 | 58 | 17.56 | 80 | 111.04 |
| | | | | 81 | 120.57 |

■ **NOTE:** These rates are rates per $1,000 for each stated age. See Chapter Three, Part V for an explanation of P.S. 58 costs and how to use this table and the table on the next page.

**TABLE OF ONE-YEAR TERM RATES FOR COST OF INSURANCE**

| Age | Male | Sex-Neutral | Female | Age | Male | Sex-Neutral | Female |
|---|---|---|---|---|---|---|---|
| 0 | 2.28 | 2.28 | 2.04 | 48 | 1.32 | 1.26 | .95 |
| 1 | .84 | .84 | .72 | 49 | 1.46 | 1.39 | 1.04 |
| 2 | .84 | .84 | .72 | 50 | 1.61 | 1.53 | 1.15 |
| 3 | .84 | .84 | .72 | 51 | 1.76 | 1.68 | 1.26 |
| 4 | .84 | .84 | .72 | 52 | 1.92 | 1.83 | 1.37 |
| 5 | .84 | .84 | .72 | 53 | 2.09 | 1.99 | 1.49 |
| 6 | .84 | .84 | .72 | 54 | 2.26 | 2.15 | 1.61 |
| 7 | .84 | .84 | .72 | 55 | 2.44 | 2.32 | 1.74 |
| 8 | .84 | .84 | .72 | 56 | 2.63 | 2.50 | 1.88 |
| 9 | .84 | .84 | .72 | 57 | 2.81 | 2.68 | 2.01 |
| 10 | .84 | .84 | .72 | 58 | 3.01 | 2.87 | 2.15 |
| 11 | .84 | .84 | .72 | 59 | 3.21 | 3.06 | 2.30 |
| 12 | .84 | .84 | .72 | 60 | 3.42 | 3.26 | 2.45 |
| 13 | .84 | .84 | .72 | 61 | 3.64 | 3.47 | 2.60 |
| 14 | .84 | .84 | .72 | 62 | 3.86 | 3.68 | 2.76 |
| 15 | .84 | .84 | .72 | 63 | 4.10 | 3.90 | 2.93 |
| 16 | .84 | .84 | .72 | 64 | 4.35 | 4.14 | 3.11 |
| 17 | .84 | .84 | .72 | 65 | 4.62 | 4.40 | 3.30 |
| 18 | .57 | .54 | .41 | 66 | 4.92 | 4.69 | 3.52 |
| 19 | .57 | .54 | .41 | 67 | 5.29 | 5.04 | 3.78 |
| 20 | .57 | .54 | .41 | 68 | 5.75 | 5.48 | 4.11 |
| 21 | .57 | .54 | .41 | 69 | 6.34 | 6.04 | 4.53 |
| 22 | .57 | .54 | .41 | 70 | 7.09 | 6.75 | 5.06 |
| 23 | .57 | .54 | .41 | 71 | 8.02 | 7.64 | 5.73 |
| 24 | .57 | .54 | .41 | 72 | 9.18 | 8.74 | 6.56 |
| 25 | .57 | .54 | .41 | 73 | 10.58 | 10.08 | 7.56 |
| 26 | .57 | .54 | .41 | 74 | 12.29 | 11.70 | 8.78 |
| 27 | .57 | .54 | .41 | 75 | 14.40 | 13.71 | 10.28 |
| 28 | .57 | .54 | .41 | 76 | 17.03 | 16.22 | 12.16 |
| 29 | .57 | .54 | .41 | 77 | 20.30 | 19.33 | 14.50 |
| 30 | .57 | .54 | .41 | 78 | 24.30 | 23.14 | 17.36 |
| 31 | .57 | .54 | .41 | 79 | 29.14 | 27.75 | 20.81 |
| 32 | .57 | .54 | .41 | 80 | 34.92 | 33.26 | 24.95 |
| 33 | .57 | .54 | .41 | 81 | 41.76 | 39.77 | 29.83 |
| 34 | .57 | .54 | .41 | 82 | 49.64 | 47.28 | 35.46 |
| 35 | .57 | .54 | .41 | 83 | 58.58 | 55.79 | 41.84 |
| 36 | .59 | .56 | .42 | 84 | 67.19 | 63.99 | 47.99 |
| 37 | .61 | .58 | .44 | 85 | 76.06 | 72.44 | 54.33 |
| 38 | .64 | .61 | .46 | 86 | 180.60 | 180.60 | 180.60 |
| 39 | .67 | .64 | .48 | 87 | 195.43 | 195.43 | 195.43 |

| Age | Male | Sex-Neutral | Female | Age | Male | Sex-Neutral | Female |
|---|---|---|---|---|---|---|---|
| 40 | .70 | .67 | .50 | 88 | 211.33 | 211.33 | 211.33 |
| 41 | .75 | .71 | .53 | 89 | 228.31 | 228.31 | 228.31 |
| 42 | .80 | .76 | .57 | 90 | 246.45 | 246.45 | 246.45 |
| 43 | .85 | .81 | .61 | 91 | 265.75 | 265.75 | 265.75 |
| 44 | .91 | .87 | .65 | 92 | 286.25 | 286.25 | 286.25 |
| 45 | 1.00 | .95 | .71 | 93 | 307.98 | 307.98 | 307.98 |
| 46 | 1.09 | 1.04 | .78 | 94 | 330.94 | 330.94 | 330.94 |
| 47 | 1.20 | 1.14 | .86 | 95 | 355.11 | 355.11 | 355.11 |

■ **NOTE:** Above are rates of a top-rated insurance company. See note on preceding table for how to use this table.

## CRUMMEY POWER BENEFITTING SPOUSE AND CHILDREN/HANGING POWERS

### ARTICLE III
### POWER OF WITHDRAWAL

**3.1 Right of Withdrawal.**

During the lifetime of the Grantor, the trust estate shall be held and disposed of as follows:

(a) The Grantor or any other person may make contributions to the trust at any time or times. For purposes of this agreement, the term "contribution" means any transfer of property to the trust for federal gift tax purposes, including property initially transferred to the trust or subsequently added thereto and payments of premiums on any insurance policy owned by the Trustee which are paid otherwise than by the Trustee. The amount of a contribution shall be its value for federal gift tax purposes.

(b) The Grantor's spouse and children who are living at the time of a contribution to the trust shall have the following rights to withdraw principal from the trust estate:

(i) The Grantor's spouse may withdraw property with a value equal to the first $5,000 of contributions made to the trust during any calendar year; and

(ii) Each child of the Grantor may withdraw from trust property an equal share of the value of the contribution which is not subject to withdrawal by the Grantor's spouse, except that a child may not withdraw more than $20,000 (or $10,000 if the Grantor is not then married) in the aggregate during any calendar year.

(c) By granting these withdrawal rights, the Grantor intends that contributions to the trust shall qualify for the federal gift tax annual exclusion as gifts of present interests.

(d) With respect to each contribution made to the trust during a calendar year:

(i) The Trustee shall notify each beneficiary of his or her withdrawal right with respect to the contribution. The Trustee may give notice after each contribution, once annually for all contributions made during the calendar year, or otherwise as the Trustee deems advisable, but in no event later than December 31 of the calendar year.

(ii) A beneficiary's withdrawal rights with respect to contributions to the trust shall continue from year to year until exercised, except that on December 31 of each year the beneficiary's aggregate withdrawal rights shall lapse as to the greater of $5,000 and 5% of the value of the trust estate, and except further that those withdrawal rights shall lapse upon the death of the beneficiary.

(e) A beneficiary may exercise a withdrawal right only by written request delivered to the Trustee. The Trustee shall make payment pursuant to a written request in cash to the extent practicable, otherwise from other trust property selected by the trustee, including policies of life insurance.

(f) Each payment to a child under this section shall be treated as an advancement and charged without interest against the share hereinafter provided for the child or his or her descendants.

The succeeding provisions of this agreement shall be subject to the terms of this section.

■ **NOTE:** The above was prepared by Stephen Margolin of Chuhak & Tecson, Chicago.

**CRUMMEY NOTICE**

November 6, 199_

Ms. Client [Beneficiary]
67 Money Street
Richtown, CA
Dear Client:

Pursuant to the terms of the MOTHER AND FATHER CLIENT IRREVOCABLE LIFE INSURANCE TRUST DATED APRIL 14, 199_ you have the right to withdraw a portion of the contributions made to the Trust during the current calendar year. In order to exercise such right, you must deliver a written request to the Trustee by December 31 of this year.

______________________________

Tommy Trustee, as Trustee
under the Father and Mother
Client Irrevocable Life
Insurance Trust dated April 14, 199_

Address of Trustee:

Mr. Tommy Trustee
1234 North Lincoln
Big City, PA 78901

■ **NOTE:** The above was prepared by Donald J. Russ, Jr. of Chuhak & Tecson, Chicago.

## LIFE EXPECTANCY TABLE IN YEARS

### 1980 COMMISIONERS STANDARD ORDINARY MORTALITY TABLE*

| Age | Male | Female | Age | Male | Female | Age | Male | Female |
|---|---|---|---|---|---|---|---|---|
| 0 | 70.83 | 75.83 | 34 | 39.54 | 43.91 | 67 | 12.76 | 15.83 |
| 1 | 70.13 | 75,04 | 35 | 38.61 | 42.98 | 68 | 12.14 | 15.10 |
| 2 | 69.20 | 74.11 | 36 | 37.69 | 42.05 | 69 | 11.54 | 14.38 |
| 3 | 68.27 | 73.17 | 37 | 36.78 | 41.12 | 70 | 10.96 | 13.67 |
| 4 | 67.34 | 72.23 | 38 | 35.87 | 40.20 | 71 | 10.39 | 12.97 |
| 5 | 66.40 | 71.28 | 39 | 34.96 | 39.28 | 72 | 9.84 | 12.26 |
| 6 | 65.46 | 70.34 | 40 | 34.05 | 38.36 | 73 | 9.30 | 11.60 |
| 7 | 64.52 | 69.39 | 41 | 33.16 | 37.46 | 74 | 8.79 | 10.95 |
| 8 | 63.57 | 68.44 | 42 | 32.26 | 36.55 | 75 | 8.31 | 10.32 |
| 9 | 62.62 | 67.48 | 43 | 31.38 | 35.66 | 76 | 7.84 | 9.71 |
| 10 | 61.66 | 66.53 | 44 | 30.50 | 34.77 | 77 | 7.40 | 9.12 |
| 11 | 60.77 | 65.58 | 45 | 29.62 | 33.88 | 78 | 6.97 | 8.55 |
| 12 | 59.75 | 64.62 | 46 | 28.76 | 33.00 | 79 | 6.57 | 8.01 |
| 13 | 58.80 | 63.67 | 47 | 27.90 | 32.12 | 80 | 6.18 | 7.48 |
| 14 | 57.86 | 62.71 | 48 | 27.04 | 31.25 | 81 | 5.80 | 6.98 |
| 15 | 56.93 | 61.76 | 49 | 26.20 | 30.39 | 82 | 5.44 | 6.49 |
| 16 | 56.00 | 60.82 | 50 | 25.36 | 29.53 | 83 | 5.09 | 6.03 |
| 17 | 55.09 | 59.87 | 51 | 24.52 | 28.67 | 84 | 4.77 | 5.59 |
| 18 | 54.18 | 58.93 | 52 | 23.70 | 27.82 | 85 | 4.46 | 5.18 |
| 19 | 53.27 | 57.98 | 53 | 22.89 | 26.98 | 86 | 4.18 | 4.80 |
| 20 | 52.37 | 57.04 | 54 | 22.08 | 26.14 | 87 | 3.91 | 4.43 |
| 21 | 51.47 | 56.10 | 55 | 21.29 | 25.31 | 88 | 3.66 | 4.09 |
| 22 | 50.57 | 55.16 | 56 | 20.51 | 24.49 | 89 | 3.41 | 3.77 |
| 23 | 49.66 | 54.22 | 57 | 19.74 | 23.67 | 90 | 3.18 | 3.45 |
| 24 | 48.75 | 53.28 | 58 | 18.99 | 22.86 | 91 | 2.94 | 3.15 |
| 25 | 47.84 | 52.34 | 59 | 18.24 | 22.05 | 92 | 2.70 | 2.85 |
| 26 | 46.93 | 51.40 | 60 | 17.51 | 21.25 | 93 | 2.44 | 2.55 |
| 27 | 46.01 | 50.46 | 61 | 16.79 | 20.44 | 94 | 2.17 | 2.24 |
| 28 | 45.09 | 49.52 | 62 | 16.08 | 19.65 | 95 | 1.87 | 1.91 |
| 29 | 44.16 | 48.59 | 63 | 15.38 | 18.86 | 96 | 1.54 | 1.56 |
| 30 | 43.24 | 47.65 | 64 | 14.70 | 18.08 | 97 | 1.20 | 1.21 |
| 31 | 42.31 | 46.71 | 65 | 14.04 | 17.32 | 98 | 0.84 | 0.84 |
| 32 | 41.38 | 45.78 | 66 | 13.39 | 16.57 | 99 | 0.50 | 0.50 |
| 33 | 40.46 | 44.84 | | | | | | |

*Table currently in use in life insurance industry

## DEATH BENEFIT AGREEMENT

THIS AGREEMENT is made this _ day of September, 199_, by and between J.O. Die & Stamping Co., Inc., a Montana corporation, hereinafter referred to as "the Company", and Joe Owner, hereinafter referred to as "the Employee".

**Recitals**

A. The Employee is currently employed by the Company and is considered to have made a valuable contribution to the Company over the past years, having discharged his employment duties in a capable and efficient manner which resulted in substantial profits to the Company.

B. The Employee is willing to remain in the employment of the Company until his retirement if the Company will agree to pay to his beneficiary designated below a death benefit in certain quarter-annual installments, all in accordance with the terms and conditions hereinafter set forth.

**Clauses**

In consideration of the mutual covenants and agreements set forth below, the parties agree as follows:

1. *Payment of Death Benefit*. The Company hereby agrees that it will pay to the person or persons hereinafter designated a death benefit on account of the death of the Employee in an amount equal to Two Hundred Fifty Thousand Dollars ($250,000.00). The said death benefit shall be payable without interest in eight (8) equal quarter-annual installments, commencing one hundred twenty (120) days following the date of the death of the Employee and continuing thereafter on the first business day of each succeeding calendar quarter until eight (8) installment payments have been made by the Company. The Company reserves the right to prepay one or more of the foregoing installments without penalty.
2. *Designation of Potential Recipients of Payments*. The aforesaid installments shall be paid by the Company to the Henrik Freitag Family Trust created pursuant to the Henrik Freitag Trust dated March 31, 1990.
3. *Employment*. The Employee agrees to remain in the employment of the Company until the earlier of his death, total disability or retirement at or after age sixty-five (65). In the event that the Employee, other than by reason of death or total disability, leaves the employment of the Company prior to his having attained age sixty-five (65), whether at the instance of the Company or himself, the obligation of the Company to pay the aforesaid death benefit shall forthwith be terminated and neither he nor the above designated recipients shall have any right whatsoever to demand or receive any of the payments for which provision is made herein. For the purposes hereof, the Employee shall be deemed to be totally disabled when, as a result of bodily injury or disease or mental disorder, he is so disabled that he is prevented from performing the principal duties of his employment and is under the regular care and attendance of a currently licensed physician or surgeon.
4. *Non-assignability*. It is agreed that neither the Employee, his legal representatives, nor his wife or descendants shall have any right to commute, sell, assign,

transfer or otherwise convey the right to receive any payments hereunder, which payments and the right thereto are expressly declared to be non-assignable and non-transferable, and in the event of any attempted assignment or transfer the Company shall have no further liability hereunder.

5. *Agreement May Not Be Rescinded or Amended.* During the lifetime of the Employee, this agreement shall not be amended, rescinded or revoked at any time in whole or in part by either party or both parties hereto.
6. *Notices.* All notices for which provision is made in this agreement shall be given in writing either by actual delivery of the notice into the hands of the party entitled to the notice or by mailing the notice by registered or certified mail, return receipt requested, in which case the notice shall be deemed to be given on the date of mailing. If a notice is mailed it shall be addressed as follows:
   a. If to the Company, to its then principal office.
   b. If to the Employee, to his then last known principal residence address. Any party hereto may change the address to which each such notice shall be so mailed by giving written notice to the other party hereto of such new address.
7. *Binding Effect.* This agreement shall be binding upon and inure to the benefit of the Company, its successors and assigns and the Employee, his heirs, personal representatives, and assigns.
8. *Applicable Law.* This agreement shall be subject to and governed by the law of the State of Illinois, irrespective of the fact that one or more of the parties now is or may become a resident of a different state.
9. *Arbitration.* Any dispute or controversy arising from or relating to this agreement shall be decided by an arbitrator in the City of Chicago by the American Arbitration Association, which decision shall be final and binding upon the parties and shall not be subject to judicial review.
10. *Descriptive Headings.* All paragraph headings, titles and subtitles contained herein are inserted for convenience of reference only and are to be ignored in any construction of the provisions hereof.

The Company has caused this agreement to be executed and the Employee has executed this agreement on the day and year first above written.

| | |
|---|---|
| (SEAL)<br>ATTEST: | J.O. Die & Stamping Co., Inc.,<br>a Montana corporation<br>By: |
| ____________________<br>Secretary | ____________________<br>President |
| | Employee: |
| | ____________________<br>Joe Owner |

## Deed of Gift

I've saved one of the best problem-solving ideas for last. Here's the problem. It happens every year. Around Christmas. The procrastinating gift-minded business owners come out of hibernation in droves. They want to make a gift of the stock of their closely held corporations, usually $10,000, $20,000 (the annual exclusion amounts depending on the owner's marital status) per donee, or some other specific dollar amount for various reasons. But what is the exact number of shares that should be gifted to equal the specific dollar amount desired? There simply is not enough time to value the business before December 31. What to do? Well, here's the answer. Use a deed of gift.

■ **CAUTION:** Always check with your attorney to make sure the deed of gift wording completes the gift under your local state law on the date of the deed. Then the valuation can be made after that date to determine the number of shares.

> Deed of Gift
>
> I, the undersigned, Father Owner, hereby give, assign and transfer to Son Owner (the "Donee") all of my right, title and interest in the following described property owned by the undersigned as follows:
>
> The largest number of whole shares of Success, Inc., a (your state) corporation, which as of the date of this Deed of Gift shall have a value which does not exceed the sum of one-sixth of the value of the Donor's and the Donor's spouse's exemption equivalent (for federal gift tax purposes) as of January 1, 199 _ plus $20,000 (the "Stock").
>
> In regard to the Stock, I hereby direct the transfer agent of the company in whose possession are all of my share certificates of Success, Inc. to accept this Deed of Gift as an Assignment Separate from Certificate for such shares and to transfer the appropriate number of shares. For purposes of reregistering the Certificate in the name of the Donee, the transfer agent is directed to reregister such shares based on the fair market value appraisal of the transfer of a minority interest in Success, Inc. as prepared by Blackman Kallick Bartelstein.
>
> By this Deed of Gift, the undersigned does transfer the Stock as of the date of this Deed of Gift and all income arising from the Stock from and after the date of this Deed of Gift.
>
> Executed this the 31st day of December, 199_ at (your city, state).
>
> Donor:
>
> ______________________________
>
> Father Owner

■ **NOTE:** In the above deed of gift the exact amount of the gift (in shares of stock) to be made to Son Owner is $220,000 (1/6 of $1,200,000 or $200,000, plus $20,000). This is why: Father Owner owned all of the stock of Success Co. His wife, Mother Owner, consented to the gifts which were made to their six children. Each child received a separate deed of gift like the one made to Son Owner.

Once Blackman Kallick Bartelstein finished the valuation, it was a simple matter to determine the exact number of shares to be transferred to Son Owner and his five brothers and sisters.

# INDEX

# ABOUT THE AUTHOR

Irving L. Blackman, CPA, is known as the father of the Transfer/Succession/Estate Planning discipline. He is a founding partner of Blackman Kallick Bartelstein (the 36th largest CPA firm in the country), which specializes in closely held businesses. Professionally, he writes, lectures and consults. He has written 10 books, including *The Book of Tax Knowledge* and *Valuing the Privately Held Business* (Probus, 1992). As an attorney, he is a sought-after speaker on the subject of business transfer/succession planning and business valuations. He consults with business owners and their professional advisors from coast to coast and sits on the advisory board of a number of family owned businesses.

His most recent book, *How the Wealthy Win the Tax Game* (self-published), is available by calling (312) 207-1040.